Standards of English in Higher Education

GW00535720

The student demographic of universities today has changed quite dramatically from even a decade ago. As universities seek to internationalise, widen participation and derive attendant reputational and financial benefits, along with greater opportunities for research collaborations and industry links, they also face a growing challenge associated with what Neil Murray terms 'the English language question'. In particular, as the proportion of students of non-English speaking backgrounds entering universities increases, there is growing concern over levels of language proficiency and what this can mean for educational standards, the student experience and, ultimately, institutional standing. *Standards of English in Higher Education: Issues, Challenges and Strategies* unpacks a number of key and interrelated issues – for example, the assessment of proficiency and the structure and nature of provision – that bear on the question of English language standards and in doing so offers a frank critical appraisal of English language in higher education today.

* Draws together in a single volume a number of key and interrelated issues around English language proficiency in today's higher education context.
* Provides a framework for ongoing discussion and debate on a critical area in higher education.
* Highlights the potential tension between the maintenance of educational standards in higher education and the need to reflect an international orientation, widen participation and maintain financial buoyancy.

Neil Murray is Reader in Applied Linguistics at the Centre for Applied Linguistics, the University of Warwick, UK, and adjunct member of the Research Centre for Languages and Cultures at the University of South Australia, where he was previously Head of Language and Literacy.

CAMBRIDGE
UNIVERSITY PRESS

University Printing House, Cambridge CB2 8BS, United Kingdom

One Liberty Plaza, 20th Floor, New York, NY 10006, USA

477 Williamstown Road, Port Melbourne, VIC 3207, Australia

4843/24, 2nd Floor, Ansari Road, Daryaganj, Delhi - 110002, India

79 Anson Road, #06-04/06, Singapore 079906

Cambridge University Press is part of the University of Cambridge.

It furthers the University's mission by disseminating knowledge in the pursuit of education, learning and research at the highest international levels of excellence.

www.cambridge.org
Information on this title: www.cambridge.org/9781108436434

First published 2016
First paperback edition 2017

A catalogue record for this publication is available from the British Library

Library of Congress Cataloging in Publication data
Murray, Neil, 1960–
Standards of English in higher education : issues, challenges and strategies /
Neil Murray.
    pages   cm
ISBN 978-1-107-03278-1 (hardback)
1. English language – Standardization.   2. English language – Study and
teaching (Higher)   I. Title.
PE1074.7.M87   2016
306.442'.21–dc23

                                                                2015026853

ISBN 978-1-107-03278-1 Hardback
ISBN 978-1-108-43643-4 Paperback

Standards of English in Higher Education

Issues, Challenges and Strategies

Neil Murray

CAMBRIDGE
UNIVERSITY PRESS

For Henry Widdowson
in modest thanks for his sheer inspiration over the years,
and for bringing applied linguistics to life for me
and for so many others in his inimitable way

Contents

Figures and Tables

Figures

Tables

Acknowledgements

I would like to thank a number of people, all of whom have contributed significantly in some way to this book.

First and foremost, I extend my thanks to the team at Cambridge University Press who have overseen the production of the book, and especially to Helen Barton, who commissioned it, demonstrated confidence in its underlying concept from the outset, and has been supportive throughout and admirably patient in the face of my requests for extended deadlines.

Thanks must also go to colleagues at the Centre for Applied Linguistics, Warwick University, as well as to the Learning & Teaching Unit and the Centre for Languages and Cultures at the University of South Australia, where many of the ideas that appear in the book crystallised and were implemented. Particular thanks are due to Ema Ushioda and Gerard Sharpling for their valuable and perceptive feedback on the manuscript, to Margaret Hicks and Liz Murphy for their support throughout the conceptualisation and implementation of the model described in the latter part of the book, and to the Language and Learning Advisors, Language and Learning Coordinators, Academic Developers and the Learning and Teaching Unit's administrative team at the University of South Australia. Other individuals who deserve my appreciation for serving as a sounding board, alerting me to new dimensions and perspectives, and helping me to reflect critically on my ideas include Cathie Elder, Tony Liddicoat, Katie Dunworth and Cynthia Kralik.

I am grateful to Alexander Murray for his help with formatting the book and to Faye Murray for her assistance with researching elements of its subject matter.

Finally, special thanks to my friend and colleague Chris Klinger for scrupulously editing the manuscript.

Acronyms and abbreviations

ACER	Australian Council for Educational Research
AEI	Australian Education International
ATAS	Academic Technology Approval Scheme
AUQ	Australian Universities Quality Agency
BALEAP	British Association of Lecturers in English for Academic Purposes
BICS	Basic Interpersonal Communication Skills
BUTEX	British Universities Transatlantic Exchange Association
CAE	Cambridge English Advanced
CALP	Cognitive Academic Language Proficiency
CEFR	Common European Framework of Reference
CPE	Cambridge English: Proficiency
DEEWR	Department of Education, Employment and Workplace Relations
DIAC	Department of Immigration And Citizenship
EAL	English as an Additional Language
EAP	English for Academic Purposes
ELP	English Language Proficiency
ESB	English-Speaking Background
ESL	English as a Second Language
ESP	English for Specific Purposes
ETS	Educational Testing Service
FE	Further Education
GPPs	Good Practice Principles
HE	Higher Education
HEFCE	Higher Education Funding Council for England
HEI	Higher Education Institution
HESA	Higher Education Statistics Agency
IEAA	International Education Association of Australia
IELTS	International English Language Testing System
LOTE	Language Other Than English
NCES	National Centre for Education Statistics
NEON	National Education Opportunities Network
NESB	Non-English-Speaking Background

NZREX	New Zealand Registration Examination
OECD	Organisation for Economic Co-operation and Development
OET	Occupational English Test
OFFA	Office For Fair Access
PLAB	Professional and Linguistic Assessments Board
PTE	Pearson Test of English
QAA	Quality Assurance Agency
RMP	Researcher Mobility Programme
SELT	Secure English Language Test
SES	Socio-Economic Status
TEQSA	Tertiary Education Quality Standards Agency
TOEFL	Test of English as a Foreign Language
TOEFL iBT	TOEFL Internet-Based Test
TOEIC	Test of English for International Communication
UKBA	United Kingdom Border Agency
UKCISA	UK Council for International Student Affairs
UKIERI	UK–India Education and Research Initiative
UKVI	United Kingdom Visas and Immigration
WUN	World Universities Network

Introduction

In an era of globalisation and ever-increasing student mobility, there are few people working in higher education today, whether as managers, academics or administrators, who are unaware of the increasing prominence of English language as a key – many would say contentious – issue in the sector. The number of English-medium universities, where all or part of the curriculum is delivered via the medium of English, is growing as institutions try to acquire a share of what is now the global enterprise of education. Significantly, these institutions are no longer confined primarily to those countries where English is used as the native tongue – what Kachru (1985) referred to as the 'inner circle' countries, in his frequently cited Concentric Circles model. Increasingly, universities worldwide are looking at the possibility of offering programmes or modules in English in an effort to attract international students, ensure their long-term viability and enhance their reputations as global institutions with an international outlook and the ability to produce graduates who are equipped to meet the expectations of employers in what is a changing, increasingly multicultural workplace, where communication skills are regarded as more important than ever.

Clearly, the efforts of these universities are being rewarded, as evidenced by the unprecedented level of student mobility and the accompanying growth in international student numbers being experienced across the sector. For many international students, the benefits of studying for a degree in countries such as the United Kingdom, the United States and Australia are considerable, and include the cachet that comes with acquiring a degree from a reputable overseas institution, along with the prospect of better employment conditions and opportunities in their countries of origin as a result of having developed a good level of English language competence during the course of their studies. However, while this influx of international students promises to benefit universities and the students they enrol, it comes with significant ramifications for all stakeholders – the university as an institution, academic staff, and the students themselves and their families – and it raises some complex but fundamental issues, many of which bear on a tension between business imperatives and the need to uphold educational standards. How universities reconcile that tension is critical, for it calls into question the extent to which their decisions are guided by a moral compass, and has the potential to alter fundamentally not just the institutions concerned but also the very nature of higher education.

One key issue with which institutions need to grapple is that of English language entry standards and how to set realistic and reasonable thresholds which ensure, so far as is possible, that there is a reasonable prospect of students being able not merely to cope with and survive the university experience but to fully integrate and flourish, both academically and socially. Failure to set standards appropriately is likely to mean that students who have paid handsomely for an overseas university education will have an unfulfilling learning experience and feel anxious and isolated, with the result that a proportion will inevitably drop out, only to return to their countries of origin with a sense of failure at having not lived up to their own, their families' and their friends' expectations. For their part, academic staff are likely to face the frustrating and demanding task of having to adjust syllabi and the pedagogy through which they are delivered in order to accommodate students with weak language skills, but without compromising the essential integrity of their courses or the degree programmes of which they are a part. Some would argue that there is an inherent and irreconcilable tension here.

Failure to set entry standards correctly and to find an appropriate balance between accommodating students with weak language skills and maintaining curriculum standards has potentially important reputational consequences for graduating universities, both in terms of the quality of their degrees and of the student experience. This in turn has implications for the employability of their graduating students and for future recruitment. Furthermore, Student Services departments are likely to find themselves having to deal with increasing numbers of students suffering stress-related illnesses, while those units responsible for developing students' English language skills will come under pressure from a growing demand for their services and the attendant implications for resources and budgets.

English language development opportunities have, perhaps unsurprisingly, taken on greater significance and visibility in recent years largely as a result of the rapid growth in international student numbers, but also in response to other factors such as attempts to widen participation in higher education. How to accommodate students who need additional English language development has become a prominent and, for many, difficult and contentious issue, and its emergence suggests, among other things, that gatekeeping tests such as IELTS and TOEFL are either not, in and of themselves, fit for purpose and/or are not being used appropriately – which again raises ethical questions as well as questions concerning the levels of assessment literacy of those responsible for setting English language entry standards. The only possible alternative interpretation is that, while it is common practice for universities to benchmark

against competitor institutions in respect of English language entry requirements, these are typically set at the minimal levels of competence deemed
necessary to cope with university study. That is, universities will often choose
to admit students on the basis of strategically setting entry requirements on the
understanding that a proportion of the students they accept will need to develop
their language proficiency during the course of their studies. Where this is the
case, there is surely a moral imperative not only to inform those students of the
need for ongoing language development post-entry but also to ensure that
adequate provisions are available to them, designed to address that need. Of
course, the intended language development may not necessarily happen – or
happen to the required extent – due to individual differences in learners'
aptitude and/or application or to the nature and extent of those language support
services and resources to which students have access.

The reality is that the rigour with which universities set their entry criteria, the
minimum proficiency levels they stipulate and, particularly, the extent and quality
of English language provision that they offer, can be highly variable. Where
universities are coming up short they are certainly not serving their students well;
neither are they, ultimately, serving their own interests and those of their staff.

It is against this background, and in light of the accompanying sense of
unease felt by many working in higher education, that there has, in recent years,
been a growing sense in countries such as the United Kingdom and Australia
that more robust regulation of English language standards and provision is
needed; indeed, there have already been moves in this direction. What is clear is
that if universities are to respond effectively to such regulation and ensure that
they are 'doing right' by their students, they will have to consider and produce
creative and informed responses to an array of complex issues and challenges:

- What is English language 'proficiency', and how – if at all – does it relate to
  domestic as well as international students for whom English is not a first
  language?
- Is pre-enrolment assessment serving its purpose sufficiently well or not, and
  if not, how might any shortcomings be rectified or at least compensated for?
- Should some form of post-enrolment assessment of English language competence be implemented, and, if so, what might be the benefits and threats
  associated with such a policy?
- What are the possible permutations for how a conceptualisation of proficiency might be implemented in terms of a model of English language
  provision, and how might such a model be resourced?
- And how can the different elements of an English language strategy work
  together in an integrated fashion so as to help ensure a positive and productive student experience?

Critically, as I have already intimated, the issue of English language standards in
higher education is highly political as well as strategic in nature, for, rightly or

wrongly, it has become inextricably linked to the fortunes of universities and ultimately, in many cases, their continued viability. The way in which institutions set their English language standards, the way in which they assess students' English language skills pre- and post-enrolment, the nature of the English language provision they offer, and the way in which they publicise and present these activities both internally and – especially – to the outside world, all serve to position them in a certain way. They say something about their brands in an era where brand image is a factor that necessarily infiltrates almost everything they do; one that is an increasingly important determinant of their survival and success in what has become a highly competitive, even cut-throat higher education marketplace where every university is vying for market share. And, again, this fact highlights a growing tension that inevitably manifests itself in managerial decision-making between actions that promise to provide competitive advantage on the one hand and, on the other, those that place sound pedagogy and the students' interests centre-stage. Furthermore, the way in which the sector as a whole reconciles this tension has wide-reaching ramifications for the broader national economic interest, for it will influence the choices made by students seeking an overseas study experience in an English-speaking environment.

This purpose of this book is to unpack these and related issues, although not with the intention of offering a set of definitive answers or an 'ideal' model. To do so would be both presumptuous and unrealistic, not least because, while there may be general principles and broad standards that need to apply irrespective of circumstances, institutional contexts inevitably vary, and what may be a reasonable and effective response in one context may not necessarily be so in another. Instead, what I seek to do in this book is to frame what I shall call the 'English language question' and to identify and deconstruct key issues in the hope that this process will both generate and inform institutional discussions as universities strive to conceptualise and implement effective change in a way that ensures they better serve the English language needs of their students. It bears repeating that, while the book highlights some of the quite considerable challenges universities face in dealing with a rapidly changing student demographic, it is important to temper this perspective with recognition that this diversity brings with it important opportunities as well, not least in enriching students' experience through more inclusive curricula and intercultural interactions that develop in them important skills that they will require post-graduation. The fact is that the changing demographic of universities is very much a reflection of change in society more generally, and by equipping students with the skills they need to operate effectively and comfortably in multicultural contexts, universities are helping ensure their future success, and this is no more true than in the world of work. It has become axiomatic that employers today particularly value well-developed communication and intercultural skills in their employees.

Although it is beyond the scope of this book, one issue which nonetheless warrants passing mention at least, by virtue of the fact that it is increasingly making itself felt across the higher education sector and concerns the issue of English language standards, is that of the English language competence of academic teaching staff: in particular, those from non-English-speaking backgrounds. While academics whose first language is not English have always been a part of the higher education landscape, the globalisation of education and universities' attempts to internationalise have meant that they have become a more prominent feature of this landscape. This of course can bring with it great benefits; however, student satisfaction surveys and anecdotal evidence suggest that, where academics' English language competence – and indeed intercultural competence – is such that they are difficult to understand and to interact with, this can have a negative impact on learning and leave students dissatisfied with part or much of their educational experience and with a jaundiced view of their graduating universities.

The chapters

The book begins by looking, in Chapter 1, at some of the key issues currently affecting higher education. I suggest that, despite not necessarily always being immediately evident, English language proficiency is nonetheless a common denominator. In light of its increased significance and thus prominence, and the variation that exists in the way universities account for it in terms of their entry standards, their post-entry measures for identifying those at greatest risk linguistically, and the nature of English language development provision they have in place, Chapter 2 considers the case for greater regulation of English language provision in universities and describes some recent initiatives designed to provide such regulation, or at least guidance on best practice. Chapter 3 analyses the notion of language proficiency and argues that a clear conceptualisation of the concept is a necessary prerequisite to the shaping of any well-informed, coherent institutional strategy for addressing the English language question as well as to meeting any regulatory requirements. The fact that a proportion of students who enrol in English-medium universities subsequently struggle to cope with the language demands of university level work, sometimes to the extent that they discontinue their studies, suggests that something is awry with the pre-entry processes, instruments and/or the way in which they are applied and used respectively by universities, and it is this that forms the focus of Chapter 4. Chapter 5, in contrast, looks at what can be done post-entry in terms of assessing students' language competence. In particular, it considers some of the pros and cons of post-enrolment language assessment (PELA) in general, as well as of some possible models of PELA and the logistical and other issues they present. Drawing very much on the conceptualisation of language proficiency articulated in Chapter 3, Chapter 6 reflects on its implications for the delivery of language development and for the centralised and decentralised models by which language services are provided in the higher education context. A particular focus of the chapter is on the embedding of academic literacies in the curriculum. Chapter 7 looks at the practicalities of implanting change of the kind implied in the preceding chapters. Among other things, it considers such factors as the institutional context and political climate, the personality, astuteness and awareness of those leading change, the implications for technology and professional development, the criticality of good communication channels and regular dissemination of information and progress towards waypoints, and the importance of evaluating innovation post-implementation. Finally, by presenting an institutional case study located in the Australian higher education context, in Chapter 8 I seek to offer some insights into how many of the principles and ideas discussed in the forgoing chapters might be realised and how, in attempting to implement any change – and, especially, large-scale institutional change – there can be considerable divergence between ideas in principle and ideas in practice. As such, innovators need to manifest two particularly crucial qualities: the ability to anticipate and the capacity to respond deftly to unexpected challenges as and when they arise.

Neil Murray

1 The 'English language question' in the context of the changing face of higher education

1.1 Introduction

Few would dispute that the nature of higher education has changed significantly over the course of the past five decades. The pace of that change has accelerated notably in the last fifteen to twenty years such that those working in the sector – and in academic faculties in particular – often feel that no sooner has the implementation of one policy begun to bed down and a sense of routine, rhythm and stability in their working practices returned, than yet another initiative is forthcoming, flowing from which are directives requiring further change, and sometimes even a complete reversal of previous policy and practice. Whether driven by government agendas or ideological shifts within education generally or the institution itself (or indeed both), and whether or not it is desirable and educationally or morally justified, this continual state of flux can be a source of frustration for those at the coalface who are often left feeling as though they never fully manage to implement one directive before they have to respond to a new one. Moreover, it can undermine innovation by engendering feelings of disorientation, cynicism and a general scepticism about the intellectual rigour and integrity underlying policy change. Further, it can lead to a reluctance by academic staff, and indeed administrators, to engage with new initiatives in the near-knowledge that, regardless of how potentially worthwhile they may be, and no matter how praiseworthy the motives driving them, they are unlikely to reach a state of maturity that will ensure the kind and degree of change envisioned by their architects.

Be this as it may, change is, and looks likely to remain, very much part and parcel of higher education as universities position themselves and attempt to respond adroitly to a fast-changing political, educational and social landscape at a time of great economic uncertainty. More than ever, they need to adopt a highly pragmatic stance on policy and practice if, in the face of such change, they are to deliver education of the highest quality while remaining competitive and financially buoyant. As I hope to demonstrate in the pages that follow, while they are certainly not mutually exclusive, efforts to achieve an acceptable balance between the maintenance of educational standards and continued viability as institutions of higher education can, nonetheless, present universities with major ethical quandaries in the face of which the decisions they ultimately make can have far-reaching implications.

1.2   Key drivers of change in higher education

1.2.1   The social justice agenda

A number of key and largely interrelated developments can be identified as relatively recent and important drivers of change within the higher education sector. One such development is what is sometimes referred to as the social justice agenda, to which governments, particularly in Western, economically developed nations (but increasingly elsewhere), have given growing prominence in terms of policy and strategy. This agenda has sought to increase, through so-called 'widening participation' initiatives (e.g. AimHigher (2004–2011) and the National Education Opportunities Network (NEON) in the United Kingdom; TRIO in the United States; and the government response to the Bradley Review in Australia), that proportion of the population who hold a higher education qualification, by striving to ensure greater access for groups that are traditionally underrepresented in the sector; in particular, those disadvantaged by the circumstances of their birth and who typically fall within the low-SES (social and economic status) category, defined variously in different constituencies.

Efforts to engage this sector of the population have been reflected in multifarious initiatives, including the setting by governments of targets specifying that percentage of the population whom it is intended should gain entry to university and/or who should hold a higher education qualification by a given date; and the encouraging of universities to set quotas on the number of students they enrol who originate from low socio-economic status (SES) backgrounds and/or who apply from state (comprehensive) schools as opposed to those independent private and grammar schools that are seen by many as the domain of the economically and socially privileged. In the United Kingdom, these targets have been linked to funding and, following substantial university fee increases in 2012, universities are now required to have in place an 'Access Agreement', approved by the Office for Fair Access (OFFA), in order to be able to charge students higher tuition fees; that is, fees above the 'basic level' of £6000, up to a maximum of £9000 (OFFA, 2013). In response to government targets, social and educational institutions and organisations have invested time and money in developing community-focused outreach programmes designed to raise the awareness and aspirations of disadvantaged and non-traditional groups; in pathway programmes – variously referred to as 'access' or 'enabling' programmes and designed to provide a means via which individuals can transition effectively into higher education, or at least get a sense of whether or not higher education is for them; and in schemes offering bursaries and other forms of financial support for the socio-economically disadvantaged. Although the existence of and commitment to such initiatives varies from country to country (see, for example, Mortensen, 2013; Merisotis, 2013; Scott, 2013), nonetheless the widening participation movement has contributed to the 'massification' of higher education (Stuart, 2002) and to the changing demographic make-up of universities such that, according to Calderon (2012), the number of students enrolled in higher education by 2030 is forecast to rise from 99.4 million in 2000 to 414.2 million in 2030 – an increase of 314%. Within the United Kingdom, the participation target of 50% of school-leavers entering higher education by 2010, set by Tony Blair's Labour Government, was almost reached in the 2011–12 academic year, according to statistics published by the Department for Business, Innovation and Skills, with 49.3% of young people entering higher education. While this figure may have been 'artificially driven up by the decision of thousands of school-leavers to go straight on to higher or further education, rather than defer their entry by a year or more, in order to beat the increase in tuition fees from £3,290 to a maximum of £9,000 a year from 2012–13' (Adams, 2013, online), nevertheless it is indicative of a continued significant rise in participation from 4% in the early 1960s and 20% in the 1980s (Klinger and Murray, 2012). In Australia, the 2008 Bradley Review recommended higher participation targets of 40% of 25- to 34-year-olds attaining a bachelor-level or higher qualification by 2020 (roughly equivalent to a 50% school-leaver participation rate), with low-SES students comprising 20% of all commencing enrolments by 2025 (Bradley, 2008). In the United States, while financial and other incentives have been put in place by the Obama government in order to increase participation and thus social mobility, there have been no specific targets set other than to have the highest proportion of college graduates in the world by the year 2020 (White House Briefing, 2009). With this in mind, it has been estimated that approximately 60% of Americans will have to earn college degrees and certificates by that time if the country is to regain its international lead. This is an indication at least of the American government's ambitions, given that the present figure is 40% (Advisory Committee on Student Financial Assistance, 2012).

The moral imperative driving the widening participation agenda conveniently intersects with the socio-economic motivations of governments seeking to increase human capital in what is now widely referred to as the global knowledge economy (Cooper, 2010). That is, where governments succeed in raising levels of participation in higher education, it is hoped and expected that a better educated, more skilled workforce will enable their respective countries to better participate and compete economically.

1.2.2   New technologies

New technologies have also had a major impact on education generally, and higher education in particular, and they have rapidly and radically altered the way students learn and teachers teach. Particularly in developed countries, the kind of traditional teacher-fronted, highly structured classrooms that are physically and temporally restrictive are giving way, in part, to increasingly sophisticated and creative electronic forms of learning that are liberating learners and altering their preconceptions, and thus expectations, of what the higher education experience means and what is possible in terms of access to higher education learning opportunities and their personal and professional development. Dedicated online or blended learning increasingly features in universities' course offerings, and distance programmes delivered via online modules and virtual classrooms are rapidly growing in popularity as audio–visual applications such as Skype and Adobe Connect reduce the constraints traditionally associated with studying at distance. As universities endeavour to extend their global reach and compete for market share, it is incumbent on them to move with the times and offer these alternative modes of delivery if they are to meet the expectations of new generations of students and not risk getting left behind in what has become a global marketplace.

The increasingly commercial dimension to higher education, which has been driven in part by its globalisation, is reflected in strategic decision-making by university senior management that increasingly places importance on market research, benchmarking, student satisfaction surveys and 'the student experience'. Today, those same technologies that can broaden the learning experience also drive the higher education sector to be more data-driven than at any time in its history, and having a handle on relevant and reliable metrics and intelligence on their own and competitor institutions can give universities a critical edge by enabling them to shape their brands and their programmes (and their delivery) in ways that are unique, offering added value to the student and positioning them as being at the vanguard of educational development and excellence. The effective integration of new technologies that enhance learning and opportunities for learning is a key element of these efforts to enhance institutional reputation, ranking and thus appeal.

1.2.3   Globalisation

Then there is globalisation itself, a phenomenon that is largely a product of technological developments and a catalyst driving universities' attempts to 'internationalise'. In an increasingly interconnected world, where air travel is now affordable for the masses and where information and communication technologies have rendered physical distance almost irrelevant in many contexts, universities that are forward-thinking and appropriately technologically equipped are finding themselves faced with new opportunities for expansion, the exploitation of which allows them to more effectively compete in an increasingly marketised sector. Technology, a willingness to embrace it, and the vision, strategy and know-how to use it creatively and purposefully, positions them well to meet the challenges of the global economy, take advantage of the changing global context, significantly enlarge their interests, broaden their financial base, and increase their income and profit margins in a way that helps secure their viability and future development. This thinking has been a driving factor in the establishment of the 2012 *Warwick–Monash Alliance*, an alliance whereby the two signatory institutions:

offer a connected experience to students wherever they come from in the world. Those students will be able to do a course made up of components from either institution, experiencing learning from Europe and/or the Asia-Pacific, and become globally aware and culturally adept graduates. We hope also to appeal to researchers of laboratories running simultaneously on either side of the world, to PhD students from both continents, and to support and research funding sources in more than one system. (Coates, 2012, accessed online)

Coates, the Joint Academic Vice-President of the two Universities and Director of the Monash–Warwick Alliance, goes on to say:

We know (and governments understand) that global challenges will not be solved by parochial thinking or small groups using the approaches they have always used. It will require bigger collaborations, transnational partnerships and a degree of inter-disciplinarity that has proved so difficult to foster within single institutions. To have even a chance to do that we need the best globally aware academics and students, those who feel Beijing, New York or Singapore are as likely to offer an answer – or the right person to work with – as the UK or Australia. These people know that time-zone and distance barriers merely mean Skype rather than coffee together. (Ibid.)

Globalisation and the general move by universities to internationalise are, of course, also the products of other factors. These include:
• Political and educational agreements and structures that allow for greater mobility across national borders and which, in cases such as the European Union, mean that students benefit from having to pay local, rather than substantially higher international, tuition fees. The Bologna Process (its original 1999 Declaration and subsequent communiqués and the 2010 Budapest–Vienna Declaration) typifies such initiatives, aspiring as it does to ensure international comparability in the standards and quality of higher education qualifications. International student mobility is rising each year and the increase in the use of English around the world has led to projections

that by 2050 there will be one billion English speakers, two thirds of whom will be non-native speakers (Irish Higher Education Quality Network, 2009).

- More widespread institutional student and staff exchange programmes such as ERASMUS/SOCRATES, Junior Year Abroad, the UK–India Education and Research Initiative (UKIERI), the British Universities Transatlantic Exchange Association (BUTEX), and the World Universities Network (WUN) Researcher Mobility Programme (RMP).
- The 'opening up' and/or rapid economic growth of countries such as China, India, Brazil and Russia, that have large populations, a proportion of whom are eager to broaden their international experience, and collectively represent significant investment opportunities and a potentially rich source of students and associated income generation.
- Government policies that drive individuals and communities to migrate as a result of political unrest and/or persecution.
- Skills shortages in certain locales, countries and regions, reflected in immigration policies designed to reduce the administrative hurdles for individuals looking to emigrate and able to demonstrate the required skills.
- Individuals' aspirations vis-à-vis their education, self-development and a better lifestyle.

Together, these factors have brought with them associated changes not merely in terms of larger international student populations but in terms of national and local demographics such that there has been a notable growth in multicultural communities in general (Vertovec (2010) speaks of 'superdiversity' in referring to the complexity of modern societies) and with it a concomitant growth of diversity in the student body both within and outside of institutions of higher education.

In responding to these developments, universities have sought to expand their outward-facing activities in an effort to broaden their domains of influence, enhance their academic reputations and put themselves on a firmer financial footing by diversifying their income streams. This has resulted in an increase in international research collaborations and other initiatives, cross-/ inter-institutional degree programmes, offshore and student exchange programmes, degree programmes by distance, and the marketing of courses in general, with a view to attracting greater numbers of international students. Moreover, it has led to the design and tailoring of degree offerings that have international appeal, reflect the needs and demands of a global market, and articulate better with programme curricula and the academic cycles of those countries from which universities source a significant number of their students. Increasingly, such activity is seen as a mark of an institution's academic prowess and evidence of its being in tune with the times and able to respond to the rapidly changing global context of education.

1.2.4   Funding

Funding, too, is an ingredient that has influenced, and continues to influence enormously, the shape of universities: how they tailor their activities and programmes, position themselves in relation to their competitors, and present themselves to the outside world. That is, the strategies that underpin these things reflect the fact that universities today are commercial entities – what Marginson and Considine (2000, p. 28) refer to as 'enterprise universities' – as much as they are educational institutions, and as such they are under unprecedented pressure to balance their books if they are to sustain their activities, and indeed continue to exist. Referring specifically to Australian universities but with far broader (even global) relevance, Marginson and Considine describe today's enterprise universities in the following terms:

> The enterprise university joins a mixed public–private economy to a quasi-business culture and to academic traditions party reconstituted, partly republican, and partly broken. This is not so much a genuine private business culture as a public sector variant in which certain of the conditions and techniques of business (such as competition, scarcity, marketing, goals defined in money terms) have been grafted onto existing bureaucracies now opened up to external pressures ... In their political economy, enterprise universities sit somewhere between the public academic institutions they were and the private companies that some imagine them to be already. (Ibid., p. 236)

There are two main income streams that govern and shape the strategic plans of universities operating within this new paradigm: student fees and research income.

Student fees   Student fees are clearly a critical factor for institutions striving to manage their budgets, at the very least balance income and expenditure, and ideally have a surplus with which to expand their physical presence and facilities as well as the resources needed to develop their research and their teaching and learning activities. However, the basis on which students fund their university studies is subject to change, in line with prevailing government and institutional policy. The decision in 2011 by the UK coalition government (implemented for the first time in the 2012–13 academic year) to raise the cap on the tuition fees universities could charge to £9000 a year, understandably raised concerns over a possible decline in student application numbers (Shepherd, 2012). Those concerns appeared to be well-founded. According to Higher Education Statistics Agency (HESA) data, between the 2011–12 and 2012–13 academic years there was a 6% decrease in total undergraduate enrolment across all modes of study (full-time and part-time) in the United Kingdom, equating to a reduction in numbers from 1,928,140 to 1,803,840 students (HESA, 2014). While these figures may have presented a somewhat misleading picture due to a glut of applications in anticipation of the fee increases and demographic factors such as a decline in the number of eighteen-year-olds (Shepherd, ibid.), they nonetheless had the effect of driving universities to further increase the vigour and impact of their overseas marketing campaigns in a move to secure greater numbers of international students and thereby compensate for this apparent drop-off in the domestic market. In fact, as reported in the 12–18 February 2015 issue of the *Times Higher Education*, student numbers have since regained their buoyancy and in the 2014–15 academic year exceeded those immediately prior to the fee increase.

Moves to increase the number of international student enrolments are, of course, by no means unique to the United Kingdom; today, in English-medium universities worldwide, international students typically represent a significant and increasing proportion of the student population in higher education. The index of change in the percentage of international students enrolled in higher education in the United Kingdom from 2005 to 2011 was 121, and in Australia 115, where 2005 is the base year (Organisation for Economic Co-operation and Development (OECD) indicators: Education at a Glance 2013, Table C4.1). This demographic shift is not only a product of globalisation, greater international collaboration between institutions and the increasingly sophisticated technologies that have become available to support different modes of study, it is also an undeniable fact (no doubt unpalatable to many) that international students, and the considerable fees they bring with them, are today something of a 'cash-cow' for universities – and indeed for the local economies of those communities in which they operate – as the media continually remind us (e.g. BBC News, 2010; Buchanan (*The Times Education*), 2013; CBC News, Canada, 2014; Fischer (*The Chronicle of Higher Education*, USA), 2012; Morgan (*Times Higher Education*), 2010; Narushima (*Sydney Morning Herald*, Australia), 2008; Paton (*Daily Telegraph*), 2012; Tan (*New Zealand Herald*), 2010). These students are an important source of income that helps assure universities' ongoing and future viability and growth. While this is not necessarily a bad thing in itself, and the students concerned do, in point of fact, choose of their own volition to study as overseas students, it does require universities to ask themselves (a) whether they are providing those students with value for money in terms of the quality of the learning experience on offer, and (b) whether the entry criteria they have in place are rigorous enough for the institution to feel confident that, having paid high fees, the students concerned have a reasonable prospect of success. These questions, to which I shall return later, take on an ethical dimension, for they require universities to carefully and objectively balance their need to be financially secure with the need to provide their students with a high quality of education and ensure that they have at their disposal the skills and supports needed to take fullest advantage of the educational opportunities before them and to realise their academic potential. This is no more true than in the case of English language proficiency: universities need to set their English language entry thresholds such that both they and the students whom they are admitting can feel confident that they have the linguistic competence to achieve at the levels of which they are capable.

Whether domestic or international, and whether or not they pay up-front via student loan schemes, students today pay substantial fees for a university education at a time of general austerity in the world at large, when employment prospects are relatively bleak and opportunities few and far between. As a result, they want – indeed expect – a return on that investment, and this fact has unequivocally had a major impact on the nature of universities and their strategic thinking. Given the financial outlay involved and a climate in which competition for jobs is fierce, today's increasingly savvy students want a near-guarantee that, at the end of their studies, they will be well positioned to enter stable employment that will ensure a decent standard of living and enable them to pay back their student loans, the magnitude of which can be in excess of £160,000 (US$300,000) for clinical degrees. This means that programmes which offer a less obvious and direct route into employment are likely to be looked upon less favourably. This relationship between economic conditions and students' choice of undergraduate university subject is highlighted in a 2010 report by the Higher Education Funding Council for England (HEFCE) focusing on changes in student choices and graduate employment, in which they state that:

Whilst applications to most subject areas have increased, those for which there has been a decrease might be indicative of responses to economic conditions. For example, programmes related to the building and finance sectors, both of which have been adversely affected by the recession, have received fewer applications. (HEFCE, 2010, p. 4)

Generally speaking, those arts, humanities and social science disciplines that traditionally were regarded as strong and respected academic subjects in themselves, constituted a valuable grounding for further studies, and provided students with the opportunity to indulge their intellectual interests and curiosity and to develop themselves more broadly as individuals, but which did not necessarily set up them up for a specific type of job or profession, are increasingly at risk in the current climate. In contrast, subjects such as business and management, information technology/computer science, psychology, health sciences and nursing are typically flourishing in the United Kingdom (*Daily Telegraph*, February 2014). The US Department of Education's National Center for Education Statistics (NCES) (2013) provides data that suggest a similar trend, with business, health professions, education and psychology featuring strongly as desirable undergraduate degree courses – although, interestingly, with social sciences and history also being highly favoured. A similar situation exists in Australia, where business management, education, health sciences, environmental science and engineering perform particularly well (Now Learning, 2013).

In effect, higher fees combined with fewer jobs have created a higher education environment where students are now 'clients' who bring with them a 'consumer' approach to studying, and seek value for money and an educational experience that they feel justifies the considerable financial outlay required to purchase that product. Few students today can afford to regard a university degree as a government/parent-funded opportunity to simply indulge their intellectual interests regardless of its currency in the job market and/or as an interregnum between school and work. Many will consider carefully whether university is really for them and whether the overall experience will be worth the investment of time and money and the pressure of knowing that they will be burdened with a debt the size of which will feel considerable, particularly to those from socio-economically disadvantaged backgrounds (Gielis, 2010). As such, universities find themselves operating in an increasingly competitive market, one in which they need to be ever more resourceful and to respond more effectively to student demand if they are to secure the enrolments needed to remain solvent and realise their plans for growth. This means that senior management needs to be increasingly pragmatic in terms of how and where to invest human and financial resources such that they are well placed to tailor and deliver their programmes in ways that are responsive to students' needs and their preferred, more varied learning styles, while also reflecting a more professional and vocational orientation. As a result, many would argue that universities today are becoming something of a hybrid of 'traditional' (i.e. pre-1992) universities and those 'new universities' that were formerly polytechnics prior to the Further and Higher Education Act of 1992 (Great Britain, 1992).

Students as 'clients': the increased pressure on the curriculum, teaching staff and support services units

As we will see, the notion of 'students as clients' is an interesting and, for many, disturbing one in that it puts strain on the curriculum, pedagogy and assessment. Having paid substantial fees 'for a service' and, in some cases, put themselves under considerable financial burden in the process, a growing number of students enrol in their course of study not only expecting a value-for-money experience but with the idea that the university has a responsibility or duty to ensure that they graduate – referred to by some as the 'marketisation of higher education' (Molesworth, Scullion and Nixon, 2010) or the 'consumer approach' (Raisman, 2001) – and this in turn can impose an unhealthy sense of obligation on academic departments and faculties, which may feel under pressure to pass the students, particularly in a climate of ever-greater regulation, performance evaluation and league tables. In June 2014, BBC Radio 4's Today programme reported on the results of a Freedom of Information request made to UK universities which provided a strong indication of changing student attitudes following the 2012 tuition fee increase. Responses to the request showed a 10% increase in the number of student complaints received by universities in the year following the fee increases. Of these, a high proportion concerned student dissatisfaction with the grades they had received, suggesting perhaps that the high cost of a university education today is leading to a situation where, for all intents and purposes, a proportion of university students see themselves as buying a university degree.

In 2009, and in relation to international students in particular, the United Kingdom's Quality Assurance Agency (QAA) published a report – *Thematic enquiries into concerns about academic quality and standards in higher education in England* – in which it cited a 2008 BBC news article on plagiarism, cheating and the language skills of international students, in response to which readers were able to post comments. The report noted:

A number of respondents identified themselves as students or academic staff with English universities. Of these, several in their postings queried how students who could not converse well in English could nonetheless produce assessed work in the language to a level that enabled them to achieve their award. Commentators elsewhere have asserted that international students are being marked 'leniently' and 'positively' because their 'full-cost fees are now a lucrative and essential source of revenue'. (QAA, 2009, pp. 13–14)

Pressure to accommodate students who lack the requisite English language skills can lead to changes in curricula which are not strictly prescribed by external bodies, changes to assessment practices, and a greater onus on academic staff and student services departments to provide students with the necessary support in an effort to ensure that they meet students' expectations as far as possible and ensure they have what they need to graduate successfully. For many, an uncomfortable and unsustainable situation now exists: academic departments and their staff face the often near-impossible task of meeting enrolment targets and graduating students without compromising or being seen to compromise academic standards, and while also ensuring that graduates are able to meet professional accreditation requirements and the demands of the workplace (Lovegrove and Clarke, 2008; Shah, Lewis and Fitzgerald, 2011). As I demonstrate in Chapter 2, evidence increasingly suggests that academic staff view this situation as serious cause for concern on a number of levels.

Firstly, it signals a drop in standards as institutions feel they have little option but to dance to the tune of students. This is counter to everything universities have traditionally stood for as the ultimate arbiters of standards, and as such it sits uncomfortably with academic faculties. Reporting on a poll conducted by the *Times Higher Education*, Baty commented as follows:

However the minute is interpreted, one thing is irrefutable. Professor Ebdon's comments highlight the vicious circle many believe is irrevocably damaging academic standards in new universities struggling for financial stability. It is a cycle of declining finances and academic quality: those universities with the fewest resources are the least popular, so they are forced to pick up the least qualified students. Such students cost more to support through higher level study and drain the coffers further if they drop out. With dropout rates above 25 per cent at 13 universities, including Luton, some say it is all but inevitable that standards will slip, almost as a prerequisite for financial security.

The message of *The Times Higher*'s (THE) poll is clear: academics believe standards are being forced down. And the survey provides the first evidence that academics are compromising or, worse, being forced to compromise their professional academic judgement to an alarming extent. (Baty, 2004)

Key findings from the poll include:

- Eighty-four per cent of respondents agreed with the statement: 'The squeeze on resources for universities is "having an adverse effect on academic standards".' Half 'strongly agreed'.
- Since 1989, universities have seen resources per student fall by 37 per cent. The student-to-staff ratio now stands at 23:1.
- The number of university places already outstrips the supply of well-qualified school-leavers, with the gap being met largely through mature and non-traditional students.
- The sector now takes thousands of overseas students who 'place different pressures on standards with divergent learning cultures and, often, language problems'.
- Almost three quarters of respondents believed that their university has been forced to accept students who 'are not capable of benefiting' from university study.
- 48 per cent of academics agreed with the statement: 'I have felt obliged to pass a student whose performance did not really merit a pass'. 42 per cent said 'decisions to fail students' work have been overruled at higher levels in the institution'.

More recently, and invoking evidence that emerged from the 2009 report *Students and Universities* and the then Select Committee on Innovation, Universities, Science and Skills, to which he submitted written and oral evidence, Geoffrey Alderman paints a similar picture, citing five factors responsible for a decline in academic standards in British universities, the first three of which read as follows:

First, the league table culture that has permeated the senior leaderships of many British universities, resulting in intolerable pressures on academic staff to pass students who should rightfully fail and to award higher classes of degrees to the undeserving.

Second, pressures to maximise non-governmental sources of income, primarily from 'full fee-paying' non-European students, to whom it is deemed prudent by these same senior leaderships to award qualifications to which they are often not entitled, so as to ensure future 'market share'.

Third, the increasing and increasingly stupid use of students' course evaluations as pivotal factors in the academic promotion process. To put it bluntly, a conscientious academic with poor student evaluations may find it difficult or even impossible to obtain promotion because her/his students do not like getting the low grades they may well richly deserve. (Alderman, 2010)

What can be termed 'the education press' has been rife with such discourse in recent years.

Secondly, balancing academic standards with financial imperatives raises ethical questions about accepting students onto degree programmes that may not necessarily be offering as rigorous an intellectual experience as students expect or, perhaps more importantly, need in terms of their future career aspirations. It is important to note that while, for the reasons mentioned above, students may expect to graduate successfully, this certainly does not necessarily mean that they wish to have, or will tolerate, a mediocre programme that is undemanding and does not provide them with a respected degree that will serve them well in terms of securing future employment and giving them the means to flourish in their chosen professions. Thus a potential tension can exist *within* the individual student which mirrors somewhat that being experienced by the institution in terms of maintaining its standards without sacrificing student numbers and success – and, in doing so, risking its own financial security and, therefore, its continued viability.

Thirdly, any compromise in standards can be frustrating and demoralising for teaching staff, who feel unable to teach a full and appropriately rigorous curriculum: one that will stretch students and provide them with what they need for their future professional and personal lives. It can also be a less rewarding and stimulating experience, for themselves as well as their students, as they feel the need to simplify – or 'dumb down' – material and devote time to providing the type of support to students that many consider should be unnecessary at tertiary level and beyond the scope of their job descriptions and expertise.

Finally, it risks putting unsustainable pressure on student support services units and systems that are, in many cases, already struggling to maintain themselves with often quite minimal human and financial resources at their disposal. Ensuring that university programmes have a full complement of students, remain financially viable and develop and retain a good reputation has to do not only with sustaining enrolment numbers but also with maintaining high retention rates and thus maximising graduate numbers. As a result, the activities of student support units that provide services such as counselling, research training and language and study skills are more important than ever as university departments find themselves under ever greater pressure to fill classes and achieve respectable completion rates. The fact is that, in an era where universities are striving to internationalise and higher education policy continues to reflect an aspiration to be more egalitarian in providing opportunity to a far larger proportion and a broader spectrum of the population, change in the sector's student demographic is perhaps inevitable. This will have implications for the curriculum, for pedagogy and for student services units on which there is a greater onus to provide an expanded support infrastructure in an effort to empower students and equip them with the understanding, skills and outlook they require to succeed in their studies.

In the past, it was largely assumed that the (approximately) four per cent of the population who entered higher education in the United Kingdom in the 1960s at the time of the Robbins Report (1963) came equipped with many of the tools they needed to get the job done and successfully graduate; and where they did not, it was generally felt that they had the capacity to 'pick it up' as they went along; to learn on the job, as it were. Indeed, the struggle to do so was seen as part of the educative process and, as such, one of the desirable qualities of a graduate: a quality that would help prepare them for their future life and employment. Regardless of whether such assumptions were ever really valid, they are certainly questionable at best in the context of higher education today, with very real consequences for student support services. Today, academic staff find themselves facing a situation where more students require more support than ever before; support which many regard not only as lying outside their realm of responsibility but, to their great frustration, as requiring expertise that they themselves simply do not have – or, if they do, the time or inclination to exercise it. Furthermore, while they are under pressure to obtain good student evaluations and results in an environment that is increasingly driven by data and metrics, and thus feel obliged to provide these kinds of supports, they also feel compromised in their ability to do so as a result of being subject to the pressures of greater bureaucracy and an all-pervasive research culture that demands more and more of their time and effort. Academics today are under no illusions that, while teaching quality may certainly be recognised and acknowledged in bids for academic promotion, in general, far greater weight is given to research grants, successful PhD completions and research outputs with tangible and measurable impact. One consequence of this is that there can be a tendency for academic staff to send struggling students to support services units that are already under-resourced in the hope that they will provide a quick fix in their stead – as a proxy of sorts. In this regard, Drennan and Beck (2000, online) have stated that:

Promotion criteria of all higher education institutions include performance in teaching, research and administration. Yet the prevailing perception is that research performance is the true discriminator ... So long as the Funding Councils favour large institutional awards for excellence in research and much smaller rewards for excellence in teaching, individual academics will chose to concentrate their activities in research activity, to the detriment of teaching. Only when the rewards are equalised will staff believe that teaching is an equal partner of research, and not its poor relation.

Lewicki and Bailey (2009) similarly acknowledge the imbalance between research and teaching in universities:

To deny that there is a tension between research and teaching activities and demands at most management education institutions would be disingenuous. But it would be equally disingenuous to deny the productive synergies and reciprocities between knowledge creation, dissemination and application. Scholarship and education are the twin pillars that serve as the foundation of most academic management education institutions. Yet there are two trends prevalent in the more prestigious research universities: that excellence in scholarship and education are both critical to faculty selection and promotability, and that one of these pillars (research) is more strongly encouraged and rewarded than the other, exacerbating the tension and impeding the realization of effective institutional balance. (2009, p. 385)

While, as Lewicki and Bailey indicate, in some quarters there have been efforts made to redress the research–teaching imbalance and that these can be productive, many would argue that the emphasis on research – now along with demonstrable impact – has, along with greater levels of competition between universities, increased in recent years, despite what the sceptical might see as an accompanying but rather superficial and apologetic nod to the 'student experience'.

Research income   Although always a defining characteristic of universities and traditionally a key part of their activities, research activity and associated funding has become a key – and in many cases *the* key – priority for universities today, as evidenced by the ever-increasing emphasis placed on it in academic staff selection and promotion review processes, the establishment of bodies within universities focused solely on identifying and publicising to academic staff grants and research opportunities, and the institution of Early Career Researcher schemes and similar such initiatives which seek to maximise the number of research-active staff. As Billig has noted, this is an age 'where research, across all disciplines, is being mass produced' and this boom in research 'is far too big to be accounted for simply by the increase in the number of academics. The job of many academics has changed so that they are now expected to publish as well as teach' (2013, p. 19).

Not only does research activity directly help sustain an important income stream as a result of new faculty bringing with them existing grants and subsequently attracting new ones, it also does so indirectly by enhancing the profile and reputation of institutions through the dissemination of research outputs – articles, books, reports etc. That is, through their research activity, universities acquire academic kudos which, in turn, makes them an attractive destination for would-be students looking to obtain a degree from a respected, high-profile institution, and thereby increase their employment opportunities and their social mobility more generally. In this regard, Billig (2013) observes that

> Widely publicised league tables rank order the so-called 'best' universities. Managers want to see their institutions ranked highly and they certainly do not wish to be seen to be slipping down the rankings. The better ranked an institution is, the greater its chance of attracting student fees from wealthy parents, securing lucrative research contracts from outside organizations, and receiving bequests from alumni. (2013, p. 20)

Thus, the kudos that comes with successful performance not only improves student recruitment prospects but also allows institutions to approach other reputable universities and industry with credibility and thus from a position of strength when seeking to initiate partnerships and collaborative projects which can, directly and indirectly, generate significant income streams and help secure continued financial health. This is exemplified by the 2012 Warwick–Monash Alliance, discussed above, and described by Coates as 'a tight, yet broad, partnership between two proud universities who will co-develop courses, co-invest in technologies and attract the best researchers who want access to the best facilities – and the best students too' (2012, p. 1).

As I highlighted earlier, the foregrounding of research to an unprecedented degree in recent years risks being at the expense of the student experience (Drennan, 2000, 2001), with academics having less time to work with individuals and small groups of students face-to-face in a way that can promote a richer, more rewarding learning experience. Despite this – or perhaps because of it – learning and teaching units are becoming a common feature of the university landscape. While the raison d'être, objectives and products of such units may be praiseworthy indeed, one wonders to what extent they exist and/or have evolved in an effort to counter the growing inability of academic staff to provide both the pedagogical and pastoral support that an increasingly diverse student body demands. While the kinds of approaches to learning that such units tend to promote and develop undoubtedly introduce efficiencies into teaching and learning and take advantage of new technologies, social media and new ways of organising oneself such that learning can be more flexible, accessible and engaging, they can also be seen as devolving responsibility by taking some of the onus for teaching and learning away from academics, who are increasingly seen as having to focus more on bolstering their research profiles. The same argument might also be made of the increased prevalence of student portfolios. There can, of course, be a considerable workload associated with developing modules and associated materials for online delivery and blended learning, setting up and moderating discussion forums and blogs, and creating podcasts etc.; however, a return on that investment of time and effort can ultimately be realised in 'release time' for academics to engage in research and related activity.

1.2.5   *International students and multicultural classrooms*

The growth in international student numbers over the past few decades, particularly in English-medium universities, has been striking and, in many cases, a cause and/or effect of those other drivers of change in higher education discussed in this chapter. Today, international students represent a sizeable proportion of the university student body and a considerable source of revenue. In 2013, the OECD reported that the number of students enrolled in tertiary education outside their country of citizenship increased more than threefold, from 1.3 million in 1990 to nearly 4.3 million in 2011, representing an average annual growth rate of almost six per cent. This, they noted, was a greater increase than the overall rise in tertiary enrolments globally and contrary to expectations of a decline in the growth rate due to the global financial crisis of 2008. Furthermore, they reported – unsurprisingly, perhaps – that international students primarily go to English-speaking countries to study, often in the fields of social sciences, business and law, with the consequence that Australia, the United Kingdom and the United States together host 36% of all foreign tertiary students enrolled worldwide.

In terms of the proportions of international students enrolled in higher education in these and other English-speaking countries, the OECD reported the following statistics:

> The United Kingdom: 15.3% of tertiary enrolments (representing nearly 35% of fee income)
> The United States: 3.5% of tertiary enrolments
> Canada: 6.5% of tertiary enrolments
> Australia: 21.5% of tertiary enrolments
> New Zealand: 14.6% of tertiary enrolments

The growth in international student numbers has been particularly marked in the United States – in a higher education sector that is privatised to a vastly greater extent than in other jurisdictions, it should be noted. Here, the number of international students enrolled in higher education increased by seven per cent to 819,644 students in 2012/13, with 55,000 more students enrolled in colleges and universities across the United States than in the previous year. The Institute of International Education reported that

this 2012/13 data marks the seventh consecutive year that Open Doors reported expansion in the total number of international students in U.S. higher education. While international students account for a relatively modest proportion of the total student body in higher education, there are nevertheless 40 percent more international students studying at U.S. colleges and universities than a decade ago, and the rate of increase has risen steadily for the past three years. (Institute of International Education, 2013, accessed online)

The increased importance of the international student market means that universities are increasingly shaping their programme offerings, delivery modes, support services and pastoral infrastructures in ways that will prove attractive to this cohort. Their success in doing so has ramifications beyond the considerable income international students bring with them in the form of tuition fees, however. A significant international student presence is an indication of how a university sees and seeks to position itself, and in particular its credentials as an institution 'of the times' with an international outlook and global reach. International students both promote that image and are enticed by it. Furthermore, as alumni, they spread the reputation of their Almae Matres and, for those who come as researchers or proceed to postgraduate studies in their home countries, some will serve as points of contact or liaison, helping to facilitate future collaborations between their graduating universities and those of their home countries. Such collaborations promise to further enhance the institution's reputation and help secure its financial health.

And English-medium degree courses are not the exclusive preserve of higher education institutions located in inner circle countries. Increasingly, as Coleman (2006) notes, they feature in many countries of the world as governments and universities recognise the benefits associated with them:

The reasons which have impelled individual HEIs, as well as regional or national governments, to introduce programmes and courses taught through the medium of English may be allocated across seven categories: CLIL, internationalization, student exchanges, teaching and research materials, staff mobility, graduate employability and the market in international students. It might be suggested that this rainbow of motives ranges from the ethical and pedagogical through the pragmatic to the commercial. Foreign language learning in itself is NOT the reason why institutions adopt English medium teaching. (Coleman, 2006, p. 4)

While international students play a significant role in creating the kind of multicultural classrooms that are increasingly commonplace, in Western countries in particular, they certainly do not account for all such diversity. The changing demographics – and their causes, as outlined above – of populations more generally in these countries means that an increasing number of domestic students of non-English-speaking backgrounds and representing a broad cultural spectrum enrol in university programmes. These students, in turn, are joined by local students for whom English *is* a first language but who fall into the 'non-traditional' category and as such may be products of widening participation initiatives, originate from a variety of socio-cultural and educational backgrounds, and bring with them a wide range of world experiences

(Richardson, 1994; Peters, Pokorny and Sheibani, 1999; Shanahan, 2000; Scevak and Cantwell, 2001; Murray and Klinger, 2012).

This changing demographic has had and continues to have implications for classroom practice and, by extension, teacher education courses and professional development activities. Academics today require a pedagogical toolkit that includes an intercultural competence that provides them with the means to negotiate cultural difference and to develop materials that both acknowledge that difference and promote the ability to traverse it, although always in a manner consistent with the requirements of the academy. And it is not just an educational imperative that dictates that they should do so; increasingly, regulation exists that seeks to govern the way in which classroom behaviour and materials reflect a push towards greater equity and inclusivity. Moreover, there is a large and growing body of literature concerned with teacher education and the development of teacher attitudes and skills that promote the sound management of multicultural and multilingual classrooms and the effective negotiation of cultural difference such that diversity is drawn upon as a strength that can enrich the teaching–learning process rather than seen as an obstacle that interferes with it (see, for example, Cochran-Smith, 2004; Hockings, 2010; Premier & Miller, 2010; Simonds et al., 2008; Tellez, 2007; White-Clark, 2005).

1.2.6 The student experience

While the role of universities as institutions of higher education has essentially remained unchanged, their efforts in recent years to tailor what they do in order to respond more relevantly to social and economic factors – and, as a corollary of this, to the market forces they shape and the requirements of an increasingly diverse student population – have resulted in an increased emphasis on outreach activity and the student experience as measured by student barometers designed to gauge levels of student satisfaction, often on an annual basis. Such initiatives both highlight and reinforce the notion of students as clients. As we have seen, more and more, today's university students see their degree programmes as an investment in their future rather than as an intellectual journey that is of value in and of itself. Not only do they want an optimal university experience (however defined), they want to feel confident of securing a job post-graduation and of having a student experience that will not only be engaging and rewarding but of practical value. Equally, however, the very same social and economic factors that drive students' study choices and expectations have meant that professional bodies and other employers are also looking for work-ready graduates who come better trained, with a comprehensive knowledge base and a set of hands-on skills that will give them the means to operate competently in the workplace.

This increased emphasis on learning product and graduate preparation is most obviously reflected in the 'Graduate Qualities' statements that universities now routinely publish as part of broader mission statements, and in league tables based on the employment statistics of first year graduates. Furthermore, it is commonly realised in curriculum renewal initiatives and extended outreach activity with industry/partners and the professions, as universities strive to increase the experiential learning of their students through work placement schemes, exchange programmes, and so on.

1.2.7   The interactivity of the drivers of higher education

When thinking about these different drivers of change in higher education today, what becomes amply clear is the fact and extent of their interactivity. Each impacts on one or more of the others in various and complex ways and, as such, in considering their influence not only within the context of higher education but also more broadly, none can be compartmentalised and sensibly discussed without invoking the others. The social justice agenda, for example, has been linked to funding through mechanisms designed to reward those universities who meet or exceed government targets for non-traditional and disadvantaged groups or, conversely, effectively penalise those who do not. Equally, it is linked to the funding of social capital and the desire of governments to increase the proportion of their populations who are productive members of society in ways that enable their respective economies to compete in an increasingly globalised knowledge economy.

Similarly, the critical issue of funding cannot be discussed today without also considering its relationship to the social justice agenda, social capital, globalisation, internationalisation and international student numbers. In the case of social justice, I have already highlighted the fact of institutional funding being tied to the meeting of quotas of hitherto disadvantaged cohorts. Cynical though it might sound, the notion of social capital dovetails rather conveniently with that of widening participation; that is, the potential benefits of widening participation extend beyond the more obviously philanthropic motive of responding to a moral imperative to make educational opportunity more equitable and accessible, to an economic one focused on making nations commercially competitive – a goal which, while promising to benefit the population at large, at a political level also serves the self-interest of governments seeking to promote their own fortunes and consolidate their power. The need to be competitive in a global economy, along with growing (and, in many cases, ageing) populations, increases the need for a larger, stronger and better qualified workforce that is able to address skills shortages where they exist. This has implications for immigration policy – a social and political issue, and increasingly and controversially an educational issue too. Although immigration policy is prone to change on a regular basis as governments come and go, countries such as the United Kingdom and Australia have instituted policies that give preferential treatment to immigrants who come with highly valued skills. In Australia, where a points-based visa system exists, such skills are specified on a *Skilled Occupation List*, and applicants who are able to demonstrate that they have the necessary skills accrue points that help them reach the threshold necessary to securing a Points Tested Skilled Migration Visa (Australian Government: Department of Immigration and Border Protection). In addition, and more pertinent to the theme of this book, in response to the Australian Government-commissioned Knight Review (Knight, 2011), university graduates of Bachelor and Masters by Coursework degrees are now able to apply for a two-year post-study work visa following the completion of their degree, while Masters by Research and PhD graduates will be able to apply for a four-year post-study work visa. Although the government explicitly distances this initiative from the skilled migration visa programme, it is likely that some international students will strategically select their degree courses according to the Skills Occupation List, in the hope that a post-study work visa could assist them to more easily and quickly acquire Australian permanent residency, should they so desire. As a result, certain discipline areas are likely to experience a higher volume of applications.

As we have seen, international student numbers are a well-recognised cash-cow for English-medium universities, in particular at a time when universities the world over are being challenged to secure adequate funding if they are to survive in an economic environment where cutbacks to the sector are widespread. Universities are finding themselves under unprecedented pressure to compensate for decreases in government funding, and enrolling greater numbers of international students is an obvious strategy to employ in response. This is especially true in the United Kingdom where the 2012 domestic student fee increases have risked disincentivising higher education, thereby forcing universities to look to international students in an effort to compensate for any funding shortfall due to decreased domestic students enrolments. It is somewhat ironic, perhaps, that despite the rhetoric about widening participation so evident in recent years, it is precisely the disadvantaged cohorts which this agenda has sought to target who are likely to feel these fee increases most keenly. Furthermore, they are the most likely to be discouraged from applying to university: a thirty to sixty thousand pound loan will seem formidable indeed to many students, particularly those who come from low-SES backgrounds and who may also lack self-confidence and the belief that they could one day earn a salary that would enable them to pay back such a sum.

1.3   English language: the common denominator

The interactivity of those factors currently shaping higher education indicates the complexity of today's world more generally and highlights the challenge of making national and institutional policy and other decisions in ways that offer the best overall compromise in contexts with multiple pressures and conflicting priorities. And this is certainly true of the microcosm that is higher education. Understanding the essential interactivity of the principal movements, themes or drivers described in this chapter is key to understanding the importance of English language in higher education today, and the associated issues and challenges with which this book is fundamentally concerned.

As the title of this section suggests, when considering the changes experienced within the higher education sector in the last five decades or so, it is English language that emerges as the common denominator. The social justice agenda, for example, has meant that students from a far broader range of socio-economic and educational backgrounds are today entering higher education in considerably greater numbers than previously and this, as we shall see, has implications for the assumptions that educators are able to make about the knowledge and skills base they bring with them, and particularly the language and academic literacy skills possessed by commencing students (Pokorny and Pokorny, 2005). By extension, there are also implications for the positioning and prominence in universities of language support units, the nature of their work, and the demands placed on them (see, for example, Klinger and Murray, 2012). Few academics would challenge the claim that there is today a far greater need to provide language development opportunities to students than there was ten years ago, let alone thirty or forty years ago. While, to some extent, this is a result of changing theoretical perspectives (see Chapters 4 and 6), it is most certainly also a product of a changing student demographic.

New technologies and the resulting access by would-be students to information on universities – their national and world rankings, programme offerings, areas of research activity and expertise, institutional links, support services etc. – along with the ever-greater availability of increasingly powerful and elegant hardware and software and the ease and speed of international communication, mean that those looking to study in English-medium universities can acquire a far better picture of the relevant institutions and thus feel much better informed and, therefore, more confident in choosing a particular institution, submitting an application and, if successful, making the move overseas. For those who wish to remain in their home countries, study by distance – either wholly or in part – is often a realistic possibility thanks to those same technologies. In particular, they have become a vehicle through which to obtain a degree, credit towards a degree, or simply an intercultural experience and/or language learning opportunity through university study in an English-speaking country. This international experience, along with improved English language skills, intercultural competence and a more global outlook, develops the individuals concerned, broadens their horizons, adds a valuable and attractive dimension to their CVs, and thus promises to increase their job prospects, particularly if allied with a degree from a reputable university.

Equally, new technologies represent a means through which institutions can develop their sphere of influence and dramatically enhance their reputations and financial standing by broadening their target market and adjusting and promoting their offerings and delivery modes so as to appeal to international students who may originate from almost any part of the world, bringing with them a smorgasbord of linguistic, educational and broader cultural expectations and dispositions. This cultural diversity is, as we have seen, a product not only of a growing international student body but also of an increase in local multicultural communities that is in part also a result of globalisation. For certain members of those communities, English may not be their first language or the primary language spoken at home.

1.3.1   The English language 'problem'

In essence then, a changing global context has fundamentally altered the shape and dynamics of higher education institutions. One important consequence is that English-medium universities in particular now find themselves having to resolve a tension between, on the one hand, the desire to attract – in addition to their traditional constituents – overseas students (with the attendant benefits) and non-traditional cohorts (the focus of the widening participation agenda); and on the other, the language problems these students can bring with them and their potential impact on the curriculum, pedagogy and institutional resources and, ultimately, the institution's reputation.

Rising numbers of non-English-speaking background (NESB) students with weak language skills entering degree programmes puts strain on academics, who can find themselves struggling to meet the demands of the curriculum and complete prescribed syllabi as a result of having to slow down and adapt concepts, tasks and even their own language in order to ensure that students comprehend the material they are attempting to teach. As discussed previously, this can lead to a process of simplification, or 'dumbing down' (see, for example Attwood, 2009; BBC News, 2012), with multiple possible consequences. It can be a source of intense frustration for those students for whom English language, and the intellectual content of the material being taught, is *not* problematic. These individuals can feel that their own educational experience is being compromised in a number of respects. Firstly, they can feel that programme content is being diluted, rendering it less challenging and engaging and so less beneficial developmentally. Secondly, they can feel bored as material which they have understood on a first pass is repeated and reformulated in order to ensure that those with weaker language proficiency understand sufficiently. Thirdly, where group or pair work is involved and students are teamed with NESB students in practicals, seminars or tutorials, there may arise a situation where, though cultural dispositions, lack of comprehension and/or confidence in their language competence, NESB students are reluctant to participate and the onus therefore falls on other members of the group to take the initiative, complete the main bulk of the task and provide feedback to the larger group. Those students who do not have proficiency issues can resent this (see, for example, Harrison and Peacock, 2010).

Baik and Greig (2009) report that, sometimes, there is also a perception that where NESB students opt for or are required to take an ESL course as an elective rather than a course related to their degree, the work they submit is assessed more sympathetically, due to their weaker language skills, than that of students taking 'regular' courses. Whether right or wrong, such perceptions have the potential in themselves to cause resentment. In other words, there are not only practical issues created by disparities in language competence; there is also created potential for interpersonal issues that can result in poor classroom chemistry, poor learning outcomes and other challenging scenarios. Furthermore, the potential for frustration and resentment on the part of students proficient in English is likely to increase given the significant fee increases to which many have been subjected and a resultant reinforcing of the sense of 'students as clients paying for a service'. Indeed, at the time of writing, two articles recently appeared in a local university newspaper, one arguing that unions needed to fight for students' right to receive a minimum number of hours of input (ten, in this case) per week, and the other quantifying the cost of staff strikes over pay to students paying £9000 a year in tuition fees. This illustrates vividly the changing financial realities facing students entering higher education and the accompanying shift in mindset: twenty years ago, the average student, required to attend eight to ten hours of lectures a week, was far more likely to look enviously upon a peer having to attend only four! Any consideration of relative value for money barely entered their thinking.

While NESB students can certainly make the classroom a more vibrant and stimulating teaching and learning environment, the challenges they can present are by no means confined to the students themselves and their non-native speaker counterparts; they can also be a source of frustration, perplexity, even embarrassment for academic staff who may feel shackled by students' inability to communicate and compromised in their ability to deliver material at a speed and in a manner they would wish. In addition, while there are those academic staff who feel that addressing students' language problems is not part of their role and who may, inadvertently or otherwise, marginalise 'problem students' in the classroom and/or direct them to language support services for a quick fix, there are others who feel inclined, even morally obliged, to help students but are also very conscious of the fact that they do not have the necessary expertise to do so. In many cases, there is a belief that students who are unable to communicate at a level of proficiency sufficient to enable them to negotiate their studies without compromising the curriculum, pedagogy and the opportunity and educational experience of their peers, should not be in the classroom at all. Of particular concern are those cases where, despite serious shortcomings with their English, students nonetheless progress through their degree programmes and graduate successfully. This can be down to methods of assessment – with multiple choice and short-answer tasks and portfolio work being less likely to highlight those students with weak language skills – but it also raises questions about the rigour with which assessed work is marked, and whether and to what extent academic staff may be being lenient in the interests of the continued financial security of the department and its reputation, and the concomitant pressure to maximise completion rates and minimise attrition levels.

Of course, while certain assessment practices and a culture of sympathetic marking may serve a department's purposes internally, they can quickly have an adverse effect on the perceptions of external stakeholders if students do not exhibit the kind of communication skills expected of an English-medium university graduate, particularly by employers. This lack of communication skills should be of great concern to academic staff and senior management, not only because it suggests that the institution is not serving its students well and is out of kilter with the kind of graduate qualities I referred to earlier, and which universities habitually publish as part of their efforts to promote and define their respective missions, but because it raises disturbing questions about the quality of the degrees the university is awarding. That is, employers are likely to be concerned upon receiving new university recruits who have completed their studies successfully yet are unable to demonstrate good general communication skills as well as a grasp of the language and discourse of their particular professions (see, for example, Birrell and Hawthorne, 1996). And that concern would derive not merely from the fact that students may struggle to understand and make themselves understood, important though this undoubtedly is, but also from the realisation that students who struggle with language in the workplace post-graduation, and who might reasonably be expected to have a higher level of proficiency as graduates than they did as undergraduates, would have been unlikely to understand much of the content of their degree studies. The fact that they successfully graduated nonetheless, is likely to set alarm bells ringing, is a great disservice to the students and, ultimately, reflects poorly on the graduating universities. I have characterised the situation as follows:

In some cases, lecturers are forced to 'tone down' their course materials and spend time addressing English language problems many regard as outside the scope of their expertise and locus of responsibility. This calls into question the quality and depth of both the knowledge base and English language competency with which these students exit their programmes of study, and thus, by extension, their future prospects. For those hoping to enter an English-speaking workforce that is increasingly multicultural regardless of geographic location, significant issues arise around their employability (see, e.g., Birrell & Healey, 2008; Burch, 2008). This is of concern not only to employers, who increasingly regard good language and communication skills as critical attributes of an effective employee, but also to graduates, who risk finding themselves at a disadvantage in the job market, and their almae matres, whose reputations are at stake. (Murray, 2010a, p. 344)

Once again, government (see Chapter 2) and media reports reflecting concerns at the threat caused to standards by students unable to communicate sufficiently well in English are rife. The following are but a taster:

From a BBC online article (BBC News Wales, op cit.)
The lecturer claims that the academic standards of some courses at British universities have suffered in recent years as universities concentrate on attracting foreign students.

'Internationalisation in itself is absolutely necessary for any modern university – however, this is not at any cost. [. . .] What we're finding is that we can't teach the students because their English language ability is so low.'

He claims pressure by university authorities to secure funding from international students means standards of some courses are lowered. It is claimed this involves students struggling with English.

'We should be focusing on quality and I would say that UK higher education has suffered significant reputational damage as a result of the recruitment policies by many universities. The question I'm asking is can we recover from this?'

Some university tutors are pressurised to accept substandard work by overseas students for financial reasons, BBC Wales has been told.

One lecturer claims exams are simplified or dropped from some Masters business courses.

From the Times Higher Education (Prof. Susan Bassnett)
I am not the only academic to have acted as an external examiner, assessor or auditor in the sector and to have seen scripts in English so poor that the students wouldn't scrape a GCSE.

I have been asked to 'disregard linguistic competence and focus on content' in some places.

Every university has been touting for international applicants, and although many are good, often excellent, students, the pressure to boost numbers means that strict selection criteria are not always observed.

Universities have colluded with this situation for years and successive governments have turned a blind eye because it has enabled them to continue to cut higher education funding. Nor are those colleagues stuck at the chalk face with students with poor language skills and irregular attendance likely to do any whistleblowing, since it is common knowledge that a lot of people's salaries are dependent on the cash cows being roped in.

As we will see in Chapter 2, professional accreditation bodies are becoming increasingly aware of this issue and, in response, are no longer viewing the fact of holding a degree as evidence of adequate English language proficiency. As a result, many are now electing to set their own English language standards, the meeting of which is a prerequisite to professional registration. In Australia, for example, the Nursing and Midwifery Board English Language Skills Registration Standard (2010) and the Education and Training Reform Act (2006) require graduates to demonstrate, via performance on the IELTS (International English Language Testing System) or the OET (Occupational English Test), that they have achieved competence in English *in addition to* the successful completion of a degree course in Australia. Thus, for graduates of professional degree courses in allied health and education, this means additional financial outlay and the necessary associated investment of time; and it looks as though other professions (e.g. accountancy) are moving in the same direction. The Registration Standards for the Medical Board of Australia state that 'all internationally qualified applicants for registration, or applicants who qualified for registration in Australia but did not complete their secondary education in English, must demonstrate that they have the necessary English language skills for registration purposes'. In the case of IELTS (academic module), a minimum score of 7.0 in each of the four components (listening, reading, writing and speaking) is required, although an overall pass in the OET, with grades A or B in each of the four components, is also acceptable, as is the successful completion of the NZREX (New Zealand Registration Examination), administered by the New Zealand Medical Council, or the PLAB test (Professional and Linguistic Assessments Board) of the General Medical Council of the United Kingdom. These results must be obtained in one sitting and 'within two years prior to applying for registration' (Medical Board of Australia, 2010, p. 1). In New Zealand the 'standard requirement for several registration agencies, such as the Medical, Dental and Pharmacy Councils, is an overall score of at least 7.5 in the Academic module, with no individual band score of less than 7.0' (Read and Wette, 2009, p. 40). In the United Kingdom, any international applicant to the Health Care and Professions Council must have achieved a 7.0 with no element below 6.5 on the IELTS and a minimum score of 100/120 on the TOEFL, unless working as a Speech and Language Therapist, where the scores are slightly higher (8.0 with no element below 7.5 on the IELTS or a minimum score of 118/120 on the TOEFL) (Health and Care Professions Council, accessed online). The General Dental Council in the United Kingdom only accepts the IELTS with applicants showing a minimum overall score of 7.0, and with a score of no less than 6.5 in any of the individual sections (General Dental Council, accessed online), while the UK Nursing and Midwifery Council requires all non-EU applicants to have achieved IELTS 7.0 overall, with at least 7.0 in all of the four sub-skills (Nursing and Midwifery Council, accessed online). The Victorian Institute of Teaching in Australia requires an overall IELTS 7.5 with the following required in each of the skill areas: speaking 8.0, listening 8.0, reading 7.0 and writing 7.0. Alternatively, it will accept the International Second Language Proficiency Rating (ISLPR) (with level 4 required in each of the four sub-skills), or the Professional English Assessment for Teachers (PEAT), with band A required in each of the four sub-skills (Victorian Institute of Teaching, accessed online). The Legal Profession Admission Board in Australia requires non-native speakers of English to demonstrate English language proficiency by taking the IELTS academic module, with an overall score of 8 and minimum sub-skill scores of 7.0 in listening, 7.0 in reading, 8 in writing and 7.5 in speaking (Legal Profession Admission Board, accessed online).

And what of the students themselves – surely the most important element in all of this? What of students who secure entry to university only to find themselves struggling to understand and make themselves understood in lectures, seminars, tutorials, practicums and placements; unable to comprehend the necessary reading materials; and lacking the confidence and ability to complete assignments of the required quality? What of those students who may have left school prematurely and who see higher education as a daunting prospect and may feel socio-culturally and educationally dislocated and lack the skills and strategies to cope with the demands of academic work at this level? As a result of their inability, often, to engage with the learning process, to make friends and to fully integrate into university life, these students can very quickly suffer anxiety, frustration, demotivation and panic. For those returning to education relatively late in life, who are the first in their families to enter education and/or who feel from the outset that university is beyond them, such feelings are perhaps too readily taken by them (and sometimes their families) as confirmation of their unsuitability and lack of capacity. As a consequence, they may decide to simply drop out. For some, that decision will no doubt be taken easily and with relief, but for others it can be painful and emotionally fraught, and can reinforce pre-existing feelings of inadequacy. In both cases, however, otherwise intellectually capable individuals fail to realise their full academic potential. For others, and particularly overseas students who may also be struggling to acculturate to university life and build a support network of friends, language challenges and the resultant difficulty in coping with their studies can be frustrating and demoralising, particularly for those who otherwise know that they have the intellectual capacity to succeed. Some may ultimately make the decision to withdraw – a decision that is rarely taken lightly, for it can carry the stigma of 'failure' within their families and cultures, and as such represent a potential source of real trauma for those concerned. This can be a compounded by feelings of shame and guilt for those whose parents have made enormous sacrifices, even life changes, in order to invest in their children's future.

1.3.2   English language as a systemic problem

The fact that these issues concerning students' English language competence are arising in many – if not all – English-medium universities today is indicative of a systemic problem, one which some would say is rooted in misplaced ideological allegiances concerning the fundamental nature of universities, their purpose and the ways in which they need to operate if they are to respond effectively to multifarious and often conflicting pressures in order to compete and thus survive. Yet while it may be almost impossible to discuss English language in higher education today without reference to particular agendas and the political and commercial interests that impinge on it, it is also important to recognise that these agendas and interests reflect the particular paradigm in which universities currently operate, and this is not necessarily one that is supported by many – even most – stakeholders in the sector; least of all, perhaps, by those who work in the area of student English language development. It is probable that most will see themselves and their students as victims of these pressures and of management policies that seek to reconcile them, and the compromises they make in the process.

What is undeniable is that many working in higher education today, whether as academics or administrators, are acutely aware of an 'English language problem' in the sector, the existence of which is surely attested to by the fact of an increase in regulation concerning the way in which universities assess their students' language ability pre- and post-enrolment and the measures many are adopting with the intention of providing students with the developmental mechanisms and resources necessary to ensuring that, once enrolled, they have the best possible chance of succeeding in their studies. As we shall see in Chapter 2, today more than ever before, universities are subject to various policy and moral imperatives and the need to demonstrate compliance in this area of their activities to higher education auditing bodies. For those institutions that are able to come up with well-conceived, theoretically informed and effectively implemented solutions to the English language problem, and to demonstrate their efficacy, the rewards are considerable, both in terms of their standing within the sector and among its regulators, and in terms of student enrolments and graduate outcomes. Clearly, universities able to boast the means and a track record of supporting students in this increasingly critical area are going to be a reassuring and thus more attractive prospect to would-be students, and as such they will have gained an important competitive edge.

1.4   Summary

This chapter has sought to provide the contextual backdrop against which any meaningful discussion of the English language issue in higher education needs to be set. In doing so it has identified and discussed a number of key factors that have shaped policy and practice in higher education in recent years; in particular, the social justice agenda – most obviously realised in the widening participation movement, new technologies, globalisation, funding mechanisms (especially student fees and research), international students and multicultural classrooms, and the considerable emphasis now placed on the student experience. I have argued that these factors interact in important and complex ways and that the issue of English language both influences and is influenced by each of them. And the stakes, for individual universities, for higher education more generally and for national economies, are high, as their reputations and future health are ultimately in question. This fact suggests that it is likely to remain prominent as an issue in the sector for the foreseeable future, and it is no doubt this realisation that has motivated the move towards greater regulation of English language standards and provision in tertiary education: the focus of Chapter 2.

2 English language: the need for and impact of policy and regulation

2.1 Introduction

The regulation of any field of endeavour from without is normally an indication that things are not being sufficiently subjected to scrutiny and regulation within an institution, sector or field of activity, or that the scale of the activity concerned and the variation in the extent to which it is scrutinised and regulated is such that some form of external regulation and monitoring needs to be imposed. Few in higher education, and in particular those involved in the design and delivery of English language programmes, would deny that English language is one such area of activity; indeed, as I indicated in Chapter 1 (1.3.1), many would argue that some form of regulation is long overdue. As we have seen, for a variety of reasons the issue of English language proficiency in the university sector is one of growing prominence as, for both financial as well as reputational reasons, institutions recognise the advantages – indeed the necessity – of increasing the proportion of international students enrolling in their degree programmes. Failure to respond to that need will almost certainly result in an inability to compete in an increasingly crowded and competitive sector and, ultimately, to survive. However, enrolling more international students can be counterproductive if high numbers ultimately fail their courses, compromise standards and have difficulty securing employment post-graduation due to an insufficient level of English language competence.

As we saw in Chapter 1, the unprecedented and increasing pressure on universities to grow international student enrolments raises a number of very legitimate but complex questions and concerns involving the way in which universities are dealing with the issue of English language standards (Arkoudis, Baik and Richardson, 2012). This chapter unpacks some of those questions and concerns with a view to better understanding the rationale behind moves in countries such as the United Kingdom and Australia to regulate and monitor institutional English language strategies through internal mechanisms and external quality assurance agencies. In doing so, it will become evident that they implicate structures, processes and procedures that come into play prior to and during the student's course of study, as well as issues of competence, performance and perception post-graduation.

2.2   The rationale for regulation

2.2.1   English language entry requirements

English language entry requirements raise at least two questions that demand careful consideration. First: are the tests used by institutions to determine whether or not students have the necessary level of language competence to study fit for purpose? That is, do they do what their developers claim they do and what universities expect them to do? A QAA report published in 2009, and discussed in greater detail later in this chapter, drew attention to this question via its recommendation that there be a review conducted of English-language tests and the development of guidance for international students about the support they could expect once enrolled in their degree programmes. In making that recommendation, it acknowledged the potential threat to standards and to the student learning experience posed by inadequate admissions procedures, and in particular tests used to determine whether or not students had sufficient competency in the language to meet the demands of their studies. The report stated:

Specific challenges have been identified with regard to the admission of students with English-language skills that are either insufficient to deal with the demands of their programme of study or have the potential to have a detrimental effect on the learning experience of all students. (QAA, 2009, p. 2)

An important secondary question that arises in relation to the veracity of the English tests used by universities to determine students' linguistic suitability for higher education study is whether universities and their staff have a sufficient understanding of the tests they approve for this purpose and the claims that their developers make of them; for no matter how valid and reliable a test may be, if it is misused and/or its results misinterpreted, then it will fail to do what its users expect and require of it.

The second question that demands consideration is whether the English language test scores required for university entry are set appropriately by institutions. And here, once again, related questions arise, in this case concerning (a) the basis on which institutions set their language requirements; (b) the propriety and integrity of the common practice of benchmarking in this regard against immediate competitor institutions or against the sector more generally, rather than according to their own knowledge and understanding of the tests themselves, particularly in relation to the varied linguistic demands of different disciplines; and (c) again, the knowledge those responsible for setting institutional English language entry requirements have of the tests they employ.

Although, as we shall see, British universities today have somewhat less of a say in how they set their English language requirements, the need for some form of regulation was highlighted in 1996 by Cownie and Addison, who conducted a study from which it emerged that although seventy-six per cent of their respondents indicated that their institution required international students to provide evidence of proficiency in English as a requirement of entry, only seventeen per cent of those institutions were seen as adhering rigidly to the standards of English which they stipulated.

2.2.2 International student pathways into universities

There are normally multiple routes available to international students seeking to enter higher education. While the vast majority of these will provide an indication of graduating students' English language competence and preparedness for tertiary study, as Coley (1999) observed with particular reference to the Australian context, sixty-one pieces of evidence were, at the time of her writing, accepted by the universities as fulfilling their English language requirements. While that number will inevitably fluctuate, it nonetheless raises questions concerning the validity of claims of (or assumed) equivalence, both explicit and implicit, of these many different kinds of evidence of language competence – an issue to which I shall return in Chapter 4, section 4.2.2, when I look in greater detail at issues relating to pre-enrolment language assessment. Clearly, though, it is a major – some might say near-impossible – task to research and produce meaningful statistics on the multiple pathways that exist, and to establish equivalence, particularly given their diverse nature, the fact that in many cases they were designed for different purposes, and the variation that exists in the contexts and ways in which they are used. Final statements of competence or grades based on formative and summative assessment as part of a foundation course academic English language curriculum, cannot, for example, be meaningfully compared with results achieved on an approved, properly validated English language test, even where both highlight similar skills. In the case of the predictive validity of tests or final course statements of competence, these can only be ascertained through conducting longitudinal research that tracks students' progress through part or all of their academic careers (Light, Xu and Mossop, 1987; Cotton and Conrow, 1998; Kerstjens and Nery, 2000; Dooey and Oliver, 2002; Ingram and Bayliss, 2007). Here, however, the fact that multiple intervening factors come into play that may influence students' performance on their degree programmes (see for example, Bellingham, 1993; Allwright and Banerjee, 1997; Cotton and Conrow, ibid.) and thus potentially confound attempts to draw useful conclusions, means that it is on trends that any analysis of such research needs to focus.

Even where students have previously been resident and/or had schooling for a specified period in countries where English is the primary language of communication, this is no guarantee of their competence in the language. Nor is their having completed a first degree at an English-medium university. At the time of writing, UK Visas and Immigration (UKVI – formally the UK Border Agency (UKBA)) requires that in order to be eligible for a visa to study at university in the United Kingdom, students should be able to demonstrate English language proficiency at B2 level in all four skill areas (reading, writing, listening and speaking) on the Council of Europe's Common European Framework of Reference for Languages: Learning, Teaching, Assessment (commonly abbreviated to CEFR) (Council of Europe, 2001). Although the completion of a first degree in the medium of English is generally taken by universities as evidence of an adequate level of English for study in higher education, the ability to demonstrate this in terms of B2 proficiency in the four skill areas is problematic unless universities choose to require all international students who have not been educated in English in an inner-circle country to take one of the UKVI-recognised Secure English Language Tests (SELTs). Yet many universities are understandably reluctant to do so, in part because it compromises their ability to be competitive by discouraging would-be students from applying to them; consequently, they need to ensure that they have a sound and defensible rationale for determining which of those international students who have completed a first degree in English can reasonably be assumed to have at least a B2 level of proficiency in the language.

2.2.3   Defining those cohorts that are the focus of regulation

An issue to which we shall return later in this chapter, and indeed in this book, concerns the fact that initiatives to regulate English language in higher education have focused almost exclusively on NESB students, a fact from which there flow important consequences for other cohorts both in terms of the assessment of English language skills and the nature of English language provision offered by universities to their students. For now, though, we will confine our attention to NESB students.

Terms such as NESB, EAL (English as an additional language) and LOTE (language(s) other than English) are inherently problematic in that they tend to convey a sense that the cohort being identified is a homogeneous group the members of which share a similar profile or demographic, when in reality they represent a very diverse and complex range of individuals and groups. This can create difficulties for any attempt at regulation, for one cannot begin to think sensibly about the processes involved in regulation without first having a clear definition of the cohort it is intended that their implementation should benefit. Equally, those seeking to comply need to know precisely with whom such regulation is concerned if they are to establish appropriate systems and procedures for demonstrating compliance.

NESB is a label that is typically and somewhat crudely applied only to international students. However, just as international students may include students for whom English is a first language, equally domestic students may include speakers of English as a second or additional language. Some of these may, in turn, be quite fluent in English yet habitually speak a language other than English at home. Other NESB students who are officially categorised as 'domestic' may be recent migrants and only have been resident in the country for a very short period such that their English language skills are not necessarily well developed. Understanding the heterogeneity of NESB students is important because it has a bearing on the conceptualisation of the provision of English language development opportunities once they have enrolled at university. In particular, it has the potential to influence the way in which one accurately and appropriately identifies who should be the beneficiaries of such provision, whether via an agreed-upon and all-inclusive definition of the cohort and/or some form of pre- and/or post-enrolment language assessment. That is, any form of regulation needs to make certain that all individuals potentially at risk linguistically are clearly defined and accounted for and that there are suitable and effective mechanisms in place to ensure that those in need get access to appropriate opportunities for English language development, the focus of the next section.

2.2.4   Opportunities for English language development

As we shall see in Chapter 4, the fact that significant numbers of students struggle with English despite having met university language entry criteria calls into question the tests themselves and the way in which universities use – and perhaps abuse – them, either through ignorance or in order to ensure they meet enrolment targets. It also calls into question the nature of the pathways via which they arrive at university and the adequacy of the English language preparation they have received. Somewhat ironically, such preparation might reasonably be regarded as adequate by those institutions graduating them (English language schools, university English language centres etc.), as well as by the students themselves, by virtue of their having successfully met university English language entry criteria; indeed, English language schools and centres will often gauge and promote the success of their programmes on this very basis. Unfortunately, however, regardless of what these graduating institutions know or choose to concern themselves with regarding the actual demands of degree studies, the truth is that all too often their students go on to begin university careers assuming, naively perhaps but certainly not unreasonably, that because they have met their receiving institution's English language conditions of entry they must, therefore, have the language skills necessary to negotiate their studies with relative ease. If and when they realise that they do not, they can feel frustrated, anxious and misled; this despite English language entry thresholds frequently being described as 'minimum requirements' by both receiving universities and testing organisations such as IELTS (Matthews, 2012; Stanley and Murray, 2013). This misalignment of perception and reality suggests not only that universities need to do more to inform their students of what English language university scores mean in real terms and in terms of their future developmental needs[1] but also, and more importantly, that gate-keeping mechanisms are flawed in some way and/or that universities accept NESB students on the understanding – not necessarily communicated sufficiently to would-be students – that they may require English language development in parallel with their degree studies. In both cases, there is an argument that there should be opportunities for these students to enhance their language skills once they enter university. Most universities recognise this and have in place various models of provision shaped according to a range of factors: their aspirations in terms of institutional brand and their commitment (and *perceived* commitment) to supporting this cohort; their structures and financial circumstances; their student demographic; their resident English language expertise and knowledge of the broader field of applied linguistics; their conceptualisation of language proficiency and what it is, in more precise terms, that these students need; and the basis on which they prioritise access to language development services. Inevitably, the settings for each of these parameters will vary between institutions, with the result that the nature and quality of provision can and does vary quite dramatically. A 2012 *Times Education* Survey showed that the variation in the annual spend by universities was considerable, with some outlaying an average of £903 per international student enrolled, and others £227. While this can reflect the fact that some universities are more discriminating and demanding in terms of the students they admit in respect of their language proficiency (those spending more admit students with greater language needs), it may also mean that students paying similar tuition fees may have very different English language learning opportunities and experiences. The QAA's 2009 report (ibid.) acknowledges this:

While institutions recognise the importance of providing English-language and other support for international students on a continuing basis, there appears to be some variation in the availability and/or effectiveness of such support mechanisms. (p. 2)

---

[1] This, of course, assumes that university staff members are sufficiently well versed in the relevant English language tests themselves to be able to impart this information to future students.

It is the job of regulation to redress such inequities for both moral and educational reasons, and the fact of the enormous pressure on universities to increase their international student numbers makes it critically important that standards of English language provision are at the very least adequate and fit for purpose, given the characteristics of the local context and, most particularly, the student demographic. In light of the elevated fees many NESB students pay, and the fact of their having met language conditions stipulated by their universities which may well necessitate further language improvement, there is a growing sense among all stakeholders – regulators, senior management, the students themselves and their parents, lecturers and departments – that they have a right to expect language development opportunities that help ensure they have the best chance of reaching their academic potential and achieving the best degrees of which they are capable.

The quality of provision needs to be determined by regulators according to the following criteria:

- Whether there is a coherent institution-wide strategy for English language development;
- Whether there is a sound, theoretically-informed rationale underpinning any such strategy;
- The efficiency and effectiveness of its organisation and administration;
- The extent of its relevance and adequacy;
- The quality of its delivery and, as a corollary of this, that of its management and English language teaching staff;
- Whether there are mechanisms in place for evaluating its effectiveness;
- Whether and to what extent it gives students access within the context of their other study commitments;
- Whether it is equitable and gives all those in need equal, or at least fair, access.

These criteria provide a broad quality assurance framework that offers guidance to universities looking to design and institute English language strategies, and they will be unpacked and discussed in detail throughout this book. In terms of a more comprehensive typography of quality criteria, this will be discussed later in this chapter (section 2.3), particularly in relation to regulatory documents published in the United Kingdom and Australia, and the British Council's English Language Accreditation Scheme (*Accreditation UK*).

2.2.5 *The training and professional development of academic staff*

While the skills of English language tutors may be an obvious focus of regulation, a less obvious one is the skills of university academic staff in general. The frustration that can be felt by academic staff who, particularly in business and science disciplines, frequently deliver lectures to and conduct seminars and tutorials with groups of students of predominantly non-English-speaking backgrounds who can struggle with the language and with the expectations of the local academic culture, was highlighted in Chapter 1. While the strength of feeling often expressed by such staff is understandable, perhaps even justified in some cases, the reality of multicultural, multilingual classrooms is certainly not about to change. This means that although universities have a duty to ensure that they have in place appropriate pre-entry gatekeeping mechanisms and post-entry forms of English language provision, there is also an obligation on institutions and their academic staff to provide and take up, respectively, professional development opportunities for up-skilling such that they are better placed to deal with the added challenges – but also potential richness – that multicultural/multilingual classrooms promise for the teaching–learning experience. Today, the skills-set required of academic staff needs to be broader and more sophisticated than ever and to reflect an awareness of the fundamental interconnectedness of language and culture. Academic staff need to appreciate, for example, how meaning and the way in which it is linguistically encoded and interpreted is culturally determined, and that classroom behaviours and learning styles are products of students' cultural upbringing and predispositions (Pütz and Neff-van Aertselaer, 2008; Joy and Kolb, 2009). Within the context of ever-increasing diversity, they need to be able to understand, manage and mediate difference not only in relation to their own interactions with students as individuals and as heterogeneous groups but also in relation to student–student interactions (Alptekin, 2002; Arkoudis and Tran, 2010; Barker, Hibbins and Farrelly, 2011; Broughan and Hunt, 2013; Carroll and Ryan, 2005; Chang, 2006; Crichton and Scarino, 2007; Crose, 2011; de Vita, 2002; Jiang, 2011; Kramsch, 1993; Leask, 2011). They need to be sensitive to cultural differences in relation to the perception, expression and realisation of concepts such as independence, autonomy and groupwork/teamwork, privacy/confidentiality, power relations, leadership, lines of responsibility and conflict resolution. As Samovar et al. observe, 'teachers who understand cultural diversity … are more likely to be successful in their multicultural classrooms' (2006, p. 2), and to that end the analysing of cultural issues can offer insights into the unconscious processes that shape individuals' perceptions of reality as well as patterns of interaction, including language use and communication (Scollon and Scollon, 2011, p. 268). As Gelb (2012, p. 1) argues, this kind of analysis 'may benefit teachers as well as learners by raising awareness of the hidden cultural assumptions and biases that they bring to the classroom', and Scollon and Scollon's 'Grammar of Context' framework and the four elements of culture it cites – ideology, socialisation, forms of discourse, and face systems – provides one tool for such analysis that can usefully inform instructional strategies.

In a somewhat similar vein, the International Education Association of Australia (IEAA, 2013) proposes a set of guiding principles (see Table 2.1)

Table 2.1. *Principles for working with linguistically and culturally diverse learners*

Principle	Realisation of principle
Focus on students as learners	• Providing prompt feedback to students on their performance, including their use of language for academic and professional purposes; • Not making assumptions about students' learning preferences based on their cultural background or their appearance; • Providing a variety of learning and assessment activities; • Providing examples, models and suggestions of ways of approaching learning in the discipline; • Facilitating the development of self-assessment and reflection on learning; • Embedding the development of academic and information literacy skills into your course; • Supporting the development of communities of learners through, for example, peer mentoring and peer-assisted study programmes.
Respect and adjust for diversity	• Finding out about incoming students' linguistic, cultural and educational backgrounds: student groups will differ, one from another, and individuals will differ within those groups; • Recognising diversity in the cultural, socio-cultural, academic and linguistic backgrounds of the local student population; • Adjusting teaching, learning and assessment activities to take into account and utilise your students' diverse cultural, socio-cultural, academic and linguistic backgrounds, work and life experiences; • Asking students about their preferred modes of learning and encouraging them to try new approaches to learning; • Maintaining a sharp eye on equivalence, fairness, inclusivity through reflective practice informed by student performance data; • Building on and using your students' cultural and social capital and individual differences; • Seeking out examples, suggestions and guidance on effective ways in which others have made adjustments to cater for student diversity.
Provide context-specific information and support	• Recognising the need to adjust teaching and service provision for learning context and student cohort; • Conducting a needs analysis at the beginning of a course and using findings to shape provision; • Referring students where necessary to specialist services, preferably tailored to the needs of your course/subject; • Seeking advice and assistance from support services staff with specialised knowledge of embedding the development of academic literacies into course and assessment design;

Table 2.1. (*cont.*)

Principle	Realisation of principle
	• Encouraging students in lectures and tutorials and/or online to ask questions about expectations in relation to assessment criteria (including the weighting of components such as grammar, vocabulary, content and structure);
	• Explaining what different task requirements mean ('evaluate', 'justify', 'analyse') and creating opportunities for students to use and critique exemplars of efforts to meet task requirements;
	• Clarifying what good performance is by providing marking rubrics which explain each criterion; clarifying expected standards or performance for specific assessment tasks;
	• Waiting after asking a question to give less confident English speakers time to formulate an answer.
Enable meaningful intercultural dialogue and engagement	• Designing cross-cultural tasks which use and link with students' knowledge and experience;
	• Providing specific preparation and support for all students to develop their cross-cultural communication skills prior to and during group tasks;
	• Ensuring appropriate support is available to develop all students' academic and social language skills;
	• Assessing the development of intercultural skills and individual students' participation in intercultural group work at regular intervals;
	• Talking to other staff teaching on the programme about how they enable and encourage intercultural engagement;
	• Involving specialists in teaching intercultural communication skills in the preparation of all students for cross-cultural group work;
	• Assessing the process as well as the outcome of cross-cultural group assignments;
	• Encouraging self-reflection and self-assessment by students as they engage in cross-cultural group assignments.
Be adaptable, flexible and responsive to evidence	• Designing assignments that allow all students, regardless of their cultural background, to draw on their life experiences as they learn;
	• Seeking regular feedback from colleagues on your effectiveness in upholding each of these Good Practice Principles: Teaching Across Cultures;
	• Engaging with literature on teaching and learning across cultures;
	• Experimenting with a variety of different approaches to teaching and monitoring their effectiveness with different groups of learners;
	• Collecting evidence and advice on your effectiveness as a teacher of diverse cultural groups from a variety of sources;

Table 2.1. (*cont.*)

Principle	Realisation of principle
Prepare students for life in a globalised world	• Seeking out colleagues from diverse backgrounds and discussing approaches to teaching with them; • Getting feedback from transnational partner staff on course content and assessment task design, in particular on whether you have inadvertently unfairly disadvantaged students from cultural backgrounds different from your own. • Critiquing the implicit assumptions of disciplinary perspectives and ways of knowing and encouraging your students to do the same; • Developing your students' understanding of the requirements of professional practice and citizenship in a globalised world; • Engaging with global problems and global issues and encouraging your students to critique these issues (including in assessment tasks); • Discussing the progressive development of the skills, knowledge and attitudes required of global citizens and professionals across the programme informally with colleagues and as part of formal periodic course and programme reviews; • Making a commitment to the development of your own and your students' intercultural communication skills.

(Adapted from IEAA (2013))

which together offer something of a roadmap for teachers and teacher educators that can help ensure that those working with students in higher education and elsewhere are equipped with the skills they need to shape the learning process in such a way that it benefits *all* students and provides a learning experience that not only maximises their academic potential but develops them more broadly as interculturally competent graduates prepared for global citizenship (Volet and Ang, 2012).

Despite issues about staff workloads that it can raise, there are signs that universities are waking up to the need for this kind of professional development as more offer courses to their staff that seek to raise awareness of the issues that arise from working with diverse student groups and to furnish them with the sensitivity and techniques needed to manage such groups effectively and thereby maximise learning and ensure the broader development of the individual. Increasingly, such development occurs within the context of graduate diploma or certificate courses in teaching in higher education that are increasingly required of staff as part of their probation, irrespective of their level of experience (see, for example, Quinn and Vorster, 2004; Ginns, Kitay and Prosser, 2008). And it is very much in universities' interests to make certain that their staff have the awareness and skills that such courses seek to promote, for students who feel marginalised and unable to engage are unlikely to integrate and achieve; some may not finish, and those who do are likely to reflect negatively on their experience. In a sector where student satisfaction, as measured by student barometers and other feedback mechanisms, is viewed as critically important for reputational and business reasons, this is regarded by senior management and academic departments as a highly undesirable state of affairs. Furthermore, it is not only the NESB students that universities risk alienating if they fail to successfully address the diversity issue. Evidence from these same student barometers have, in some cases, indicated a strength of feeling that is striking among ESB students who feel dissatisfied and angry because they see their own education as being seriously compromised by the growing number of students with inadequate levels of English and/or who are disinclined to voice opinions or take the initiative in groups due to cultural predispositions – specifically, the result very often of their being products of collectivist-oriented rather than individualist-oriented cultures (see Hofstede, 1991, p. 51). Specifically, these ESB students often resent being placed in groups where their NESB counterparts are unable to participate fully because of language or cultural factors and where, as a result, they end up having to take the lead and, often, do the great bulk of the work. Indeed, they frequently feel they have no option but to assume the greater share of responsibility in tasks and group projects if they are to produce acceptable outcomes and achieve good marks (Dunne, 2009, 2013; Harrison and Peacock, 2010). This was one of a number of emergent themes identified in a study by Harrison and Peacock (ibid.), who took an Integrated Threat Theory perspective (Stephan and Stephan, 2000) on their data, and which included: unsatisfactory peer learning experiences; fear about lower group work marks; concerns about 'swamping' by unfamiliar others; absence of shared cultural reference points; language barriers and the need for 'mindful' communication; fear of causing offence; fear of inadvertent racism and related peer disapproval; lack of differentiation between individuals; and the special position of 'Chinese' students (p. 887). Even where ESB students do opt to take the lead in group tasks, they sometimes feel unable to produce their best work because they are held back and unable to benefit from the input of peers who may be unable or reluctant to express views that could make a valuable and original contribution.

The United Kingdom's Quality Assurance Agency's (QAA's) 2009 report on quality and standards in higher education highlighted this problem, quoting a visiting lecturer as saying that 'This [lack of language competence among international students] inevitably interferes with the learning experience of other students.' (p. 14). The report refers to press and media reports, one of which cites material taken from an internal institutional discussion forum, which reported that 'international students with poor English language skills have led to a "plague of plagiarism", and their presence is "downgrading" the experience of home students as lecturers have to give basic English lessons' (2009, p. 12). It continues:

The 'interference' mechanism was not specified, but in other articles and discussion threads the assertion is frequently repeated, sometimes with the explanation that students whose first language is English are expected to provide additional language support for those for whom English is a second language, and that the additional support needs of international students were detracting from the learning experience of their peers. During focus group discussions, a number of participants from across the groups supported the notion that where issues relating to cultural differences to academic study and language ability arise, they affect not only the learning opportunities of international students but also those of 'home' students. (2009, p. 14)

Furthermore, as Baik and Greig note, ESB students' feelings intensify when NESB students cluster together for course tasks and activities or receive 'special' attention in the form of credit-bearing English courses that their native-speaker peers sometimes perceive as soft options (Baik and Greig, 2009, p. 405). This observation is also reflected in the QAA's report:

The challenges to the learning experiences of all students posed by the inconsistency with which international students are able to communicate with staff and other students was raised in each of the focus group discussions. Home students in this context were reported to feel 'disadvantaged' when academic staff appeared to make dispensations for international students' language capabilities, and where they perceived that they are likely to receive lower overall marks for group work when teamed with some international students. (2009, p. 17)

While there is little doubt that, in some cases at least, universities have a case to answer in terms of their English language entry criteria and the skills of their academic staff, there is also evidence of a lack of understanding – and thus tolerance – among ESB students about those cultural behaviours of their peers that are out of sync with what is familiar to them as native speakers, naturally au fait with local cultural behavioural norms. In a world where education is now globalised, intercultural interactions between both native and non-native speakers of English as well as between non-native speakers have become commonplace, particularly in institutions where there are high proportions of international students (see, for example, Tight, 2013), and it is in the interests of all of such students, academic staff and universities that intercultural awareness is developed in the academic community at large and that its value and importance, within not only the educational setting but also the workplace, is promulgated among all stakeholders. In this regard, Harrison and Peacock (ibid., pp. 878–9) speak of two specific (and 'challenging') components of the 'internationalisation at home' agenda: the integration of international students and the intercultural development of UK students. University strategy, including the training and professional development of staff, is an essential prerequisite to ensuring that these two challenges are quickly and effectively addressed to the benefit of the educational experience of both NESB and ESB student cohorts.

Universities currently face a dilemma: on the one hand there are imperatives driving the demand for international students, such as the six per cent drop in undergraduate student enrolments in the United Kingdom between the 2011–12 and 2012–13 academic years as a result of the substantial increases in student fees implemented in 2012 (HESA, 2014; see also section 1.2.4). On the other, the influx of international students that promises to compensate for reduced domestic student enrolments compounds the aggravation felt by domestic students about significantly increased fees by creating resentment over what they regard as a diluted educational experience brought about by the poor language and cultural skills of their peers – thereby threatening to lower domestic student numbers further still. Ironically, this could eventually lead to a situation where international students feel that one of the main benefits of an education in an English-medium university has been lost: namely, the opportunity to study with and learn the local language and culture of English-speaking students. In some cases, even the potential advantages of using English as a lingua franca and developing intercultural competence through interacting in multicultural/multilingual groups are lost where one particular ethnic and linguistic group dominates. In other words, universities potentially stand to alienate parts of all sections of the student population if they fail to resolve these tensions.

To further complicate the picture, the financial impact of any fall in enrolment numbers associated with particular student groups is addressed not only through compensatory strategies that target alternative or additional student cohorts and markets, but also through strategies that seek to increase research funding by strongly encouraging academic departments to put ever greater effort into the submission of grant applications. This time-consuming activity, while undoubtedly an important and necessary part of academia, nonetheless risks detracting further from the student experience, for due also to the increasing bureaucratic and managerial role academics are today expected to assume (and typified by the recent requirement to take responsibility for monitoring students' movements for visa purposes), they find themselves unable to devote as much time as they might wish to their students, particularly taught undergraduate and postgraduate students. In the case of postgraduate research students, the pressure to reduce PhD completion times, along with the potential that this dimension of their work has in terms of research outputs and associated impact, encourages greater involvement with and commitment to these students for these things promise to bring with them often very tangible reputational and financial benefits to universities, as well as academic kudos and opportunities for promotion and career progression for academic staff.

The fact that the training of academic staff and the strategies of universities to reconcile the above tensions have the potential to significantly affect the student experience, and in particular their learning, would appear to constitute a compelling argument for regulation focusing on this area of activity. Yet there is another area that should, arguably, also be a focus of regulation: namely the professional development of administrative staff involved in processes and decision-making concerning the setting and monitoring of institutional English language entry criteria. If universities are to make informed admissions decisions and advise students, education agents and other bodies outside and within the university effectively both prior to and during the students' studies, it would seem reasonable to expect them to have at least a modicum of understanding of, and conversancy in, those gatekeeping tests that are at the heart of these processes. This issue of 'assessment literacy', what it means and how it might be developed, is one I shall revisit in section 4.2.2.

2.2.6   Striking a balance between research and teaching activity

As we have seen, the student experience has the potential to be compromised not only by the multicultural, multilingual make-up of classrooms and a lack of intercultural competence among peers, academic staff and administrators, but also by a failure to achieve an appropriate balance between research and teaching activity. This again highlights the various tensions that universities today struggle to reconcile. Students typically wish to obtain degrees from universities with good reputations. Those reputations are built more than ever on research quality, and as such academics are encouraged and increasingly expected to obtain grants and produce research of the highest order and to be able to demonstrate the impact of their research. Applying for research grants and authoring high quality books, journal articles and reports are notoriously and necessarily time-consuming activities; they need to be, due to the extent of competition from academics and practitioners across the world who are similarly striving to find suitable and prestigious outlets for their work and to develop their academic careers. Only those whose work is deemed relevant and significant and manifests the appropriate level of rigour and overall quality are likely to meet with success; and that success not only spells opportunities for career development, it generates income for the university that can be invested into further research and other areas of its activities and infrastructure, which, in turn, enhance its institutional profile and with it the opportunity to generate *further* income.

Ironically, this often means that those same students who desire a degree from a prestigious university can be a casualty of this emphasis on research. In this respect, it is a situation that can be seen as somewhat analogous to that of the PhD student who desires a high-profile supervisor with an international reputation: although he or she may benefit from the association and expertise that is likely to come with such an individual, they may have very limited access to that expertise as a result of their supervisor's lack of availability due to other commitments commensurate with their academic status. All students deserve and pay for the support of academic staff, but it is often international students, and particularly those with weak language skills, who suffer most from a lack of such support, for it can be very difficult for them to follow lectures, engage in seminars, understand reading materials, interact with their fellow students and benefit from a sense of integration and the confidence to approach and use the increasingly limited support of tutors whose time is likely to be at a premium. Consequently, they can very quickly find themselves falling further and further behind and in need not only of academic tutoring but also encouragement and moral support. This leads to their feeling demoralised and a sense of injustice that, having paid high fees, their interests and needs are left unmet. For their part, staff – particularly those who feel a sense of vocation and a commitment to students and to teaching and learning – can feel frustrated and dismayed at not being able to give these students the time and care they need. While there are no doubt some academics who are able to strike an effective balance between research and teaching activity, for many it can prove very difficult indeed. In her discussion of the institutional habitus, Thomas (2002) alludes to this relationship between research and teaching and learning in the following terms:

Relationships between students and teaching staff seem to be fundamental to attitudes towards learning and coping with academic difficulties. Within a particular 'field' individuals, groups and institutions exist in structural relations to each other, which are mediated by habitus, thus the relations between staff and students are key to under-standing the institutional habitus. This point is supported by James (1998: 109), who argues that contrary to the way student experience is usually conceptualized in HE in the UK, the student experience has to be understood in relation to practices of teaching and research, as part of a larger picture. In other words, the way in which the HE field is structured is significant, and he points to the tension between research and teaching, and the lack of parity of academic status and economic capital. Research with HEIs that have a good track record in both recruiting and retaining under-represented groups suggested that the former polytechnics accorded higher status to teaching, which had benefits for these student groups in particular, but that this priority was being challenged by the need for more academics to be research active, and for all institutions to perform well in the research assessment exercise. (Thomas, 2002, p. 432)

So, the situation is complex. Universities need to remain viable and interna-tional students are an important means by which to do so. In order to better attract these students, they need to have developed a reputation, and the most effective way of doing so is through high quality, high impact research. Paradoxically, having attracted the students, these high-end universities can struggle to provide a high quality student experience, and, in time, one suspects that this will impact negatively on their attractiveness to would-be students and thus their future prospects.

Blended learning has, of course, offered universities one very useful mechanism for compensating for the richness of face-to-face interaction, and indeed it offers very tangible benefits to students in general and to NESB students in particular. In the case of the latter, through online materials, podcasts, discussion forums etc., it allows students to hear and read material multiple times, to interact with peers and lecturers and to integrate more fully. However, it is not a panacea and cannot be treated as a mechanism for avoiding the kind of experience and personal support that these students often need and which can most effectively be provided through physical face-to-face contact. One might also argue that, while efforts to promote a so-called 'teaching–research nexus' by looking at creative ways of incorporating research activity and findings into the delivery of all degree programmes promise to provide students with valuable graduate skills in conceptualisation, organisation and analysis, they can also be viewed more cynically as a pragmatic way of resolving the tension between research and teaching–learning activity. As such, their effectiveness demands careful monitoring.

Regulation, then, needs to ensure that universities have created an acceptable balance between research and teaching and learning, for failure by universities to do so has implications for all students and particularly NESB students, who risk exiting higher education with a considerably diluted educational experi-ence. If universities accept NESB students then they have an obligation to inject money into services that support them as necessary.

2.2.7   *Meeting the needs and expectations of students and employers*

While a higher education experience promises to bring with it general benefits in terms of the individual's personal development, it is also designed to give students a good grounding in their area of study and, increasingly, provide them not only with discipline knowledge but also workplace skills that will make them an attractive proposition to potential employers and help ensure that they perform and achieve well in their chosen professions. Once again, the extent to which universities succeed in doing this is measured in part via employment statistics that feed into league tables, and it is the case that, over time, certain universities appear to acquire a reputation for producing well-rounded and desirable graduates: something of which they are understandably proud and which they are keen to publicise.

Four related graduate qualities that have become especially prized by employers in recent years are team or group skills, leadership skills, intercultural skills and communication skills, and many universities are thinking creatively about how they might integrate the development of these skills into the curriculum. At the heart of these graduate qualities lies language, the common denominator. If students succeed in completing their degree programmes with weak language skills, this not only calls into question their employability – particularly if they are to work in English-speaking contexts – but also the extent and depth of their knowledge base and, by extension, the rigour of the programmes from which they have graduated. Ultimately, it not only calls into question the standards of their graduating universities but, should it become prevalent, has the potential to threaten the reputation of higher education more generally in the country concerned by casting doubt on its quality and value. This fact alone would appear to constitute a good case for some form of regulation, instigated at a national level, involving language standards.

The uncomfortable reality, then, is that universities are increasingly finding themselves between a rock and a hard place as they struggle to resolve the tension between maintaining standards and remaining financially viable. The setting of English language entry standards and the provision of English language development opportunities post-enrolment lie at the heart of this tension as universities assign ever-greater importance to the recruitment of international students. Furthermore, if the ability to remain financially viable is increasingly dependent, in part, on increasing research activity, then there also arises a tension between financial imperatives on the one hand and the student experience on the other; that is, as academic staff divert their energies increasingly towards research activity, this – along with the management and administrative load they are increasingly expected to shoulder – means inevitably that they have less capacity to focus on their teaching activities and the needs, both academic and pastoral, of their students.

The kind of regulation described in the remainder of this chapter could and should go some way to alleviating these tensions by helping to ensure that students who enrol in university degree programmes have the language skills – and, where necessary, the support mechanisms available to them – to work more autonomously. While these things should not be seen as a substitute for contact with academic tutors, they should help take some of the pressure off academic staff by allowing them to create a better balance between teaching and research; one that benefits both themselves and their students. In particular, the initiatives described should help to obviate a situation where universities strategically undercut each other's English language entry criteria in order to gain a competitive advantage and thus a greater market share, regardless of the potentially detrimental effect on the teaching–learning process. They promise to do this by (a) creating a more level playing field by requiring universities to operate according to externally prescribed minimum English language thresholds deemed acceptable for study in higher education, and (b) specifying, and in some cases mandating, the extent and nature of those English language development opportunities that should be made available to students.

2.3 Regulation as it is currently realised

Partly due to a situation they see as increasingly unsustainable within their institutions and partly in response to external regulatory pressure from education departments, visa and immigration departments or government quality agencies, many universities today have elected to revise the way in which they deal with the issue of English language. For some, this has meant re-evaluating pre-enrolment processes and procedures, including the monitoring of entry pathways and the regular reviewing of English language entry criteria by international offices in consultation with admissions officers and English language specialists. While many also review their post-enrolment English language provision periodically, this tends not to be evaluated at an institutional level and is instead left to those 'experts' residing in the institutions' English language units. There is, by and large, little interest on the part of the broader university community in the way in which these units conduct their activities – the level of rigour they manifest and the extent to which they conform to principles of good practice – and little inclination to interfere. Of more concern to them is the ability of English language units to serve as points of referral to which departments can direct (some would say 'offload') students who are seen as problematic due to their weak language skills. While this is perhaps beginning to change as universities and their departments realise the high stakes relating to English language in a context of growing cultural and linguistic diversity, changing policy regarding immigration in countries such as the United Kingdom and Australia, and the now considerable emphasis placed on the student experience, it remains prevalent nonetheless. This chapter, however, concerns itself primarily with regulation at the national level and the way in which change here can drive changes in practices at the institutional level. I shall begin by considering the Australian context where developments have been notably progressive in respect of regulation and approaches to addressing the English language question.

2.3.1   Regulation in Australia

Australia is known as a country of immigrants and exemplifies 'the multicultural society', with 27.7% (6.4 million) of its resident population having been born overseas (Australian Bureau of Statistics, 2013) compared to 10% in 1945, when the population numbered just 7 million. According to Cook (2008), the growth in student mobility between 1999 and 2004 was 43%, with Australia's on-campus international student numbers increasing by 95% over the same period. Today, Australia's education and training industry is worth over $16 billion and the 490,000 foreign students who studied in Australian institutions in 2009 represent a considerable source of income (Burgess, 2010). Indeed, in 2007 the OECD cited Australia as the country with the highest percentage of international students, due largely to its status as an English-speaking country, its comparative affordability and its high academic standards (Banks and Lawrence, 2008, p. 33). In 2013, 19.8% of tertiary students enrolled were from another country (OECD, 2013). Given these statistics, it is perhaps unsurprising that Australia is at the vanguard of scholarship centring on interculturality, multilingualism, identity and the development of English language competence within this context (Lo Bianco, Crozet and Liddicoat, 2009; Scarino, 2009; Liddicoat and Scarino, 2013; Lo Bianco, 2010; Murray and Scarino, 2014).

As with most other countries where English-medium universities are the norm, the quality of English language provision and the routes through which students enter university are both highly variable, and it was this fact, in conjunction with the increasingly diverse student demographic that characterises higher education today, that prompted a move to greater regulation. In August 2007, driven in part by a high-profile report on the English language levels of overseas students graduating from Australian universities (Birrell, 2006) and the considerable media attention associated with this, a national symposium, attended by representatives from all Australian universities, was convened by Australian Education International (AEI) and the International Education Association of Australia (IEAA) to debate the topic of the English language competence of international students. Flowing from that event, entitled *English Language Competence of International Students*, was the formulation of and dissemination across the higher education sector of a document entitled *Good Practice Principles for English language proficiency for international students in Australian universities* (GPPs) (2009; see Appendix A for the full document). This document was the outcome of a project funded by the Department of Education, Employment and Workplace Relations (DEEWR) and undertaken by a steering committee convened by the Australian Universities Quality Agency (AUQA). It acknowledged the challenges presented by the ever-swelling number of students entering higher education for whom English is not a first language, and its purpose was to enhance the quality of English language provision at universities by having a sector-wide mechanism for its monitoring and evaluation.

The document reads:

The expectation of the project Steering Committee is that universities will consider the Principles as they would consider other guidelines on good practice. As part of AUQA quality audits universities can expect to be asked about the way they have addressed the Principles, just as they are likely to be asked by AUQA auditors about their application of a range of other external reference documents for the university sector. (DEEWR 2009, p. 2)

The GPPs were informed by six 'key ideas':
- With widening participation across tertiary education and the increasing numbers of international students, it can no longer be assumed that students enter their university study with the level of academic language proficiency required to participate effectively in their studies.
- Irrespective of the English language entry requirements of the university, most students, in particular those from language backgrounds other than English, will require English language development throughout the course of their studies.
- Different disciplines have different discourses of academic inquiry.
- Students' English language proficiency can be developed through appropriate course design, supplemented where necessary by other developmental activity.
- Development of academic language and learning is more likely to occur when it is linked to need (e.g. academic activities, assessment tasks).
- English language proficiency is one part of the wider graduate attribute agenda since English language communication skills are crucial for graduate employment.

The GPPs comprised ten board priniciples (see Table 2.2), organised according to theme and against which were articulated a set of 'good practices'.

In their introduction to the GPPs, DEEWR stated that 'the examples of good practices given in the thematic guide are examples only and not intended to be prescriptive. They are provided to assist universities and other institutions in

Table 2.2. *DEEWR's Good Practice Principles for English language proficiency for international students in Australian Universities*

The Good Practice Principles for English language proficiency for international students in Australian universities (DEEWR, 2009)

Theme 1: University-wide Strategy, Policy and Resourcing
1. Universities are responsible for ensuring that their students are sufficiently competent in the English language to participate effectively in their university studies.
2. Resourcing for English language development is adequate to meet students' needs throughout their studies.

Theme 2: Prospective Students and Entry Standards
3. Students have responsibilities for further developing their English language proficiency during their study at university and are advised of these responsibilities prior to enrolment.
4. Universities ensure that the English language entry pathways they approve for the admission of students enable these students to participate effectively in their studies.

Theme 3: Curriculum Design and Delivery
5. English language proficiency and communication skills are important graduate attributes for all students.
6. Development of English language proficiency is integrated with curriculum design, assessment practices and course delivery through a variety of methods.
7. Students' English language development needs are diagnosed early in their studies and addressed, with ongoing opportunities for self-assessment.

Theme 4: Transition and Social and Academic Interaction
8. International students are supported from the outset to adapt to their academic, sociocultural and linguistic environments.
9. International students are encouraged and supported to enhance their English language development through effective social interaction on and off campus.

Theme 5: Quality Assurance
10. Universities use evidence from a variety of sources to monitor and improve their English language development activities.

reviewing and improving their own activities' (2009, p. 2). In light of the fact that they would form the basis on which future AUQA inspectors were to evaluate universities' English language provision, the Principles themselves – as opposed to the examples of their realisation provided by the document's authors – were not viewed by universities and other stakeholders as similarly subject to local interpretation. They were seen as non-negotiable and this led to a tangible sense of urgency as universities felt compelled to review their provision in an effort to ensure that their practices aligned sufficiently with the guidelines laid out in the GPPs. The document, the principles it articulated, the challenges those principles presented and the pros and cons of various strategic permutations designed in response, have been the focus of numerous conferences, interest groups, academic articles, media publications, institutional policy/strategy documents and pilot studies – both intra- and inter-institutional (see, for example, Dunworth, 2010; Dawson, 2011; Barrett-Lennard, Dunworth and Harris, 2011; Harper, Prentice and Wilson, 2011; University of Sydney, n.d.; Murray and Hicks, 2013; Dunworth, Drury, Kralik and Moore, 2013).

One result of this activity and the reflection it provoked was a re-assessment of the GPPs document itself, with a view to giving greater definition to the ideas expressed therein and to rectifying any shortcomings and omissions. Under the auspices of the Tertiary Education Quality Standards Agency (TEQSA) (the successor to AUQA, established in 2012) a steering committee was formed and invited to turn the Good Practice Principles into 'standards'. The resulting document, *English language standards for Higher Education* (2012; see Appendix B), reflected a refinement or 'tightening up' of the original document and left no doubt as to its status and the expectations of its authors vis-à-vis its potential significance for future university audits. With the original 'Principles' expected to become 'Standards', the implication was clearly that, if and when the document was officially sanctioned, provision evaluated by inspectors as being less than rigorous would be seen as a reflection of inadequate standards and the institutions concerned effectively put on notice as a result. The underlying discourse thus effectively read: If you fail to meet the expectations implicit in the standards, you will be deemed to have underperformed and consequences will follow.

Like its predecessor, the GPPs, The *English language standards for Higher Education* document listed for each of the six 'standards' articulated a set of 'examples of good practice'. Where it differed, however, was in the prefacing of each such set of examples with a list of expectations relating to the standard concerned (see Table 2.3).

At the time of writing, the English language standards for Higher Education have not been formally sanctioned by TEQSA, at least not in the form they were articulated by the steering committee. Instead, expectations concerning English language have been articulated in far broader terms within a wider-ranging Higher Education Standards Framework, which includes Threshold Standards. In this regard, the Association of Language and Learning 'Degrees of Proficiency' project website notes:

Of particular relevance to student language proficiency are the Higher Education Standards Framework (Threshold Standards) Course Accreditation Standards 1.2, 3.2 and 5.6, which include the requirement that courses of study provide for the development of English language proficiency as a 'key graduate attribute'. TEQSA is responsible for conducting Quality Assessments in higher education and will be focusing initially on English language proficiency. The Terms of Reference for the quality assessments are available from the TEQSA website. In summary, TEQSA will report on:

Table 2.3. *DEEWR's English language standards for Higher Education*

English language standards for Higher Education (DEEWR Steering Committee, 2012)

Standard 1
The provider ensures that its students are sufficiently proficient in the English language to participate effectively in their higher education studies on entry.

Expectations
• The provider recognises that appropriate English language standards on entry are not of themselves adequate to ensure students' English language proficiency on graduation, and considers entry standards, the needs of the course of study and the support that is provided as a coherent whole.
• The higher education provider adheres to a formal policy that specifies English language entry criteria, including criteria for direct entry pathways, which are appropriate for the level of studies and the discipline and which are consistent with research evidence, including the recommendations of relevant testing organisations.
• The provider verifies the accuracy and authenticity of the evidence provided by prospective students to satisfy its English language entry criteria.
• The provider systematically monitors the performance of students by entry pathway or by cohort and makes appropriate changes to entry criteria to ensure that it admits only those students who are able to participate effectively on entry.
• The higher education provider gives feedback to direct entry pathway providers on the comparative academic performance of students who have entered through pathway provisions and on the provider's satisfaction with the English language proficiency of entering students from the pathway provider.
• If the provider uses a test of English language proficiency to determine student entry, the provider is able to demonstrate the security, reliability and validity of the test that is applied.

Standard 2
The provider ensures that prospective and current students are informed about their responsibilities for further developing their English language proficiency during their higher education studies.

Expectations
• The provider formally acknowledges significant responsibility for the ongoing development of its students' English language proficiency and provides explicit advice to students of the nature and level of support that will be given to help them meet expectations of graduate English language proficiency.
• The provider ensures that students know they must play an active role in developing their English language proficiency during their studies.
• The provider's education agents understand the provider's expectations for further development of students' English language proficiency.
• The provider's onshore and offshore educational partners understand the provider's expectations for further development of students' English language proficiency.

Standard 3
The provider ensures that resourcing for English language development meets students' needs throughout their studies.

Expectations
• The higher education provider identifies students' individual English language development needs early in their studies and addresses these needs.
• The provider ensures there are adequate resources for appropriately-qualified academic language and learning staff to meet the language and learning needs of students.

Table 2.3. (*cont.*)

English language standards for Higher Education (DEEWR Steering Committee, 2012)

- The provider ensures there is adequate expertise available to assist academic staff to integrate English language proficiency into curricula and teaching.
- The provider ensures that academic staff know how to and are able to access professional assistance for the development of curricula, assessment tasks and teaching to develop English language proficiency in specific academic disciplinary contexts.
- The provider ensures that academic staff have opportunities to revise curricula and teaching to integrate English language proficiency with discipline-specific learning.

Standard 4
The provider actively develops students' English language proficiency during their studies.

Expectations
- The provider ensures that development by students of their English language proficiency is integrated into curriculum design, assessment practices and course delivery.
- Course learning outcomes include English language proficiency outcomes that are taught and assessed during the course and take account of the proficiency that is required of graduates in the discipline for employment or further study.
- The provider gives attention to all aspects of English language proficiency in assessment methods, e.g. attention to listening, speaking, reading and writing.
- The curriculum takes into account time for students to develop their English language proficiency within overall expected student workloads.
- The provider has considered how best to use work placements or practica to assist students to develop their English language proficiency in professional or employment settings.
- Course approvals and reviews consider the extent to which English language proficiency outcomes are designed into curricula, assessment and teaching.
- The provider ensures effective interaction of students from differing cultural and language backgrounds in regular academic activities.
- The provider ensures that students are encouraged and supported to enhance their English language development through effective intercultural social interaction in a range of formal and informal settings.

Standard 5
The provider ensures that students are appropriately proficient in English when they graduate.

Expectations
- The higher education provider states clearly to students and other stakeholders its expectations of its graduates, including its expectations regarding English language proficiency encompassing a range of communication skills.
- English language proficiency is an explicit component of academic standards for the course of study and is aligned to disciplinary standards.
- The provider obtains regular information from students on the extent to which they consider their English language proficiency is improving.
- The provider has ongoing dialogue with industry and with professional accreditation and registration bodies about their expectations regarding English language proficiency and the English language proficiency of the provider's graduates.

Standard 6
The provider uses evidence from a variety of sources to monitor and improve its support for the development of students' English language proficiency.

Table 2.3. (*cont.*)

English language standards for Higher Education (DEEWR Steering Committee, 2012)

Expectations
- The provider regularly compares its policies and practices for English language development against those of comparable institutions nationally and internationally and considers these in developing policies and practices that reflect the specific needs of its students and the requirements of specific discipline areas.
- The provider systematically monitors the extent to which its academics consider students' English language proficiency on entry is appropriate and is developed through their studies.
- The provider systematically monitors the extent to which its graduates believe their English language proficiency was developed throughout their higher education studies.
- The provider makes adjustments as appropriate to its entry standards, resourcing, curricula, assessment practices or teaching to better meet students' needs for development of their English language proficiency.

- Overall institutional strategies or philosophies
- Communication with prospective and current students on language issues
- Minimum English language entry levels
- Post-entry language development strategies and their evaluation
- Tracking and performance measures
- Processes used to identify those in need of particular language development assistance
- Descriptions of and monitoring of language outcomes
- English language proficiency as a graduate attribute.

('Degrees of Proficiency' project website, as hosted by the Association of Academic Language and Learning)

2.3.2   Regulation in the United Kingdom

In April 2009, the same year that the Good Practice Principles document appeared in Australia, a report (referred to earlier in this chapter) was published by the United Kingdom's Quality Assurance Agency for Higher Education (QAA) entitled *Thematic enquiries into concerns about academic quality and standards in higher education in England* (2009). In that document, the QAA – the United Kingdom's higher education standards agency and thus its equivalent of AUQA/ TEQSA – identified as one of its themes 'International students – admission and language requirements'. In a summary statement of this theme it noted that there was evidence to suggest that the following three actions were required:
- A review of the efficacy and appropriateness of established schemes for testing the English language skills of international students, in

determining English language competence and support needs before acceptance on to higher education programmes and while studying in the United Kingdom.

- Institutions, either individually or collectively, should provide clear guidance to international students and their advisers about higher education teaching, learning and assessment practices in the United Kingdom and, further, both facilitate international students' understanding of these expectations and support them in making the transition to studying in the United Kingdom.
- A general statement or guidance about the support arrangements that international students should expect from higher education institutions, including English language support and personal and academic support, be developed.

Although rather less detailed and prescriptive, and while constituting part of a document the focus of which extends beyond issues of English language proficiency, these key actions nonetheless broadly coincide with DEEWR's Good Practice Principles. Specifically, common between the two is a concern that suitable safeguards should exist to ensure that students have a level of competence in English, prior to entry, sufficient to enable them to cope with the demands of their studies. Similarly, both documents require that receiving institutions have adequate resources available to provide international students with the support they need to further develop their language skills. They also share an emphasis on the need to help students adapt more generally to the local higher education context. Furthermore, in recognising the need (a) for appropriate post-entry language support and (b) for the integrity of pre-entry levels of English referred to above, both documents appear implicitly to acknowledge shortcomings of those tests widely used as gatekeeping mechanisms to assess students' English language competence and/or the fact that English language entry requirements are set as they are in the knowledge that students will *need* language support post-entry.

The GPPs and English Language Standards, however, appear to go a step further than the QAA's Thematic Enquiries in a number of important respects. Firstly, they propose post-entry English language assessment as a way of identifying individual students' language needs early on in their studies – an idea we will revisit in Chapter 5 and which, again, suggests that its authors were cognisant of the fact that many students slip through the net cast by pre-enrolment testing mechanisms. Furthermore, in addition to highlighting the need to review testing schemes used by universities to determine the English language competence and support needs of international students prior to their acceptance onto degree programmes, the GPPs also make clear the need to evaluate the various pathways by which students enter university and the veracity of claims made, whether implicitly or explicitly, regarding the English language proficiency of students exiting preparatory programmes, and their suitability for tertiary level study. While the QAA's Thematic Enquiries and the GPPs both emphasise that students should be made aware of the expectations of them as they enter higher education in the United Kingdom, the GPPs are more explicit with respect to English language proficiency, stating that 'Students have responsibilities for further developing their English language proficiency during their study at university and are advised of these responsibilities prior to enrolment'. Principle 6 of the GPPs ('Development of English language proficiency is integrated with curriculum design, assessment practices and course delivery through a variety of methods') is at least suggestive of the idea that English language requirements may differ depending on the course of study and discipline and that English should thus be developed within the context of the discipline.

One of the 'expectations' listed under TEQSA's Standard 3 offers a rather more explicit formulation of this idea, stating as it does that 'The provider ensures that academic staff have opportunities to revise curricula and teaching to integrate English language proficiency with discipline-specific learning'. This level of granularity and, in particular, the notion that language and discipline are intimately related and that language thus needs to be taught within the context of the relevant discipline is absent from the more general guidelines provided by the QAA's Thematic Enquiries. This greater granularity can also be seen in the fact that while the QAA's Thematic Enquiries highlight the need for enhanced academic support mechanisms at the programme level for international students and their specific requirements, the GPPs are much more prescriptive in terms of how this should occur through curricula and assessment revision and design where English language proficiency is an integral component of programme learning outcomes, and is aligned to discipline-specific standards.

Informing its three quite broad recommended actions, listed above, the QAA document discusses a number of more specific issues and concerns that highlight the need for regulation and some of the areas of focus (see Table 2.4).

The authors of the Thematic Enquiries document were careful to point out that the issues identified should not be interpreted as painting a picture of failure across the sector. Indeed, citing two papers from its *Outcomes from institutional audit* series, in 2006 and 2008, which looked at evidence from a total of 129 Institutional audits on institutions' arrangements for international students, it noted that it:

found much good practice in the way that institutions were supporting their international students. The second paper observed that, overall, 'the audit reports show that institutions are aware of the substantial learning and cultural issues involved in recruiting large numbers of international students, many of whose first language is not English, and are adopting strategic approaches to their support'. (QAA, 2009, p. 12)

Table 2.4. *Key issues and concerns highlighted in the QAA's 2009 Thematic Enquiries document*

Thematic enquiries into concerns about academic quality and standards in higher education in England: Some key issues and concerns

- The need to provide fair and accurate information to international students (as applicants) about the facilities and support on their campuses.
- The need for a coordinated approach to enhance academic and personal support mechanisms at both central and programme level to ensure that the particular needs of international students are met. According to a study conducted by the UK Council for International Student Affairs (UKCISA), in 2007 eight per cent of universities offered no in-sessional English language support.
- The need (implied) for internal diagnostic English language testing arrangements.
- A range of difficulties being encountered by the students and the staff teaching increasing numbers of international students.
- Instances of plagiarism (and associated disputes) as a result of weak English language skills, and insufficient understanding of academic culture and institutional assessment regulations in general.
- A 'downgrading' of the home student experience as lecturers have to give basic English lessons to students with weak English.
- A willingness to accept students who do not meet the minimum stated language requirements – as indicated by sixty-two per cent of institutions surveyed in the above 2007 UKCISA study – and the potential tension created by the high-fee-paying status of international students.
- A perception by some that gatekeeping tests such as IELTS do not prepare students for the particular language demands of their course of study.
- A proportion of institutions offering no in-sessional provision in language or study skills (eight per cent, according to the same UKCISA study).
- Many institutions setting language standards that are too low.
- A lack of equity in the way in which work is graded – with international students being treated more sympathetically due to the high fees they pay.
- Reported irregularities by institutions and individuals in university and college admissions processes, and reports of malpractice on the part of applicants.
- The need for institutions to develop and monitor policies and procedures involving student recruitment and, in particular, the verification of entry requirements.

2.4   Assessing compliance with English language standards

One interesting question concerns the basis on which auditors acting on behalf of regulators such as TEQSA and the QAA assess whether institutions have met the specified required standards. What, for example, will they use as criteria against which to evaluate each of the standards articulated and the various degrees of compliance? And what will be the make-up of institutional audit teams in terms of the qualifications of their members, vis-à-vis their suitability to pass judgement on that provision?

In the United Kingdom, one possible route that has been discussed in recent years concerns the use of the British Council's English Language Accreditation Scheme, *Accreditation UK*. This quality assurance scheme operates as a partnership between the British Council and English UK and is open to language schools, home tuition providers, further education (FE) and higher education (HE) institutions, international study centres and independent schools, and it not only identifies key inspection criteria but also specifies in very clear terms, via an itemised list, the extent to which institutions will be judged to have met each of these criteria. One criterion worthy of particular note is that of 'academic staff profiles'; while the British Council's Scheme stipulates the formal qualifications expected of English language instructors, this is conspicuously absent from the AUQA/TEQSA and QAA regulatory documents.

Although it is voluntary, many university English language units are listed as recommended providers of English languages services by virtue of having successfully met accreditation requirements. This is not only intended to provide students with reassurance and a useful indication of the standards they can expect at those accredited institutions, it also gives the institutions themselves a business edge as well as the motivation to improve and maintain their standards. The Accreditation UK Handbook describes the purposes of the Scheme as being:

- to develop, establish and maintain quality standards for English language provision delivered in the United Kingdom for international students;
- to accredit all organisations providing English language courses in the United Kingdom which meet the Scheme criteria and standards; and
- to provide an assurance of the quality of English language providers accredited under the Scheme to international students and their advisers (British Council, 2014, p. 5).

Accredited institutions are re-inspected every four years against the criteria presented in Table 2.5.[2] The table in full, including the list of forms of evidence used to determine the extent of compliance with these criteria, can be found in Appendix C.

The British Council Scheme raises some legitimate questions. Its field of application, for example, is very broad, covering all types of English language operations and institutions. While all of the criteria and the vast majority of the inspection areas would certainly appear to apply specifically to the higher education environment, it could be argued that it would need to be expanded if it is to provide suitable coverage of all areas relevant to the teaching of English in universities. For example, consideration may need to be given to the issues of monitoring entry pathways, setting English language entry standards, the nature of staff qualifications and experience, and the structure of provision such that,

---

[2] A full version of the Accreditation UK Handbook can be accessed online at: www.britishcoun cil.org/accreditation_uk_handbook_2014–15.pdf.

Table 2.5. *Inspection criteria for British Council accreditation*

Criterion	Specific inspection areas
Management	• Legal and statutory regulation • Staff management • Student administration • Quality assurance • Publicity – information available before enrolment
Resources and environment	• Premises and facilities • Learning resources
Teaching and learning	• Academic staff profile • Academic management • Course design and implementation • Learner management • Teaching
Welfare and student services	• Care of students • Accommodation • Leisure opportunities
Care of under 18s	

(Accreditation UK Handbook 2014–15. © British Council 2014. Reprinted with permission)

where appropriate, they reflect more precisely an EAP/ESP and academic literacies orientation – an issue that will be discussed in much greater detail in Chapters 3 and 6 of this volume. In this regard, there has been some discussion in the UK EAP community suggesting that the BALEAP (British Association of Lecturers in English for Academic Purposes) inspection scheme may be more appropriate given its more specific focus, described by the organisation as 'designed to establish and sustain the standard required of specialist courses in English for Academic Purposes' (BALEAP website). Like the British Council scheme, institutions accredited by BALEAP are inspected every four years and the areas audited include: management and administration; staffing; resources and facilities; course design; teaching and learning; assessment; student welfare; and course evaluation.[3]

Whichever scheme, if any, were to be adopted, confidence in its scope and relevance is crucial if it is to secure buy-in from all stakeholders and serve its purpose as a regulatory mechanism. While the British Council Scheme may not necessarily be ideal for application in the higher education context, it certainly provides something of a blueprint: an idea of the sort of instrument that regulators need if they are to be relevant, comprehensive and even-handed in their auditing of institutions.

---

[3] The BALEAP Accreditation Scheme Handbook can be accessed online at: www.baleap.org.uk /media/uploads/pdfs/baleap-accreditation-scheme-handbook.pdf.

2.5   Summary

This chapter has considered the rationale for increased regulation relating to English language standards in higher education in light of changing student demographics, the motivation for universities to increase the size of their international student body, and the tensions that can arise as a result. Those tensions concern at least the following:

- both domestic and international students' perceptions of their learning experience;
- changing expectations concerning the skills set that academic staff need to operate effectively in multicultural/multilingual classrooms, and the importance of achieving a balance between the different facets of their role, and in particular between teaching/pastoral and research-oriented activity;
- balancing the language requirements of immigration departments with institutional and departmental language criteria and business imperatives; and
- weighing the financial and reputational benefits flowing from larger numbers of international students and the projection of an image of internationalisation, with the need to meet institutional ethical responsibilities by accepting onto degree programmes only those students with a reasonable prospect of success, and combining effective gate-keeping mechanisms pre-enrolment with language development opportunities that help ensure such success post-enrolment.

Documents such as the *Good Practice Principles for English language proficiency for international students in Australian universities* and *Thematic enquiries into concerns about academic quality and standards in higher education in England* represent two recent efforts to provide effective regulatory frameworks in countries where English is the medium of instruction and the proportion of international students particularly high. Unquestionably, these frameworks reflect a recognition of the growing significance of the English language issue in higher education and its associated tensions, and of the need to address the notoriously disparate and idiosyncratic ways in which universities have hitherto dealt with it and the resultant variability in the quality of provision. Lack of regulation has meant a lack of standards and thus of motivation on the part of some universities to review their institutional practices, to the potential detriment of the student experience and the reputation and success of the universities themselves. For the reasons articulated in this chapter and in Chapter 1, this situation is no longer sustainable: the internationalisation of education is set to continue and the stakes are likely to become even higher. The Australian and UK initiatives are encouraging in that they have embedded regulation of this important area within broader higher education quality assurance mechanisms, and in doing so have gone some way to helping ensure that good practice is implemented and adhered to by all institutions of higher education.

3 Seeking definitional clarity: what is 'English language proficiency'?

3.1 Proficiency in context

Having contextualised the issue of English language in higher education in Chapters 1 and 2, the remainder of this book will look at the principles, practices and challenges relating to pre- and post-enrolment English language assessment; different permutations – and their respective implications – concerning English language development opportunities for those enrolled in degree programmes; and strategic approaches to the political complexities that are inevitably faced by those seeking to bring about significant change in this area within the current university climate. Before embarking on any such discussion, however, clarity needs to be brought to the somewhat elusive construct of 'language proficiency', without which it becomes virtually impossible to have a meaningful and coherent discussion of the situation of English in higher education and to formulate theoretically well-informed proposals concerning the assessment of English language and the systematic and targeted provision of appropriate, effective and sustainable initiatives concerning English language development (Dunworth, 2013; Dunworth, Drury, Kralik and Moore, 2013; Humphreys and Gribble, 2013). That such proposals should be well-informed and systematic is important, for it helps ensure that they are well-received by stakeholders internal to the university and more easily defensible to auditors working within regulatory frameworks and seeking to uphold standards.

In its 2013 government report, *Five Years On: English Language Competence of International Students*, the International Education Association of Australia (IEAA) acknowledged the challenges posed across the higher education sector by English language proficiency (ELP) definitions and terminology, noting that there had been a tendency to rely on test scores to describe proficiency levels and implicitly emphasising the fact that this is not the same thing as a clear articulation of the construct of language proficiency itself. The report continues:

ELP in higher education is being debated but … we are still struggling with our terminology and definitions. What is clear is that ELP in higher education settings is

69

complex and challenging to define (Barrett-Lennard et al., 2011) and also that we have no agreed definition either of the construct itself or of the level of the construct that is appropriate (Dunworth, 2010; Webb, 2012). (IEAA, 2013, p. 83)

The definition of proficiency proposed in the Good Practice Principles (GPP) document discussed in Chapter 2 is fairly typical of the rather vague, 'catch-all' language in which proficiency is treated in such reports. There it is described as follows:

the ability of students to use the English language to make and communicate meaning in spoken and written contexts while completing their university studies. Such uses may range from a simple task such as discussing work with fellow students, to complex tasks such as writing an academic paper or delivering a speech to a professional audience. This view of proficiency as the ability to organise language to carry out a variety of communication tasks distinguishes the use of 'English language proficiency' from a narrow focus on language as a formal system concerned only with correct use of grammar and sentence structure. The project Steering Committee recognises that in many contexts the terms 'English language proficiency' and 'English language competence' are used interchangeably. (DEEWR, 2009, p. 1)

While the IEAA notes that this definition is intended as a working definition for the non-specialist and acknowledges the efforts of the GPP's authors to move beyond the sometimes overly narrow conception of proficiency as comprising the 'more atomistic levels of language related to sentence level grammatical competence', and to contextualise ELP within the university setting, it nonetheless offers little to elucidate and provide a more sophisticated understanding of the construct. Particularly significantly, as the IEAA report observes, DEEWR's definition has 'been criticised for its failure to capture important distinctions between ELP and academic literacy, (Harper, Prentice and Wilson, 2011; Murray, 2012). The need for such a distinction will form an important part of the discussion in this chapter.

Over the course of the next few pages and, subsequently, through Chapters 4 and 5, I shall make a case for a tripartite division of what are overlapping and interactive competences which together provide a conceptualisation of proficiency that has formed the basis for a model of provision currently being implemented at a university in South Australia (see, for example, Murray, 2010a, 2010b, 2014; Murray and Hicks, 2014; Murray and Nallaya, 2014). As will become evident as the argument unfolds, the rationale for that conceptualisation is informed by a combination of both theoretical considerations and the practical constraints that govern what is and is not possible within higher education settings; for example, the extent to which curricula are prescribed or flexible and open to adaptation. During what was an extended process of consultation that constituted a critical part of mustering support in the early stages of what was termed the *English Language Proficiency Project*, this tripartite articulation was well received by staff across the university and viewed as being helpful in clarifying a concept that was seen by many as unclear and which was understood in diverse ways (Harper, 2013, p. 155).

The question of how one defines language proficiency is, of course, not a new one; indeed, in terms of recent history it has been the subject of considerable debate in the applied linguistics literature, and attempts to formulate a widely accepted and detailed definition of the nature of proficiency have been closely informed by developments in the area of language assessment; after all, one cannot establish valid instruments with which to measure proficiency in the absence of a clear definition of the construct itself. Although there has certainly been a very practical dimension driving attempts to 'capture' what it is that constitutes proficiency, there has also been a more theoretical debate which in part has raged somewhat in isolation from questions of real-world application and which has loomed large and had significant impact on how we think about language acquisition and use, as well as how we assess our knowledge of and ability to use language. In terms of the latter, and as North noted in 2000, a seminal moment in the evolution of our conceptualisation of proficiency came in the early 1970s, courtesy of the American anthropologist Dell Hymes, whose response to the groundbreaking work of Noam Chomsky a decade earlier is now part of applied linguistics' folklore. Its significance is such that it certainly warrants mention here, along with the important developmental work it spawned in the years that followed.

3.1.1   Chomsky and Hymes: from competence to communicative competence

As a rationalist concerned with the universal cognitive mechanisms responsible for language behaviour, Chomsky deliberately chose to interpret linguistic competence within the framework of an ideal speaker-listener,

in a completely homogeneous speech community, who knows its language perfectly and is unaffected by such grammatically irrelevant conditions as memory limitation, distractions, shifts of attention and interest, and errors (random and characteristics) in applying his knowledge of the language in actual performance. (Chomsky, 1965, p. 3)

By distilling language from the conditions of its use and so idealising it, Chomsky was able to disregard the problems associated with accounting for the relationships between form and function in context; considerations which he saw as irrelevant and undesirable given the precision necessarily involved in a formal and universal account of the rules which govern creativity in language; rules which, he claimed, 'have the formal properties that they do have by virtue of the structure of the human mind' (Lyons, 1981, p. 231). His consequent decision to restrict his enquiry to a notion of *competence* synonymous with the potential to be grammatical, while assigning to *performance* all forms of variation and deviation from a standard, was the cue that provoked Hymes' reverberant response.

Hymes saw the need for a description of language to '*transcend* the notions of perfect competence, homogeneous speech community, and independence of sociocultural features' (1972, p. 274; italics added). As such, his theory of *communicative competence* was intended not as a rejection of Chomsky's notion of competence but rather as an extension or development of it, according to which the kinds of performance factors surrounding any speech event were seen as an integral part of a theory of communication. Idealising *a* language and describing it (as Chomsky had done) solely according to its grammatical characteristics as manifested by a *homogeneous* population of its users was, in Hymes' view, naïve on a number of counts:

- Within and across those cultures that share a common language there exists a good deal of variability in the nature and perception of linguistic ability. As such, to refer to a *standard* variety against which linguistic competence might be judged is misleading, particularly as sociocultural and socio-economic factors would appear in part to dictate, or demarcate, what is or is not the same language, and not merely linguistic features. To equate a speech community with the language of its members 'rules out the heterogeneity of a speech community, diversity of role among speakers, and stylistic or social meaning' (Berns, 1990, p. 31).
- With the exception of certain élite or professional groups, there is no such thing as a homogeneous speech community at a macro level, as Chomsky suggests. Within any single language community there exist various socio-economic groups, each sharing different grammatical, phonological, lexical and registerial norms, yet they may understand each other perfectly well while also recognising a *range* of linguistic styles for use in different contexts within a set of shared norms.
- The notion of 'differential competence' means that we may feel able to participate more fluently in certain discourse domains than others. A community may, as Hymes observed, 'find Kurdish the medium in which most things can best be expressed, but Arabic the better medium for religious truth' (Hymes, 1972, p. 275). Likewise, 'users of Berber may find Arabic superior to Berber for all purposes except intimate domestic conversation' (ibid.).
- What may appear to the grammarian as degenerate language may, in Hymes' words, be 'the artful accomplishment of a social act', or 'the patterned spontaneous evidence of problem-solving and conceptual thought' (ibid., p. 272). Furthermore, some occasions, he states, 'call for being appropriately ungrammatical' (ibid., p. 277).

In essence, at the heart of these and similar such issues was a recognition that by having deliberately dissociated himself from the sociocultural/situational particularities intrinsic to the language use in context, Chomsky had left unaccounted for a critical element of what makes us competent users of a language. This realisation of the need for any account of language use to encompass a sociolinguistic dimension is reflected in Hymes' commonly cited statement that 'There are rules of use without which the rules of grammar would be useless.' Both competencies, he argued, are 'part of the same developmental matrix', and as such linguistic theory needs to:

account for the fact that a normal child acquires knowledge of sentences, not only as grammatical, but also as appropriate. He or she acquires competence as to when to speak, when not, and as to what to talk about with whom, when, where, in what manner. (Hymes, 1972, p. 277)

It was this need to understand the non-grammatical aspect of the 'developmental matrix' which motivated that area of enquiry known as the ethnography of communication: the study of those sociocultural realities that govern the way in which we mean and are appropriate with language. This was an area that had various precedents – most notably in the work of Malinowski, The Prague School, Firth, and Austin and Searle – which reflected a common concern that linguists should 'include statements about the way in which language is used in social interaction, and how it varies in accordance with its social function' (Allen, 1975, p. 39). Thus Malinowski, in his ethnographic study of the Trobriand Islanders, was conscious of the significance of what he termed the *context of situation* in language use, noting that 'the situation in which words are uttered can never be passed over as irrelevant to the linguistic expression' (1923, p. 306). The Prague school was likewise concerned with the relationship between the formal linguistic system and what Vachek had referred to as 'extra-lingual reality', or situational characteristics (1966, p. 7). Firth (1957a), meanwhile, proposed a distinction between *formal meaning* (the relations between structural items in a sentence) and *situational meaning* (the product of the interaction between structural items and all other non-verbal contextual elements of the communicative situation) – a distinction later referred to by Widdowson (1990) as one between 'semantic' and 'pragmatic' meaning. Halliday (1975) later referred to the process of getting to grips with and manipulating this form–context relationship in order to perform social acts or functions as 'learning how to mean'.

Austin's (1962) contribution to the 'language and context' debate (elaborated upon by Searle, 1969) came from within the discipline of philosophy in the form of Speech Act Theory, to which Hymes makes reference in his celebrated and influential article of 1972. Speech act theory has been described as:

concerned with the functional units of speech [i.e. speech acts] and the ways in which they derive their meaning not from grammatical form but from the rules of interpretation that prevail in a given speech community. (Savignon, 1983, p. 14)

As was later highlighted in Grice's (1975) Theory of Implicature, the functions or 'acts' performed by an utterance may be numerous and not always apparent in the surface structure of what is said. For example, 'It's cold in here' may function as an assertion about the temperature inside a room, a warning not to bring the baby in, or as a request to turn on the heater (Bachman, 1990, p. 90). Each of these represents a different speech act. Moreover, numerous different forms may be used to perform the same act; Fraser and Nolan (1981), for example, identified eighteen distinct strategies as possible ways of making the same request.

Searle (1969) distinguished three types of speech act: utterance acts (simply saying something), propositional acts (referring to or expressing predication about something) and illocutionary acts (the function(s) performed in saying something). Accordingly, an utterance's meaning can be described in terms of its propositional content (reference and predication), its illocutionary *force* (the intended illocutionary act), or its perlocutionary effect (its effect on the hearer). The success or otherwise in conveying or interpreting the correct (i.e. appropriate) illocutionary force of an utterance is dependent upon two factors: (1) the degree of directness with which the speaker signals the illocutionary force he intends, and (2) the contextual clues accompanying the utterance. Clearly these two factors are related; the more indirect the speaker is, the more important becomes the context to the listener's interpretation of what is said. As Bachman points out, for the speaker,

the choice from among several alternative utterances of differing degrees of directness will . . . be a function of both the speaker's illocutionary competence, and his sensitivity to the characteristics of the specific context, which is part of sociolinguistic competence. (Bachman, 1990, p. 91)

The notion that effective and appropriate communication depends upon an understanding of force – a function of the relationship between what is said and the situation of its utterance – clearly dovetailed with the contextual concerns of Malinowski, The Prague School, Firth, Hymes and Halliday. Prompted by what he saw as Chomsky's 'Garden of Eden' conception of competence, Hymes was able to harness and give new currency, and indeed structure, to these sociolinguistically oriented strands of thought. So as to account for the 'rules of use' that are a natural corollary of language in context and provide a more comprehensive account of language behaviour, Hymes modified and effectively superseded Chomsky's limited notion of competence in two ways:
1. He extended it beyond the merely grammatical to include three additional parameters. In so doing, he formalised the concept of *communicative*

competence, thereby giving it greater influence and helping ensure its place as an enduring fixture in applied linguistics.

2. He conceptualised communicative competence as comprising not only *knowledge* of the grammatical and sociolinguistic rules governing language use, but also the *ability* to access that knowledge given environmental and cognitive constraints of the kind Chomsky relegated to performance and consciously ignored, but which 'frame' all natural communication.

Hymes (1971, p. 12) saw communicative competence as comprising four parameters:

- Whether (and to what extent) something is formally *possible*;
- Whether (and to what extent) something is *feasible*;
- Whether (and to what extent) something is *appropriate* in relation to a context in which it is used and evaluated;
- Whether (and to what extent) something is in fact done, actually *performed*, and what its doing entails.

He stated: 'Knowledge also is to be understood as subtending all four parameters of communication just noted. There is knowledge of each. Ability for use also may relate to all four parameters' (1972, pp. 282–3).

It is noteworthy that Hymes' framework can be viewed as a convenient heuristic tool with which one can identify the three general approaches that have been taken historically in defining the conditions of adequacy of a linguistic description. Thus Chomsky, for example, could be said to have been concerned merely with the possible (parameter 1) at the expense of performance considerations implicit in the notions of feasibility, appropriacy and attestedness. Those of Hallidayan persuasion, on the other hand, see a need to account for both the possible and the appropriate (parameters 1 and 3), for language is seen as being informed by the appropriate; it is an encoding of those social functions that language has evolved to serve. Finally, advocates of corpus linguistics equate the possible with the attested (parameters 1 and 4), believing as they do that the only language which is real is that which actually occurs.

3.1.2 Canale and Swain's framework

The emergence of communicative competence thus became a critical moment in the evolution of the construct of language proficiency. With the shift towards a communicative paradigm in language teaching gaining momentum during the 1970s, the question of how to *test* communicative ability took on a new significance. Indeed, as early as 1968, Spolsky had already debated the relationship between functionalism and assessment, observing:

A more promising approach might be to work for a functional definition of levels: we should aim not to test how much of a language someone knows, but test his ability to operate in a specific sociolinguistic situation with specified ease or effect. The preparation of proficiency tests like this would not start from a list of language items, but from a statement of language function. (1968, p. 93)

Somewhat later, Wilkins (1976) likewise expressed his concern with establishing a means of testing learners' communicative proficiency:

We do not know how to establish the communicative proficiency of the learner . . . while some people are experimenting with the notional syllabus as such, others should be attempting to develop new testing techniques that should, ideally accompany it. (1976, p. 82)

If the question of how to test communicative ability was to be satisfactorily answered, there had to be some means of describing what that ability entailed, for, as Spolsky was to note:

One cannot develop sound language tests without a method of defining what it means to know a language, for until you have decided what you are measuring, you cannot claim to have measured it. (1989, pp. 138–59)

Spolsky himself proposed what was widely seen as an elaboration of Hymes' description of communicative competence, suggesting that five dimensions together constituted a complete description of the individual's communicative competence, namely:
* Linguistic dimension: lexicon, semantics, grammar, phonology;
* Channels: oral-aural, speech-writing, gesture;
* Code dimension: (a) varieties available – languages, regional dialects, social dialects, styles, registers; (b) control of code selection rules;
* Topic dimension: what can be talked about;
* Setting dimension: ability to function in various domains (home, school, work, community, etc.) (1978, p. 126).

It was, however, Canale and Swain's (1980) description of communicative competence which was to become the most influential and widely accepted as a useful and transparent basis for curriculum design, methodology and materials development. Driven again by the need for a clear conceptualisation of communicative competence for the purpose of assessment, Canale and Swain's framework identified three components of communicative competence:
* *Grammatical Competence* – mastery of the structural properties of language;
* *Sociolinguistic Competence* – the understanding of social context and rules of appropriacy upon which effective and successful communication is based;
* *Strategic Competence* – the ability to compensate for obstacles to performance and to initiate, terminate, maintain, repair and redirect communication.

This framework was subsequently refined by Canale (1983) who added a further component:

• *Discourse Competence* – the interpretation/production of language in terms of its relationship to the discourse as a whole and according to inferencing skills based on an understanding of principles of cohesion and coherence.

This made more explicit an element of communication previously embedded within sociolinguistic competence.

3.1.3 Bachman's framework of 'communicative language ability'

Designed for reasons similar to those motivating Canale and Swain, namely as a sound basis on which to develop tests of communicative proficiency in foreign languages, Bachman (1990) proposed a notably more detailed account of communicative competence – what he called 'communicative language ability' – consisting of five elements:

• knowledge structures (that is, knowledge of the world);
• language competence;
• strategic competence;
• psychophysiological mechanisms; and
• context of situation.

Language competence he divided into organisational competence (comprising grammatical competence and textual competence) and pragmatic competence (comprising illocutionary competence and sociolinguistic competence). Reflecting Bachman and Palmer's (1996) model of communicative language ability, this was later superseded in 1996 by Bachman's division of language ability into the two categories of language knowledge (the domain of information related specifically to language ability) and strategic competence (the metacognitive strategies engaged during language processing). Language knowledge comprises organisational (grammatical and textual) knowledge and pragmatic (propositional, functional and sociolinguistic) knowledge. The metacognitive strategies that make up strategic competence include assessment, goal-setting and planning.

It is significant that Bachman (1990, 2002) shifts his terminology away from 'language proficiency' (generally treated as synonymous with communicative competence, it should be noted) when creating his models of language use and language ability. In this regard, Katz, Low, Stack and Tsang (2004) comment:

In relating his models to language testing, Bachman (1990) recognises that test methods and the background characteristics of language learners influence scores as much as the students' language skills. Thus, his models of language use and ability come closer to recognising the influence of sociocultural context for the language learner than Cummins. And similar to Colliers' model of language acquisition for school, it distinguishes between linguistic and academic development. (2004, p. 19)

3.1.4   English as a lingua franca (ELF)

One intriguing – and, for some, problematic – issue that bears on the question of language proficiency – and thus on frameworks of communicative competence that attempt to define the construct and which inform the way in which languages are taught and the basis of their assessment – concerns the legitimacy of the view that any particular variety or varieties of English – and especially those spoken by its native speakers – are somehow more correct and thus desirable, and collectively mark the standard to which learners should therefore aspire. In the last fifteen to twenty years, there has been an important and growing body of research and a notable increase in applied linguistics discourse associated with what I shall call the 'English as a lingua franca "perspective"', which takes issue with this monolithic view that upholds native-speaker English as somehow superior to other varieties (see Jenkins, Cogo and Dewey, 2011, for a useful overview). Underpinning this perspective is the realisation that with globalisation, English has become a truly international language, not only in terms of its spread and the range of its domains of use but also by virtue of the fact that today the majority of interactions in English are between non-native speakers of the language (Seidlhofer, 2005). This fact has led scholars such as Widdowson to argue that English is no longer the property of its native speakers and that 'how English develops in the world is no business whatever of native speakers in England, the United States, or anywhere else' (1994, p. 385). Similar sentiments have been echoed by other scholars, with Rajagopolan, for example, stating that 'World English (WE) belongs to everyone who speaks it, but it is nobody's mother tongue' (2004, p. 111), and Matsuda claiming that provided it is learned as an international language, English should neither come from an inner circle country nor be taught as an inner circle language (2003). In fact, House (2009) has suggested that English language has largely outgrown the norms of the Kachruvian 'inner circle' and has become not only a useful default means of communication but often also a means of national, regional and local renaissance and resistance by its new expert non-native users.

The arguments for adopting a plurilithic rather than a monolithic view of English have not been based solely on a pragmatic reaction to reality on the ground, as it were, but also have a basis in an ideological critique that sees the mystification of existing power relations as 'central to maintaining the unassailable advantages English gives to core English-speaking nations (Pennycook, 1994, 1998; Canagarajah, 1999, 2005; Phillipson, 1992, 2009; Tollefson, 1991, 1995) and, more insidiously, to ensuring the consecration of linguistic and cultural privilege (Bhatt, 2002)' (Crichton and Murray, 2014). Bhatt exemplifies this critique as follows:

the hierarchical structure needed to sustain the sacred imagined [English] community can only be guaranteed if Standard English is accepted by all members as inevitable and the speakers of this standard accepted as uncontested authorities of English language use. How is this ideological manipulation and indoctrination in fact accomplished? . . . Expert discourse establishes a habit of thought which makes the standard variety of English (British/American) desirable, necessary, normal, natural, universal, and essential, and all other varieties instances of deficit and deviation. The key ideological process is a naturalizing move that drains the conceptual of its historical content, making it seem universal and timelessly true. (Bhatt, 2002, p. 74)

The ELF perspective necessarily calls into question articulations of communicative competence such as those outlined above on the grounds that they are based on precisely the kind of native speaker norms to which its proponents take exception (Widdowson, 2003); that is, what is grammatically correct or appropriate language, for example, is judged to be so in relation to native speaker behaviour. Similarly, a good deal of second language acquisition research is seen as discredited on the grounds that constructs such as 'fossilization', 'interlanguage', 'foreigner talk' likewise presuppose a target competence of an idealised native speaker (see, for example, House, 2003). In this vein, and of particular interest given the focus of this book, Jenkins (2013) has recently questioned the norms to which the academic community in particular subscribes in English-medium universities, arguing that as institutions that pride themselves on their 'international' credentials they nonetheless continue to uphold a view of English that is anything but international, retaining as it does standards that fail to reflect the increasingly international nature of today's higher education student body – effectively a microcosm of the wider world in which, as we have seen, English is realised in numerous and diverse varieties by and between different communities and individuals. Jenkins' stance and more politically oriented critique complements the substantial empirical work of Mauranen (see, for example, Conrad and Mauranen, 2003; Mauranen, Hynninen and Ranta, 2010; Mauranen, 2013), and in particular the ELFA (English as a Lingua Franca in Academic Settings) and WrELFA (Written English as a Lingua Franca in Academic Settings) corpus projects, both located at the University of Helsinki.

While the reality of English and its use in today's world cannot be disputed, ELF is nevertheless contentious territory for many, not only because it is confrontational in calling into question deeply held – even unconscious – ideas and beliefs and in destabilising feelings of identity and belonging, but also because it raises challenging questions that arise from a consideration of its practical implications. While it is not the purpose of this book to offer a critical appraisal of the ELP perspective, I will briefly mention some of the thornier issues that have been a focus of concern by those sceptical of ELF. Firstly, concerns have been expressed, for example by Kuo (2006 – see also Jenkins'

2012 response), that where mutual intelligibility rather than conformity to a standard is the goal of ELF interactions, this risks promoting a less nuanced, more utilitarian form of communication that would not meet the needs and expectations of professions such as law and medicine, where precision in meaning can be particularly critical. The same might be said of academia, and, rightly or wrongly, these stakeholders will be resistant to change, with the result that English language learners seeking to enter these and other such professions will themselves be uneasy about learning English according to an ideology that does not align with the expectations of these stakeholders and to which they may not, anyway, subscribe.

Then there are pedagogical questions concerning how one deals with a culturally and linguistically heterogeneous class of students studying for academic, professional or other purposes. What does one actually teach and how does one determine was is and is not acceptable language? It may be possible, for example, for two students from different L1 backgrounds to negotiate meaning and complete tasks satisfactorily, yet for either one of those students to fail to do so with another class member from a different L1 background. How does the teacher then intervene and on what basis? Can competence only sensibly be understood in terms of the individual's capacity to negotiate interactions, by, inter alia, accommodating and traversing any differences between their own variety of English and cultural frame of reference, and that of their interlocutor? This, of course, has an important bearing on another key issue, namely that of assessment. Moving between varieties of English, whether as teachers or learners, raises the question of the basis on which informed judgments can be made as to the acceptability of learners' production and interpretation of spoken and written texts, and scholars such as Elder and Davies have been outspoken in their views in this regard:

Calls for new approaches to the assessment of ELF (Jenkins, 2005; Lowenberg, 2002) have thus far come from those outside the professional language testing field unfamiliar with the constraints and requirements of language testing that we have alluded to in the discussion of issues of measurement here. These approaches are stronger on politics than applied linguistic realities and appear to be a push by claimants from outer and expanding circles for ownership of English (Higgins, 2003), or perhaps a plea for official recognition of their legitimacy as users of English and acknowledgment of validity of their intra- and cross-nationally negotiated language identities. (2006, p. 296)

Without doubt, the question of assessment within the context of ELF has considerable implications for high-stakes international English language tests such as IELTS, TOEFL and CPE, which, as we have seen, are widely used as gatekeeping mechanisms by higher education institutions, border/immigration agencies and professional organisations. These and other such tests are constructed according to native speaker norms and the implicit assumption that students will (indeed should) have studied 'standard English'. Until and unless there is a broad change of attitude and culture beyond applied linguistics and its germane sub-disciplines such that testing organisations, universities, agencies and professional accreditation bodies buy into the ground-level reality of diversity and its implications (and do so virtually simultaneously, for that is what will be required if any individual stakeholder is not to feel vulnerable), it is unlikely that it will gain traction at the implementation level. Crichton and Murray have articulated the situation as follows:

This, in turn, means that there will be little change to what is taught in the classroom, for pedagogy needs to serve the perceived needs and expectations of receiving institutions and the perceived needs, expectations and aspirations of the students themselves. However, there arises a chicken and egg problem, in that there is no meaningful way of establishing standards in assessment without first having some conceptualisation of what it means to be communicatively competent as an ELF speaker, and therefore of what ELF materials need to look like. If international assessment is to acknowledge the reality of diverse linguistic ecologies and communicative competence and its assessment is to be operationalised in pedagogy and assessment ... then the challenge and opportunity afforded to teachers and materials designers is to reflect this in how they design and deliver effective English language programmes. (2014, pp. 40–41)

Clearly, it will take a good deal of time, perseverance and sustained research and argument to change ingrained institutional beliefs and practices – and even then ELF will face an uphill struggle if it is to face-off powerful stakeholders, such as testing organisations, publishers of English language resources and semi-political bodies such as the British Council, who have a high stake in maintaining the status quo and who may see their very existence as being under threat from any move away from native speaker norms and the traditional language requirements of academia. Critically in relation to this book, and particularly the current chapter, even if, ultimately, ELF proves to be an important driver of change in teaching and assessment practices in higher education, there will still be a need to distinguish between general proficiency – however defined and according to whatever notion of communicative competence – academic literacy and professional communication skills (see below).

3.2   English for Specific Purposes, BICS and CALP, and academic literacies

3.2.1   English for higher education studies

In considering the notion of language proficiency in relation to English within the higher education context in English-medium universities, alongside the concept of communicative competence and its various articulations, three other developments are especially noteworthy. The first of these was English for Specific Purposes (ESP) (Mackay and Mountford, 1978; Hutchinson and Waters, 1987), an area of inquiry associated most notably with the work of John Munby and Peter Strevens in the 1970s–80s and which inquired into the question, prompted by functionalists such as Hymes and Halliday, of 'What system (if any) is being used to arrive at the specification of the English deemed appropriate for specific purposes?' (Munby, 1978, p. 1). How does one model those factors that require consideration in designing a course of language learning that will provide the learner with the kind of target communicative competence he requires given the ultimate context in which he expects to use the language? This relationship between language and context was at the very heart of ESP, an area that bred an increased awareness of the limitations of ideas about language teaching current at the time and encouraged language course designers and materials writers to consider how language related to external circumstances and to different discourse domains; that is, how it encoded and expressed the concepts and communicative conventions of different speech communities. As such, the concepts of contextualisation, the speech act, register etc. associated with 'external language' that were becoming prominent in applied linguistics circles were already implicitly very much part and parcel of ESP inquiry.

3.2.2   BICS vs CALP

The second development was a distinction made by Jim Cummins (1980a, 1980b) between Basic Interpersonal Communication Skills (BICS) and Cognitive Academic Language Proficiency (CALP) and essentially based on the observation that it was 'problematic to incorporate all aspects of language use or performance into just one dimension of general or global language proficiency' (Cummins, 2008, p. 71). While BICS was used by Cummins to refer to the individual's conversational fluency in a language and the day-to-day language needed to interact socially with other people, the notion of CALP was used in relation specifically to the social context of schooling – hence the term '*academic* proficiency', defined by Cummins as 'the extent to which an individual has access to and command of the oral and written academic registers of schooling' (Cummins, 2000, p. 67). Baker (2011) explains:

BICS is said to occur when there are contextual supports and props for language delivery. Face-to-face '**context embedded**' situations provide, for example, non-verbal support to secure understanding. Actions with eyes and hands, instant feedback, cues and clues support verbal language. CALP, on the other hand, is said to occur in '**context reduced**' academic situations. Where higher order thinking skills (e.g. analysis, synthesis, evaluation) are required in the curriculum, language is **'disembedded'** [boldface in original] from a meaningful, supportive context. Where language is 'disembedded' the situation is often referred to as **'context reduced'**. (Baker, 2011, p. 170)

The BICS/CALP distinction was made in the context of bilingual education programmes as a response to the question of 'how much proficiency in a language is required to follow instruction through that language' (Cummins, 2000, p. 2) and, by extension, to the more fundamental question of how we conceptualise language proficiency and how it is related to academic development (Cummins, 1979). It was, in the words of Cummins,

intended to draw attention to the very different time periods typically required by immigrant children to acquire conversational fluency in their second language as compared to grade-appropriate academic proficiency in that language. Conversational fluency is often acquired to a functional level within about two years of initial exposure to the second language whereas at least five years is usually required to catch up to native speakers in academic aspects of the second language. (Collier, 1987; Klesmer, 1994; Cummins, 1981a) (Cummins, online n.d., p. 1)

In particular, it was

intended to warn against premature exit of minority students (in the United States) from bilingual to mainstream English-only programs on the basis of attainment of surface level fluency in English. In other words, the distinction highlighted the fact that educators' conflating of these aspects of proficiency was a major factor in the creation of academic difficulties for minority students. (Cummins, 2000, p. 3)

In other words, Cummins was concerned to highlight the danger of assuming that non-native speakers who have attained a high degree of fluency and accuracy in everyday spoken English have the corresponding academic language proficiency; a proficiency that is more cognitively demanding and in which contextual cues are less in evidence, and the development of which takes longer as a result (Klesmer, 1994; Shohamy, Levine, Spolsky, Kere-Levy, Inbar and Shemesh, 2002; Hakuta, Butler and Witt, 2002; Thomas and Collier, 2002).

While it has been the subject of considerable critical appraisal (Edelsky et al., 1983; Martin-Jones and Romaine, 1986; Romaine, 1989; Wiley, 1996; Hulstijn, 2011), to much of which Cummins has himself responded vigorously (see, for example, Cummins, 2000), the notion of CALP nonetheless intersected with and built on Munby's (and others') ESP work by recognising and focusing on the specific demands of different domains of language use – in this case academic English, or what is now commonly referred to as English for Academic Purposes (EAP), and by drawing on insights provided by their antecedents, namely those developments that promoted the functional perspective on language that drove the communicative movement with its critical focus on context and appropriacy.

3.2.3   Academic literacies

Since Cummins originally proposed his BICS/CALP distinction, another key development took place in the late 1990s which has had an important influence on the way in which language proficiency is understood in academic settings, and in the higher education context in particular: the academic literacy movement. In certain respects, this might legitimately be viewed as something of a natural extension or elaboration of work in ESP in that it recognises that the world of academia has its own particular discourses which, in Bourdieu's (1989) terms, form part of the institutional habitus and demand of those entering its community that they accommodate to that habitus by coming with and/or developing the kind of cultural capital (Bourdieu, 1986; but see also Ryan and Hellmundt, 2005; Sheridan, 2011) that enables them to become, and operate effectively as, legitimate members of that community. Sheridan (2011) states:

In essence, cultural capital is the relationship between individual agency and the influence and legacy of family and institutions. Such capital includes linguistic knowledge, speech patterns, conceptual knowledge, informal interpersonal skills, habits and manners and educational credentials so that cultural capital contains a mix of personal, social and academic elements. (p. 130)

Although, to varying degrees, all students will need to increase their cultural capital as they negotiate their degree studies, with regard to international students in particular Sheridan observes:

International students, arriving with their own particular cultural capital gained and ingrained over time, thus engage with their new higher level institution which has its own practices and expectations around teaching and learning. Where these fit into the existing institutional and disciplinary culture, a student achieves personal goals. Clearly, increased levels of student diversity imply a lack of such comfortable fit for some students leading to a gap in the relationship between parts of the student body and academics' expectations in the context of their higher level institution. (Ibid.)

By implication, where the practices and expectations that make up the individual's cultural capital do not align well with institutional and disciplinary culture, this threatens to hinder their development, or 'achievement of personal goals'.

The emergence of work on academic literacies was important in that it helped to highlight and define the notion of disciplinary culture and in doing so provided a new theoretical lens through which to consider language and the construct of language proficiency. This, as we shall see, has in turn influenced the way in which language development has been approached in university settings in particular in recent years, and both the conceptualisation of proficiency and the model of provision I articulate later in this chapter and elucidate further in subsequent chapters. Significantly, Sheridan's reference to 'student diversity' reintroduces here the widening participation agenda discussed in Chapter 1 and serves as an opportunity to emphasise that the need to be conversant in academic literacies is relevant to *all* students (Preece and Godfrey, 2004), not only international students with whom it had tended, wrongly, to be exclusively associated – a point to which I shall return.

Grounded in the New Literacy Studies/Literacy as Social Practice, which conceptualised literacy as social practice rather than an asocial set of generic skills, academic literacies research focuses on higher education and on the dissonance – or, at least, lack of alignment – between students and lecturers in respect of academic literacies. The approach it adopts is frequently discussed in counterpoint to the study skills approach to student literacy in academic contexts, described by Sheridan as 'an individual cognitive skill where the formal features of writing are learnt and easily applied across different contexts. Such features would typically be a focus on sentence structure, creating a paragraph and punctuation' (2011, p. 130). It is the study skills model which has been most prevalent in the last three decades in university English language units and university preparatory programmes where EAP is the 'staple' teaching activity, and it is an approach which assumes that:

literacy is a set of itemised skills which students have to learn and which are then transferable to other contexts. The focus is on attempts to 'fix' problems with student learning, which are treated as a kind of pathology. The theory of language on which it is based emphasises surface features, grammar and spelling. (Lea and Street, 1998, p. 158)

In other words, the study skills approach takes a one-size-fits-all view of academic literacy, which articulates a skills set or set of practices in generic terms and tends to dislocate those skills from particular disciplinary contexts, or 'microworlds'. Its perspective is 'unitary and monolithic' and does not take into account the 'conflicting and contested nature of academic literacies' (Henderson and Hirst, 2006, p. 1). Furthermore, it is an approach which is increasingly seen as, and criticised for, propagating a deficit model of teaching and learning, a fact highlighted thus by Henderson and Hirst in their description of the approach:

'academic literacy' is strongly associated with academic skills advisers, learning support, or some form of centralised learning centre. And in these contexts, academic literacy is defined as a generic set of skills (for example, grammar and editing) and types of writing (for example, essay writing, scientific reports and reference lists) that students need in order to be successful. Procedural guides lead students step by step in the construction of particular text-types. Additionally, academic support courses are often targeted at particular groups, such as 'under-represented groups' and indigenous students. As a result, academic literacy is generally constructed within discourses of deficit and remediation. Similar findings were reported by Green, Hammer and Stephens (2005) following their interviews with academics in one university. That is, the 'problem' is seen as located within students rather than with teaching practices, and the 'solution' to the problem focuses on student deficits that require remedial intervention from support staff. (2007, p. 26)

The academic literacies model, in contrast, is less crude and insensitive and, in the words of Lea and Street (1998), with whom its development is most closely associated,

sees the literacy demands of the curriculum as involving a variety of communicative practices, including genres, fields and disciplines. From the student point of view a dominant feature of academic literacy practices is the requirement to switch practices between one setting and another, to deploy a repertoire of linguistic practices appropriate to each setting, and to handle the social meanings and identities that each evokes. (p. 159)

These 'settings', or disciplines, are, as Rex and McEachen (1999) noted, recognised not only by specialised vocabularies, concepts and knowledges but also by accepted and valued patterns of meaning-making activity (genres, rhetorical structures, argument formulations, narrative devices, etc.) and ways of contesting meaning – areas in which seminal work has been done by scholars such as Hyland (2000, 2006, 2007, 2008) and Swales (1990), and recently by Nesi and Gardner (2012). As they become members of their university and, more specifically, their disciplinary communities of practice, students are learning to:

participate in a variety of socially constituted traditions of meaning-making that are valued in cultures of which they are a part. These traditions include not just concepts and associated vocabulary, but also rhetorical structures, the patterns of action, that are part of any tradition of meaning-making. They include characteristic ways of reaching consensus and expressing disagreement, of formulating arguments, of providing evidence, as well as characteristic genres for organizing thought and conversational action. In mastering such traditions, students learn not only to operate with them, but also how to change them. (Rex and McEachen, ibid. p. 69)

This was an idea that had been expressed earlier, if in somewhat less precise terms and in relation specifically to international students, by Cownie and Addison, who remarked that:

Success on an academic course also involves becoming integrated in to a new academic culture, with all its hidden expectations of written and spoken language. Such knowledge cannot necessarily be acquired before a student arrives in the UK, because published language learning materials, aiming to cater for as wide an audience as possible, are unable to cater to the precise needs of a student following a particular course in a particular institution. (1996, p. 221)

The academic literacies approach goes beyond merely the acquisition of the formal features of writing to include 'both epistemological issues and social processes, including power relations among people, institutions and social identities' (Lea and Street, 2006, p. 369). It recognises that that the literacies associated with particular contexts/disciplines comprise not only a set of skills but also social and cultural practices and discourses (Bizzell, 1982, 1992; Coffin et al., 2003; Curry and Lillis, 2003; Lea and Street, 2000; Lillis, 2001) in which those entering those disciplines need to become conversant if they are to become bone fide members of their communities of practice (Lave and Wenger, 1991). Citing Rex and McEachen (1999), Henderson and Hirst point out that 'this means that students have to know "how to engage with and construct texts strategically and procedurally within particular interactional contexts", because literacies represent socially developed and culturally embedded ways of using text to serve particular cultural or social purposes' (2007, p. 27). Curry and Lillis (2003) rationalise this underlying notion of contextualised social practice as follows:

First, student writing is always embedded within relationships around teaching and learning and these relationships influence, not least, the extent to which students come to write successfully in higher education. Second, the conventions governing exactly what constitutes 'appropriate academic writing' are social to the extent that these have developed within specific academic and disciplinary communities over time. Third, student academic writing is a social practice in that the writers, students, are learning not only to communicate in particular ways, but are learning how to 'be' particular kinds of people: that is, to write 'as academics', 'as geographers', 'as social scientists'. Thus academic writing is also about personal and social identity. (Curry and Lillis, 2003, p. 11)

Academic literacies, then, are – as the phrase suggests – essentially pluralistic in nature; sets of practices associated with each discipline which together help to construct, reinforce and perpetuate the culture of that discipline and help define and differentiate it from other disciplines; and students need to acquire the cultural capital that those practices collectively represent. Through doing so and learning how to know, they become empowered (Lillis, 1997, p. 191). Thus, an academic literacies approach takes the notions of institutional habitus, cultural capital and ESP a step further, effectively arguing that within the higher education habitus, there exist multiple disciplines each with its own habitus and requiring students wishing to gain membership of its sub-community of practice to develop the particular set of practices – the sub-cultural capital – that enables them to do so.

3.3   A tripartite model of language proficiency

There have been a number of models which have sought to shed light on the nature of language proficiency in particular relation to the higher education context (see, for example, Harper, Prentice and Wilson, 2011; and O'Loughlin and Arkoudis, 2009, as cited in Arkoudis, Baik and Richardson, 2012). The tripartite model of proficiency I propose here, the implementation of which is described in detail in Chapter 8, was a strategic response to the 'English language question' formulated within the Australian higher education context and it draws on all of the historical developments outlined above. It comprises:

• General proficiency;
• Academic literacy;
• Professional communication skills.[1]

Dunworth et al. (2013, pp. 14–15) have suggested that this tripartite model reflects a basic 'communicative paradigm', evident in alternative articulations and which recognises 'three major domains of English language use relevant to students in higher education: everyday contexts, academic contexts and professional contexts'.

3.3.1   General proficiency

General proficiency approximates to Cummins' Basic Interpersonal Communication Skills; that is, those skills that furnish the individual with the capacity to negotiate the demands of everyday communication in social contexts. It takes as its starting point the notion of communicative competence and refers to a set of generic skills and abilities broadly captured in frameworks of communicative competence such as those described above and reflected in learning that focuses on areas including grammar and syntax, general listening skills, vocabulary development, general reading and writing skills, the development of communication strategies and fluency, and the pragmatics of communication and associated concerns with politeness, implicature and inference (see Murray, 2010a). These generic skills and abilities represent an investment in language that can be 'cashed in' in *any* potential context of use. For university students of non-English-speaking backgrounds, they provide an entrée to engagement with the university experience generally (i.e. both socially and academically) without which students can feel marginalised, isolated and unfulfilled, and their importance to academic success is well documented in the literature (Light et al., 1987; Johnson, 1988; Elder, 1993; Tonkin, 1995).

3.3.2   Academic literacy

Academic literacy refers to students' conversancy in the particular set of literacy practices relevant to the discipline area within which their course of

---

[1] This appears to approximate to Harper, Prentice and Wilson's (2011) 'professional proficiency'. However, the term 'professional proficiency' risks blurring the distinction between academic literacies and my notion of 'professional communication skills'.

study is located. It is something with which few if any undergraduate students, whether domestic or international, will enter university sufficiently equipped, particularly in cases where their degree subject areas have no equivalent in the secondary education curriculum (e.g. philosophy, sociology, astronomy) and they have therefore had little if any opportunity to develop an appreciation and working understanding, however modest, of those practices pertinent to their tertiary studies. Many, particularly those who have attended English language university foundation courses, will have acquired some awareness of the general principles that determine and are determined by institutional expectations around the use of English; that is, they will frequently have some grounding in the kind of generic study skills (sometimes tellingly referred to as 'generic EAP'[2]) that appear to approximate to Cummins' notion of Cognitive Academic Language Proficiency and which are frequently presented in juxtaposition to academic literacies, as we have seen. However, given the increasingly diverse educational and cultural backgrounds from which university students originate, receiving departments can make few assumptions about *any* individual student's academic literacy (Kirkness, 2006; Matthews, n.d.; Murray, 2010a; Nesi and Gardner, 2006) and there is a strong case, therefore, underlying the growing call for academic literacies to be embedded in the curriculum such that *all* students benefit from tuition designed to ensure that they acquire the particular literacies they need to study effectively in their discipline area and become bona fide members of its community of practice. Van Schalkwyk, Bitzer and van der Walt (2009, p. 189) speak of first-year students missing 'the discipline-specific codes that characterise the discourse [of the discipline], making the process of acquisition [of academic literacy] more difficult'. In their study, they found that:

What emerged was an understanding of students, particularly less prepared students, having to negotiate a series of boundaries in order to assume membership of the larger academic community, on the one hand, as well as the different disciplines, each with its own conventions and discourse, on the other. In this context, the potential of an aligned and integrated academic literacy module to enable such negotiation would appear to have relevance. (van Schalkwyk, Bitzer and van der Walt, 2009, p. 189)

By embedding academic literacies in the curriculum, they are learned within the context of the discipline and presented as an integral part of their degree studies, where they take on an immediacy, relevance and 'authenticity' (Baik and Greig, 2009; Clerehan, 2003; Curnow and Liddicoat, 2008; Kirkness, 2006; Matthews, n.d.; Warren, 2002; Wingate, 2006; Wingate, Andon and

---

[2] The notion 'generic EAP', implies the existence of specific kinds of EAP and as such appears to acknowledge the kind of approach adopted within the academic literacies school of thought. Furthermore, the increasing frequency with which the phrase is being used suggests growing recognition of the pluralistic perspective associated with the academic literacies approach.

Cogo, 2011). Citing Arkoudis, Baik and Richardson (2012), Kennelly, Maldoni and Davies (2010), Mort and Drury (2012) and Steppenbelt and Barrett-Lennard (2008), Dunworth et al. (2013, p. 14) have noted that in studies which have looked at initiatives to embed academic literacies within disciplines 'there is a positive trend emerging that this approach has a positive impact on student learning, at least as measured by academic results'.

As Klinger and Murray observe, 'by embedding academic literacy in this way, it is no longer constructed within discourses of deficit and remediation; it is for – and seen to be for – everyone and is thus inclusive and non-stigmatising' (2012, p. 37). Such embedding does, however, have considerable implications for the role of academic staff and for the way in which language issues are perceived and acted upon by academic staff who have traditionally tended to view any and all language problems as outside their locus of responsibility and area of expertise and who consequently, as a matter of course, refer students with weak language skills to English language units. The need to change this mindset, the strategies needed to do so, and the implications for the role of English language service units in universities are issues that will be addressed in Chapter 6, *From Assessment to Provision*. In the meantime, however, it is worth noting that there is an argument for saying that a broad move away from generic EAP provision towards an academic literacies approach that is – and is seen by students as being – more obviously relevant to their immediate learning needs, promises to help rectify the notoriously erratic attendance that tends to characterise generic EAP in-sessional English language development classes (see Lobo and Gurney, 2014, for a good discussion of this issue). Such classes often do little more than recycle information that many students will already have been taught on university English language foundation programmes and other study skills-based preparatory EAP programmes. As such they can represent more a source of frustration than of benefit to students, many of whom struggle, anyway, to attend due to the pressures of their regular course-work; indeed, ironically, it is often those most in need of help with their English who are least able to afford the time required to access provision and attend in-sessional classes because they are frequently struggling to keep their heads above water and keep pace with their degree studies as a result of weak English.

Given that those newly enrolled students who have attended preparatory EAP programmes will almost certainly have been exposed to a study skills approach (or generic EAP) that is out of kilter with the notion of academic literacy as something intimately and fundamentally tied to a particular domain of application, it is likely that many will have to unlearn some of what they have absorbed in those programmes if they are to meet the requirements of their disciplines.

The nature of the relationship between general proficiency and academic literacy is one that demands clarification. As I have already mentioned, the three facets or 'competencies' of which the construct of proficiency is comprised inevitably impact on each other, and in theorising and considering the pedagogies of one, the others are likely to be invoked. However, the three competencies are also distinct. What is certainly true is that having advanced English language proficiency does not equate to having well-developed academic literacy: students may be highly proficient users of English, but lack the academic literacies pertinent to their disciplines and necessary to performing well in their studies. I have argued elsewhere that:

Although there is an argument for saying that proficiency is part of academic literacy and should therefore be developed within that framework, there is also a rationale for distinguishing the two: Even if their language exhibits dialectal forms not in sync with academic and professional standards and expectations, ESB students are, by definition, fully proficient, yet they share a need with NESB students for academic literacy tuition, as we have seen. This fact implies a different if related set of abilities underlying proficiency and academic literacy. (Murray, 2010a, p. 352)

I have proposed elsewhere (Murray, 2010a, 2010b, 2012, 2013) that general proficiency is a prerequisite to the development of academic literacy and have been criticised for this on the grounds that it represents a 'vertical conception of language development' and 'suggests that there exists a threshold level which students must traverse in order to participate in academic or professional literacies' (Harper, Prentice and Wilson, 2011, p. 41). This criticism is misplaced, I believe, and based on a misinterpretation. In fact, I would espouse a view that supports both a vertical and horizontal conceptualisation of development. The point I had made originally was that if academic literacy is to be embedded in the curriculum and taught by academic staff, then in order for that to happen effectively and for students to understand and be able to engage with concepts in academic literacy that can be complex both in themselves and to explain, students need to have attained a certain level of general proficiency in English that makes this possible; and, in this respect, language development can be seen as vertical in nature. However, a student's ongoing general proficiency development will both inform and be informed by their developing academic literacies. In this respect, language development can be characterised as horizontal.

3.3.3 Professional communication skills

The third component of proficiency that completes the tripartite model is professional communication skills. These derive from the idea that students need to develop the skills and strategies needed to communicate effectively in the workplace; skills upon which they will be judged both as graduates looking to secure professional jobs and as employees. As we have seen, the ability of students to communicate in a rapidly changing, increasingly culturally and linguistically diverse work environment is one of most desirable skills that employers look for in graduates, a fact reflected in its increased salience in universities' graduate qualities frameworks and the 'person specifications' statements typically included in job application packs. Universities want to be able, with confidence, to send out the message to potential employers that their graduates are an attractive proposition precisely because they have the communication skills needed to negotiate effectively a work environment that is increasingly complex demographically, interpersonally as well as in terms of regulation and compliance.

The importance of professional communication skills is not, however, confined to the success they promote among graduates entering the workplace; they can be critical to students' successfully navigating and completing their degree programmes. This is particularly the case where those programmes include practicums or work placements in professions where good communication skills might be regarded as especially critical; for example, medicine, nursing, the allied health professions and education.

Professional communication skills comprise a number of interrelated skills, competences, and orientations as follows:

1. *Intercultural competence*: Intercultural competence refers to the ability to work well across cultures and to manage and accommodate cultural difference and unfamiliarity, intergroup dynamics, and the tensions and conflicts that can accompany this process (see, for example, Alptekin, 2002; Deardorff, 2006; Kramsch, 1993; Perry and Southwell, 2011; Stier, 2003, 2006).[3] It is defined by Fantini and Tirmizi (2006) as 'a complex of abilities needed to perform *effectively* and *appropriately* when interacting with others who are linguistically and culturally different from oneself' (p. 12). Byram, Nichols and Stevens (2001) see intercultural competence as comprising knowledge, skills and attitudes 'complemented by the values one holds because of one's belonging to a number of social groups' (p. 5). They suggest that it is the attitudes of the intercultural speaker and mediator that are the foundation of intercultural competence, and they define these as:

Curiosity and openness: readiness to suspend disbelief about other cultures and belief about one's own. This means a willingness to relativise one's own values, beliefs and behaviours [see point 2 below], not to assume that they are the only possible and naturally correct ones, and to be able to see how they might look from the perspective of an outsider who has a different set of values, beliefs and behaviours. This can be called the ability to 'decentre'. (p. 5)

---

[3] For a discussion of the development of intercultural competence within the higher education context, see, for example, Summers and Volet, 2008; Stier, 2003, 2006; Cotton, George and Joyner, 2013.

By 'knowledge' Byram et al. are referring to knowledge of 'social groups and their products and practices in one's own and in one's interlocutor's country, and of the general processes of societal and individual interaction' (p. 6). They emphasise that this includes knowledge about how other people see oneself as well as some knowledge about other people. Skills they see as being twofold in nature: the skills of interpreting and relating (to 'interpret a document or event from another culture, to explain it and relate it to documents or events from one's own' (p. 6)), and the skills of discovery and interaction (the ability 'to acquire new knowledge of a culture and cultural practices and the ability to operate knowledge, attitudes and skills under the constraints of real-time communication and interaction' (p. 6)).

The final aspect of intercultural competence highlighted by Byram et al. is what they call 'critical cultural awareness', that is 'the ability to evaluate, critically and on the basis of explicit criteria, perspectives, practices and products in one's own and other cultures and countries' (p. 7).

Intercultural competence, then, requires flexibility, open-mindedness and a tolerance of ambiguity, and it is a crucial mediator of difference in a number of key areas where so-called critical incidents are likely to arise; these include, but are not confined to, sexual orientation, independence, autonomy and teamwork, leadership, lines of responsibility, conflict resolution, power relations and notions of hierarchy, and privacy/confidentiality.

2. *A cultural relativistic orientation*: Closely related to but distinct from intercultural competence, this refers to an individual's perception of the world and their place in it in global, relativistic terms rather than from an ethnocentric perspective where there is a tendency to evaluate other groups according to the values and standards of one's own ethnic group, often accompanied by a conviction that one's own group is superior. Cultural relativism and the ability to 'decentre', in Byram et al.'s terms, suggests a more neutral ethical stance rather than one biased either towards a xeno-centric orientation, where the individual manifests a preference for the products, styles or ideas of a culture/cultures other than his or her own (Horton and Hunt, 1976; Stier, 2010), or an ethnocentric orientation (Sumner, 1906; LeVine and Campbell, 1972; Tajfel and Turner, 1979), where the individual's own group is regarded by them as 'the center of everything, and all others are scaled and rated with reference to it' (Sumner, 1906, p. 13).

3. *Interpersonal skills*: Interpersonal skills have to do with the individual's ability to relate to and interact with others effectively and harmoniously for the purpose of establishing and maintaining good relationships, both as an end in itself and also as a way of expediently and expeditiously achieving goals in the workplace. The development of good interpersonal skills entails an appreciation and sound application of those principles governing the

negotiation of relationships – of politeness (Brown and Levinson, 1987; Lakoff, 1973; Watts, 2003); face and the capacity to understand and respond to the face-wants of one's interlocutor (Goffman, 1955, 1967); turn-taking strategies; an awareness of self and other and the ability to empathise and to listen effectively (Adler, Rosenfeld and Proctor, 2012; Watson, 1996). Importantly, it also requires recognition of the fact that the way in which these principles are realised is culturally variable, often with significant implications for the expression and interpretation of meaning (Murray, 2010c). Without such recognition, and the ability and inclination to accommodate that it promotes, relationships are likely to break down.

4. *Conversancy in the discourses and behaviours associated with particular domains*: This refers to the ability to understand and use spoken and written language in a way appropriate to and for the specific purposes associated with particular contexts of use, and to take on different roles, assume different behaviours, and interact appropriately and effectively according to those contexts. Such conversancy requires sensitivity to contextual norms and thus expectations, and the willingness and capacity to adjust one's own behaviours accordingly.

5. *Non-verbal communication skills*: Based on the pioneering work of Birdwhistell (1952, 1970), non-verbal communication – what he referred to as 'kinesics' – is concerned with 'the study of body-motion as related to the non-verbal aspects of interpersonal communication' (1952, p. 9), or what Neuliep has more recently described as 'Messages people send to others that do not contain words, such as messages sent through body motions; vocal qualities; and the use of time, space, artifacts, dress, and even smell' (Neuliep, 2006, p. 286). In Hallidayan terms, non-verbal communication is behaviour other than verbal behaviour which has meaning potential. While the bases for claims that such behaviour accounts for around 93% of all meaning in a social situation have been questioned, nonetheless, Berko et al. acknowledge that 'both children and adults rely more on non-verbal cues than on verbal cues in interpreting the messages of others' (2007, p. 58). Just as there is a grammar of verbal communication, so there is also a grammar of kinesics, Birdwhistell argued. What one might term the parameters of that grammar have been articulated by Burgoon (1994) as sevenfold:
   (1) kinesics or body movements, including facial expressions and eye contact;
   (2) vocalics or paralanguage that includes volume, rate, pitch and timbre;
   (3) personal appearance;
   (4) our physical environment and the artefacts or objects that compose it;
   (5) proxemics or personal space;
   (6) haptics or touch; and
   (7) chronemics or time.

To this list Burgoon et al. add signs or emblems. These parameters together produce a 'semantics' of non-verbal communication (Burgoon, Jensen, Meservy, Kruse and Nunamaker, 2005) and an understanding of them, and in particular their culture-specific nature, is an important factor in successfully interacting in multicultural contexts such as the global workplace.

6. *Group and leadership skills*: Harry S. Truman apparently described a leader as 'a person who gets other people to do what they don't want to do and like it'. A rather more insightful definition, perhaps, is provided by the Collaborative Leadership Network, which describes leadership in the following terms:

Leadership is a reciprocal process of motivating individuals and mobilizing resources in pursuit of goals shared by members of a group, organization, or community. As an aspect of group innovation and problem-solving behaviour, leadership involves the clarification of group goals, the communication of strategies for goal achievement, the initiation of structure in interaction and expectation, and the assumption of responsibility for results. (n.d., www.leadershipskillsandvalues.com/lessons-and-readings/defi nitions-of-leadership)

Group skills – part of what makes a good leader but certainly not confined to those in positions of leadership (see, for example, Baron, Kerr and Miller, 1996; Lumsden and Lumsden, 1997) – broadly refers to those attitudes and strategies that enable an individual to integrate with those with whom he or she is interacting on a regular basis or for a given task, and to integrate or make to feel integrated others in the group. Group skills build a sense of cohesion among a set of individuals through the displaying of a number of traits highlighted in Table 3.1.

Clearly, language lies at the very heart of these six skills, competences and orientations that collectively make up Professional Communication Skills. They inevitably assume a level of general proficiency in English manifested in language that is sophisticated and nuanced, and, in the case of item 4, they draw on knowledge of those academic literacies relevant to the activities of the particular profession concerned. Nevertheless, the inclusion of professional communication skills as an discrete component in the model of proficiency proposed here is based on the idea that it is perfectly conceivable that a given individual may have advanced levels of general proficiency – indeed even be a native speaker, and be highly conversant in the academic literacies of his or her discipline – yet not necessarily have well-developed professional communication skills. That is, professional communication skills can legitimately be regarded as something other than general proficiency and academic literacy.

As with academic literacy, there is a quite compelling argument for embedding professional communication skills in the curriculum and presenting them within the context of students' discipline areas so as to help ensure that they are

Table 3.1. *Traits associated with developed group skills*

Trait	Characteristics
Openness	Receptivity to new ideas, diverse viewpoints and the variety of individuals present within the group, particularly those with different interests and backgrounds. An ability to listen to others and elicit their ideas and to balance the need for cohesion within a group with the need for individual expression.
Trust and self-disclosure	The ability to promote a sense of mutual trust such that there is a willingness to self-disclose and be honest yet respectful. Trust also grows as group members demonstrate personal accountability for the tasks they have been assigned.
Support	The ability to demonstrate and inspire support in the accomplishment of group goals and to display team loyalty and a desire to assist members who are experiencing difficulties. The ability to see others as collaborators rather than as competitors.
Respect	Group members communicate their opinions in a way that respects others, focusing on 'What can we learn?' rather than 'Who is to blame?' See constructive feedback in the process section for more details.
Individual responsibility and accountability	All group members agree on what needs to be done and by whom. Each student then determines what he or she needs to do and takes responsibility to complete the task(s). They can be held accountable for their tasks, and they hold others accountable for theirs.
Constructive feedback	Group members are able to give and receive feedback about group ideas. Giving constructive feedback requires focusing on ideas and behaviours, instead of individuals, being as positive as possible, and offering suggestions for improvement. Receiving feedback requires listening well, asking for clarification if the comment is unclear, and being open to change and other ideas.
Problem solving	Group members help the group to develop and use strategies central to their group goals. As such, they can facilitate group decision making and deal productively with conflict. In extreme cases, they know when to approach the professor for additional advice and help.
Management and organisation	Group members know how to plan and manage a task, how to manage their time, and how to run a meeting. For example, they ensure that meeting goals are set, that an agenda is created and followed, and that everyone has an opportunity to participate. They stay focused on the task and help others to do so too.
Knowledge of roles	Group members know which roles can be filled within a group (e.g. facilitator, idea-generator, summariser, evaluator, mediator, encourager, recorder) and are aware of which role(s) they and others are best suited for. They are also willing to rotate roles to maximise their own and others' group learning experience.

(Adapted from the Centre for Teaching Excellence, University of Waterloo, Canada) most relevant to their current and future needs. The content of communication skills components needs to be informed by answers to the question, 'What communication skills do these students need in order to enter, operate in and succeed in their chosen professions?'

3.4 Summary

Drawing on historical developments in communicative competence theory and ESP, and invoking a distinction in the literature between Basic Interpersonal Communication Skills (BICS) and Cognitive Academic Language Proficiency (CALP), this chapter has articulated a tripartite model of 'English language proficiency', a construct that has been variously defined and which, as a result, is variously understood. The model articulated seeks to give clarity and unity to the construct on the grounds that, without it, efforts to meaningfully engage all potential stakeholders and to develop a systematic, coherent and theoretically informed institution-wide model of English language provision are unlikely to be fruitful and to satisfy auditors seeking to uphold standards in this increasingly relevant – some would say problematic – area of higher education.

The model comprises three interrelated and interactive components: general proficiency, which invokes those parameters of language knowledge and ability associated with a number of key frameworks of communicative competence found in the literature; academic literacies, which sees reading and writing not in the kind of generic terms associated with a study skills approach but in terms of cultural and social practices that are discipline specific and involve 'both epistemological issues and social processes, including power relations among people, institutions and social identities' (Lea and Street, 2006, p. 369); and professional communication skills, which are informed by the changing contextual landscape of the professional workplace and the increased emphasis employers are consequently placing on a range of interpersonal skills and competencies that have language ability at their heart.

I have argued that all students, whether international or domestic and regardless of their first language background, require – indeed have a right to expect – academic literacy and professional communication skills development opportunities, as success in their studies, and subsequently in the workplace, is dependent upon their conversancy in these areas. This being the case, tuition in academic literacy and professional communication skills should not be offered merely as incidental 'bolt-on' activities delivered centrally as extracurricula activities (Bennett, 2000); they should be regarded as central or core to students' higher education experience and should not be separated from the process and content of learning (Wingate, 2006).

In concluding their discussion of the issues relating to defining English language proficiency and the different models of proficiency that have been proposed within the Australian context, the authors of the IEAA's 2013 Outcomes Report, *Five Years On: English Language Competence of International Students*, state the following:

Despite disparities between the models, similarities can be extrapolated. Firstly, they each highlight the fact that ELP in higher education is complex and multidimensional. Secondly, they suggest that different stages of the student lifecycle may require a focus on a different dimension. Thirdly, an informal domain of general or everyday language appears necessary *in addition to* language for more formal academic or professional purposes, which is in line with the received view of language use as socially- and contextually situated (Bachman and Palmer, 2010; Hyland, 2007). This view also fits employers' perceptions (Arkoudis et al., 2009), who identified both general and specific occupation language skills as necessary, including 'high-level workplace communication skills with an emphasis on social and oral English, with literacy and cross-cultural skills' (Arkoudis et al., 2009, p. 16). A key issue, however, is the difference in language use in different disciplines and professions with their varying norms and conventions (Hyland, 2007), and such diverse needs have hampered efforts to devise shared definitions. (p. 83)

I would suggest that the kind of componential model I have described here offers the sort of shared definition of which the IEAA speaks, while recognising disciplinary and professional variation in norms and conventions and thereby helping ensure that, through a process of embedding – articulated in greater detail in Chapter 6 – students, whether of English-speaking or non-English-speaking backgrounds, benefit from ample opportunities to acquire the particular language that is of greatest relevance and benefit to them.

One important outstanding issue, however, is how to ensure that students have the general proficiency to be able to benefit from embedded tuition in academic literacies and professional communication skills, as well as integrate into university life more generally. This issue will form the focus of Chapters 4 and 5.

4   Pre-enrolment language assessment and English language conditions of entry

4.1   Introduction

Within the context of the regulation of English language standards in higher education, reference was made in Chapter 2 to the increasing role of immigration departments in the establishing of university entry threshold proficiency levels. In countries such as the United Kingdom, this development has proven to be highly significant and it highlights a tension at the political level between a desire by some governments to be seen to be taking robust measures to control levels of immigration, instances of *illegal* immigration and employment and the issuing of student visas on the one hand, and on the other a desire to create a buoyant economy though promoting the virtues of their respective higher education sectors through political discourse and, in the case of the United Kingdom, institutions such as the British Council that promote British educational and cultural interests internationally. That is, while the British government, for example, seeks to extol the virtues and benefits of the educational experience offered by its universities as a way of promoting Britain and generating business and thus income for the national economy and for higher education institutions through international student fees,[1] it has, simultaneously, been making it more challenging for international students to obtain visas permitting them to enter the country for the purpose of studying. In 2011, the Home Office UK Border Agency issued a press release announcing changes to its immigration rules affecting Tier 4 (the student tier) of the points-based system it employs. Among other things, these changes:

- restricted work entitlements to migrants studying at higher educational institutions (HEIs) and publicly funded further education colleges only;
- restricted the sponsorship of dependents to those studying at postgraduate level at HEIs on courses lasting at least twelve months, and government-sponsored students on courses lasting at least six months;

---

[1] A research paper by the UK government's Department for Business Innovation and Skills valued higher education exports at approximately £8 million in 2011.

- stipulated minimum English language levels required for study in the United Kingdom both at degree level and above as well as below degree level (including pre-sessional courses);
- required education providers to vouch that a new course represented genuine academic progression;
- ensured that maintenance funds were genuinely available to the applicant, by introducing a declaration on the visa application form;
- committed the then UKBA (later UKVI (Visa and Immigration)) to publish a list of financial institutions that they considered, on the basis of experience, did not verify financial statements to their satisfaction in more than fifty per cent of a sample of cases;
- introduced a streamlined application process for low-risk nationals applying to attend courses with so-called Highly Trusted Sponsors;
- extended the list of courses for which students must receive ATAS (Academic Technology Approval Scheme) clearance; and
- clarified the position of overseas universities with campuses in the United Kingdom.

These rules have since been subject to further and ongoing changes, and have tended towards even greater stringency.

While it could be argued that these kinds of more robust immigration policies actually help regulate English language standards in higher education by stipulating minimum English language requirements,[2] they have the potential to be manipulated by governments as a way of gaining a marketing edge in a space where Kachru's 'inner circle' countries are continually vying for competitive advantage in the hope of benefiting from the considerable income these students represent. In other words, economic considerations could incline governments to lower language entry standards. In 2011, for example, Australia saw a dramatic decline in its international student enrolment numbers following a tightening up of immigration regulations: a decline which effectively handed the marketing initiative to the United Kingdom and North America. Since then, in part as a response to the higher education lobby, it has backtracked somewhat in an effort to recoup some of its lost market share; yet, ironically, at the exact same time as Australia was attempting to redress a problem of its own making, the UK government decided to increase its visa restrictions, thereby inadvertently assisting Australia to claw back its losses by making the United Kingdom a less attractive destination where the opportunity to study requires the negotiation of considerably more formidable hurdles and an understanding by educational agents and would-be students and their parents of immigration rules that can seem opaque and off-

---

[2] In the United Kingdom, the UKVI currently requires all non-EU students to meet a minimum B2 level overall on the Common European Framework of Reference (CEFR), with at least B2 proficiency in each of the four skills of speaking, listening, reading and writing.

putting to those unfamiliar with them. Indeed, anecdotal evidence suggests strongly that even those who negotiate these rules on an almost daily basis – UK universities and their academic and administrative staff – can find them difficult to understand and apply, and spend a good deal of time and money making absolutely certain that they are following them to the letter. The consequences of failure to do so were highlighted in August 2012 when the United Kingdom's London Metropolitan University had its licence to recruit non-EU overseas students revoked in a highly publicised case, following claims by the UKBA that it had 'failed to address serious and systemic failings' in its visa practices that had been identified six months previously. The then Immigration Minister, Damian Green, claimed that London Metropolitan University had failed in three particular areas:

- More than a quarter of the 101 students sampled were studying at the university when they had no leave to remain in this country;
- Some 20 of 50 checked files found 'no proper evidence' that the students' mandatory English levels had been reached;
- And some 142 of 250 sampled records (57%) had attendance monitoring issues, which meant it was impossible for the university to know whether students were turning up for classes or not (Richardson, BBC News: Education and Family, 30 August 2012).

Although the decision was appealed and revocation of the University's visa licence subsequently withdrawn in Spring 2013, subject to a twelve-month probationary period and following a number of systemic and administrative improvements (Baker, 2013), the immediate fallout from the UKBA's original decision to prohibit the university from recruiting was severe: not only was the University's licence revoked but approximately 2000 enrolled students found themselves facing a situation where they had to find an alternative institution to sponsor them or be told that they would be removed from the United Kingdom.

Coincidentally, at the very time of writing the previous paragraph, an email arrived in my inbox which serves to highlight, yet again, the pressure on universities to maintain watertight entry procedures or face the consequences. It is from an organisation (Business Forums International) offering a workshop to this end, and it reads as follows:

Document Verification Workshop for Overseas Students and Staff

Dear Colleague

I am writing with the latest details and dates of our one day workshop specifically researched and written for universities, colleges and schools that employ overseas staff and enrol overseas students.

As I am sure you are aware, your institution has a responsibility to prevent illegal working, provide evidence of an employee's Right to Work and comply fully with UKBA regulations. The failure to do so can lead to punitive fines and a removal of your licence to hire migrant workers. It is also vital that academic institutions vigorously check their overseas students' documents and academic records. Sponsoring students who hold fake passports, visas and educational certificates opens your organisation to wealth of potential problems that could result following any UKBA audit.

BFI's Document Verification Workshop for Universities, Schools & Colleges will provide International, Admissions and HR teams with practical, hands-on training in recognising fraudulent documents; enabling attendees to get to grips with the legal responsibilities surrounding document verification for applicants: staff & students, spotting fake qualifications and ID documents, giving each delegate the chance to handle and compare fake and real examples.

Highlights include:
Legal overview of institution's responsibilities;
- UKBA regulation
- Discrimination
- Data protection

Combating education fraud;
- What countries and agencies to watch out for
- Real life examples of fake degrees and diplomas

Masterclass in identity checks;
- Passports
- Photo ID and driving licences
- Birth certificates
- Supporting documents
- Stamps
- Visas

(Business Forums International, 2013)

Unedifying though it may be, the issue of pre-entry English language assessment, the focus of this chapter, is inextricably linked to the question of standards and the lure of overseas fees and their potential, at least, to unduly influence decisions, processes and procedures concerning student admissions. That is, it highlights the tension, discussed in Chapter 3 within the context of regulation, between ethical considerations and the maintenance of standards on the one hand, and the pressure to respond to institutional financial imperatives on the other. While its primary purpose is to control illegal immigration, the kind of immigration legislation to which I have made reference arguably serves something of a secondary purpose by helping ensure that students enter higher education with a minimum level of English language proficiency as measured by a recognised Secure English

Language Test (SELT) such as IELTS and TOEFL.[3] However, meeting the minimum proficiency level stipulated by immigration departments and agencies such as UKVI is not the same thing as meeting the minimum language requirements stipulated by universities and their individual departments and typically set differentially according to the perceived language demands of particular programmes. In reality, many university departments set their minimum English language entry requirements above the minimum level required for visa purposes. The key question, however, is whether their own English language conditions of entry are set appropriately so as to ensure that students who meet those conditions have at least a reasonable chance of graduating successfully, assuming that they put in reasonable effort, however defined. This question takes on particular poignancy given the UK Council for International Students Affairs' (UKCISA) finding, cited by the QAA (2009), that sixty-two per cent of the sixty-six institutions it surveyed said they would admit students with less than the minimum stated language requirements (p. 12). And, as the following extracts from the QAA's report attest, anecdotal evidence from those at the coalface suggests not only that this does indeed occur but also that, even where minimum requirements *are* met, students often still struggle subsequently to cope with their studies:

An article published in the press in 2006 argued that the minimum International English Language Testing System (IELTS) scores required by many universities were not appropriate 'to ensure students could keep pace with the expectations of academics, particularly on postgraduate courses', and that the adoption of low 'language requirements [was] the result of international students' status as a "lucrative source of income" for institutions in the UK'. The author argued that universities needed 'to provide a greater level of support to enable overseas students to deal with the challenges of daily teaching as well as to help them to undertake dissertations and larger enquiries in English'. (pp. 12–13)

All representatives of organisations interviewed for the Enquiry considered competency in English to be an important factor in the recruitment and admission of international students. Interviewees were aware of the use by institutions of the IELTS, although some noted that not all institutions found the system to be as helpful as it could be in determining students' language capabilities ... Participants in the 'academic' and the 'student' focus groups (which included international student representatives) commented that IELTS scores do not necessarily correlate well with a student's ability to understand conversational English, including local dialects and accents, or their ability to understand subject-specific vocabulary. It was further noted that international students beginning a programme of study in the UK may benefit from ongoing support to enable them to develop their language skills. (p. 13)

---

[3] At the time of writing, UKVI's Secure English Language Tests are: IELTS (Academic), Pearson PTE (Academic), Cambridge IGCSE, Cambridge ESOL and TOEFL (IBT). Other approved tests include City & Guilds ESOL, TOEIC, BEC, ILEC, ICFE and BULATS.

Throughout 2007, press and media reports increasingly focused on the link between the admission of growing numbers of international students to universities and a range of difficulties being encountered by the students and the staff teaching them. (p. 12)

The following extract, while referring to institutional entry requirements generally, given the immediate context in which it appears, certainly implies at the very least that the concerns expressed apply to English language entry requirements:

Institutions' policies and practice regarding the admission of international students were cited by several members of focus groups convened for the Enquiry as the reason behind several of the recent challenges appearing in the media about academic standards and quality of students' learning experiences. Many participants, particularly in the groups composed of academics and students, reported that institutions do not, variably, set, enforce or verify entrance requirements for international students sufficiently to ensure that they are able to succeed with the programme of study. Discretion applied by institutions in making individual admission decisions for international students was felt to be higher in some, but not all, institutions for international students than for home students. Differences in the degree of discretion exercised by institutions were attributed to the fulfilment of institutional quotas and the need for institutions to generate income. (p. 16)

According to a *Times Higher Education* survey conducted via a Freedom on Information request, 'nearly two in three UK universities are setting English language requirements below the recommended level for undergraduate students from outside the European Union' (Matthews, *Times Higher Education*, 23 August 2012).

The fact that, despite having met institutional English language entry requirements, a significant number of students for whom English is not a first language appear to struggle with the demands of their studies (see, for example, McDowell and Merrylees, 1998; Coley, 1999; Jamieson et al., 2000; Bretag, 2007) indicates problems in one or more of the following areas:

- the English language tests themselves that are employed by universities to serve as gatekeeping mechanisms designed to ensure that only those students who have the language skills needed to succeed in their degree studies are admitted;
- the way in which such gatekeeping tests are understood and used by universities (an issue related, in part, to that of assessment literacy among those tasked with setting English language thresholds (Davies, 2008; Pill and Harding, 2013; Spolsky, 2008; Taylor, 2009));
- the rigour with which universities uphold the standards they have put in place (where these exceed UKVI requirements, in the case of the United Kingdom); and
- the security surrounding the administration of high-stakes gatekeeping tests.

Let us now consider each of these areas in turn.

4.2 A critique of pre-enrolment English language tests

4.2.1 Are English language gatekeeping tests fit for purpose?

The fact that universities use gatekeeping tests such as IELTS, TOEFL and PTE at all indicates a belief that they tell test users (the students and their receiving institutions/departments) something about students' linguistic suitability or preparedness for higher education study – the underlying premise being that a certain degree of English language competence is a pre-requisite to academic success and that scores on such tests serve as predictors of students' linguistic performance in academic contexts – and, indirectly at least, of their academic performance therefore; that is, they have 'predictive validity', defined by Bachman as:

> The extent to which test performance replicates some specified non-test language performance. This approach thus seeks to develop tests that mirror the 'reality' of non-test language use, and its prime concerns are: (1) the appearance or perception of the test and how this may affect test performance and test use (so-called 'face validity'), and (2) the accuracy with which test performance predicts future non-test performance (test utility). (Bachman, 1990, p. 301)

In the higher education context with which we are concerned here, what Bachman calls 'future non-test performance' refers to students' academic performance post-enrolment. Predictive validity studies have thus attempted to answer the question 'What is the evidence that students accepted at a certain grade on this test have sufficient language proficiency to perform satisfactorily on their course of study?' (Bool, Dunmore, Tonkyn, Schmitt and Ward-Goodbody, 2003, p. 4) – a context-specific articulation of Messick's broader question of whether test scores 'have utility for the proposed purposes in the applied settings' (Messick, 1996, p. 247). Typically, these studies look at whether and to what extent the sub-tests of, for example, IELTS (i.e. reading, writing, speaking and listening) correlate to a measure of academic achievement – often students' grade point average across their first and/or second semesters of study at university (see, for example, Bayliss and Ingram, 2006; Cotton and Conrow, 1998; Kerstjens and Nery, 2000).

Despite numerous such studies having been conducted in recent years, designed to investigate the predictive validity of gatekeeping tests, results have been mixed and the territory remains contentious as a result, not least because of the many intervening variables, both linguistic and non-linguistic, that have the potential to influence academic performance and success and which therefore make it difficult to draw unambiguous causal links between language proficiency as measured by such tests, and subsequent academic performance (Criper and Davies, 1988; Cotton and Conrow, 1998; Dooey and Oliver, 2002; Elder, 1993; Fox, 2004; Graham, 1987; Hill, Storch and

Lynch, 1999; Ingram and Bayliss, 2007; Kerstjens and Nery, 2000; Light et al., 1987; Palmer and Woodford, 1978; Park, 2003; Paul 2007; Rea-Dickens, Kiely and Yu, 2007; Woodrow, 2006). Such variables include:

- the extent of the individual's understanding of university culture;
- their degree of integration into academic life;
- their motivation levels;
- the extent of their professional experience;
- their level of self-confidence and willingness to interact in class;
- the sophistication of their critical thinking skills;
- the degree of peer support available to them;
- the type of degree they are studying and how linguistically demanding it is;
- the inherent complexity of the content of their degree;
- their capacity to independently manage their studies;
- their ability to work with those of different genders, age groups and social and cultural backgrounds;
- the institutional support infrastructure and the availability and take-up of language support services in particular; and
- sociocultural and psychosocial factors.

Studies that have found little or no correlation between scores on gatekeeping tests and subsequent academic performance include those of Fiocco (1992), Gibson and Rusek (1992), Cotton and Conrow (1998), Dooey (1999) and Dooey and Oliver (2002). In contrast, studies conducted by Bellingham (1993), Elder (1993), Ferguson and White (1993), Hill, Storch and Lynch (1999), Kerstjens and Nery (2000) and Feast (2002) have found a generally positive correlation between IELTS and grade point averages (GPAs), be they of variable degrees of strength. A number of studies have indicated that ELP is a better predictor of academic success for lower proficiency than for higher proficiency students (Graham, 1987; Elder, 1993) and that the relationship is strongest at the end of the first semester (Light et al., 1987; Elder, 1993).

The results of these and other such studies certainly do not provide anything like incontrovertible evidence that tests such as IELTS, TOEFL and PTE provide a reliable indication of students' future academic performance. While the kinds of variables specified earlier, when viewed collectively, go some way to explaining these less than conclusive results and highlight the difficulty of establishing meaningful correlations with confidence, there is, I would argue, another critical factor that fatally undermines the integrity of gatekeeping tests; and it is a factor that bears on the distinctions articulated in Chapter 3 between general proficiency, academic literacy and professional communication skills. The high-profile gatekeeping tests that are currently employed by English-medium universities the world over focus on generic EAP and, as we have seen, this fails to take account of the particularity of literacy practices within specific disciplines and associated with an academic literacies perspective; that is, they can be seen as lacking 'content validity' by failing to provide a truly 'repre-sentative sample of the domain to be tested' (Bachman, 1990, p. 306). Universities and the tests they employ thus essentially – some would say *necessarily*, given the considerable practical challenges of doing otherwise – take a broad-brush approach, and as such the ability to provide an accurate indication of future performance is necessarily compromised, for that perfor-mance is largely dependent on students' conversancy in those practices perti-nent to their particular disciplines and with which, I have argued, we cannot assume or expect students to come equipped to university; hence the need to embed tuition in academic literacies within the curriculum. In other words, while they may be valid in terms of measuring test-takers' generic academic English skills, the pre-enrolment tests currently used by English-medium universities as screening mechanisms lack authenticity for they do not suffi-ciently reflect the actual language requirements of students' future degree programmes.

It would seem unreasonable, then, to expect pre-entry gatekeeping tests to have high levels of predictive validity if, in certain important respects, the language demands they make of students differ from those that students face post-entry, during the course of their degree studies. Paradoxically, while a solution to this misalignment may appear to lie in the development of a series of more nuanced gatekeeping tests that reflect the particular language demands of different disciplines, and which could also better serve the purposes of profes-sional accreditation organisations, this would seem to be equally inappropriate given that such discipline-specific tests would assume language knowledge that many students will not yet have acquired. More critically, however, the pro-blem arises that secondary school curricula can vary significantly between different countries, and this would make it challenging, at the very least, to design a series of tests based on accurate assumptions about prior student learning and which would suit all cohorts originating from whichever educa-tional contexts.

While questionable predictive validity must raise doubts about the extent to which gatekeeping tests are fit for purpose, alternative practicable means by which to assess students' suitability for degree studies are hard to discern. Furthermore, while many would no doubt argue that the weaknesses of such tests have always been widely acknowledged by the academic community, and while they may be quite blunt instruments, generally speaking they do a reasonably good job under the circumstances, both for universities as well as for students, for whom they provide a standard via which to compare different universities' English language entry requirements and measure their own language development.

Although the idea of students taking English language tests based on the discipline area in which they intend to study and tailored accordingly might appear a logical option, in practice it makes little sense if (a) we cannot assume that students will come equipped with adequate conversancy in the literacy practices of their future disciplines, as a result of diverse educational experiences, and (b) those literacy practices will therefore need to be taught to them anyway, embedded in the curriculum.

4.2.2   How are gatekeeping tests understood and used by universities?

So, it would appear that while gatekeeping tests are not ideally suited for purpose, they do *serve* a purpose; one that cannot easily be better served by alternative instruments. What is important is that the tests, their strengths and their weaknesses are sufficiently understood by those who use them. Arkoudis, Baik and Richardson (2012) suggest that 'All staff involved in setting and administering English language requirements should be made aware of the meaning, limitations and relationship of test scores on different standardised tests, including their limited predictability for future academic performance' (p. 36). I would argue for casting the net wider still to include universities and their administrators, their marketing teams and their academic departments and admissions tutors. I would also propose that, when viewed as initial screening mechanisms that operate in parallel with some form of post-enrolment assessment (see Chapter 5), the case for retaining gatekeeping tests is bolstered.

The idea that users of tests such as IELTS, TOEFL and PTE within higher education should understand what the tests claim to be able to do and what their scores indicate in real terms is something that has not been given adequate prominence in the sector. To a large extent this is a product of the way in which universities set their English language entry requirements. Typically, universities benchmark against competitor institutions following the deliberations of a committee or working group set up for this very purpose and often including at least one member from the institution's English language support unit on the grounds that they are well-versed in the various tests and therefore well placed to advise the committee. Such committees also tend to include representation from the institution's International Office or equivalent, and have reference to qualifications categorised by country, language residency criteria,[4] tables of competitors' language requirements, and English language test equivalence tables. The validity of such tables is often dubious at best (see Davies et al., 1999; Taylor, 2004) for, as Arkoudis, Baik and Richardson (2012) observe, 'assessing language ability involves reference to the context in which language is used, the objectives users are trying to achieve, the actions they undertake to achieve these objectives and the knowledge and skills they make use of'

---

[4] See Fox (2005) for a discussion of language residency criteria and their relationship to academic performance at university.

(p. 25). These things can be highly variable, an observation not lost on Davies et al. (1999), who argue:

Strictly speaking, this concept [equivalence] is unjustifiable, since each test is designed for a different purpose and a different population, and may view and assess language traits in different ways as well as describing test-taker performance differently. (1999, p. 199)

The International Education Association of Australia echoes these sentiments as follows:

The continued rapid growth in international student mobility worldwide means that additional tests of English language proficiency are likely to emerge to meet a market need. Diversity here, as in other spheres, is becoming the norm. For institutions and their staff, the proliferation and greater diversity of English language tests, together with the continuing difficulty in the absence of rigorous equivalency studies to agree the measures of equivalence for test scores on different tests (see below), means that determinations about suitable English language requirements and assessments of proficiency levels for entry are likely to become even more challenging than they currently are. (2013, p. 32)

Despite problems inherent in establishing test equivalence, in Australia, testing organisations whose tests have been accepted for purposes of student visa assessment have all been required by the Department of Immigration and Citizenship (DIAC) to undertake research in order to demonstrate equivalence with IELTS. In the United Kingdom, CEFR has been adopted as the benchmark against which IELTS, TOEFL, CAE and PTE are referenced, yet as Murray and Arkoudis observe:

there is considerable breadth in the range of scores that equate to each of the CEFR reference levels, so much so that 'it is impossible to determine the precise equivalency of different test scores in the absence of a rigorous study'. (Arkoudis, Baik and Richardson, 2012, p. 27)
    Moreover, the problem with the comparison of the major standardised test results with the CEFR frameworks are that different meanings can be given from different research perspectives to the word descriptions of the various CEFR levels. Interpretation of IELTS scores for example are more generous than for Pearson (PTE Academic) or TOEFL scores, whose equivalence results for CEFR are similar. IELTS appears not to publish research studies to back up the IELTS equivalences so it is not possible to know how they are arrived at.
    The incommensurability of outcomes on the wide variety of English language tests raises serious questions about quality assurance in the use of a variety of test scores for selection purposes. (Murray and Arkoudis, 2013, pp. 31–2)

Unfortunately, the process of benchmarking against competitor institutions is problematic because, once again, it is liable to compromised by the tension highlighted in Chapter 2 between the need to uphold academic standards, on the one hand, and, on the other, the need to answer to commercial/financial pressures that are increasingly making themselves felt across the sector. That is, even where the membership of committees established with a remit to set English language standards is knowledgeable about the tests upon which it confers, its decisions are likely to be influenced to some degree by consideration of their impact on enrolment numbers and the need to capture market share. This means that, rather than setting requirements according to what is deemed to be an appropriate level of language competence required to negotiate the demands of university study, such committees almost invariably – perhaps also inevitably – tend to set them at minimum recommended levels, or slightly lower, so as not to risk losing market share through being out of kilter with their competitors and through being perceived by would-be students as placing an unwelcome hurdle in the way of their transition into the university.[5] The expectation, it seems, is that students who enter at the lower end of the language proficiency spectrum will draw on institutional in-sessional language support and will simply need to be resourceful enough to make up any linguistic shortfall during the course of their studies – an expectation accompanied, perhaps, by a largely unspoken assumption that there will likely be a small percentage of students who will fall by the wayside as 'acceptable casualties' of a system that generally works well enough for the great majority and to which there is no obvious and better alternative. Such thinking fails to recognise sufficiently the reality of a steadily increasing international student population in English-medium universities and the accompanying increase in the number of students requiring in-sessional language support in a climate where, despite benefiting from the high fees international students bring with them, universities are nevertheless often reluctant to invest to the extent required in units designed to provide that support – a point alluded to in clauses 48 and 56 of the QAA's 2009 report (p. 15). Once again, this raises ethical questions concerning the basis on which these students are accepted by universities onto degree programmes in the first place.

The questions of what academic staff and university administrators, as test users, understand of gatekeeping tests and how to usefully deepen their understanding of them are intriguing ones. Typically, their decision-making will be informed by the following (although it is by no means the case that all those involved in such decision-making will have knowledge of all of these things):

- Claims made by the testing organisations that produce the tests about their rigour and suitability.
- The skills components of the tests and the types of tasks test-takers are required to complete.

---

[5] Conversely, it should be noted that while such instances may be rare indeed, a case for *lowering* English language requirements below the sector norm might also be regarded by university senior management as risk-laden, and thus undesirable, by presenting an image of the university as an institution with low standards and lacking in academic ambition.

- A set of performance descriptors ('can-do' statements) intended to give some indication of the capabilities of students who have achieved different levels of competency on the tests.

One element that tends to be absent from the users' toolkit, however, is a *sense* of what different test scores represent in real performance terms, not as captured in a rigid set of descriptors such as those found in the CEFR and to which test levels are frequently indexed (for example, the PTE) but as developed by English language teachers through years of working to improve the academic and general language skills of students and assisting them to achieve to the required standard on the various proficiency tests used by universities, employers and professional bodies. Over time, this experiential knowledge gives English language teachers an almost implicit or instinctive understanding of what a particular score means in terms of an individual's capacity to communicate; an understanding that is holistic rather than informed by a set of discrete can-do statements which imply, incorrectly, that within a given band a student can be expected to be able to perform all of the functions specified, when in reality that may well not be the case. Furthermore, anecdotal evidence suggests that, while they may be used in the construction of syllabi to inform teaching–learning goals, few language teachers with a modicum of experience under their belts refer to such descriptors in their daily work except, sometimes, for purposes of standard-setting and moderation, for they are not particularly user-friendly and do not lend themselves to memorisation. Instead, most teachers invoke their experience when making decisions, concerning the streaming of students, for example.

While it would be unreasonable to expect academic staff and administrators to have the same level of understanding of proficiency tests as English language teachers, for whom it is a fundamental and indispensable aspect of their professional repertoire or knowledge base, there may be ways of enabling them to acquire a more developed *sense* of what test scores mean, similar to that which language teachers develop through ongoing contact with students and their continual exposure to tests and test scores. It may, for example, be possible over time to raise the awareness of academic staff by including NESB students' English language test scores (and sub-skills scores, where relevant) on attendance registers so that it becomes easier for those staff to continually associate students with their academic performance and their English language test scores, and to compare the performance of different individuals, thereby acquiring a sense of what test scores mean in both absolute and relative terms.

Similarly, administrators working with NESB students and making decisions revolving around language proficiency could be given easy access to the English language scores of students with whom they will be having contact so that, again, they could begin to associate particular scores with certain levels of communicative competence. Alternatively, or in addition, English language test scores could be included on NESB students' university ID cards or on essay submissions so that similar associations could be made. While this would, justifiably, raise concerns about discrimination and stigmatisation, it could be optional for students. The main point here, however, is that with creative thinking, there are possible ways of helping to ensure that, over time, academic and administrative staff begin to develop communicative 'profiles' based on frequent and continual associations made between test scores and their experience of students' communicative performances in their interactions with them. These profiles will, in effect, furnish academics and administrators with a predictive facility, albeit one that has not been subject to formal processes of validation.

It seems possible, then, that without placing an undue burden and unreasonable expectations on them, the assessment literacy of university academic and administrative staff involved in decision-making involving standards and the setting of appropriate thresholds can be enhanced by:

- ensuring that they are familiar with the literature provided by testing bodies on their respective tests, including the composition of the tests and the demands they make of test-takers;
- some knowledge of the performance descriptors for the different levels of the test – although it is somewhat difficult to discern the utility of this; and
- raising awareness of what test scores mean in real performance terms by creatively highlighting the association between test scores and students' performance in staff–student interactions and thereby promoting the formation of communicative profiles that serve as intuitive reference points.

The setting of English language entry standards according to sector norms which may not be appropriate but from which few if any institutions are likely to deviate significantly, subject as they are to high-stakes business considerations, raises the very real question of what point there is in developing, via these kinds of strategies, a deeper understanding among relevant stakeholders of gatekeeping tests and the scores they generate. Perhaps one line of justification derives from the increased tendency for universities to adjust or 'calibrate' their English language requirements according to discipline areas and the extent to which these are perceived as being more or less dependent on language skills. Practices here have varied and continue to do so, with some institutions categorising degrees of language dependency or language-richness in very broad terms (e.g. social sciences, arts and humanities disciplines versus the physical and biological sciences) and others doing so in a more nuanced manner according to specific disciplines or even particular degree programmes, while also specifying component skills requirements in addition to an overall test score requirement – a practice known as 'profiling'[6] (see, for example,

---

[6] See Clapham (2001) for a good discussion of this practice.
    The specification of component scores in profiling has also been adopted by the UKVI which, as of September 2013, stipulates that in order to secure a Tier 4 necessary for study in higher education, students must have an overall CEFR proficiency of at least B2 (IELTS 5.5 or

Queen Mary, University of London, accessed online). While this has courted controversy by suggesting, for example, that language skills are less critical within pure science subjects – a view at odds with the academic literacies approach discussed in Chapter 3 – it has nevertheless arguably served to increase the utility of gatekeeping tests by sharpening what are essentially blunt instruments and helping ensure that the proficiency demands made on students at point of entry are a more accurate reflection of the demands of their future studies. Even where institutions are setting their entry levels at minimum or below-minimum proficiency levels, a more sophisticated understanding of the tests might, arguably, assist those setting entry standards to differentiate in a more principled way between the language requirements of different academic disciplines.

Another problem with pre-enrolment assessment of English language competence concerns an issue raised in Chapter 2, namely the fact that numerous different measures are accepted by universities as evidence of English language proficiency (Coley, 1999, cited 61 in Australia) and it is, for all intents and purposes, impossible to make meaningful comparisons between, for example, a grade assigned on a university English language foundation/preparatory programme (sometimes accompanied by a rubric describing what it represents in performance terms) and an IELTS grade. While, in the United Kingdom, the Home Office has tightened up regulation in order to address this problem through requiring students to provide evidence of English language proficiency via one of its specified Secure English Language Tests (SELTs) or be prepared to demonstrate that performance on any substitute measure is equivalent, in Australia the strategy has been somewhat different. There, the emphasis has been more on universities tracking the performance of students entering via different pathways and taking responsibility for closing off those pathways that produce students who consistently underperform as undergraduates. In DEEWR's 2009 *Good Practice Principles* document, Principle 4 stated that universities should 'ensure that the English language entry pathways they approve for the admission of students enable these students to participate effectively in their studies' (2009, p.3). This idea was echoed in DEEWR's 2012 *English language standards for Higher Education* document, which stated the 'expectations' that:

• The provider systematically monitors the performance of students by entry pathway or by cohort and makes appropriate changes to entry criteria to ensure that it admits only those students who are able to participate effectively on entry.
• The higher education provider gives feedback to direct entry pathway providers on the comparative academic performance of students who have

equivalent), with no less than 5.5 in any of the four component scores (reading, writing, listening and speaking) in the case of IELTS.

entered through pathway provisions and on the provider's satisfaction with the English language proficiency of entering students from the pathway provider. (2012, p. 4)

This idea of monitoring or 'tracking' student performance post-entry promises to increase senior management's and academics' understanding of how useful or otherwise different gatekeeping tests are and what test scores mean in performance terms. On this basis, it could be argued that test comparability is not critical so long as institutions are confident that a particular score on a particular test or language development programme is likely to translate into a particular kind of performance, thus enabling universities to set their thresholds accordingly. It would, however, mean that universities would need to limit the tests and pathways they recognise to those they have been able to evaluate through the monitoring of those students who have flowed from them; and, for most universities, practicalities and pragmatism will mean that these are the tests/pathways that produce the greatest number of students, are most universally recognised, and have the greatest currency.

Language residency requirements, applied by most universities to immigrant students for whom English is not a first language, can also be a weak link in the student enrolment process, particularly where these are not stipulated precisely enough or where individuals who are non-native speakers of English, but have acquired citizenship, are not required to provide evidence of language proficiency upon application to university. In such cases, language problems can surface post-entry, particularly where students have obtained citizenship only shortly before applying to university and/or for whom English is not the primary language of communication at home or of individuals' broader social interactions. This situation is highlighted by Brooks and Adams (1999), who reported that thirty per cent of Macquarie University students were local and lived in homes where languages other than English were spoken.

4.2.3   Upholding English language standards

I have discussed how universities face a considerable dilemma when they go about setting their English language entry requirements, forced as they are to achieve what they regard as an acceptable balance between upholding their ethical responsibilities to the students they admit (or indeed reject) by accepting only those they deem to have a reasonable chance of successfully completing their studies, and the need to answer to financial imperatives and achieve enrolment targets that ensure they are able not only to continue to exist but to meet their strategic goals, sustain their development needs and remain competitive. Arguably, the need to achieve such a balance is less critical for some than others, as I have suggested elsewhere:

The idea is occasionally mooted that were universities to raise the IELTS bar, 'the English problem' would be solved and PLA thus rendered unnecessary. However, this idea is regarded as highly problematic by institutions, most of which are reluctant to unilaterally increase their IELTS requirements as this would mean losing a competitive edge. Arguably, the less eminent universities stand to lose more: Whereas those that top the league tables can depend on their reputations to ensure healthy numbers of higher end applicants and thus have the luxury of being able to be more selective, others that traditionally attract students from the middle or lower end of the ability range and/or students from more diverse socioeconomic backgrounds risk having to turn away many applicants and not filling their quota of places as a result. Furthermore, the different profiles of universities and their individual schools mean that it is doubtful they would reach agreement on IELTS benchmarks anyway. (Murray, 2010a, pp. 346–7)

So-called 'redbrick' or Ivy League universities will always attract the most able students and have the luxury of experiencing high demand for their places. As such, they can afford to be highly selective and to raise their English language standards in the near knowledge that they will consistently manage to fill their places with the brightest, most gifted students, regardless. Ironically, it is these institutions that are often best placed financially to support a strong English language service, yet the least likely to require such a service, or require it to the same extent. In other words, these often wealthier institutions can legitimately offer quite small-scale English language provision and benefit from the proportionately lower costs associated with resourcing it.

The integrity of gatekeeping tests such as IELTS, TOEFL and PTE is, however, dependent not only on the way in which English language standards or thresholds are set at the institutional level, but also on the extent to which individual departments uphold those standards. This issue takes on particular poignancy in situations where departments may be experiencing dwindling numbers in an increasingly ruthless broader institutional and sector climate where margins are tighter than ever and where departments deemed to be underperforming (and, put crudely, losing money or generating little or no profit) are legitimate targets for closure. Inevitably, such departments will feel under considerable pressure to be lenient in the decisions they make concerning applicants to their programmes.

While stricter regulation appears to be continually reducing the extent to which decision-making is left in the hands of departments and individuals, considerable scope still exists for discretion to be applied, and the wisdom and even-handedness with which this happens will inevitably vary. While UKVI, for example, requires that all students intending to study in higher education meet its minimum IELTS (or equivalent) requirement, the many universities who opt to profile English language entry requirements according to discipline area are at liberty, within the constraints set by UKVI, to set English language standards as they see fit according to their perception of how relatively language rich the different discipline areas are. What is mandated is only that those standards must meet the minimum entry requirements stipulated by UKVI for the purpose of issuing the student-to-be with the so-called Tier 4 visa that is needed to study in higher education. So, even where external regulation exists, there is room for discretion and thus error, and one cannot assume either that departments set their own English language requirements appropriately according to programme demands or that, even where they are set appropriately,[7] they are universally and consistently applied.

This is not to say that there should be no room for special dispensations; indeed, UKVI allows for such eventualities, highlighting as they do the idea of 'giftedness', where universities can apply discretion in cases where a particular student shows, and can be demonstrated to show, exceptional academic/intellectual potential. However, while universities no doubt welcome the retention of a modicum of autonomy in such cases, there exists a degree of fuzziness surrounding them. For example, even where a student is regarded as gifted, presumably they still require a level of language competence that will enable them to negotiate the demands of their studies, whether as an undergraduate or a postgraduate. But what is the minimum acceptable in these cases if it is not the minimum required for all other 'regular' students applying to the same programme(s)? In other words, how much can or should universities and departments compromise on their minimum required standards in the interests of enrolling a student who, despite being linguistically weak, has the potential nonetheless to develop themselves and benefit the university and the discipline? These are difficult questions and it may well be that they simply have to be answered on a case-by-case basis. However, where a student falls below the minimum UKVI standard but is given a dispensation on the basis of giftedness, the receiving university will need to be able to demonstrate in any future audit the basis on which that dispensation was given and to justify it to the satisfaction of auditors. That will be challenging indeed unless the universities and their auditors share clear terms of reference.

4.2.4   Test security

Although test security has always been a consideration in the development of high-stakes tests such as IELTS and TOEFL, its prominence as an issue has increased in recent years largely as a consequence of two interrelated factors.

---

[7] As I have indicated, how institutions and their departments determine appropriateness is itself a complex question that requires at the very least an understanding by all stakeholders of the nature of gatekeeping tests and what their scores represent in performance terms; some meaningful measure of the 'language richness' of their programmes and the courses of which they are compromised; and a means of tracking students' performance through their university career and correlating this with their English language entry scores.

Firstly, due to the globalisation of education, the economic development of regions such as Asia and South America (exemplified in the growing fortunes of India and Brazil, respectively) and the opening up of countries such as China and Russia, the number of students wishing to study in English-medium universities has increased dramatically and the potential rewards associated with doing so are often considerable (see Chapter 1). Secondly, accompanying this increase in numbers has been an increase in the perceived need to ensure, for both academic and visa purposes, that students are entering the country of study and their target universities legitimately. Stories have been rife in the media of students – even agencies – providing false credentials and/or having friends assume their identities and sit tests on their behalf. This phenomenon is increasingly widespread in the sector, and there are few (if any) universities that will not have had some experience of it. While such cases would previously have tended only to come to light (if at all) following the observation, post-entry, of a notable discrepancy between a student's ability to cope with the language demands of their degree programme and their English language entry test score, today there is greater likelihood of their being identified pre-entry during the application process. In the United Kingdom this is certainly due, in part, to efforts by UKVI to reduce the incidence of illegal immigration by clamping down on students seeking to secure study visas under false pretences, and they have done this by placing much of the onus on receiving institutions to ensure that they put in place watertight procedures by which to establish the veracity or otherwise of applicants' English language credentials and apply those procedures fastidiously. As we have seen, failure to do so can have serious ramifications for universities' right to accept international students, with potentially huge implications for their ability to generate income.

Establishing rigorous credential verification processes, however, is a worthless activity unless gatekeeping tests are themselves secure, and there have in recent years been widely-publicised concerns expressed over the security weaknesses surrounding these tests, particularly since they have become computer-based and thus, arguably, more susceptible to abuse.[8] Such concerns are only magnified by recognition of the fact that some international students are often desperate to secure places in English-medium universities, as to do so can provide a near guarantee of excellent job prospects often in prestigious and well-paid professions in their home countries, along with other significant

---

[8] Following allegations of fraud relating to one of its suite of tests (TOEIC), the UK government only recently (March 2014) announced that it has not extended its licence agreement with the Educational Testing Service (ETS) to provide Secure English Language Testing as required in the student visa application process. As a result, at the time of writing, TOEIC and TOEFL iBT testing will no longer be offered for UK visa-granting purposes. This has had significant and unwelcome ramifications for ETS, universities and those of their applicants who submitted TOEFL test scores as evidence of English proficiency.

lifestyle benefits. For others it can be seen as a stepping-stone to a new life living and working in their future country of study and an escape for them – perhaps even their families – from their current circumstances. These motivations can be very strong indeed and, consequently, testing bodies and test users need to be confident that the tests they design and employ are as secure as they can be.

Given the commercial, proprietary nature of the standardised tests used for entry purposes, it is in the interests of their developers that they are seen to be secure, for only those that are demonstrably secure are likely to be regarded as valid and reliable indicators of applicants' legitimacy and future academic performance are likely to be deemed acceptable for visa/university entry purposes. Students will not opt to sit tests that have not been approved and thus are not recognised by immigration authorities or academic institutions, and it is therefore in the financial interests of test organisations such as IELTS, ETS, Cambridge ESOL and Pearson to ensure that their tests are secure and that they can demonstrate this to stakeholders.

The increasing importance to test users of test security, and its commercial significance for test developers, has meant that there has been a concerted effort to introduce new technology into test administration processes. This has been realised most recently and obviously in the introduction of state-of-the-art biometric security measures designed to ensure that test takers are who they say they are. It is certainly no coincidence that Pearson has been a trail-blazer here by placing considerable emphasis on this aspect in promoting its PTE (Academic): a relatively new addition to the suite of gatekeeping tests available to universities and students and, as such, one that will need to quickly build up credibility with those constituents. This has no doubt been a positive development; one that has motivated other test providers to look further at how they too can improve their test security. Test users are certainly the benefactors of such competition. However, test developers and test users will need to remain vigilant, for as with credit card fraud, efforts to apply more sophisticated technological solutions to the question of English language test security will inevitably be countered to some extent by ever-more elaborate schemes for cheating by those intent on achieving their academic and life goals by whatever means, and by those organisations looking to profit from these aspirations.

4.3   Summary

This chapter has looked at some of the key issues surrounding the assessment of English language proficiency of students looking to enter English-medium institutions of higher education. Its point of departure was that, despite having met universities' English language entry criteria as specified in terms of performance thresholds in high-currency gatekeeping tests such as IELTS and TOEFL, a significant proportion of students subsequently struggle with the language demands of their degree programmes. This suggests, prima facie, that fragilities exist in one or more of the following areas: the veracity of the tests themselves, the way in which they are understood and used by universities, the rigour with which universities uphold the English language entry standards they set, and the integrity of security surrounding the administration of the tests. Having analysed each of these factors in turn, and while acknowledging that by and large these gatekeeping tests would appear to serve their purpose reasonably well, it is not difficult to see how, together, they have the potential to undermine the principle that those students whom universities choose to accept onto their degree programmes should be able to enter confident that they have the language skills necessary to succeed in their chosen fields of study. The fact that there is ample evidence, based on pre-enrolment assessment instruments and processes and on the perceptions of many working in higher education, that this principle is to some extent being compromised should be a cause for concern.

Of the four factors identified and discussed, it is perhaps that of the essential nature of the tests themselves – and, in particular, their predictive validity – that is, perhaps, least amenable to change, not least because it would require a significant change of focus and associated investment on the part of testing organisations if, as I have argued, increased predictive validity requires account to be taken of the language of individual disciplines. Specifically, it would require a series of more nuanced tests and, as a prerequisite to this, significant attitudinal and inter-institutional consultation, collaboration and agreement on policy change. Certainly without such agreement and great single-mindedness, testing bodies such as IELTS, Cambridge ESOL, Pearson and ETS are unlikely to take the initiative, conduct the necessary research and invest in the relevant test development. Nor will individual universities act unilaterally or as part of an interested group to bring about such change in a climate where intense market competition would render such action a high-risk strategy. Instead, the initiative would need to be supported sector-wide. The critical question is at what point the extent of shortcomings with the current 'system' and the proportion of students who slip through the net and end up struggling to cope with the language demands of their studies is such that it serves to motivate a change of this magnitude; and there will likely be differing views on this.

What is not – and should not be – contentious, however, is the idea that universities have an educational and ethical responsibility to ensure that, whatever instruments they use to assess applicants' levels of English language proficiency, those instruments should be both valid, reliable and applied with as much veracity as possible. If that means moving away from a generic EAP model of testing to a more discipline-specific one, then it must surely bear serious consideration. Furthermore, it accords with the recommendation (clause 44) of the QAA that 'a review be conducted of the efficacy and appropriateness of established schemes for testing the English language skills of international students, in determining English language competence and support needs before acceptance on to higher education programmes and while studying in the UK' (2009, p. 14).

One alternative to trying to bring about the kind of more radical change associated with the development of a suite of discipline-specific tests – something that would not, anyway, be a panacea by any means – is to consider ways of refining and increasing the integrity of current pre-enrolment processes, in parallel with the institution of a post-enrolment English language assessment regimen and more robust, effective and well-funded models of in-sessional English language provision. Chapters 5 and 6 look, in turn, at post-enrolment language assessment and provision.

5   Post-enrolment language assessment: challenges and opportunities

5.1   Introduction

Whether or not the higher education sector and language testing organisations ultimately opt to go down the road of developing the kind of more nuanced, discipline-oriented English language tests discussed in Chapter 4, it seems unlikely that the problem of students successfully meeting language entry criteria, only to struggle subsequently with the language demands of their studies, will dissipate entirely. Studying to the test, issues involving test security and factors such as test reliability and performance on the day, which contribute to a margin of error, are always likely to blight pre-enrolment language assessment. Furthermore, as we saw in Chapters 3 and 4, currently the technical, financial and political factors that have the potential to impact negatively on the effectiveness of gatekeeping tests are many and complex. Consequently, there will likely always be a proportion of students who successfully enrol in degree courses but who are at risk linguistically, and this raises the question of whether and how universities can at least manage the fallout that arises from this situation. One solution that is gaining traction, particularly in Australia and New Zealand, is that of post-enrolment language assessment, commonly referred to as 'PELA'. In a study looking at the use of PELA in thirty-eight Australian universities, Dunworth (2009) reported that more than forty per cent of the surveyed universities administered some form of post-enrolment language assessment, with another twelve universities proposing their introduction. While, as we shall see, different universities have adopted different models of PELA, they share a common discourse and are underpinned by common principles. Those at the vanguard include the University of Melbourne (DELA (Diagnostic English Language Assessment)), Curtin University of Technology (UniEnglish), the University of South Australia (ELSAT) and the University of Auckland (DELNA (Diagnostic English Language Needs Assessment)). It is certainly not coincidental that a number of these boast resident expertise in testing: expertise that has been drawn on by other universities contemplating the institution of PELA.

While the notion of post-enrolment English language assessment may feel like closing the gate after the horse has bolted, it has been the subject of considerable discussion and debate both within and across institutions in Australia, as well as in government-commissioned bodies and professional organisations such as the Higher Education Research & Development Society of Australia (HERDSA) and the Association for Academic Language Learning (AALL), and their respective journals (e.g. Bonanno and Jones, 2007; Dunworth, ibid.; Dunworth, Drury, Kralik and Moore, 2013; Elder and von Randow, 2008; Murray, 2010a, 2014; Ransom, 2009; Read, 2013; Read and von Randow, 2013). An important catalyst in this dialogue was the publication of the *Good Practice Principles for English language proficiency for international students in Australian universities* (2009; see chapter 2) by a steering committee convened by the Australian Universities Quality Agency (AUQA) at the behest of the Department of Education, Employment and Workplace Relations. Principles 1 and 7 in particular relate to the issue of the language assessment of students, with Principle 7 explicitly referring to some form of post-enrolment language assessment:

[Principle] 1. Universities are responsible for ensuring that their students are sufficiently competent in the English language to participate effectively in their university studies.

  [Principle] 7. Students' English language development needs are diagnosed early in their studies and addressed, with ongoing opportunities for self-assessment. (AUQA, 2009, p. 3)

In its *English language standards for Higher Education* document, TEQSA (AUQA's successor) similarly makes reference to the idea of assessment post-entry, though with less emphasis on its happening shortly after enrolment and more on its integration within course units. Thus, under Standard 5 ('The provider ensures that students are appropriately proficient in English when they graduate'), the document's authors state:

The provider uses stated criteria to assess students' English language proficiency within assessment of course units.

Interestingly, by proposing, in its *Standards* document, the assessment of proficiency within the assessment of course units, TEQSA appears to have effectively moved away from – or at least de-emphasised – the idea of English language assessment shortly after students' enrolment – or 'early in their studies' (GPP 7).

5.2   The advantages of post-enrolment language assessment

5.2.1   Strategic/political considerations

The case for PELA would appear to be quite compelling, for it brings with it a number of advantages. From a strategic point of view, it allows the institution to demonstrate to all stakeholders, including auditing bodies, its determination to comply with officially sanctioned articulations of standards, where these exist.

This has implications for the evaluation of its performance and for the regard in which it is held by individuals and organisations external to the university. More specifically, it indicates that the university understands and is responsive to the needs of its students and takes seriously its ethical and educational responsibilities. This not only reflects well on the institution but is also reassuring to potential students, particularly those who lack confidence and feel anxious about their level of competence in English.

While one might view these considerations cynically as being informed by the well-being and, in particular, the financial security of the university, such well-being would seem legitimate if founded on principles that help ensure that the institution is, to the fullest extent possible, realising a duty of care to its students and providing them with a positive and maximally fulfilling higher education experience. This is, after all, the raison d'être of universities. Put simply, if a university is responding effectively to the educational and pastoral needs of its students and can demonstrate that it is doing so by identifying their language needs and, where necessary, responding appropriately, then it seems only right that it should be judged favourably on that basis and benefit reputationally accordingly.

5.2.2   Identifying students at risk linguistically

Most obviously, PELA provides a vehicle through which to identify those students who are at risk linguistically but who, due to one or more of the frailties discussed in Chapter 4 surrounding pre-enrolment testing regimes (test security, status as domestic students, variability in the nature and quality of tests and English language preparatory programmes, commercial or business pressures etc.), have nonetheless managed to secure places on degree programmes. Having identified the most linguistically vulnerable students, universities can and must then ensure that appropriate support programmes and accompanying human and material resources are put in place to promote their English language development.

5.2.3   Assessing students on a level playing field

Importantly, PELA enables receiving institutions to counter the problem of students having met universities' English language requirements via multiple different means, be they different tests or different foundation or other preparatory programmes. It does this by using a common instrument that allows for the assessment of students on a level playing field, and thereby goes some way to addressing the problematic issue, discussed in section 4.2.2, of equivalence between these many different gatekeeping tests and programmes recognised by universities as measures of applicants' English language competence.

5.2.4   *Providing equitable access to English language provision*

By rendering irrelevant (at point of entry, at least) the problematic issue of multiple English language pathways into universities by enabling students to be assessed on a level playing field, PELA has the potential to offer an equitable basis on which to make a determination as to who should get access to support resources that are invariably subject to budgetary and other constraints. In so doing, it can help ensure that those most in need of English language development opportunities post-entry get priority access to those resources that are available. That is, PELA can serve effectively as a screening mechanism: a filter that helps make certain that resources go to those who stand to benefit most from them, and who might otherwise struggle to cope with their course demands and thus possibly exit their studies prematurely. This relationship between PELA and provision is one that will be explored further in Chapter 6.

5.2.5   *Allowing for local, discipline-based tailoring of assessment*

In cases where a decision is taken by a given university not to adopt and employ universally, throughout the institution, a single assessment instrument (an issue we will explore later in this chapter), PELA can still be a valuable mechanism in the hands of individual faculties or departments, which can assess their own students' English language competence through methods tailored according to local circumstances. This could mean, for example, that language assessment tasks reflect the particular genres in which students will need to communicate during their studies and subsequently in their professions.[1] Similarly, it could mean that where a given department is relatively small, it may have the luxury of being able to employ a more resource-intensive method of assessment whereby students' speaking and listening abilities might be measured through face-to-face meetings or interviews, or a piece of written work might be carefully assessed in order to identify generic and individual weaknesses. Depending on the way in which provision is structured, such information could then be used to determine the focus of language development classes.

One potential difficulty with this kind of model of localised assessment is that, where PELA is used as a mechanism for determining access to centralised English language provision, it risks rendering inequitable the basis on which such determinations are made, for measures of student performance would be based on different local instruments the equivalence of which is highly unlikely to have been established.

---

[1] This would effectively be a post-enrolment version of the kind of discipline-based tests discussed in Chapter 4 (4.2.1) in relation to pre-enrolment. In the case of PELA, however, discipline-based assessment would be used more for diagnostic purposes and as such would be less subject to the kind of criticisms that might be levelled against pre-enrolment discipline-based assessment.

5.3   The risks of post-enrolment language assessment

5.3.1   *PELA as a marketing liability*

Unsurprisingly, perhaps, university senior management tend to approach the idea of any form of PELA with great caution, particularly where it is the subject of institutional policy and mandated for certain student cohorts – a situation to which I shall return shortly. First and foremost, they regard it as a marketing liability for two main reasons. Firstly, it puts at risk the institution's brand or image and positions it in the market in a particular and, for many, undesirable way. In essence, the concern is that PELA sends out a message that the university takes students who are linguistically weak, and this calls into question the institution's standards both in terms of the quality of their entrants and, by extension, their graduates. In a higher education sector that has become increasingly global and marketised, and thus more competitive and cut-throat than ever, brand has become everything – for it is the university's name and what it represents that ultimately attracts students, staff, research funding, inter-institutional collaborations, links with industry, and the benefits that flow from these things. Today, universities that are unproductive in just one of these areas are vulnerable.

PELA is also seen by senior management as risk-laden in that it is likely to be off-putting to potential applicants, who may (a) view it as an additional and undesirable hurdle to be jumped despite having successfully entered university, and (b) feel threatened, particularly if they are worried that their language skills may prove to be less than adequate according to any such assessment. These students may consequently decide to apply to alternative institutions that present an easier and thus, for many, more attractive option by offering a less onerous route into higher education. PELA is consequently seen as a possible threat to market share and, therefore, to income.

As Brigulio (2005) has noted, PELA also raises a face-validity issue by sending out what might be seen as conflicting messages. I have articulated this elsewhere (Murray, 2010a) as follows:

Perhaps most important, it [post-enrolment language assessment] raises face validity issues around students being required to undergo a post-enrolment English language assessment procedure who have already succeeded in meeting universities' IELTS entry requirements (Briguglio, 2005). This sends out a confusing and contradictory message: 'You have met the English proficiency level we deem necessary for you to enter our institution and cope with the rigours of academic study at this level, but we wish to check that you are not at risk due to weak English'. (p. 348)

Universities, of course, do not wish to be seen as inconsistent and therefore need to reconcile the notions of pre- and post-enrolment assessment of English in a way that is meaningful to potential students in particular.

While PELA should be justified first and foremost on educational grounds, if it is to meet with the approval of senior management then any proposal needs to allay these very legitimate concerns, for the risks underlying them are certainly very real. Pragmatism would suggest that the most effective way of doing so is by characterising PELA as a marketing tool that can be strategically presented to stakeholders internal and external to the university as evidence of a caring and responsible university, cognisant of its students' needs, in tune with the times, and which recognises the increasingly international flavour of higher education today and the need to produce well-rounded graduates with good communication skills; a university which is prepared and able to respond smartly and appropriately to the changing context in which it operates. In essence, PELA needs to be presented in a way that conveys the image of a university as a trail-blazer, responsive to a changing higher education landscape and workplace expectations, and with a management that is ready to adapt institutional practices accordingly in the interests of a richer educational experience for its students and, consequently, improved career prospects. Specifically in relation to the kind of confusing message PELA risks sending to potential applicants to university, it is important that institutions that adopt PELA are transparent in their presentation of it and openly acknowledge that – despite measures taken by testing bodies and the universities themselves to ensure, as far as is practically possible, that only those students with suitable levels of language competency secure places on their degree programmes – the reality is that, for a variety of reasons, some students will nevertheless struggle. As such, the university employs PELA in order to ensure that those students who need help to cope with the language demands of their higher education study are given the relevant support.

The marketing risks associated with PELA can also be reduced if the process is not formalised through a policy-driven post-enrolment regime that entails mandatory assessment that is administered universally and centrally at a specified time. In other words, if PELA is organised and administered locally by individual faculties or departments, its profile is reduced. This, of course, also means that its advantages cannot be heralded for the benefit of the university. Essentially, the university needs to decide which strategy to adopt and where the greatest advantage lies: should it increase the visibility of PELA in the hope that it can present the university in a positive way and attract students by reassuring them that the university is aware of potential language issues and prepared to address them; or should it avoid the possible disadvantages of increased visibility while still deriving the benefits that PELA offers?

5.3.2   Resource and cost implications

There are also cost implications associated with PELA. Depending on the nature of the assessment these will vary. If, for example, a test is required, it is likely that it will need to be developed and piloted; and, if it is to be done properly, this work will in all probability need to be outsourced to those with recognised expertise in language testing and assessment. Where a test is developed by a third party, there may well be costs incurred not only as a result of the development process itself but also in the form of ongoing licensing fees that give the test user the right to employ the test. Furthermore, multiple versions of the same test will need to be written and, therefore, for the institution commissioning this work there will be ongoing costs associated with this developmental work.

There will also be costs associated with administering the test. Potentially, these could emanate from a number of sources, as follows:

- If the assessment is to be conducted electronically, there may need to be investment in additional computer suites or workstations, particularly if large numbers of students are to be assessed simultaneously and test security is an issue.
- Although it may be included in the costs associated with development of the assessment instrument, where assessment is computer-based and lends itself to electronic marking – thereby reducing the load on human resources – there will be costs associated with developing the technical means to do this.
- Where marking is done manually, this will involve cost in terms of the draw on human resources and the investment of time required, not just for the marking itself but also for the conducting of standardisation sessions that will help to ensure that all markers are working to same norms, and for any moderation that needs to take place subsequently.

5.3.3 Dealing with failure in assessment

Consideration also needs to be given to the implications for the institution should large numbers of assessed students be identified as 'at risk' due to weak English language skills. What if large numbers of students fall below the established threshold? This has possible implications for the reputation of the university (see section 5.3.1) as well as financial implications that arise from the need for resource provision (see section 5.3.2); after all, there is no point in assessing students if those identified as being at risk are not then given access to suitable language development opportunities. Indeed, to deprive these students of such opportunities would undermine the credibility of the institution and its English language initiative, and call into question its clarity of thinking and the commitment it has to those students and to the English agenda more generally. Furthermore, it would seriously undermine any justification for PELA on the ethical and educational grounds that might be used to underlie the presentation of the exercise to would-be students in the way I have suggested above (5.3.1).

Whatever form of assessment universities decide to adopt, they need to set their thresholds appropriately; that is, in a way that ensures that those who meet or exceed those thresholds will be able to cope with the demands of their studies, while those who fail to reach them and are appropriately identified as being at risk will have access to suitable language development opportunities. This can prove challenging, particularly given that different disciplines tend to place different linguistic demands on students, as we have seen. What is important is that institutions do not see their thresholds as being subject to manipulation and a way of failing only as many students as their English language resources will support. In essence, if a university is to adopt PELA, it needs to be fully cognisant of the financial implications and prepared to fund, to a meaningful degree, suitable English language provision for those identified as being in need of it.

5.4   Key decisions concerning post-enrolment language assessment

If and when an in-principle decision has been taken to adopt PELA, there will be a range of questions that universities will then need to consider.

5.4.1   Who should PELA target?

While the answer to this question may seem obvious, in light of the increasingly diverse nature of the student body in higher education it is an increasingly important and relevant question. Today's emphasis on improving access for those from non-traditional and disadvantaged backgrounds means that a growing number of students enter university lacking the kind of cultural capital (see section 3.2.3) that helps ensure they have a relatively trouble-free experience. Klinger and Murray argue that:

> Whereas commencing students from higher socio-economic status backgrounds tend to have a repertoire of cultural and social resources that can help them to feel at home at university (Margolis, Soldatenko, Acker and Gair, 2001), first-year students from low socio-economic backgrounds tend to be less equipped to accommodate to the cultural capital of the institution and are more likely to admit difficulty in comprehending content and adapting to teaching styles at university (James, Krause and Jenkins, 2010). Hence they cannot reasonably anticipate and meet their lecturers' expectations and thus have their chances of academic success dramatically reduced. (Klinger and Murray 2012, pp. 31–2)

Aschaffenburg and Mass (1997) define cultural capital as 'proficiency in and familiarity with dominant cultural codes and practices' (p. 573), while Collier and Morgan (2008) allude to it in their drawing of a distinction between students understanding their role as students and mastering that role, and the impact of students' background and cultural capital on their ability to appreciate the 'tacit understandings' and 'implicit expectations' (p. 426) that are integral to the culture of the academy and its community of practice.

In similar vein, and drawing on the work of Bourdieu (1977, 1984), Thomas refers to the 'institutional habitus' and speaks of educational institutions favouring knowledge and experiences of dominant social groups to the detriment of other groups. She argues that these institutions:

determine what values, language and knowledge are regarded as legitimate, and therefore ascribe success and award qualifications on this basis. Consequently, pedagogy is not an instrument of teaching, so much as of socialization and reinforcing status. This process ensures that the values of the dominant class are perpetuated and individuals who are inculcated in the dominant culture are the most likely to succeed, while other students are penalized. (Thomas, 2002, p. 431)

Thomas goes on to say that students may be more inclined to withdraw early if the institutional habitus leads to feelings that their own 'social and cultural practices are inappropriate' and their 'tacit knowledge is undervalued'.

Part of the cultural capital students require if they are to succeed in higher education comprises the language skills to produce written work that meets the expectations of the academy. While that will include the academic literacies pertinent to their disciplines (something which, I have argued in Chapter 3, we cannot reasonably expect the majority of students to have at point of entry and which therefore need to be embedded in the curriculum), it also includes the ability to meet the conventions of formal writing with which some non-traditional students may be unfamiliar. This once again raises the question of what we mean by the term 'proficiency'. These native English speakers are, for sure, fully proficient speakers of the language and would rightly take exception to being told otherwise; however, their language may exhibit dialectal features not in keeping with the expectations of the academy, and the fact that they can lack an understanding of the cultural capital needed to survive at university means they are less well placed than traditional students to recognise what is and is not acceptable language (Murray, 2013). There is an increasing call, evident in the literature (e.g. Johnson, 2008; Larcombe and Malkin, 2008; Preece and Godfrey, 2004; Read and von Randow, 2013; Wingate, Andon and Cogo, 2011), for the need to respond to the language needs of native-speaker students and not to assume that any issues with English language are simply confined to students for whom English is not a first language. In this regard, Sheridan notes that:

Academic literacy is an issue, however, that spreads beyond a designated group of 'international' students (Green 2007; Johnson 2008) and Larcombe and Malkin (2008) caution against considering that only international students would have academic writing needs and that institutions 'adopt measures that assess the communicative skills of all commencing students' (p. 320). (Sheridan, 2011, p. 132)

This is a view echoed by Read and von Randow:

> there is growing recognition that the need for an enhanced level of academic language proficiency is not confined to international students but applies to many domestic students in the countries concerned as well. The successful completion of secondary school qualifications may not provide sufficient evidence that matriculating students have the necessary level of language proficiency or academic literacy to ensure adequate achievement in their university studies. (2013, p. 90)

If it often said that access is meaningless without success[2] (Hughes, Karp, Fermin and Bailey, 2005; Engle and Tinto, 2008; Gidley, Hampson, Wheeler and Bereded-Samuel, 2010); as such it is incumbent on universities to provide language development to non-traditional students where this is necessary to ensure their success. And this moral imperative is based not merely on the duty or responsibility that institutions have to maximise the potential of the students they choose to accept onto their programmes, but also upon notions of equitability: if those students for whom English is not a first language should have the right to access opportunities to develop the language skills that will help ensure their success, then it is only right that other students who are also potentially at risk as a result of language-related issues should also benefit from similar opportunities. PELA should be for everyone, and the question of how to involve native speakers of English without stigmatising them is one that needs to be addressed with sensitivity. PELA for universal application also raises the question of whether both cohorts – native- and non-native speakers – can and should be tested on the same basis and whether each has particular needs that effectively differentiate them for the purposes of both post-enrolment assessment and, by extension, provision. These are questions I shall return to in Chapter 8, where I present a case study describing a model of post-enrolment testing and provision implemented in Australia.

5.4.2   Should PELA be mandated?

Having established that PELA has potential relevance to all student cohorts, another critical decision is whether or not it should be mandated. Mandating PELA for all students has a number of advantages:

- It ensures that nobody slips through the net; for example, domestic students who may be quite recent immigrants and/or students who lack the kind of cultural capital discussed above.
- It circumvents the problem of assumed equivalence between the various different gate-keeping tests employed by universities as evidence of proficiency.

---

[2] Tinto (2008) similarly argues that 'access without support is not opportunity'.

- It protects universities which might be subject to accusations of discrimination were they to restrict PELA to particular cohorts. Universities would be ill-advised, for example, to identify linguistically vulnerable students by 'foreign-sounding' names or postal codes of socio-economically deprived areas.
- It is less likely to stigmatise cohorts who would otherwise be singled out for PELA; this means not only those non-English-speaking students who would normally be the default targets of such English language initiatives, but also non-traditional students who are the focus of the widening participation agenda and who may already feel stigmatised and lack self-confidence (Christie, Tett, Cree, Hounsell and McCune, 2008; Maes, Sztalberg and Sylin, 2011).
- It provides a basis for determining which students should attend credit-bearing or non-credit-bearing English language development programmes, where these are stipulated as a requirement for those who perform below a predetermined threshold.

Mandating PELA, however, also brings with it the following significant challenges:
- The shaping by any given university of a strategy designed to present it in a positive light notwithstanding, PELA has the potential to act as a disincentive for students considering applying to that university. Students, many of whom will already have invested significant time and money in improving their language skills to a level that meets institutional entry requirements, are likely to see mandatory PELA as a further hoop through which they are required to jump. For those who are already highly proficient in English, it will be seen as irrelevant, possibly demeaning, and an unwelcome and unnecessary distraction from the primary business of getting on with their degree studies. In her analysis of data collected on universities' attitudes to PELA, Dunworth comments:

Those who were concerned about the negative impact on students also expressed the belief that students may perceive that they were being seen as 'deficient' in some way when they had already met the university's English language entry requirements; or that they were being presented with 'yet another hurdle to get through'. As a consequence, students might … become discouraged from attending university. (Dunworth, 2009, p. A-8)

- Whether mandatory or not, evidence suggests (e.g. Dunworth, ibid.; Ransom, 2009) that, regardless of universities' reassurance to the contrary, students worry that if they perform poorly on the assessment it will appear on their academic record and thus have the potential to compromise their transcript and even their degree grade.
- Given the potential numbers involved, mandatory PELA presents significant logistical issues concerning administration and security – issues discussed in more detail below.

- It is unclear how and on what basis one would secure compliance (see, for example, Bright and von Randow, 2004) and what, if any, punitive measures can or should be taken against those students who opt out of the exercise. Ransom (ibid.) articulates the problem in terms of the following questions:

To what degree should faculties [or the university at large] let students reap the benefits or consequences of their decisions? How often should faculties communicate with students before it becomes a case of harassment? Should there be a university-wide response to non-compliance? (2009, p. 22)

- As we have seen, one way of at least *encouraging*, if not securing, compliance is by presenting PELA as offering added value and being in students' interests and reflective of the university's desire to help them realise their full potential. In addition, however, students will need reassurance that poor performance in the assessment will not jeopardise their grades or result in expulsion from their degree programmes but rather provide a route to free language support and greater likelihood of success in their degree studies and beyond. In an increasingly litigious era where students are paying high fees and are effectively viewed – and see themselves – as clients expecting a quality service and a virtual guarantee of successful graduation (see section 2.4.1), some institutions are now requiring students to sign an affidavit to the effect that responsibility to improve their English language skills resides as much with themselves as with the university. The intention is that this should not only protect the university from accusations of poor practice regarding entry processes and the provision of appropriate support but also motivate the students to be autonomous agents and take responsibility for their learning/academic development.
- Finally, there is, as I have indicated above, the question of how universities deal with large numbers of students who fail PELA, without artificially lowering the threshold and thereby effectively making a mockery of the whole exercise.

5.4.3   *Which skills should PELA assess?*

Any decision concerning the skills focus of PELA has to be driven by what can realistically be made available in terms of subsequent provision; there is, after all, little point in diagnosing students' weaknesses in particular skill areas if there is no means available by which to address those weaknesses. Essentially, this highlights something of a chicken-and-egg problem: on the one hand, there is an argument for saying that the focus of PELA should be determined according to the availability of resources, focusing only on the skill(s) that are most critical to students' academic success. These are almost always regarded as writing and reading – and in particular writing, due to the fact that most assessed coursework is written, although other modes of assessment have certainly become more prominent in recent years, in part as the result of efforts to emphasise not merely students' content knowledge but the kinds of transferable skills they are likely to need as graduates. The growing importance of presentation skills, for example, has meant that presentations are growing in popularity as an assessment method, as Freeman and Lewis (1998) observe:

Presentations have become a popular method of assessing. In part, this reflects the importance of presentation skills in the workplace today. Almost anyone in a skilled job will find themselves presenting material, if only to close colleagues. (pp. 90–1)

On the other hand, there is an argument for saying that PELA should drive provision; that is, PELA should assess all four skill areas (writing, reading, listening and speaking) and wherever there are significant and widespread weaknesses, provision should be designed and resourced to address them. While this would appear to be the most responsible, pedagogically sensible option, the reality is that universities will essentially be forced to take a pragmatic stance due to limited resources as a result of funding limitations. They will, therefore, not entirely unreasonably, tend to give precedence to the skill of writing. It is interesting to note, in fact, that while it may not necessarily be a factor in universities' thinking on this issue, a strong focus on writing can to an extent be justified not on the basis of management pragmatism but on the basis of student pragmatism as well; that is, while management may prioritise writing because the fact of limited resources requires them to invest in tuition that will deliver the best overall academic returns (an essentially utilitarian perspective), students also welcome an emphasis on writing because their main goal is to perform well on assessed coursework which is, for many of them, primarily written. Indeed, students who have limited time to attend in-sessional English classes due to their mainstream degree course commitments often express a preference for writing instruction or vote with their feet when deciding how to invest their time most productively in the in-sessional English language tuition opportunities on offer. To some extent, the same is true of reading, for in order to produce good, well-reasoned and well-evidenced written work, especially under time constraints/exam conditions, or to write critiques of articles, for example, students will need to develop effective read-ing skills. The fact that effective reading skills are a prerequisite to successful writing is one reason why the two skills are frequently taught in tandem, in the same way that speaking and listening tend to be.

Another argument that might be mustered in support of a PELA focus on reading and writing is the relative ease with which tasks focussing on these skill areas can be administered and marked; they lend themselves, for example, to electronic delivery and even to some degree of electronic marking, as we will see in the model described in Chapter 8. The skills of listening and speaking are, in contrast, more problematic, for not only does their assessment involve determining thresholds and investing time in standardisation procedures designed to help ensure grading is even across assessors, but it can also be highly labour-intensive if conducted face-to-face with students, even where those students are assessed in pairs or groups (see, for example, Ducasse, 2010; Ducasse and Brown, 2009; Foot 1999; Saville and Hargreaves, 1999; Wallis, 1995).[3] Furthermore, although the electronic assessment of listening and speaking skills is certainly possible, and has been the approach adopted by Pearson in the Pearson Test of English (PTE), the cost of buying in third-party technology, software and the expertise needed to utilise it is almost certain to be prohibitive for the vast majority of universities, particularly given the unfavourable economies of scale that prevail at this quite early stage in the life of that technology, when its use is still very limited. Even in cases where employing local institutional language assessment expertise may be a possibility, the cost of developing a suitably well-conceived and well-constructed speaking/listening assessment exercise designed for electronic delivery is a complex and time-consuming activity that also requires considerable technical knowledge.

One alternative is to monitor students' listening and speaking skills 'informally' early on in their programmes of study, via group work activities (discussions, debates, analytical and critical thinking tasks, etc.) to which all students are expected – perhaps even required – to contribute, and/or presentations. This would however be subject to the same challenges as formally assessing students in pairs or groups[3] and would thus be of questionable validity as a vehicle through which to determine who should get access to language development opportunities. Furthermore, it would mean a delay in getting any such assistance to those ultimately deemed to be in need of it.

It is, of course, possible to employ practice IELTS or TOEFL tests to assess students' listening skills post-enrolment – tests that are routinely delivered and marked electronically. However, such tests preclude the assessment of listening, as it occurs in authentic interactional contexts, and instead present it as 'static' rather than dynamic and reactive, simply requiring the test-taker to respond appropriately to a given stimulus. They do not require them to adapt their understanding, make pragmatic inferences etc., according to the changing nature of the ongoing discourse, and this shortcoming needs to be factored into any decision-making concerning the focus of PELA and the relative value of focusing on the different skills areas.

---

[3] Assessing students in pairs (or groups) is not without its well-documented challenges, not least of which is the difficulty of matching students of similar proficiency levels in order not to unduly disadvantage – or indeed advantage – one or other of the pair or indeed both students. The weaker student, for example, may feel overwhelmed by the stronger and reluctant to engage, and thus be unable to perform to his/her true level of competence, while the stronger may also feel frustrated at not being able to demonstrate their listening and/or speaking skills if their partner is unable to respond effectively and 'keep up' with them.

The balance of argument would certainly seem to be in favour of PELA that focuses either on reading and writing skills or writing skills only, and as such the remainder of this chapter takes as its point of departure the assumption that, for those universities who choose to implement some form of PELA, one or other of these options is most likely to be adopted.

5.4.4   What form should PELA take?

(a) *The test option*   Having determined that writing, or reading and writing, is likely to constitute the focus of PELA, the question arises as to what form PELA should take. In Australia, following publication of the *Good Practice Principles* in 2009, and in particular its reference to the 'diagnosis' of students' English early in their studies (see above), there was considerable activity across the higher education sector relating to the idea of a post-enrolment proficiency *test* of some kind. This arose, in part, from a legitimate concern that the 'Principles' would become 'standards' and universities would therefore be expected to demonstrate to auditors that they had in place a systematic process of post-enrolment English language assessment. Actions triggered by the Good Practice Principles, and indeed some of the dialogue within the sector that preceded the document's publication, included:

- The setting up of working groups with a remit to produce a strategy that promised to respond to the English language issue and, as part of that, to conduct feasibility studies concerning the institution of a post-enrolment language test (see Dunworth, 2009).
- Attempts to identify existing tests that might usefully serve the purposes of PELA.
- Efforts to locate individuals and organisations with the necessary expertise in language testing and test development, who would be able and willing to develop a suitable test that was both valid and reliable. In a number of institutions, there was a desire for a test that could potentially serve the purposes of PELA across the entire student population and which, therefore, needed to be able to discriminate not only between the proficiency levels of non-native speakers but also between native and non-native speakers. Where language testing experts were willing to engage in this work, agreements were subject to negotiations, in particular with regard to the licensing out of the test and the development of multiple versions (see 5.3.2).
- The piloting and trialling of different tests to ascertain whether they were fit for purpose and to identify some of the logistical problems relating to implementation and the pros and cons of different modes of delivery (discussed below).
- The sharing of experience via professional organisations and fora in an effort to overcome challenges and establish testing regimes that were both workable and cost-effective (Dunworth, ibid.).

Some of the more specific questions that arose during the course of these activities and with which almost all universities have found themselves grappling serve as useful reference points for institutions considering instituting a post-enrolment English language testing regime, and there is developing a useful and growing literature in this area (Barrett-Lennard, Dunworth and Harris, 2011; Dunworth, 2009; Murray, 2010a, 2012; Ransom, 2009; Read, 2013, 2015).

How should the test be administered and marked?   Essentially, a post-enrolment English language test can be administered and marked either face-to-face/manually or electronically. As I have indicated, delivery of the test electronically presents quite considerable technical challenges, a number of which are articulated in Murray (2014) and in the case study described in Chapter 8 of this volume. While these challenges can sometimes be solved locally by university technicians, in the majority of cases they will likely require universities to outsource this work and to incur significant costs as a result, if they are to acquire a test that is elegantly designed in terms of actual delivery and which operates consistently and without glitches. This third party option was elected by the University of Auckland, where reports suggest that PELA, in the form of the DELNA, has since been running successfully since its inception in the 1990s and following a series of subsequent adaptations (see Elder and Erlam, 2001; Elder and von Randow, 2002; Elder, 2003; Elder, Bright and Bennett, 2007; Read, 2008; Elder and von Randow, 2008; Read and von Randow, 2013).

If the test can successfully be designed for electronic delivery via a suitable platform, there is certainly the potential for efficiencies to be gained as the draw on human resources is likely to be less than with face-to-face delivery. However, if significant numbers of students sit the test (whether mandated or not), this can present considerable difficulties in terms of the provision of sufficient workstations and, if security is deemed to be an issue (see below), sufficient staff to invigilate. Furthermore, a large number of test-takers is likely to mean that there would need to be multiple testing sessions, which in turn would necessitate the availability of multiple versions of the same test in order to maintain security. The development of these parallel versions would incur additional costs. It is worth emphasising here a point to which I shall return later: namely, that if post-enrolment testing is to be linked to provision by serving as a determinant of access to certain forms of provision, such as face-to-face, this is actually likely to render irrelevant the problem of security, for unless the attendance of English language development classes is obligatory for those who fail the test, and assuming that some students may not wish to devote time to such obligatory classes regardless of their language needs, it is arguably in students' interests to perform poorly on PELA if, by doing so, they gain access to provision that might otherwise be denied them. Simply put, why worry about security when it would not be in most students' interests to cheat anyway?

The greatest efficiency gains are perhaps more likely to be achieved through the electronic marking of the tests than through their delivery. While, for the reasons outlined above, the automatic marking of writing scripts is unlikely to be adopted by most universities due to inherent complexities and the cost of software[4] that is still arguably still at a trialling stage and unproven, reading skills, in contrast, are more amenable to automatic marking, particularly if tested via multiple choice and cloze exercises.

Should the test be administered at a set time/set times?   The question of when a post-enrolment test should be administered is intimately linked to that of whether or not PELA should be mandated. If it is not mandated on the grounds that students should take responsibility for their own learning, then issues of security become less relevant – perhaps even irrelevant. Students would take the test as and when they chose, and would only elect to do so if they themselves felt their language may be in need of improvement. One advantage of this approach is that, prior to sitting the test, a good proportion of these students will likely have acquired their own sense of whether they are coping linguistically with their programmes of study, and for those who are concerned that they are not (as opposed to those looking more for reassurance or affirmation), they will feel a greater sense of commitment to an assessment process into which they have opted of their own volition.

One implication of an 'as-and-when', individualistic approach to post-enrolment testing is that it lends itself more to an electronic mode of delivery where students can log in to the relevant test site from any workstation, whether in the university, at home or elsewhere, using their student enrolment numbers, and complete the test at their convenience. This is likely to encourage students with weaker language skills to opt in, for in addition to being less threatening, the fact that it is online has the potential to allay concerns that poor performance will appear on their academic records. Furthermore, although there will be peak periods when larger numbers of students opt to take the test, an as-and-when rolling approach has the added benefit of the marking load associated with the exercise being more spread out and less intensive that would otherwise be the case.

Another implication of the as-and-when approach is that an administrative process would need to be established for dealing with completed tests and for ensuring that those identified as being at risk are fed through to the relevant language development schemes available to them. Where electronic marking is

---

[4] For example, Pearson Education's WriteToLearn technology.

not available, academic staff responsible for marking the tests require a system that alerts them when a student has taken the test and which, ideally, does so automatically via email or via a repository where records are automatically maintained and updated and which is checked on a regular basis. Once the test is marked, students need to be informed of their result and, where relevant, advised on the nature of any language classes available to them and how to access those classes. Equally, provision needs to be organised on the understanding that new students will continually be coming through the system and that those responsible for processing them and allocating places should be able to do so systematically and equitably.

If an institution decides to make the test mandatory, whether for all students or for particular cohorts,[5] then it will need to decide when to schedule testing sessions. There are arguments for testing shortly after students have enrolled, although after initial orientation when students tend to have fewer distractions. Such early testing helps ensure, so far as is possible given the developmental nature of language, that students get the help they need in a timely manner and, in particular, in advance of their first pieces of assessed coursework. In this regard, AUQA's (2009) Good Practice Principles state:

irrespective of universities' English language entry requirements, students now enter university with quite widely varying degrees of English language proficiency. Early assessment of students' English language development needs means that students and staff identify these needs at a time when they can start to be addressed, rather than at a point when the stakes are much higher. At least 18 Australian universities are now adopting or examining tools for early diagnosis of students' English language development needs. (p. 9)

There is also an argument, however, for delaying mandatory testing until students themselves have a sense of the adequacy or otherwise of their language skills, perhaps following feedback on assignments, on discovering an inability to engage effectively with course readings, or after poor learning experiences in lectures or seminars as a result of under-developed speaking and listening skills. As I have already indicated, students who recognise that they are struggling because of weak English are more likely to endorse the idea of assessment and, perhaps more importantly, more likely to take up the provision that is on offer subsequently where that provision is not required but merely recommended for those who perform poorly on the test. Students recognition of their own language frailties can be a powerful motivator, and one that is especially important for those who feel unjustifiably confident in their language skills, whether by virtue

---

[5] The Universities of Auckland and Melbourne, for example, require all students who enter with an IELTS score of less than 7.0 or equivalent to take their post-enrolment English language tests. This, of course, again raises questions of the equivalence of the often numerous kinds of measures accepted as evidence of English language proficiency.

of the fact of their having met institutional English language entry requirements – requirements which, as we have seen, are often questionable and subject to various pressures and institutional/departmental interests – or for other reasons.

How often should students be allowed to sit the test? Given that most mandatory testing is likely to take place only once, at the beginning of the academic year, not least because of resource and cost implications, the question of how often students should be allowed to sit a post-enrolment test is of greatest relevance in cases where assessment is not mandated but optional. Furthermore, as we have seen, optional testing is likely to be electronic in nature so as to make it maximally accessible and thus more appealing to students.

The frequency of testing is important, particularly if those who perform poorly on the test are required to attend (possibly credit-bearing) English language support programmes on which they may have to perform satisfactorily in order to progress in their degree programmes, for once again there are resourcing and cost implications. If a student sits the test once and performs poorly, they can simply retake it as soon as they choose and this can put an unreasonable burden on those marking the test, where this is not done electronically. Limiting the frequency and times when students can take the test also helps ensure that they engage seriously with the test.

A final point in favour of post-enrolment assessment via an English language test concerns its potential to serve as a mechanism through which students can self-assess as they move through their academic careers. As we have seen, one of the costs incurred by utilising a test for post-enrolment assessment is that of the development of multiple versions of the same test. One result of this is that, over time and in addition to their institutional use as instruments through which to identify at-risk students and thus determine the scale of provision required, a bank of tests will accumulate, which can also be used by students for self-assessment purposes.

Should the test be a screening or a diagnostic test? Different individuals and institutions are likely to have different views on whether to opt for a screening or a diagnostic test. A valid, reliable and easily administered screening test is probably the more cost-effective option given that the development of a valid and reliable diagnostic test, capable of providing genuinely useful insights into test-takers' language that can inform pedagogical decisions, will be more expensive to develop. The decision, however, of which option to go for will perhaps be most influenced by whether or not students who are identified as being at risk are expected to attend formal English language development classes post-assessment. Where there is greater emphasis placed on learner autonomy and students taking a greater measure of responsibility for their own learning, institutions may be more inclined to favour a diagnostic test, such as the MASUS[6] (Measuring the Academic Skills of University of Students; Bonanno and Jones, 2007), that informs the test-taker (ideally electronically) of their particular strengths and weaknesses and which is supported by comprehensive online and other support materials that empower them and give them the means to address those weaknesses identified. Bonanno and Jones see such a diagnostic test as providing the test-taker with a 'literacy profile' and being:

particularly useful with first year students who bring with them differing experiences and standards of literacy, and in many cases are slow to recognise the expectations of tertiary institutions. Early explicit feedback provided in the context of this diagnostic procedure can result in rapid identification for the student of the strengths and weaknesses of their written communication from a tertiary, discipline-based perspective. (2007, p. 1)

Significantly, as the above extract suggests, Bonanno and Jones see the MASUS as providing diagnostic information on literacy and generic skills, and this fact means that it lends itself to the kind of localised testing discussed earlier in section 5.2.5 and which can reflect the particularities of language that characterise different disciplines. This notion of identifying strengths and weaknesses in writing in relation not only to the expectations of tertiary education in general but to those of individual disciplines exemplifies the intersection of general proficiency and academic literacy and their interactivity as discussed in Chapter 3.

Should thresholds be variable?   There may be an argument for setting test cut-scores differently according to perceptions of how language-rich or language-critical particular programmes and related future professions are deemed to be and thus how linguistically demanding they are. In cases where they are regarded as more language-rich or language-critical – for example, degree programmes/professions such as Law, Philosophy, Medicine and Pharmacy – the thresholds could be set higher.

What would appear to be less amenable to variation are the tests themselves, for, as we have seen, if it is the intention that different tests should be employed by different faculties or departments as filtering mechanisms through which to determine access to English language development opportunities that are *delivered centrally*, the very fact of test variation would mean that such access could not be determined on an equitable basis. However, where language provision is *also* decentralised, this issue would not arise: within a particular locale, students would be assessed using a similar instrument and only those students within that locale and who the test indicates are at risk would have access to provision that is shaped and delivered locally.

---

[6] See MASUS Project Reports, 1993–1995; Webb and Bonanno, 1994, 1995; Webb, English and Bonanno, 1995.

What if students deliberately fail the test?   We saw earlier, in the context of test administration and security, that where performance on a post-enrolment language test is linked to students' entitlement to access limited provision it is not in their interests to cheat, unless, despite inadequate levels of proficiency, they would prefer to risk devoting all their time and energy to their 'regular' degree coursework in the hope that their language weaknesses will not significantly compromise their overall performance in their studies. On the contrary, there is perhaps a greater likelihood that students will deliberately underperform on any post-enrolment test in the hope that this will guarantee them access to such provision. Indeed, this was a concern in my own university in Australia where a post-enrolment regime was established as part of a broader institutional model of English language assessment and provision, described in Chapter 8. In a recent article, I commented on this issue of deliberately underperforming in a post-enrolment assessment exercise in the following terms:

This access or 'filtering' function meant that there was little motivation for students to cheat on what was, anyway, an optional test; indeed, there was more concern expressed by some of the English language team – and other university stakeholders who were consulted – that students might be inclined to fail deliberately in order to secure such access. On reflection, however, it was considered unlikely that such an eventuality would materialise on the grounds that students confident in their language ability would tend to be more interested in successfully engaging with their coursework than in receiving language support services from which, on balance, they would be likely to derive less benefit. This perception was reinforced somewhat in that where students did attend 1:1 consultations post-test, they seemed genuinely to be at the weaker end of the spectrum and to be in need of assistance with their language. (Murray, 2014, p. 330)

The fact is that, whether or not institutions make the sitting of a post-enrolment test compulsory, it is almost impossible to legislate for students deliberately underperforming in cases where performance on the test is the basis on which access to provision – or certain more resource-intensive forms of provision – is granted. The Australian initiative to which I refer above, suggests that this is not an issue of any great magnitude; yet, even if it were, there are no simple solutions. For example, the idea of *requiring* those who do not meet the threshold to attend in-sessional English language development classes in which 'adequate' performance, however defined, is a prerequisite of their academic progression through their degree programme, brings with it considerable difficulties. While it would certainly encourage the vast majority of students to perform to their true competence as far as possible, it would only work if the test were mandated. If it were not mandated but optional it would simply serve as a disincentive for any students who might otherwise have considered sitting the test. Simply put, if students risk being penalised as a result of performing poorly on an optional test, they simply will not sit the test; and that would prevent those in genuine need from benefitting from any language development opportunities on offer.

5.4.5.   What form should PELA take?

(b) The coursework option   While a post-enrolment English language test brings with it a number of benefits, it is certainly challenging and can be expensive, and this will no doubt persuade many who recognise a need for PELA to look elsewhere in their search for a suitable mechanism by which to assess students' English language competence.

Two alternatives, each of which has been adopted by universities, involve using a piece of written work produced as part of students' 'regular' programme of study and not as an English language assessment exercise per se. Once again, the emphasis is on writing or reading *and* writing, where readings are used as source material for a subsequent written task. The first approach involves students simply producing a short written text solely for the purpose of assessing their language, which is holistically marked according to agreed criteria specified as descriptors associated with particular competency bands. Here, there would be a pre-agreed threshold above which a student would need to perform in order to be deemed sufficiently proficient. The second approach is to have students produce an early piece of assessed coursework and use that as the basis for judgements as to the adequacy or otherwise of their English language proficiency (Harris, 2009; Murray, 2010a). One advantage with both of these approaches is that they can target *all* students – native and non-native speakers – and thereby both avoid accusations of discrimination and stigmatisation, while also capturing all those potentially as risk and liable to benefit from language development opportunities. Furthermore, by assessing students as a normal part of their course, this diminishes the possible adverse marketing and reputational effects of large-scale institutional testing (see section 5.3.1) by 'camouflaging' the process. This can help allay senior management concerns to a degree.

A particular advantage of option two over option one is that, because it is assessed and will count towards their grade, the written work students produce is likely to be a more accurate reflection of their competence, for rather than deliberately failing in order to gain automatic access to English language provision, they will be aiming to produce work of the highest quality of which they are capable in order to secure as high a grade as possible and maintain a strong academic transcript. However, the fact that it is assessed coursework means that it will need to be marked by both content lecturers and English language support staff and, where PELA is implemented on an institution-wide basis, this amounts to a heavy workload that English language units will need to manage; one that will materialise over a fairly short period of time. One way of avoiding these workload and thus resourcing issues is to have content lecturers rather than English language tutors make judgements on students' English language proficiency. This strategy, however, brings with it other difficulties:

Firstly, the basis on which academic staff will make judgements on students' language proficiency is still likely to be subject to variability between individuals according to a number of factors. These may include the academic's own first language background, level of proficiency and expectations, how important they deem proficiency to be within the context of their discipline, and whether they believe that formal correctness should be subordinate to functionalism and comprehensibility. Secondly, academic staff might see it as being in their own interests, as well as those of their students, to place the proficiency bar fairly high in order to ensure both that they themselves are not burdened with the problem of students with weak English, and that those students who they believe may benefit from English language provision, but who in point of fact are not at risk (or, at least, not priority cases), get access to language development opportunities. In other words, it is too easy for academic staff making judgements about the adequacy of their students' English to use the assessment exercise to direct students to language services units and in so doing to divest themselves of responsibility. The fact that a number of universities, such as the University of Technology Sydney, have adopted the first approach of a short written task marked holistically suggests that it does not present an unmanageable marking load.

There would, however, appear to be at least two challenges arising from the idea of using a piece of written coursework to assess students' proficiency post-enrolment. The first concerns timing: an issue with which almost all university English language units grapple as a consequence of having insufficient resources to deliver, in a timely fashion, language development to all those students who need it. Although there is an argument for teaching particular disciplinary literacies as and when they naturally arise in the curriculum, in relation to general proficiency, 'in a timely fashion' means as early as possible in students' academic careers. If a piece of assessed coursework it to be used, it needs to be completed early on and, if it is to count towards the student's grade, ideally be based on input of some kind – whether oral or written – that is generated from the curriculum. The student will need a reasonable amount of time in which to produce the assignment, which then needs to be assessed and feedback provided. By the time those students identified as being at risk actually receive any language learning provision beyond self-access resources, it is likely to be well into the academic term or semester. Although language development cannot be expected to happen overnight, this delay can nonetheless be problematic, particularly as by the time students receive feedback they may already be facing considerable language-related challenges, along with the prospect of having to submit further assignments imminently. As we have seen, this means that those in need of assistance find themselves struggling to keep their heads above water and, ironically, despite being the most vulnerable, they are the least likely to feel able to take up any non-mandated language development opportunities the university has to offer, for to do so would risk coming up short in other aspects of their studies that they naturally perceive as more urgent and the main reason for their being at university in the first place.

The second possible challenge associated with the idea of using a piece of written coursework to assess students' proficiency post-enrolment arises from the fact that students will be set different writing tasks depending on the department with which they are enrolled and the course they are taking in which the task is located. As with localised testing, this similarly has the potential to be problematic in cases where access to resources is limited and students' performance on the writing task used as a filtering mechanism for determining who should have priority access; that is, it becomes difficult, if not impossible, to validly compare student performance on two different writing tasks and thus make decisions, on an equitable basis, that have implications for students' access to English language support.

5.4.6   Can we do without PELA?

Another way of phrasing this question is 'Can we maintain the status quo?', for in the case of many institutions there is no formal and systematic process in place for assessing students' English language proficiency post-enrolment. Despite the quite compelling advantages of PELA, maintaining the status quo remains an option, if perhaps a risk-laden one given the trend towards increased regulation of standards of English language in higher education and the high stakes in terms of institutional reputation, graduate employment and workplace expectations. If a university chooses to take this option, however, but wishes to ensure nonetheless that students are given English language development opportunities, they may simply elect to require all students who have met minimum language entry requirements but fall below a predetermined threshold to take a proficiency course or series of courses – credit-bearing or otherwise – and make their academic progression dependent upon their performing successfully (however defined) on those courses (see, for example, Brady, 2013; Lobo and Gurney, 2014). This approach has been adopted by a very small minority of universities[7] but brings challenges of its own.

Firstly, as we have seen, students are often accepted into universities on the basis of a range of different measures of proficiency, the equivalence of which is often questionable. This means that it is perfectly possible for two students, who may have significantly different levels of proficiency, both being required to attend an English language development course, despite one of them not requiring it. As a result, not only will classes sometimes comprise students of

---

[7] Lobo and Gurney (2014) discuss such a programme at Griffith University.

language abilities that are so diverse as to create a pedagogically challenging environment, but also resources will not necessarily be going to those in greatest need of them.

Secondly, it is not difficult to envisage a situation where the number of students who fail to perform to an adequate standard on the mandatory English language course(s) and are unable to progress through their degree programme is such that it creates a backlog.[8] Clearly, this has the potential to create considerable logistical, financial and political fallout: logistical in that there would be an ever-increasing demand for English language resources required to support these students and a proportionate growth in the population of students within the year of the degree programme in which students are failing their English language courses, and which could force departments to turn away new students; financial in that there would inevitably be increased costs associated with the need for greater demand for English language resources; and political because departments experiencing the backlog, as well as university senior management, would rightly be concerned not only about the risk to the academic reputation of the department and the institution more generally of students failing to progress, but also the fact that the prospect of being unable to progress would discourage would-be students from applying to the university and raise significant visa problems as a result of extended periods of study. This latter problem thus also brings with it financial and administrative implications.

Thirdly, requiring only those students who have failed to demonstrate a specified level of English language proficiency to undertake English language development classes would mean that a proportion of students who are potentially at risk may slip through the net. This is particularly true, for example, of (a) students of non-English-speaking backgrounds who have been resident locally for a period of time and who are therefore registered as domestic students, despite the fact that their English may still be weak; and (b) non-traditional domestic students who have entered university and who may not have the cultural capital needed to fully realise their potential (see section 5.4.1), and in particular an awareness of the language expectations of the academy and the means to meet those expectations. The only way to ensure that all potentially at-risk students are captured is either by requiring all students to attend a credit-bearing English language proficiency course embedded in the curriculum – an extravagant, inefficient solution given that many students would not need such development opportunities and would resent the fact of its diverting them from their main course of study – or by simply maintaining the kind of student referral system currently adopted by many universities. The trouble with this latter option is that it alleviates academic staff of all responsibility by giving

---

[8] See *What if students fail the test?*, in this chapter.

them the option of simply offloading 'problem' students to English language units. Furthermore, it is inherently inequitable, for it in no way ensures that those students most at risk, and therefore in greatest need of language development opportunities, get access to them. That is, the basis on which one tutor might refer a student may be entirely different from that on which another does so. As we have seen, PELA, in contrast, offers at the very least the possibility of a level playing field.

The difficulties generated by a system that requires students in need of language development to take a proficiency course (or courses) in parallel with their degree studies can be circumnavigated by requiring students to take the course but without making progress through their degree programmes dependent on performing to a certain standard by the time of its conclusion. An obvious shortcoming with this approach is that there is no sanction for students who choose not to push themselves and who are, consequently, unlikely to derive the necessary benefit from the course.

5.5   Summary

In this chapter I have tried to articulate some of the key issues and considerations surrounding post-enrolment language assessment. Specifically, I have presented its advantages and disadvantages, both from the perspective of senior management and those at the coalface tasked with delivering English language services in universities. In the second part of the chapter I have sought to identify and unpack some of the critical questions that universities considering PELA will, in all likelihood, need to address.

What is amply clear is that this is challenging, contentious and complex territory, and it is unsurprising, therefore, that where it has been the subject of discussion and debate in the sector, it has caused much reflection, uncertainty and unease. This fact has driven professional debate within and between institutions and in the relevant professional literature, and one senses that universities in countries such as Australia, where it has been raging for nearly ten years, are reluctant to jump too soon and ambivalent about being at the vanguard where not only the rewards but also the risks of misjudgement and failure are potentially greatest. Universities are thus both consulting and also keeping a very watchful eye on each other's activities in this space, looking to take their cue as and when they deem it appropriate and wise to do so.

What post-enrolment language assessment serves to highlight very tangibly is the tension that can and usually does exist between the principles and practical realities guiding the policies and expectations of policymakers and those responsible for delivering English language services on the one hand, and the forces that drive and simultaneously constrain decisions at the higher levels of university management on the other. That tension inevitably extends beyond the issues of pre- and post-enrolment assessment to the nature and extent of English language provision once students have undergone one or both of these processes. Chapter 7 looks in detail at some of the considerations that affect one such model of provision that takes into account the conceptualisation of English language proficiency articulated in Chapter 3.

6 From assessment to provision

6.1 Introduction

Taking as my point of departure the tripartite conceptualisation of English language proficiency articulated in Chapter 3 and comprising general proficiency, academic literacy and professional communication skills, in this chapter I seek to present some of the considerations, constraints and opportunities likely to arise in the process of implementing, within the higher education context, a model of English language provision that draws on that framework. While I would not presume to offer an 'ideal' model of language provision, I hope that, even where readers may be unsympathetic to my conceptualisation, they nonetheless derive some benefit from the analysis offered of factors impacting on the implementation of this particular model and some of the general principles and considerations that emerge and which promise to inform other such initiatives involving curriculum innovation (see also Chapter 7) in respect of English language.

Over the next few pages, I will look specifically at the notion of embedding academic literacies and of providing academic literacy support through extra-curricular means; different permutations for delivering general proficiency tuition; and the question of how to structure such provision, both administratively and managerially, in an effort to ensure that it is maximally effective in achieving its purpose. I shall begin by looking at the last of these issues, as this inevitably impacts on discussion of the other two.

6.2 Structuring English language provision in universities

Generally speaking, within the university context, English language provision tends to be centralised and delivered via an English language unit of some kind. This might be a dedicated centre – usually categorised as and frequently operating along the lines of a service department rather than a traditional academic department. Alternatively, it might be part of a larger department where it is located alongside award-bearing programmes in cognate disciplines such as TESOL, Applied Linguistics or Education, and which offers degree programmes and/or professional certificate or diploma programmes such Cambridge Assessment's CELTA (Certificate in English Language Teaching to Adults) or the DELTA (Diploma in English Language Teaching to Adults). This latter arrangement is frequently seen as beneficial to all interests: the English language courses managed within such departments are seen as providing convenient and valuable opportunities for staff and students on degree programmes to conduct classroom-based, teacher-focused or ELT management-centred research, as well as allowing a practicum component to be included in taught programmes with a teacher-training focus. Similarly, the award-bearing programmes and research activities of the department are seen as providing data, insight and expertise that can be used to both enhance the quality of the English language teaching activities of the department and to support the professional development of the teachers involved in those activities.

Despite these kinds of synergies, there are, it seems to me, good reasons to move from this kind of centralised model of English language provision to a decentralised one, particularly given the model of English language proficiency I have proposed. One way of structuring such decentralised provision is to retain central management of the institution's English language operation but delegate a degree of management responsibility to local representatives who would oversee provision within their locale. 'Locale' can usefully be thought of in terms of faculties; that is, each university faculty would have a manager aligned with it, along with a team of English language tutors. The manager would oversee all aspects of provision and thus be responsible for negotiating the form and focus of provision within their particular faculty, engaging as the first point of contact in political and strategic discussions within the faculty, and reporting to their line manager, the Director of English language services (or equivalent), who would be centrally based. The team of local managers would meet regularly with the Director to share experiences, discuss policy and issues arising, and ensure that, despite being decentralised, there is an evenness of provision and decisions are being implemented consistently within and between faculties. Broader strategic decisions would be taken by the Director in consultation with university senior management, and there would thus be a two-way flow of information from the faculty level to senior management and vice versa, with the Director effectively acting in part as a conduit of information.

This arrangement brings with it a number of distinct advantages. First, by aligning teams with particular faculties, English language tutors and their managers are well placed to develop productive working relationships with academic and professional staff in their respective divisions and to develop their discipline knowledge and keep abreast of the literacy requirements of those disciplines of which their faculties are comprised. As a result, they are better able to provide more tailored and thus relevant forms of support, both face-to-face and electronic. This in turn means that English support resources can be used more efficiently as it is likely that, particularly where attendance is not compulsory, levels of attendance will be buoyant and attrition rates lower than those typically experienced within generic in-sessional English language classes (Lobo and Gurney, 2014).

A second advantage is that English language tutors would feel more integrated if they were a permanent feature of the faculty's architecture and as such would be more likely to be looked upon as 'part of the team' and thus find themselves privy to, and better able to influence and respond to, local issues and attitudes. Through personal connections and a presence on relevant committees, such as faculty Teaching and Learning Committees, they would be keyed into debates and developments within the faculty and its respective schools, and therefore better able to make informed contributions, pedagogical and otherwise, according to the local context. This, in turn, would increase the profile of the university's English language activities by improving academics' understanding of those activities and their value, and increasing their respect for the expertise of those delivering them – something many professional English language teachers feel is often in short supply in the higher education context, due in no small part to the fact that few have academic contracts and that the majority are, therefore, neither required nor permitted to engage in teaching on degree programmes, supervision or research activity. As such, many English language tutors feel undervalued and believe that their status within their institutions does not reflect their professional expertise and the importance of what they do. This was an issue that emerged strongly in Cownie and Addison's 1996 study, in which one respondent – an English language tutor – described English as 'the Cinderella of all the disciplines'. They continued:

There is a feeling that you can pick anyone from the pavement to teach English because they speak English don't they? And when you get someone who's really good with a strong methodology and leadership, it's difficult for that person to get recognition in that field. (1996, p.229)

This status problem tends to be reflected in the preponderance of part-time and hourly-paid contracts among English language teaching staff.

Localising provision also serves to help emphasise the fundamental relationship between academic literacies and disciplines, while de-emphasising the misleading construction of academic literacy in terms of a set of 'bolt-on' general skills that equip students to cope with the academic demands of their studies regardless of the specific literacy requirements of their area of academic and professional focus (Wingate, 2006). Neumann (2001) recognises this when she states that:

On the whole, institutional support for student learning skills and staff development in Australia, and until recently in the US and UK, are also provided centrally. Within such centralised provision generic courses predominate. However, the research discussed would suggest that student study skills may be better delivered within broad disciplinary contexts. (p. 143)

Greater integration within the faculty in terms of professional and personal relationships, acknowledgement by their peers of their contribution, and their awareness of local issues and knowledge of the disciplines, also means that faculty-based English language teams would stand to have greater influence, which it turn promises to make it easier for them to help drive and steer the embedding of academic literacies in their respective faculties. As will become evident in the remainder of this book, this is challenging work indeed and the extent of English language tutors' integration into the faculty can be an important if not critical determinant of its success or failure.

As suggested above, the localising of provision would not preclude coopera-tion between faculty-aligned English language tutors across the university in the form of consultation, the sharing of ideas, experiences and strategies, and collaboration in professional development activities. Equally, while a stable 'core' of English language provision across faculties might be decided upon centrally through such consultation (see section 6.4), the model would also allow for a degree of local decision-making, and thus flexibility, in respect of other optional (i.e. non-core) forms of English language support. For example, credit-bearing proficiency courses, which require space in curricula and asso-ciated funding, may not be an option for some schools/faculties, while for others it may be regarded as desirable or even essential.

6.3   Embedding academic literacies in the curriculum

I have argued, as have others, that universities cannot and should not assume that newly-enrolled students, whatever their provenance, come to their degree studies conversant in the academic literacies of their disciplines; that is to say, in the particular sets of literacy practices that help define those disciplines and enable students to negotiate their academic and professional demands and expectations and, in doing so, become bona fide members of their respective communities of practice. I have also argued, by extension, that if such an assumption cannot be made, then it is incumbent on universities to ensure that all students have the opportunity to develop those literacies and that this can most effectively happen through their being embedded in the curriculum. Furthermore, the fact of being embedded renders pointless their inclusion in any post-enrolment English language assessment exercise, for there is little value in identifying those at risk in this area of proficiency if (a) there is no expectation of students having those literacies at the outset of their higher education careers, and (b) all students will, anyway, benefit from academic literacy tuition provided as an integral part of the curriculum.

6.3.1   Innovation

Any innovation that involves significant change to the curriculum is a major undertaking and, as such, one that universities do not take lightly. If it is to happen at all, a number of conditions need to be met. Most critically, in the sense of being a prerequisite to any subsequent steps towards change, the culture of the institution needs to be one that is open to change where it is deemed desirable and to the benefit of the institution and its students. The culture of the institution is essentially shaped by its senior management, who then seek to proliferate that culture throughout the institution. The university's leadership needs to be dynamic, forward-thinking and willing to take calculated risks. At a time where universities are under enormous financial pressure and operate in an increasingly competitive marketplace, the reality is that what is 'deemed desirable and to the benefit of the institution and its students' must ultimately be made to square with what will give the institution a competitive edge. This means that any curriculum change must be seen to deliver – or, at the point of conception, have the potential to deliver – a better student experience and potentially better employability outcomes. If it proves to do so, then the university's reputation stands to benefit and it will have been justified. Plainly, any risk associated with innovation is reduced, however, where it is mandated as a result of regulatory changes that apply to the sector as a whole. While universities may collectively oppose such changes, the fact that universal compliance is compulsory reduces the risk to any individual institution.

Regardless of regulatory change, innovation is frequently cited as an indicator of good leadership (Stoller, 2009; Harris, 2009) on the grounds that good leaders recognise the need for healthy and successful organisations to be appropriately responsive to changes to the context within which they operate. Consequently, they are dynamic, enterprising and creative, and desire to be at the vanguard of change. Conversely, poor leadership is associated with mediocrity, satisfaction with the status quo, listlessness and a more laissez-faire approach to the organisation, which results in minimal change to its structures and practices and failure to change with the times. The danger here is that the organisation will be seen as stagnant and uncompetitive and get left behind by its competitors. In other words, while there may be risk associated with innovation, the risk associated with *failure* to innovate may ultimately prove more detrimental to the organisation's well-being.

Institutional leadership that embraces change for the betterment of the institution is a necessary but certainly not a sufficient condition for effective innovation. Of equal if not greater importance is the need for those at the coalface who are responsible for implementing the innovation to have bought into it, and in particular the rationale underpinning it. Chapter 7 will consider in detail how such buy-in can be achieved and some of the critical factors involved, with particular reference to the implementation of the kind of English language initiatives that constitute the focus of this book. For now, though, it is enough to say that without the support and commitment of those tasked with implementing the innovation, it is doomed to failure, particularly in a large institution such as a university where micro-management of such projects is more difficult and recourse to punitive measures likely to be counter-productive by provoking a reaction and sacrificing the kind of goodwill and commitment needed to ensure the change envisaged comes about. Effective institutional change needs to be mandated top-down but with a rationale that is comprehensible and relates to the experience of those implementing that change on the ground. Importantly, it needs to offer the promise of improving their experience as educators and/or the student experience; only then does it have the potential at least to create the commitment, enthusiasm and thus traction necessary for successful implementation.

The embedding of academic literacies in the curriculum certainly comes with the challenges typical of any curricular innovation. Despite being motivated by the need to address a language issue with which academic staff are increasingly faced and as a result of which many experience considerable frustration, nevertheless the prospect of embedding academic literacies in the curriculum such that they are taught by their normal content lecturers as opposed to English language specialist staff, is for many a daunting one and one that provokes pushback on a number of counts.

Firstly, any curricular change tends to be treated with a mixture of caution and scepticism for various reasons. Most obviously, any kind of curriculum change is a considerable undertaking that inevitably has implications for departments and the practices of academic staff. Often this will amount to (sometimes considerable) changes to syllabi and even adjustments to pedagogical practices. Any such change to the status quo is rarely welcomed, regardless of the underlying motives and the potential to bring about positive transformation, and it always comes with an increase in workload associated with effecting the change. This additional workload is particularly unappetising to those who have experienced curriculum change on numerous previous occasions, especially where results have been mixed or poor as a result of poor steering, conceptualisation and/or implementation. Frequent curriculum change leaves academic staff feeling as though they are unable to gain any kind of continuity in their course design and delivery, and a reluctance to embark on further change is understandable, particularly in cases where it is the result of an apparent government or institutional U-turn that leaves those tasked with implementing it feeling like victims of fickle and inconsistent policymaking. In these circumstances, any kind of curriculum innovation, no matter how praiseworthy and well-informed it may be, has to overcome the obstacle of a sceptical audience who will frequently view such change as further evidence of a mercurial sector that feels obliged to respond to whatever political and/or educational agenda is fashionable at the time and being promoted as good practice, whether by government, the higher education sector, employment and industry, or the senior management of the institution itself.

As I have indicated, scepticism can also be a product not simply of a curriculum that seems to be in a constant state of flux due to policy shifts and bandwagons, but of the frequent failure of previous innovations to come to fruition despite the favour – and indeed resources – heaped upon them initially. Such failure can be the result of pre-existing cynicism and lack of buy-in, insufficient time for change to bed in, the arrival of a new policy that contradicts or supersedes it, or its champions leaving the institution or taking on new roles that preclude their continued involvement in the initiative.

Scepticism can also arise from a perceived disconnect between what senior management may consider a sound idea in principle, on the one hand, and what is practicable given constraints and complexities that are often best understood by those on the ground, who may be far more in tune with the challenges and consequences of implementation. That is, there can be a sense among those tasked with implementing innovation that senior management sit in an ivory tower and determine policy without having an adequate sense of the realities on the ground. And, as I have indicated, the more often innovation is attempted and fails, the more sceptical those expected to implement it become and thus the less likely it is to succeed.

For many, then, this will be the situation faced by those wishing to embed academic literacies in the curriculum. What it means for innovation strategy at an institutional level is the subject of Chapter 7; the focus here is on practicalities – the considerations and processes – relating to embedding academic literacies in particular and ensuring that all students have the tools they need both to meet the specific needs of their degree programmes and thereby achieve their academic potential to the fullest extent possible, and to prepare them for the professional world of work.

6.3.2   *Embedding academic literacies as a collaborative enterprise*

A prerequisite to embedding academic literacies is an understanding of the rationale for the innovation. Without a rationale, uptake and commitment are difficult to achieve, as Wingate (2006) indicates in her explanation of the persistence of a study skills approach to English language development in higher education:

There seem to be four main reasons why the predominant approach to developing learning at universities is the bolt-on model of developing study skills. The first two are interrelated and concern the difficulties involved in implementing the embedded approach: the organizational and managerial challenges in coordinating progressive skills development throughout degree courses (Drummond et al., 1999), and the reluctance of many academic staff to concern themselves with student learning (Biggs, 1996) or with developing work-related skills (Drew, 1998; Bennett et al., 2000). Embedding skills, as described by Drummond et al. (ibid.), relies on the commitment of all academics teaching in degree courses, and therefore requires staff consultation and development measures. (p. 459)

In order for those tasked with implementing the embedding of academic literacies to buy into its underlying rationale, they need a clear understanding of what academic literacy means. Personal experience acquired at the University of South Australia (described in the case study presented in Chapter 8, but see also Murray and Hicks, 2014) and through discussions with colleagues in higher education and at conferences and other fora, suggests that explaining academic literacy contrastively in relation to general proficiency, as articulated in Chapter 3, is extremely helpful in clarifying the notion to academic staff and senior management. A clearer understanding of what academic literacy refers to and its importance for students' development and academic success, on the one hand, is reinforced by the desire and commitment to improve students' language skills and address the increasing sense of frustration and concern that many academics feel in relation to what I have termed the English language question. That is, there is both an educational dimension to the desire to improve the English language situation and maintain academic standards by giving the students the tools they need to get the job done without compromising the curriculum and its delivery, as well as a personal and ethical dimension motivated by a combination of self-interest and the wish to ease a problem many see as burdensome and untenable.

Having, hopefully, created a receptive audience committed to, or at least prepared to engage constructively with the process of embedding, the next phase involves identifying the particular academic literacy sets pertinent to the various discipline areas and a determination of the principles via which they are to be embedded in curricula. This is an area that has been the focus of recent work by Gardner and Nesi (2013) and Nesi and Gardner (2012) with respect to students' writing tasks and which draws on the seminal work of Swales and Hyland on genre theory (see, for example, Hyland, 2000, 2006, 2007, 2008; Swales, 1990). Importantly, the identification of these literacy sets needs to be a *collaborative* enterprise to which academic staff and English language tutors each bring and recognise in their counterparts the particular expertise they possess, and in which 'English language tutors work with academic staff to (a) identify those academic literacies in which staff would likely be highly

conversant but not necessarily able to articulate; (b) map the literacies identified onto the curriculum and assessment practices ... and (c), provide metho-
dological training, where required, along with resources to support
development' (Murray and Hicks, 2014, p.6).

Clearly, while English language tutors may have acquired specialist knowledge of the language of particular disciplines through ESP teaching, in general
they will not, nor can they be expected to, have the kind of in-depth disciplinary
knowledge assumed of academic staff responsible for the delivery of their
degree programme content. Equally, academic staff cannot be expected to have
an understanding of language, language use, and indeed pedagogy,[1] to the
extent expected and required of English language staff, particularly in relation
to academic literacies and the process of their embedding. What bears remem-
bering in this collaboration is the fact that although academic staff may have
'procedural knowledge' (Anderson, 1983, 1985) of the academic literacies of
their disciplines, they may not necessarily have 'declarative knowledge'. It is
therefore, in part, the role of the English language tutors to help make explicit
implicit knowledge that is manifested procedurally day in and day out in the
course of academics' professional lives but which they may be unable to
articulate. Percy and Skillen (2000) have referred to this inability to articulate
in the following terms:

In the CAUT commissioned report *First Year on Campus*, McInnis, James and
McNaught (1995) discuss students' first year transition, as 'characterised by ... a series
of gaps and gulfs, especially between school and university, and between students and
academics'. These 'gaps and gulfs', in part, represent two sources of confusion: the
students' lack of familiarity with the academic learning context (generic skills) and the
conventions and discourse of their discipline (discipline-specific skills); and discipline
staff's inability to clearly articulate their tacit knowledge of the discourse and conventions of their discipline and to provide students with developmental and timely feedback. (p. 244)

I have suggested elsewhere (Murray, 2012; Murray and Hicks, 2014) that this
phenomenon of academic staff being unable to articulate 'their tacit knowledge
of the discourse and conventions of their discipline' is somewhat analogous to
that of a first language speaker who, despite using their language on a daily
basis, being wholly fluent in and able to conduct their affairs effectively and

---

[1] It is noteworthy that there is growing recognition – even concern, in an era where the quality of
the student experience is paramount – of the fact that academic staff frequently have no formal
teaching qualifications, despite often being highly qualified, experienced, published and with
excellent research records in their respected fields. This anomaly is increasingly being addressed
by universities through the requirement of all newly appointed staff who lack an appropriate
teaching qualification having to undertake a course on teaching in higher education, and typically
certified internally. In many cases, completion of such courses is a condition of having successfully completed their probationary period. Occasionally successful completion of the course is
also retrospective and thus a requirement of all staff appointed after a specified date.

efficiently through it, is likely, nevertheless, to be unable to articulate the rules of use that underlie their competence, unless they are a linguist or have a particular interest in language.

Having identified the set of literacies relevant to the discipline, the next task is to adopt and implement an approach to embedding those literacies in the curriculum (Bohemia, Farrell, Power and Salter, 2007; Curnow and Liddicoat, 2008; Percy and Skillen, 2000; Wingate, Andon and Cogo, 2011). The approach I outline here is based on that reported by Curnow and Liddicoat (ibid.) in which they begin by considering assessment and then work backwards. As they observe, while academic literacy has a 'core role' in the construction of knowledge in university settings, it tends to get ignored in teaching and assessment approaches, in favour of a narrower focus on content (Hirst, Henderson, Allan, Bode and Kocatepe, 2004; Newman, Trenchs-Parera and Pujol, 2003; Lea 1999; Rex and McEachan, 1999). While Curnow and Liddicoat's focus was on an undergraduate programme in Applied Linguistics, its underlying principles are generalisable and applicable to all other disciplines.

The first stage of embedding involves determining, for each degree programme, the academic literacy practices students would be expected to have developed upon completion of that programme and distributing these practices between the different assessment items across those core courses in which they arise most naturally in terms of being a prerequisite to engaging with their content. While these literacy practices may also emerge and be called upon in other optional or elective courses, assessment of them needs to occur in *at least* the core courses so as to ensure that *all* students both receive tuition in them and have their conversancy in them assessed. This in turn provides clarity and assurance regarding the disciplinary skills set with which the programme's graduates exit their studies. Citing Moore and Hough (2007) and Entwistle and Tait (1995), Curnow and Liddicoat (2008) are at pains to point out that there is a need to recognise the essentially symbiotic relationship between academic literacy and discipline content in course delivery and assessment:

The assessment [of the Applied Linguistics major] requires students to engage strongly with academic research articles (the majority of course readings, as textbooks are not used); they are expected not only to read and understand the content, but also to focus on such things as how the content is conveyed and the way in which the argumentation was structured. In coming to understand applied linguistics, students need to have not only 'content' knowledge, but to know discipline-specific ways of creating, transforming and reporting discipline knowledge, which cannot be taught, except together with the 'content' itself. (Ibid., p. 2)

As Curnow and Liddicoat go on to emphasise, assessment involves more than the development of tasks designed to elicit knowledge or performance, important though this is; it also involves a number of other, interrelated activities

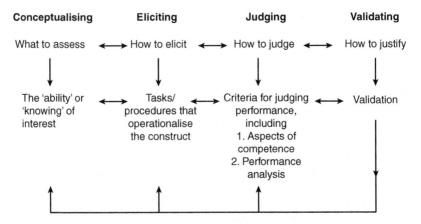

Figure 6.1 The assessment process as characterised by Liddicoat and Scarino (2010)

frequently underplayed in assessment codes of practice and including the conceptualisation of the construct to be assessed, the judging of students' work and the validation of those judgements (see Figure 6.1). It is the process of conceptualisation that is arguably most critical and which should therefore lead assessment design, for any lack of clarity here will undermine all other assessment processes. Liddicoat and Scarino (2010, p. 53) represent these processes in the following terms:

In redesigning assessment to reflect the integration of academic literacies that are to be embedded in the curriculum, the processes of conceptualising and eliciting are key and content tutors need to come together as a team, together with English language tutors well versed in academic literacy and, ideally, with relevant ESP experience, to:

- specify the learning outcomes they expect students to achieve across all the core courses of their degree programme;[2]
- understand those learning outcomes in terms of the particular literacy practices they entail – as we have seen, these may be discipline-specific or cross-disciplinary;
- ascertain how those literacy practices will be used post-graduation, whether in academic or employment contexts; and
- consider how the relevant literacies identified interrelate.

---

[2] This will often happen to some degree due to the requirement by most institutions to specify learning outcomes when articulating module proposals, including such things as communication skills, subject-specific/professional skills and cognitive skills, and associated teaching and learning methods and modes of assessment.

The last point is important, for not only will all of the pertinent literacies not be able to be covered in a single course, they will also not necessarily naturally emerge as required knowledge in any given course; and if the literacies are to be most effectively acquired then they need to have the kind of relevance and meaning that comes from arising authentically as and when needed. Equally, some literacies will occur in more than one course, and even across two or more years – a situation which may result in recycling. Such recycling, however, is to be welcomed as it will help reinforce students' understanding of those literacies and emphasise their relevance to different contexts within the same discipline. Without an understanding of how the different literacies interrelate it becomes impossible to organise them within the curriculum and across different courses in a logically sequenced manner.

By way of an example, in their Applied Linguistics major, Curnow and Liddicoat identified the following key academic literacies which, together, support a view of academic literacy within that discipline (as realised in their particular programme) as 'the capacity of students to be consumers and producers of language-focused research' (ibid., p. 3):

> Critical reading of research
> Analysis of research writing
> Synthesis of research from multiple sources
> Constructing an argument using the research of others
> Analysing language data
> Constructing an argument from language examples
> Understanding the process of research development
> Designing and implementing research projects
> Communicating research findings

The idea is that other disciplines would need to replicate this process and create a similar inventory according to their own understanding of academic literacy and the consequent learner goals that will be the subject of assessment.

If assessment is to be meaningful and effective, the tasks employed need to have a clearly defined purpose, for without such a purpose the development of sensible assessment criteria is impossible. Presentations that only provide a vehicle for the rehearsal of information are unhelpful, as is the requirement for students to answer reading comprehension questions merely as a way of ensuring that they read articles set. The purposes of such individual tasks need to be clearly articulated and key into a larger picture of academic literacies as integrated across the curriculum in a logical, coherent and cumulative fashion – what Drummond et al. refer to as 'a coordinated and structured provision running through the different levels of any programme of study' (1999, p. 14). They each need to be seen by academic staff and students as following a clear trajectory towards clearly articulated goals the value of which is amply evident. Moreover, each task needs to be preceded by tutorials that model the particular literacies they are designed to assess. Curnow and Liddicoat describe in some detail how this worked in the Language and Culture course that formed part of the Applied Linguistics programme on which they report. For illustrative purposes, I quote them extensively here:

the specific academic literacy focus in Language and Culture is on critical reading, analysing research writing, synthesising research from different sources and constructing an argument using the research of others. Each of these literacies is the focus of a separate assessment task, with the tasks combining the academic literacy focus and a content focus. While the separate tasks have a focus on separate academic literacies, each one develops students' learning in a cumulative fashion. The various literacies are modelled in tutorials in the lead-up to the particular task.
    The first task is a guided reading task based on a single research article, whose topic is naturally relevant to the course content. The emphasis is on identifying and analysing the arguments and evidence used in the article and abstracting information from across different components of the article. The second task is a focused essay-like response, based once again on a single research article. However in this task, students must use the research article to address a question which is not the focus of the article itself, with the essay topic being related to the reading, but not about the reading. Thus, students must locate and use information from the article for new purposes – knowledge transformation. This task requires the critical reading from the previous task as its starting point and develops it further. While each of the first two tasks relies on a single research article, the third task has an emphasis on synthesising arguments and evidence from multiple sources. It is a development from the previous task, as students once again must use research articles to address a question which is not the focus of any of the articles, but here they must synthesis the arguments and evidence from three different sources to produce a short essay-like response. Finally, students undertake a conventional essay, which requires them to locate sources of their own. The development of the essay requires the students to read their sources critically (Task 1) transform the knowledge from those sources for their own specific purposes (Task 2) and integrate the different sources together in a coherent way to advance their argument (Task 3). (Curnow and Liddicoat, 2008, p. 4)

As I suggested earlier, part of what makes the embedding of academic literacies within curricula a collaborative enterprise is the likely need for academic staff responsible for teaching course content to undergo at least some professional development such that they are able to model academic literacies to students during tutorials or via other teaching modes. The idea of teaching something which many will regard as outside of their remit and area of expertise will almost inevitably encounter considerable resistance. There are, however, two things that need bearing in mind here. Firstly, although traditionally such teaching has not been the responsibility of academic staff but has instead been diverted to English language units that are generally seen as having the requisite expertise, it is not unreasonable to expect academic staff to teach academic literacies, seeing as (a) they are fundamental to navigating and engaging with the discipline; (b) academic staff have the necessary knowledge of those literacies – be it often procedural rather than declarative – and are 'bona fide' members of its community of practice; and (c) while not necessarily desirable (or sustainable within the model I am proposing), English language tutors will nonetheless often only have a generic knowledge of academic literacy but lack knowledge of the specific literacies pertaining to particular disciplines. It is also worthy of note that with academic staff assuming responsibility for teaching academic literacies, the need may appear to be obviated somewhat for the kind of so-called 'tailored' in-sessional English classes sometimes provided to individual departments and which strive to provide language development classes that respond to the needs of those particular students. In practice, however, such classes will often comprise either a combination of academic literacy *and* general proficiency tuition, or merely general proficiency but for a dedicated group; as such they can serve an important function and complement the academic literacy work of academic staff.

Secondly, with astute management of this change to practices, provided that academic staff are persuaded by the rationale behind their expanded role and responsibilities, many will recognise the need and welcome the opportunity for professional development that provides them with the means to carry out that role effectively. Once English language tutors have clarified to academic staff the broad notion of academic literacies and subsequently assisted them with articulating those of their discipline, a transitional period will likely be needed during which English language tutors model lessons on academic literacy for the benefit of academic staff. These lessons can be delivered in person and/or made available via a series of podcasts which might also be adapted for use as resource materials by the students themselves. In the initial phases of the transition, English language tutors can sit in and give feedback on tutorials in which academic staff teach the literacies that have been identified and embedded in the curriculum. In addition, they can continue to support the efforts of academic staff in this regard through the provision of staff and student workshops and the development of online materials focusing of the relevant academic literacies and developed in consultation and collaboration with academic staff. Such consultation and collaboration is one of the keys to instilling in academic staff a sense of ownership that can bring with it both a greater commitment to the change process and a better understanding and appreciation of what it is seeking to achieve (Murray and Nallaya, 2014).

6.4 Dealing with general proficiency

While embedding academic literacies in the curriculum is the most effective and practicable way to ensure that all students benefit from the opportunity to develop those literacies that are critically important to their capacity to fully engage with their disciplines, general proficiency cannot and need not be treated similarly for the following two reasons:

- Not all students will require general proficiency tuition and to make it available to all students would therefore be considered by university management as extravagant, wasteful of resources and thus misguided, regardless of the financial health of their institutions. Consequently, the investment necessary for such an initiative would be unlikely to be forthcoming.
- Resourcing issues aside, those students who are competent speakers of English would resent having to devote time to classes that bear no relation to their degrees, and this would have implications for recruitment and student satisfaction ratings.
- Particularly in programmes where curricula are squeezed and heavily prescribed, there may be little room in the timetable to schedule classes in general English language proficiency.

It is the very fact of variation in students' levels of general language proficiency, allied with the constraints imposed by limited resources and curricula, that underpins the case for instituting post-enrolment assessment of English language proficiency. Yet, irrespective of whether or not some form of PELA is adopted, for those students who are identified as being in need of general proficiency tuition, the question arises as to how that provision might be structured and the form it might take.

6.4.1   Credit- and non-credit-bearing courses

For those students deemed to be in need of general English language proficiency development, one option is to run a series of credit-bearing elective courses, scheduled during regular hours, for which they are required to register and which, where circumstances permit, can provide a systematic, coherent and ongoing programme of support that is more resource-efficient than some other forms of provision such as one-on-one consultations. Being regular credit-bearing courses would mean that they circumvent the problems, discussed in section 5.4.6, associated with requiring students to pass such courses, and in particular the problematic logistical, financial and political implications of such a policy. The potential risk of losing credit would serve to help ensure that students who might otherwise feel disinclined to attend or apply themselves fully to their learning would be motivated to engage. Decisions concerning the basis on which students should awarded a pass or fail grade on such courses would need to be the subject of discussion and could be made based on the evaluation of their performance either in absolute terms or in relative terms (i.e. gains in proficiency).

As I have already indicated, if general English language proficiency development opportunities are to be offered in the form of credit-bearing elective courses, something else will almost certainly need to give in the curriculum in order to accommodate them. Finding space for such electives in curricula that may be heavily prescribed and/or already squeezed by other institutional teaching and learning initiatives concerning such things as career management skills, graduate qualities and experiential learning often presents considerable challenges, and in some cases insurmountable ones.

And there are other thorny issues with which to contend. There could, for example, be something of a face-validity issue if English language elective courses were to be mandated: 'mandatory elective courses' is a nonsensical notion in that 'elective' presupposes choice and the freedom to select, whereas, in this case, none would exist. There is also the face-validity issue, highlighted in Chapter 5, that arises from requiring students to take elective English language development courses despite their having met institutional language entry conditions that would suggest they have already developed, pre-enrolment, the English language skills needed to study successfully.

More importantly perhaps, and regardless of whether or not credit-bearing elective English language development courses are mandated, Murray and Hicks (2014) highlight the equity issues that can arise in cases where general English language proficiency elective courses are made compulsory for those students deemed to be at risk linguistically. They argue that, despite having met institutional English language entry conditions, such students are effectively being denied the opportunity to take alternative elective courses which are likely to be of greater interest to them and more directly relevant to their degree studies.

Equity issues arising from credit-bearing English language electives also have the potential to affect those students who are not linguistically at risk but who may, nonetheless, feel disadvantaged for other reasons. For example, as discussed in Chapter 2 within the context of policy and regulation, Baik and Greig (2009, p. 405) and the QAA (2009, p. 17) respectively suggest that such students sometimes perceive English language courses as less demanding ('soft options') than other 'regular' elective courses and that lecturers on such courses tend to make special dispensations and be more sympathetic in assessing students' work. Simply put, there is a perception among some that it is easier for individuals enrolled in credit-bearing elective courses that focus on English language development to gain higher course grades than it is for students enrolled on other elective courses. Whether or not they are true, such perceptions can add to the frustration of more linguistically proficient students who, as we have seen, sometimes feel that their own educational experience is being compromised by students who struggle to engage with academic work and, in particular, who can find it difficult to contribute to seminars and group tasks, thereby placing a heavier burden on the shoulders of those who are more linguistically proficient.

Despite possibly offering a viable alternative – or indeed a complement – to their credit-bearing counterparts, *non-credit-bearing* general English language proficiency courses bring challenges of their own. Whether or not they are mandated, the very fact that they are not credit-bearing means that levels of attendance may be low and there may therefore need to be some incentive – perhaps in the form of a certificate for those who either pass the course or demonstrate sufficient performance gains, however measured – particularly given the problems involved in enforcing compliance.[3] As with credit-bearing courses, it may prove difficult to find space in curricula for non-credit-bearing English courses, and one option, therefore, could be to schedule such provision outside of regular hours. While this avoids encroaching on the curriculum, it raises other issues. Even with attendance incentives in place, students' other commitments, both academic and social, may impact on their willingness and/ or ability to attend. Furthermore, after-hours classes scheduled during the semester are likely to be unattractive to teaching staff.

Whether credit-bearing or non-credit-bearing, there are two further issues that bear consideration. The first concerns the streaming of students according to proficiency level and the means by which this might reasonably be done, particularly if there is no form of standardised post-enrolment English language assessment – a quite complex issue in itself, as we saw in Chapter 5. The second is that, even if the kinds of challenges outlined here can be overcome, unless those students most in need of English language development have the opportunity to attend a series of such courses, the developmental nature of language would mean that a single one-off course is likely, anyway, to have only a modest impact on their proficiency. This raises the question, discussed in the next section, of what other forms of English language provision might be made available that could serve to supplement such courses.

6.4.2   Intensive courses

Intensive courses run between terms or semesters offer another option for provision. Being extra-curricular and delivered outside of normal teaching hours, they circumvent the problem of crowded and/or heavily prescribed curricula and can, therefore, make it easier for students to attend as they are likely to be less subject to other study demands associated with their degree programmes. While it would have the disadvantage of delaying intervention and thus necessitate other interim measures to assist students with their language needs, conversely it would have the advantage of allowing students a period to 'settle in' and acquire their own sense of the adequacy or otherwise of

---

[3] These problems are essentially the same as those discussed in relation to post-enrolment language assessment (see section 5.4.2).

their English language proficiency. As mentioned previously, this can be important, for students are often unaware of the linguistic demands of their studies and the fact that, despite having met English language entry conditions, their language proficiency levels are below those needed to cope comfortably. As a result, a proportion of those students who require language development would not necessarily take up the opportunities on offer. Furthermore, students' social calendars might, once again, also discourage them from attending.

One very real drawback with intensive courses that are run during term or semester breaks arises from the fact that, increasingly, students are using such periods to engage in paid employment. While international students are subject to visa conditions that typically either prohibit or restrict their employment, home students feeling the substantial burden of high fees and who may need to support their studies and/or their families, may feel unable to take advantage of these kinds of language courses or to attend them on a regular basis. Moreover, international students will often wish – or feel obligated – to return home during term/semester breaks, and for these individuals the prospect of missing the opportunity to improve their English is unlikely to dissuade them from doing so.

6.4.3   Workshops and 'clinics'

Workshops provide a useful addition to the repertoire of English language units. These can be used both to support the academic literacy tuition provided within the curriculum by academic content tutors, as well as to enhance students' general language proficiency. They can be run centrally and/or locally, although local delivery once again allows for the tailoring of content to reflect local disciplines both in terms of working with the particular literacies relevant to those disciplines and embedding points of learning relating to general proficiency within language contexts that are the focus of those disciplines.

English language proficiency workshops in particular can run on different bases, one of which is to organise an annual programme scheduled at the outset of the academic year and comprising a series of workshops offered on a cyclical basis and addressing key language issues with which students commonly have difficulty. Alternatively, proficiency workshops can be more reactive, effectively serving as clinics at which students can suggest topics, raise issues and request help with particular language-related problems they may be having in their work. Depending on whether they are pre-planned or reactive in nature, the focus of workshops can thus be informed by commonly-occurring problems in students' writing, speech etc. as perceived through tutors' years of experience as well as through PELA, where it exists, and by students' own perceptions of their weaknesses. Feedback on students' written coursework can also be a fruitful source of information on particular weaknesses in students' writing, and it is to this that I turn next.

6.4.4   Feedback on students' written work

One way of promoting students' language development is by providing feedback on their written work (ideally assessed assignments, as it is here that they are most likely to perform to their full competence). Because the potential scale of the workload this entails for English language tutors could become overwhelming, it needs to be managed through a system which ensures that only those students in greatest need get such feedback, or at least that the quantity of feedback is scaled to reflect relative need; a point to which I shall return in Chapter 8.

In the interests of efficiency, and in particular ease of communication and ease of access on the part of students, feedback would be provided electronically via a standardised mark sheet comprising, among other things, a comprehensive set of tick-box categories reflecting different types of error that would also feature in a linked database which would be updated automatically as different categories and types are ticked by language tutors. Through this database, the relative frequencies of different errors could be ascertained and that information could then serve to determine the focus of proficiency workshops and online resources. That is, standardisation of the mark sheet would help ensure that teacher feedback aligns with those categories that feature in the database, and, in turn, that workshops and online materials are developed which effectively address those language issues most salient in students' work. Initially, the mark sheet would be subject to tweaking as the volume of feedback increases and new categories emerge. This utilitarian approach helps ensure that what is taught is of greatest relevance to the greatest number.

One way in which English language tutors' workloads can be managed within this system, and how the feedback that students receive can be integrated with online resources (the subject of the next section) so as to most effectively assist students as they attempt to address their weaknesses, is discussed in section 8.3.5 within the context of the Australian case study.

6.4.5   Online resources

Today, in most countries of the world, it is virtually impossible to think about the delivery of English language without also thinking about the provision of electronic language learning/teaching resources, frequently referred to as computer-assisted language learning (or CALL), and defined by Levy as 'the search for and study of applications of the computer in language teaching and learning'

(1997, p. 1) and by Egbert as 'learners learning language in any context with, through and around computer technologies' (2005, p. 4). It is not the purpose of this section to discuss at a micro-level the design and content of a website offering such resources; that would warrant a book unto itself. Instead, I would like to consider briefly, at a macro-level, how electronic English language resources might be organised in manner that is consistent with both the tripartite conceptualisation of proficiency articulated in Chapter 3 and a decentralised model of language provision as discussed at the start of this chapter.

The first thing to say is that although the notion of academic literacies presupposes language and language use that is discipline-specific and thus involves resources and their organisation that reflect this, there is also a case for organising general proficiency materials on a similar, discipline-specific basis. Online resources might, for example, be organised at a faculty level according to which there would be one English language portal within which there are individual faculty streams. Each faculty stream would contain three kinds of resources: academic literacy resources, general proficiency resources, and professional communication skills resources. For reasons of ease of navigation, particularly for students who may be studying joint degrees across different faculties, there is advantage to standardising this format; however, within this basic structure, the nature of the content and the way in which each of the three strands develops will necessarily differ according to faculty if it is to reflect their particular language requirements.

A point to emphasise here is that just as academic literacy and professional communication skills resources should be relevant to the communicative needs of the particular disciplines of the faculty, so too should general proficiency resources. In order for this to happen, points of grammar, for example, that are being presented need to be embedded within language contexts that reflect discipline content. This has a number of advantages. Firstly, it reinforces the fundamental relationship between language and discipline; secondly, it gives an organised, integrated and bespoke feel to each faculty's English language website; thirdly, it offers a sense of immediacy and authenticity to students who are, consequently, more likely to see it as relevant and, therefore, to engage with and thus learn from it; and finally, by embedding points of learning within discipline-related contexts rather than generic contexts, students get additional exposure to the language and discourse of their discipline.

While the disciplines within a given faculty are likely to share language and literacy practices, there will also exist degrees of variation between them. This means that even a website where resources are tailored to faculties will be something of a blunt instrument, for it will not be nuanced enough, in its initial iteration at least, to account for the idiosyncrasies of every conceivable discipline within the faculties. However, the idea is that each faculty website should undergo a process of continual evolution and refinement such that, over time, resources increasingly reflect the particularities of individual disciplines.[4] This is clearly a longer-term project and one that needs to be managed locally, and once again this is where a decentralised model of English language provision can pay dividends. While the standard format or template of the English language website itself needs to be agreed centrally by the Director of Language Services (or equivalent) in consultation with the faculty English Language Coordinators and their teams,[5] the way in which each faculty website develops within that format is a product of local decision-making between the English language faculty Coordinators and their respective teams, the members of which should feel that they have a voice in shaping provision. What is certain is that there needs to be somebody – an individual or task force – assigned with responsibility for (a) policing the websites and ensuring that they conform to the format mandated centrally by the university, and (b) making certain that all resources undergo a similar vetting process prior to posting in order to ensure they are well-coordinated, presented in an integrated fashion, of sufficiently high quality, and exhibit little in the way of redundancy.

In many cases, the ability to create engaging and effective online resources that respond to students' learning styles and expectations and which are diverse and not overly text-based – a common complaint – will necessitate staff training in order to familiarise them with, and give them confidence in using, the relevant hardware and software, and in working with their institution's preferred delivery platform.

6.4.6   One-on-one consultations

One-on-one consultations with English language tutors are another quite widespread form of English language provision offered by universities, one that can be used to help students address particular problems with their language proficiency, or indeed their academic literacy. The basis on which students gain access to such appointments can vary between different institutions, but increasingly they are seen as a resource-intensive and thus costly option; as a result, where they do exist, there is a strong argument to limit access in a way that such provision is equitable but not all-consuming given the other potential demands on English language support staff. The case study presented in

---

[4] In the case of general proficiency, there will be some redundancy across the faculty disciplines with respect to the items being taught, as opposed to the contexts in which they are embedded. However, the same explanations of points of grammar, for example, can be used across those disciplines, even if they are then illustrated via different and tailored contexts. Furthermore, having examples within different online discipline streams means that students will have access to a greater number and range of examples, even if some of them may not relate specifically to their own discipline.

[5] Decisions on website design will almost certainly be constrained, to a large extent, by university regulations that dictate a level of conformity to an institutional template.

Chapter 8 suggests one model of one-to-one appointments that rationalises its provision by linking it to post-enrolment language assessment in the manner alluded to in section 5.2.5.

None of the forms of English language provision cited in this section are mutually exclusive of course, and the likelihood is that, given the contextual variation that exists between faculties and departments in respect of such things as the curriculum and financial constraints, ultimately any permutation of provision will need to be multi-pronged in design and offer a *suite* of interventions, if it is to be a practical and equitable solution to the question of how to most effectively provide those students who require it with suitable general language proficiency support. The kind of decentralised model of provision I proposed at the outset of this chapter would mean that faculty Coordinators would be tuned in to local conditions and well placed to tailor the shape of both general English language and academic literacy activities accordingly. That is, in consultation with the relevant academic staff and students, they could tailor the content and delivery of workshops, negotiate credit- and non-credit-bearing courses, provide language-related feedback on assignments, design the website and other resources, and oversee any post-enrolment English language assessment exercise far more effectively locally than if provision were designed and delivered centrally.

6.5   Funding provision

One question all institutions face – and periodically revisit – is that of the funding model they should adopt for their English language teaching operations. Although in the United Kingdom, for example, some higher education institutions have opted to outsource their English language provision to third party organisations such as INTO and Kaplan, I am concerned here with internal provision and will only observe that, while such organisations are able to fund often impressive physical and learning resources, there have been concerns raised over teachers' employment conditions, something which in turn can impact negatively on morale and ultimately the quality of the service being provided to students. Furthermore, these organisations operate largely independently, a fact which calls into question their ability to respond to the local needs of faculties and departments, with particular implications for the provision of academic literacy support.

One thing tends to hold true: universities generally appear reluctant to fund English language support – or at least to fund it to the extent required to support the language needs of students potentially at risk either from dropping out of their studies or not achieving at the academic level of which they are intellectually capable. While this would seem unreasonable given the widely acknowledged shortcomings of the English language gatekeeping mechanisms universities employ to ensure that commencing students have sufficient language competence to succeed (discussed in detail in Chapter 4), this reluctance to fund English language support can be a product of one or more of the following:

- A desire by universities not to draw attention to the linguistic shortcomings of their students;
- The tendency of English language units – particularly those unaligned with academic departments – to offer relatively meagre returns in terms of institutional kudos. Staff are typically employed on teaching-only contracts and thus not normally required to engage in research activity that can help generate such kudos and improve institutional rankings;
- A sense among senior management and even individual departments that English language provision is support or service work (and not necessarily critical support/service work) rather than a part of academia proper. This is reflected in the fact that, unless they are part of a larger concern such as Applied Linguistics, TESOL, English or Education, many do not have departmental status but are instead categorised as 'centres' or 'units'. This, in conjunction with the non-award-bearing programmes that are typically the staple English language units, and their teaching-only staff, means that English language units are often regarded as outliers for they do not fit the traditional mould of an academic department and are thus seen as problematic and treated differently accordingly. Indeed, it is for this very reason that outsourcing English language operations is seen by some university management as an attractive proposition.
- A belief that gatekeeping tests work sufficiently well and that, while a small minority of students may choose or be forced to withdraw from their studies as a result of weak English, the vast majority will have the wherewithal to increase their language competence, where necessary, during the course of their studies to the extent required for them to progress through and graduate.[6]

This situation appears to present us with something of a chicken and egg problem: staff working in English language units are not normally required to produce research. They are therefore not regarded as academics proper and entitled to academic contracts; nor are their units formally recognised as academic departments unless they are part of a larger collective, and even then, the English language element may sometimes be subject to different funding arrangements. Because English language units are not academic departments, the academic requirements and opportunities for the promotion of English teachers are limited. As a result, the motivation to produce research which

---

[6] As we have seen, students' ability to graduate can indicate that standards are being compromised.

might ultimately help bolster the case for those units to qualify as academic departments is lacking.

Be this as it may, the kind of decentralised model of English language provision I am suggesting could be funded in a number of different ways, possibly in combination.

6.5.1   Self-funding

Self-funded English language units are not uncommon, in part due to the very fact that they are not traditional academic departments and therefore not subject to the same funding principles and mechanisms. As such, the need for them to balance their books is often especially important and, consequently, income-generating courses tend to accompany and thus fund non-income-generating courses – normally in-sessional English language provision. Although many within these units see this as unreasonable given that they are necessarily servicing the needs of the wider university, specifically the academic departments that admit those students who stands to benefit from the services they provide, it remains the reality nonetheless. While income-generating courses such as pre-sessional, foundation and test-preparation courses may be academically oriented, others may instead have a general English orientation, thereby increasing possible income streams by appealing to broader markets. In essence, these kinds of English language units run largely as commercial enterprises and the universities whose students' needs they service are content for them to operate on that basis *because* they are somewhat anomalous and so long as they remain financially healthy. Where they succeed in doing so, the university will typically top-slice them; where they do not, the temptation to outsource provision is surely heightened – an option which brings is own potential hazards, as I have indicated.

6.5.2   Faculty/departmental funding

An alternative funding model is based on the idea that individual faculties or departments should fund provision. The main attraction of this arrangement is that it aligns well with the idea of decentralised provision. That is, faculties pay for having access to language development services located within the faculty and dedicated and tailored to the particular needs of the faculty and its constituent departments. This means that faculties and their departments are more likely to feel that they are getting value for money and are benefiting locally and tangibly from returns on their investment through provision that is relevant to them and specifically available to their students.

This option is, however, prone to certain challenges. Most prominent among these is the fact that different departments are likely to have different levels of need with respect to English language support for their students and those least in need of such support may be reluctant to fund the provision, particularly if they are already financially burdened. Unfortunately, the basis on which they make this decision is not necessarily well informed, for two reasons: firstly, even where their students may require English language development, the department may not wish to acknowledge and draw attention to the fact for reputational reasons and out of concern that it may give the impression that they accept students who lack sufficient language competence; and secondly, they may not necessarily be well placed to judge the level of need of their students. For example, as we have seen, there is a tendency to incorrectly assume that science subjects demand relatively low levels of language proficiency.

6.5.3   International Office funding

Although, as I have mentioned, the question of English language development is one which potentially concerns all students, and not only international students of non-English-speaking backgrounds, Universities' International Offices tend, nonetheless, to have close working relationships with English language units, partly because institutional collaborations and other initiatives are frequently brokered by these offices and sometimes hinge on there being an English language development component either as preparation for the main event (e.g. an English language programme for a group of government-funded Iraqi PhD scholarship students) or as a language development course designed to run in parallel with it. Other reasons for the often close ties include the joint involvement with such things as the setting and monitoring of institutional English language entry standards and compliance with respect to visa requirements.

Essentially, then, international students are very much the core business of International Offices and English language centres; consequently a synergistic and reciprocal relationship normally exists between the two. It is for this reason that International Offices may choose to fund or part-fund English language teaching activities within the university, particularly where these service the needs of students enrolled in the university. By providing those services, English language units support the university's international recruitment efforts, enhance its business opportunities, and help ensure that its enrolled students receive the kind of in-sessional English language development that helps them meet the demands of their programmes, feel integrated and have a fulfilling social life, and thus have a positive learning experience as a result.

6.5.4   Student-funded provision

Although most, if not all, universities provide online English language materials that students can access and work through at their own pace as and when they need to, face-to-face teaching, including one-on-one consultations, workshops and proficiency courses, could be made available to students on a fee-paying basis. Students could either pay a one-off fee that would entitle them to access to all such forms of provision, or pay a fee 'per unit' taken.

If provision is made available on the former, one-off fee basis, this could be incorporated into the students' fees, although in principle this would seem unfair as it would mean that, regardless of whether or not they were aware of the fact, those students not requiring English language development services would be funding those who do. However, if the cost of funding provision were *not* incorporated into students' fees, there would almost inevitably be a negative reaction from students who have met their universities' English language entry criteria and who would in all likelihood feel aggrieved at then having to fund the cost of language development in order reach the academic standards expected of them.

Unsurprisingly perhaps, the student-funded English language support model is relatively rare, most probably because it does not sit comfortably or present the institution in a very positive light in an era when universities are so intensely focused on providing added value and measuring up in terms of the student experience.

6.6   Evaluating the effectiveness of provision and tracking student progress

Whatever form English language provision takes, if funding is generated via mechanisms other than the students themselves and is to be ongoing, then it is imperative that its efficacy can be demonstrated, not only for the purpose of future funding but also to help provide assurance that the service is relevant and the structures and pedagogy through which it is delivered are effective. This, of course, is easier said than done, and presents for universities and English language units the same challenge that test developers face in attempting to measure the predictive validity of gate-keeping tests (see the foregoing discussion in section 4.2.1): there are many intervening variables that cloud the picture and make it difficult to make secure statements and provide unambiguous data; this in an age where universities are preoccupied – some would say obsessed – with performance metrics. Today, more than ever before, if an activity is not measurable and cannot, therefore, be shown unequivocally to contribute to the institution's well-being and development, it is likely to be regarded as unviable. As a consequence, it will typically be subject to re-evaluation and/or have its funding reduced or, at worst, withdrawn. This reflects a disturbing incongruity that arises from the fact that institutions, not unreasonably, require evidence of need before they commit funding, despite knowing that English language entry standards are generally set at minimum levels of proficiency which assume that students at the low end of the proficiency spectrum but who meet those standards will need further language development post-entry, according to the guidance offered by testing bodies such as IELTS.

So how *can* the efficacy of English language provision be measured? For sure, the kind of categorical data typically sought by university management is likely to be elusive, particularly given the many intervening variables potentially affecting student performance that militate against the drawing of unequivocal cause–effect statements. Perhaps, one of the most likely sources of evidence is to be found in the identification of trends across as large a population of students who have received English language tuition as possible, thereby counteracting the effects of individual variation and allowing for claims to be made about the efficacy of provision that have increased veracity. Those trends ideally need to be observable in data derived from multiple sources, thereby allowing for triangulation and enabling more secure claims to be made about provision. Evaluating provision in this way would constitute a longitudinal project in which performance would need to be tracked during the course of the students' lifecycle.

6.6.1   *Data derived from evaluation points*

One form of data could be based on a series of evaluation points either spanning the entire duration of students' degree courses or spanning the period during which they are utilising the English language provision available to them. Performance could, for example, be measured according to grades obtained on assessed coursework, such as essays and presentations. In this case, assessment could either be on the content itself (with language proficiency being implicit in that grade) or on the language element of the task (although the artificial separation of language and content is problematic). Alternatively, evaluation points could simply consist of an English language assessment exercise that is separate and distinct from students' academic coursework. That exercise could be a test of which there are multiple versions.[7] An internationally recognised exit test such as IELTS might also be used as an indication of any general proficiency gains made by comparing entry and exit scores (see, for example, Berry and Lewkowicz, 2000; Qian, 2007; Zhengdong, 2009, in relation to the Hong Kong higher education context). However, again, the fact of the considerable intervening time (three or four years for most students) during which one would expect students, anyway, to 'pick up' the language to some a degree merely through

---

[7] As indicated in Chapter 4, the tests used for PELA could potentially also be used for this purpose or for the purpose of student self-assessment.

academic and social exposure, would cast doubt on the soundness of any conclusions drawn and therefore constitute an argument for more regular, periodic assessment of students' language skills.

One problem inherent in the idea of language proficiency being implicit in coursework grades awarded by academic content tutors is the fact that different course tutors might prioritise English language differently or grade it according to different criteria. This and the fact that different students within the cohort concerned would be getting input of differing quality and quantity, depending on their opportunities and efforts to learn language, suggests a need to identify trends across the cohort in an effort to compensate for the kind of individual variation between students that will always exist.

6.6.2   Staff and student feedback

Staff and student feedback offer other means by which to gauge increases in students' language skills. Through questionnaires and/or focus groups, information can be gleaned from students as to whether and how they found the provision they accessed beneficial to their language development and the extent to which they themselves feel that their language competence (general proficiency, academic literacy and professional communication skills) has improved. Similarly, English language tutors and academic staff can be canvassed for their views both on the increases in competence evident in individual students (possibly a sample set) and, more generally, across the English language learning cohort as a whole.

6.6.3   In-sessional attendance levels

Levels of engagement with English language learning, as evidenced through the use of online resources and hard copy resources and the attendance of in-sessional English language classes, workshops and consultations, can also be measures of the success of any given model of language provision. Due very often to other pressures in their academic and personal lives, students are, necessarily, highly pragmatic in terms of how they invest their time and energy, and they will quickly opt out of activities they feel do not yield a tangible return. I have already indicated earlier in this chapter how this can be, and often is, the case with in-sessional English language classes that offer generic English for academic purposes tuition. Students will often have had their fill of such pre-admission tuition as part of their efforts to meet language entry requirements and prepare themselves linguistically for their upcoming course of study, and they have a low tolerance for in-sessional classes that merely offer more of the same at a time when they are juggling other study demands. This tends to be reflected in the high attrition rates that characterise these classes and is, as I have suggested, an argument for discipline-specific language tuition that is more likely to meet their immediate needs.

6.6.4   A pilot study

Finally, although a pilot study is unlikely to be of a duration long enough to enable conclusions to be drawn about the efficacy of the model of provision it is intended to trial, it can nonetheless serve to demonstrate whether the model is systemically viable; that is, whether it works in organisational as opposed to pedagogical terms and can be effectively delivered within the university context with its multifarious demands and constraints.

6.6.5   Comparative analysis

While none of these methods of evaluation will, in isolation, offer a reliable picture of the efficacy of the model of English language provision adopted by an institution, together they might reasonably be expected to provide a strong indication at the very least; and that is perhaps the most one can expect given the numerous confounding factors. Ideally, they will already have been implemented and associated records would thus provide baseline data that would allow for a comparative analysis to be conducted of the efficacy of provision available under the preceding model and that offered by the new model, once the latter has bedded in sufficiently for valid judgements and comparisons to be made. In cases where such data on the preceding model has not been collected, however, the extensive lead-up time associated with piloting and securing approval for any significant and large-scale innovation is typically such that it may be feasible to collect it in the interim period.

6.7   Summary

In discussing the shape of English language provision in higher education, I have taken as my starting point in this chapter the tripartite division of competencies outlined in Chapter 3, which together constitute a framework within which to conceptualise provision. I have focused in particular on the areas of general proficiency and academic literacy and suggested that these are best supported through a decentralised model of provision that allows for a more bespoke approach that is of greater relevance to students, and as such promises to be more engaging and thus promote increased learning.[8] I have suggested a number of mechanisms through which language development can be realised, given this model, and have discussed in some detail the basis on which

---

[8] I would – and have – argued that the same is true of professional communication skills.

academic literacies can be embedded in curricula in the manner proposed in Chapter 3. What is clear is that academic staff delivering degree content will need to play the leading role in imparting to students the academic literacy skills pertinent to their disciplines, and that this will require them to understand the rationale informing this approach, in addition to professional development that will enable them to implement it successfully. English language tutors will, in contrast and in a break with tradition, play more of a support role.

However English language proficiency is conceptualised, and whatever the model of provision adopted, funding is an inevitable part of the equation, and each institution will need to determine how to approach this issue, whether it be via English language units' income generating courses, a supplementary student fee (either built into tuition fees or charged as an additional language course registration fee), the university's international office, or contributions from individual faculty or departmental budgets. None of these options is without its challenges; yet solutions need to be found, and while these will almost certainly be compromises, the alternative – no provision or ineffective provision – is not acceptable or even sustainable in a context where a climate of increased regulation of standards combines with a changing student demographic that sees the proportion of students for whom English is not a first language at an all-time high.

As I (and many others) have indicated, mustering the necessary support and approval for any institutional model of English language provision, effecting the proposed changes post-approval attracting and sustaining the necessary funding, will inevitably bring with it the kinds of challenges associated with any large scale, significant innovation in a sizeable institution. It is these challenges, and in particular the political hurdles and strategies for negotiating them, that form the focus of Chapter 7.

7   Innovation in English language provision: driving and navigating institutional change

7.1   The higher education sector as a particular context for innovation

While not all change necessarily amounts to innovation, and there are scholars who articulate differences between the two terms (e.g. De Lano, Riley and Crookes, 1994; Kennedy, 1999), in this chapter, and following Murray (2008), Wedell (2009) and Waters (2009), I use the words 'innovation' and 'change' synonymously.

Innovation is often cited as one of the hallmarks of good leadership (see, for example, Stoller, 2009) and, conversely, the lack of innovation as a 'recipe for disaster' (Goldsmith and Clutterbuck, 1984). White (1987) argues that, while it may be distasteful to some, ELT is an industry like any other, and thus Goldsmith and Clutterbuck's observation is as relevant to the ELT context as it is to other areas of industry. His argument reads as follows:

That ELT is an 'industry', let alone a mature one, may not appeal to teachers, who probably regard themselves as educationalists and not as industrialists. Yet, ELT is a service industry, supplying people with a service—English language teaching—and a commodity—the English language. So, although we may not be used to thinking in management terms, the effective running of any ELT enterprise is subject to essentially the same considerations as apply in any other industry. (White, 1987, p. 211)

While I would argue that it is legitimate to interpret White's reference to the 'ELT industry' as encompassing English language provision within higher education, it is the case that change within that context, and on the kind of institution-wide scale with which this book is concerned, raises a number of issues that would not necessarily arise with innovation in ELT on a more modest scale and within smaller organisations such as language schools. This is due, in part, to the unprecedented complexity of institutions of higher education today in terms of the following factors:

- The increase in regulation governing practices and the concomitant increase in institutional bureaucracy designed, in part, to guard against sanctions that can result from failure to comply. This is typified by the enormous bureaucracy surrounding UK universities' efforts to ensure that they meet the UKVI requirements (see section 2.2.2). Such regulation and the potential dangers of failure to comply with stated good practice can have the effect of stifling innovation by reducing universities' appetite for risk.

- The diverse needs and perceptions of needs within different departments of the institution. This can result in multiple agendas and thus different attitudes towards a given innovation. Reconciling those differences can be problematic, if not impossible, with the result that efforts to progress proposals for change can be stymied.
- The interdependence of various operational aspects of the university. This means that any proposal for change can rarely be confined to one area of its operations and will normally impact a range of constituencies within the institution. The result is that the number of potential stakeholders increases and thus also the difficulty of securing sufficient buy-in to make the proposal viable.
- The need to protect reputation and brand and to position the institution strategically. Any potential risk here that is seen as arising from the proposed innovation will need to be sanctioned by the uppermost echelons of university management.

Together, these factors exert formidable constraints on universities and lead them to approach any proposals for significant change with understandable caution. As such, those attempting to bring about change in a way that mitigates these factors need to be prepared for what is likely to be a protracted affair as they begin to navigate the various institutional processes that exist to serve as safeguards against the potential risks inherent in any major change. As I seek to show in this chapter, success in navigating those processes is dependent upon considerably more than simply the merits of the innovation itself. It needs to be the consequence of an alignment, whether by design or coincidence, of different and overlapping elements: personal, institutional and political, and organisational. For each of these, where the conditions needed for successful innovation do not pre-exist, they need to be created. It also bears mentioning that although at times I will refer in this chapter to 'the innovator', in reality most if not all large-scale innovations involve a team of people who share a belief in the proposed changes, and while there will typically be one main driver who leads or 'fronts' the initiative, the effort to secure adoption of the innovation by the institution will normally be a collective one.

7.2   Creating the conditions for innovation

7.2.1   The personal dimension

The success of any innovation in any institution has as much to do with the makeup of those leading it as it does with the merits of the innovation itself. It is essential that those who drive innovation – so-called 'change agents' (Robbins and DeCenzo, 2001) – are able to demonstrate certain key traits if their efforts are to result in adoption and successful implementation. What Rogers (1983, cited in Markee, 1993) observes about adopters of innovation is equally true of drivers; namely that:

individuals with particular psychological profiles tend to display specific adoption behaviors. For example, individuals who adopt early tend to travel widely and are usually well-educated and upwardly mobile; they tend to seek out and be open to new ideas, and they tend to have a high degree of exposure to mass media. Their contacts with other people are often extensive, and they are usually able to tolerate high levels of uncertainty. Laggards, on the other hand, tend to display diametrically opposite characteristics while the people in between exhibit intermediary traits. (Markee, 1993, p. 236)

Unquestionably, drivers of innovation need to have a certain force of personality; a charisma of sorts that commands the attention and respect of others and inclines them to be sympathetic to what they hear, even in cases where the rationale for and implications of the innovation may be odds with their personal beliefs and desires. They need, essentially, to have a strong sense of self-belief, carry conviction and be able to instil in others belief and confidence in what they are proposing. Conger (1998) makes this point strongly by juxtaposing these personal characteristics with the arguments that the innovator employs in an effort to secure buy-in:

In persuading people to change their minds, great arguments matter . . . But arguments, per se, are only one part of the equation. Other factors matter just as much, such as the persuader's credibility and his or her ability to create a proper, mutually beneficial frame for a position, connect on the right emotional level with an audience, and communicate through vivid language that makes arguments come alive. (1998, p. 87)

In addition to being strong and engaging personalities with considerable self-belief, innovators need to be endowed with certain other leadership qualities. Just as charisma and the ability to get others to follow can be regarded as one such quality, so too can those of commitment, perseverance, tenacity and empathy. Without these and other qualities, any hope of gaining the endorsement of senior management and peers across the institution will in all probability be a forlorn one, for institutional change rarely comes easily. There will be pushback, and innovators need to be prepared to keep faith, although while keeping an open mind, listening to detractors and critical voices, and revising their proposals where they deem it necessary. Should they be unsuccessful in garnering the required support for their proposal first time around, they should be ready to reintroduce it following any judicious and strategic revisions. The very fact of having listened to colleagues within and across the university community and adjusted the proposal accordingly can be perceived as positive and ultimately help the proposal to gain traction. However, if not carefully managed, it can also be seen as weakness and invite further criticism and calls for change that can lead to a dilution of the original idea to such an extent that it loses its essential integrity and its potential to be effective in what it seeks to achieve. In this sense, innovators have to keep in touch with their original vision while having the capacity to reflect on it objectively in light of others' input, the confidence to adjust it where necessary, and the strength of vision to know when they risk being seduced by arguments that fundamentally undermine that vision and answer to other agendas.

Furthermore, it can be difficult to convince academics and administrative staff to sign up to significant change that will result in what they may see as an upsetting of the apple cart by necessitating alterations to practices with which they are familiar and comfortable. This is particularly true in an environment such as higher education, where policy seems to be continually changing and where, as a result, any stability that has been achieved is highly prized and thus reluctantly relinquished. Citing Plant (1987), Shen (2008) lists the following factors as being important in terms of their potential to 'fuel resistance and unwillingness to change':

• Fear of the unknown;
• Lack of information;
• Threat to core skills and competence;
• Threat to power base;
• Fear of failure;
• Reluctance to experiment;
• Reluctance to let go.

Although anecdotal evidence suggests that those individuals who have the necessary force of personality to drive institutional change tend to be concerned less with being liked than with bringing about transformation that they believe in – and in which they frequently feel fervently that others should also believe – it can, nonetheless, help to bring about such transformation if one is able to combine an ability to have others warm to you with the kind of single-mindedness and absolute commitment to ideas that typically characterises change agents.

If he or she is to be credible, the innovator needs to be able to demonstrate a thorough and coherent understanding of the innovation they seek to promote and of the context within which it is to be located. This involves not only the display of relevant knowledge and understanding but, equally importantly, the ability to communicate it in a way that is accessible to others who may have neither the necessary disciplinary knowledge nor familiarity with its associated terminology. Thus, in the model of English language provision described in Chapter 6, those driving change – and indeed the English language teachers tasked with implementing it – need to be fully apprised of the innovation and knowledgeable about the disciplinary contexts in which it is to be applied: the local political landscape, pertinent issues and debates, available resources, the relevant academic literacies, programme expectations and assessment practices, areas of language particularly critical to students' success, and perceived areas of common weaknesses in students' language in relation to their communicative needs. They also need to be able to explain the innovation in terms that do not presuppose knowledge of applied linguistics.

Furthermore, English language innovators need, ideally, to be connected with their counterparts and others working within a similar field in other higher education institutions, particularly where a process of similar change has been undertaken or is in the process of being undertaken. This emphasis on reciprocal and collaborative professional as well as social relationships as a key variable in adoption is reflected in social interaction and linkage models of innovation (Havelock 1970, 1971; Rogers and Shoemaker, 1971; Conger, 1998) which 'stress the connections that exist between change agents and users of innovations' (Markee, 1993, p. 238). While these models tend to focus on the social interaction between members of the adopting group within an institution (how connected or disconnected they are from peers who might influence their decision; the role of informal personal contacts as a mechanism for exchanging information about innovations; and the importance of group membership and reference-group identification as predictors of individual adoption), the importance of dialogue between – as well as across – institutions should not be underestimated. Among other things, it allows for experience to be exchanged and for the innovator to use their knowledge of other institutions as potential leverage for bringing pressure to bear on their own institution: if institutions see their immediate competitors taking steps to move forward in terms of how they deal with the English language issue, and prepared to face up to the risks associated with doing so, they are more likely to take notice and to feel reassured that there is likely merit in rethinking their own approach and engaging enthusiastically with the idea of change. Moreover, while an institution might not necessarily be at the forefront of change, they stand to benefit nonetheless by learning from the successes and failures of others. In so doing, they can move forward more confidently and are better placed to develop their own approach – adjusted, where appropriate, according to the particular characteristics of their own institutional context – in a way that can legitimately be described as innovative.

7.2.2   The political dimension

How the innovator negotiates the political realities of the institution within which they are striving to bring about change, and the probability of success, depends on a myriad factors all of which are impacted upon to a greater or lesser degree by the kind of personal traits described above. Success in negotiating the political landscape will, therefore, be a product of demonstrating these qualities in combination with institutional knowledge and strategic awareness.

One key factor that is largely outside the control of the innovator, but of which he or she needs an appreciation, is the nature of the university's leadership: in particular, its aspirations and the extent to which it is prepared to entertain risk as a necessary by-product of embarking on changes which promise to realise those aspirations and, ultimately, enhance its reputation and brand as an institution that is forward-thinking, innovative and at the forefront of change in higher education. Along with ideological, historical, political, economic and administrative variables, this attitudinal variable forms part of the sociocultural context in which the innovation is situated (Cooper, 1989; Markee, 1986, 1993), and the innovator needs to be cognizant of it because it not only places constraints on what is and is not likely to be possible, but also needs to inform their approach in presenting their ideas to senior management in such a way as to maximise receptivity.

It is easier to secure buy-in for proposed changes in a culture where change is welcomed provided it can be demonstrated to have the potential to improve the university's standing and thus to give it a competitive edge and the additional security this can bring. In contrast, universities that err on the side of conservatism – or indeed see conservatism as a competitive advantage deriving from the image it engenders of provenance and longevity, and, by association, stature, augustness and stability – and which are more risk-averse, are likely to present the innovator with more substantial hurdles to overcome and to require them to draw in greater measure on the personal qualities described in section 7.2.1. Regardless of how risk-averse an institution is, any proposal for change will always need to include a realistic assessment of associated risks, along with suggestions as to how they can be most effectively managed. As I have indicated in Chapter 5, the idea of mandatory post-enrolment English language assessment, for example, brings with it distinct risks by potentially undermining an institution's brand and deterring students who may see it as an additional and unwelcome hurdle to be faced when transitioning into higher education.

One of the ways in which university senior management can assess potential risk is if the proposed innovation has been implemented elsewhere in the same or similar form. Where this has occurred, it can offer insights into the consequences of implementation that may suggest that the benefits have the potential to outweigh the costs (financial or otherwise). However, this alone would not and should not be sufficient reason to adopt the innovation, as regardless of whether the innovation has been implemented elsewhere and of the insights that process has generated, the fact that no two institutions are ever precisely the same makes it imperative that it is initially implemented on a limited scale as a pilot exercise within the institution considering adoption, for what may work in one institution will not necessarily work in another. This ability to pilot the innovation by 'trying it out in stages' (Markee, 1993, p. 236), perhaps within one faculty initially, is what Rogers refers to as its 'trialability'; and the ability to demonstrate trialability, and ultimately the efficacy of the innovation, is an important determinant of whether or not the university's senior management will initially endorse it in principle, and ultimately in practice should the trial prove successful and thus help validate the changes envisaged.

A point made by Harris (2009) in her discussion of creative leadership is that creativity in the form of innovation is more likely to be realised in institutions where it is the product of collective rather than individual endeavour and there exists a strong sense of community, high levels of trust and a norm of 'no-blame innovation' should things go wrong (p. 10). An English language model of provision, such as that outlined in Chapter 6, which is to be implemented on an institution-wide basis within a university, is unlikely to benefit from such a sense of community, for the size of the institution and the many often conflicting agendas tend to militate against it, as does the fact that the stakes are potentially very high in terms of the institution's image and reputation, as we have seen. Nonetheless, having a well-informed, well-led and well-coordinated team that is able to secure support from the majority of stakeholders by presenting the innovation as responding to a common – and commonly felt – problem is clearly more likely to meet with success. Conger argues:

> Even before starting to persuade, the best persuaders we have encountered closely study the issues that matter to their colleagues. They use conversations, meetings, and other forms of dialogue to collect essential information. They are good at listening. They test their ideas with trusted confidants, and they ask questions of the people they will later be persuading. Those steps help them think through the arguments, the evidence, and the perspectives they will present. (1998, p. 92)

If the innovator is to negotiate the university's political landscape successfully, they need to be politically astute. This includes having a good understanding of the processes through which any proposal for change at the institutional level will need to pass and what this means for the way in which it will be vetted and by whom. Familiarity with the institution's systems, processes and procedures enables the innovator to adapt the presentation of the proposed innovation in such a way that it addresses the respective concerns of those bodies and the ways in which they conduct their business. It can be shaped strategically such that in presentation it is seen to respond to their agendas. Importantly, knowledge of the terrain the proposal will need to traverse during the course of its journey towards acceptance and, hopefully, implementation, allows the innovator to lay essential groundwork by nurturing relationships with those sitting on the various relevant committees and other key individuals whose blessing is required if the proposal is to advance and who, similarly, may have their own agendas. Again, they need to display complete control of the proposal and of their discipline, and through knowledge of the committees and their membership try to anticipate queries and questions. Equally, as we have seen, the innovation needs to speak to the broader issues of concern to the university's senior management; in particular, graduate employability and the student experience. Clearly, language, communication and intercultural competence are at the heart of these things and as such will need to be exploited.

Machiavellian though it might sound, political astuteness also extends to the negotiation, explicit or implicit, of quid pro quos. By understanding the agendas of individuals who can influence the passage of the innovation, the innovator is able to position themselves in relation to those individuals' agendas such that they acquire leverage by expressing and showing support in a way that morally obligates them to return the favour. The reality is that, in higher education institutions, innovation is in large part about politics and politicking, and while this may appear distasteful to some, the truth is that it is precisely through this kind of activity that a good deal of business gets done. Educational institutions are certainly no more immune to political machinations than any other organisation and, while it may not necessarily result in the best policy and practice, those who opt out of this approach to 'doing business' are unlikely to achieve any large-scale change no matter how meritorious it may be.

Critically important though it is, achieving significant change requires more than the support of the various institutional committees and of key individuals whose opinions carry weight. There needs to be garnered the broader backing of the wider academic community so that a groundswell of opinion arises in support of the innovation which will inevitably filter through to those with responsibility for making a determination as to whether or not to pursue it. For a driver of innovation, a number of key traits can help to smooth the passage of the innovation, for collectively they furnish the innovator with the kind of credibility to which I have already made reference (Benoit and Graham, 2005; Gabris, Golembiewski and Ihrke, 2001; Rogers, 2010). These include:

- being visible and active within and across the institution, via membership of committees, for example;
- having a degree of academic and managerial seniority;
- having a reputation for measuredness and sound thinking;
- having discipline knowledge relevant to the innovation; and
- having the kind of charisma and force of personality referred to earlier (7.2.1).

Crucially, the innovation tends naturally to take on, almost by default, some of the credibility that these traits bestow on the innovator, even before he or she has presented their rationale for change to the broader university community.

Reputation and track record, however, can only take things so far, and there will need to be a sound and convincing rationale if those who will be affected by the proposed change are to be supportive of it. Embedding academic literacies in the curriculum, for example, is, as we have seen, a major undertaking that will impact a large section of the university population; as such, it will require cogent arguments eloquently presented. Crucially, it will need to demonstrate convincingly how the receivers of change and their students will benefit; how the adoption of the innovation improves significantly upon the status quo; and how the benefits promise to outweigh the challenges of implementation.

An essential element that lends credibility to both the innovator and the innovation is the need to understand – and be seen to understand and be empathetic towards – the receivers' circumstances in relation to the proposed change, and specifically the challenges they face with respect to the existing situation. Demonstrating awareness and empathy is part of what Goleman has referred to 'emotional intelligence' (Goleman 1995; Goleman, Boyatzis and McKee, 2013), and, I would argue, is a prerequisite to winning the support of those who will, ultimately, be tasked with implementation. Essentially, if they feel the innovator fully understands their predicament, they are more inclined to have greater faith in and thus be more sympathetic to his or her proposed solution. An important dimension to demonstrating empathy, which will assist the innovator(s) to carry future users with them, is the need to be seen to be consulting with those users and not exclusively with committees and those who ultimately have the authority to approve the innovation. That is, users need to feel they are part of the change process and have ownership of it, and eliciting their views and demonstrably factoring them into the design, implementation and ongoing development of the innovation will be an essential ingredient to its success. Waters and Vilches (2001, p. 134) see this consultation process as responding to what they refer to as the 'socialization needs' of the innovation.

It seems reasonable to postulate that those in higher education proposing change concerning the ways in which their institutions approach the issue of English language in particular are potentially at an advantage in that they are likely to find themselves appealing to a receptive audience and thus able to approach innovation with greater confidence and assurance than might otherwise be the case. As I have suggested in Chapters 1 and 2, there is increasing frustration among academic staff with what is seen by many as an untenable situation with respect to English: one that threatens standards both in terms of tutors' ability to deliver the curriculum in the form and at a level they deem appropriate, as well as students' levels of achievement and the qualifications, knowledge and skills with which they graduate. Students who perform relatively poorly in their programmes and who struggle to meet the expectations of employers due to weak language skills and insufficient subject knowledge and practical skills as a result of a compromised, watered-down curriculum and workplace experience, reflect poorly on their graduating departments and universities. This is of concern not only to the departments and tutors involved but also to the university, whose academic standing risks being called into question, with obvious consequences for recruitment, research opportunities, links and partnerships with industry and opportunities for experiential learning. These things are a source of concern for all, and academic departments and their staff feel this keenly and see them as a threat to their personal and collective well-being. As such, an important question that senior managers and all adopters need to ask themselves is: 'can we afford *not* to implement the innovation?' That is, any cost–benefit analysis needs, from the innovator's point of view, to make the case for adoption by showing not only that the inevitable costs incurred with implementation are significantly outweighed by the potential benefits to students, staff, departments and the university at large, but also that the costs incurred by maintaining the status quo and *failing* to innovate are unacceptable.

Finally the university needs to feel confident that the proposed innovation is not so complex and difficult to use that it is impractical and unsustainable. Even if management recognises that there is a case for change, they tend to opt for the solution that brings the greatest benefit with the least upheaval. In other words, the 'best solution' is seen in relative not absolute terms, and it is up to the innovator to ensure that the proposed innovation is effective yet elegant.

7.2.3   The organisational dimension

Convincing the institution – and particularly its senior management – that innovation which seeks to improve its approach to the assessment and provision of English language development opportunities and ensure that it meets regulatory requirements, speaks to other of its key agendas and is thus in the university's interests, is an essential prerequisite to the establishment of structures and procedures that must underpin any favourable reception among all stakeholder groups. Unless the need for change is apparent to all concerned, the proposed model is unlikely to gain traction. The kind of rationale I referred to above, and which lends essential credibility to any proposal, requires that those individuals driving the change are fully apprised of the relevant regulations, policies, issues and literature concerning English language and literacy, and able to bring to the project a sound theoretical and research base, drawing on the necessary metrics in order to bolster the case for change. Furthermore, they need to be able to display their awareness of these factors, along with their conversancy in the area of language and academic literacy, in a way that promotes understanding of and receptivity to the innovation without employing disciplinary jargon that can make their ideas inaccessible to those who are not applied linguists, whether senior management committee members or those on the ground who will, ultimately, be tasked with implementing it. That is, a fine balance needs to be struck between, on the one hand, drawing sufficiently on theoretical constructs and demonstrating authority and project control, and, on the other, ensuring that the innovation and its rationale are presented accessibly in a manner that resonates with stakeholders. This is an issue we will revisit later.

Essential to taking successful carriage of any innovation is the formation of a project management team and, within that team, the clear delineation of lines of responsibility. Without a well-ordered and well-led team at the helm, there is considerable potential for the initiative to be fatally undermined. Firstly, a poorly coordinated team is likely to be perceived as inept, and that can only undermine stakeholders' confidence in the proposed innovation. Secondly, unclear lines of responsibility within the team will almost certainly result in a lack of efficiency due to unnecessary repetition, redundancy and the subsequent need to bring clarity where there is confusion. Thirdly, a well-led team with clear lines of responsibility will also help to ensure that a consistent message is being conveyed to stakeholders and that there are no 'loose cannons' conveying messages at odds with 'the party line', which could lead to negative reactions based on misunderstanding. As we will see shortly, the team needs to consult very carefully in order to establish unambiguously what precisely it is they are seeking to do, why and how they will do it, and who will be responsible for the various different aspects of the project. In this regard, Nicholls (1983) states that:

it is of crucial importance that teachers working together to plan innovation should be prepared to discuss the meanings of ideas and principles underlying their innovations in order to establish, among other things, that they are at least talking about the same thing. (1983)

Regular feedback sessions by team members will also help to ensure that lines of responsibility are being maintained as well as provide an opportunity to reflect on progress and on the current status of all aspects of the project.

One of the key objectives of the project team, then, is to formulate, through careful and thorough consultation, a well-articulated project plan that will ultimately be subject to review in light of progress made and the response it elicits from stakeholders – particularly from institutional committees and groups – and which instils a sense of ownership within the team and includes a clear roll-out strategy, with waypoints and realistic associated timeframes by which specified goals are to be achieved.

A key part of any such roll-out strategy is a good communication strategy through which the proposed innovation will be disseminated to stakeholders (Hyland and Beckett, 2009; Leeuwis and Aarts, 2011; Pfeffermann, Minshall and Mortara, 2013). This involves a number of crucial elements. As we have seen, a prerequisite to effectively presenting the innovation to others is a crystal clear understanding of the innovation itself and its relevance, underlying rationale and associated theoretical underpinnings. I have also emphasised that having a clear conceptualisation of the innovation, its rationale and the issues at stake is of little value unless these things can be articulated during the dissemination phase in a way that is accessible to audiences and does not presuppose expert knowledge they are unlikely to possess. The need for innovators and users to have a sufficient understanding of the change being proposed, along with its rationale, is referred to as *familiarisation* by Waters and Vilches (2001), who state:

This [familiarization] involves the innovation implementation team, on the one hand, in becoming properly familiar with the innovation situation, and on the other, in the potential innovation users likewise being adequately informed about the background to, rationale for, and possible direction of the innovation. (p. 134)

Furthermore, information and the way the innovation is presented will need to be tailored to the particular audience on any given occasion if it is to be digestible, for what may be alluring to and help secure the support of one group of stakeholders may not necessarily do so for another group with different agendas and concerns. Consequently, the ability to tailor the way in which the innovation is presented requires the kind of broader institutional awareness and political astuteness highlighted earlier.

Consideration also needs to be given to the way in which information is shared with the community. It may be, for example, that while an overview of the proposed innovation and its rationale is needed during the initial awareness-raising phase of the project, it may be disadvantageous to provide excessive detail, for this risks overloading an audience that may, anyway, struggle to get to grips with the basic proposal, its underlying reasoning and some of the key concepts to which they will need to be exposed in order to fully appreciate that rationale. The risks with overloading include:

- 'turning off' the audience as key ideas become obscured by detail and they lose any sense of orientation and of the broader picture;
- overwhelming the audience, who are already likely to feel wary about 'another innovation' and what it will mean for their workload; and
- irritation with those proposing change, who may be perceived as being out of tune with and thus unable to relate sufficiently well to their audience.

Ultimately, overloading – which results from a failure to adjust the message so that information is released in a timely and digestible manner – can alienate those stakeholders whose support the innovator is striving to obtain.

A good communication strategy also requires a certain amount of staging; that is the process of making a determination of which groups and committees need to vet and be consulted on the proposed innovation and in what order, so as to elicit feedback, ensure greater likelihood of approval at each stage by each group/committee, and refine the conceptualisation of the innovation and its presentation before moving up the 'approval food chain'. This not only pro-vides the opportunity to render the idea more rigorous and thus less vulnerable to subsequent criticism, it also lends it added potency and credibility by virtue of having undergone the scrutiny of other institutional committees (such as teaching and learning committees, language teaching units, quality assurance groups with a focus on internationalisation, and international offices) and, hopefully, secured their broad support. Essentially, innovation on an institution-wide scale, such as that proposed in Chapter 6, will need to be approved by the university's senior management group, and they will expect the innovators to have done their homework, both in terms of the conceptualisation and piloting of the proposal but also in terms of having subjected it to the scrutiny of the various relevant committees and providing evidence of having subsequently modified it on the basis of feedback received during that process.

I have emphasised the need for change agents to be prepared and able to clearly articulate their ideas and the rationale underpinning them. There is also a need, however, to make clear the ramifications of those ideas: how they will be implemented and the implications of this for those at the coalface – English language tutors, academic staff delivering degree courses, and, to a lesser extent, admissions tutors, marketing departments, International Offices and compliance committees concerned with English language entry standards. Everard and Morris state:

All who are affected by the change need a clear picture of what it will mean for them: what will they be doing differently, after the change has been implemented? They want to know specifically what it means *in practice* for them. (1985, p. 188)

While the proposed changes may be viewed by these stakeholders as heralding additional work, the process of dissemination of the innovation needs to be open and seen to be responsive to their needs, concerns and suggestions. This will not only help gain their buy-in but also help ensure that the proposal stands to benefit from their critical appraisal and ownership of it. White articulates this idea in the following terms:

So, then, reaching a mutual understanding is fundamental. But it is also important that all participants feel that they have contributed towards the formulation of the innovation, that they are part of it and that it is part of them. People who are not informed of new developments will tend to lack responsibility towards the innovation. Goldsmith and Clutterbuck (1984, p. 69) quote Jan Carlsson, chief executive of the Scandinavian airline SAS: 'Those who have no information can take no responsibility. Those who have information have no choice but to take responsibility'. (1987, p. 213)

Critical appraisal by stakeholders can and should, then, be viewed constructively as an opportunity to reflect on and, where necessary, improve and refine the proposal where this is possible without fundamentally changing it. As Everard and Morris (1985, p. 188) noted, this process of dialogue and questioning serves the function of illuminative evaluation by bringing clarity of understanding to the proposed innovation. Furthermore, being seen to be responsive in this way to stakeholder feedback can serve to bolster support while also providing reassurance to senior management – who are frequently also keenly sensitive to the reaction that ideas may provoke in other groups within the wider university community – that the proposal has had a good hearing elsewhere, has run the gauntlet of scrutiny from a variety of interested parties within the institution and, where deemed appropriate, has undergone modifications as a result.

While the proposed model of English language provision may be seen as ideal by those agitating for change, it is unlikely that it will be accepted and adopted in its entirety. Indeed, it is rare that any innovation is ultimately implemented in precisely the form it was originally conceived. This makes it advisable for those proposing the innovation to have considered one or two alternatives – variations on the basic theme, which needs to remain fundamentally intact but be seen to have built into it the flexibility to adapt to contingencies and to the different micro-contexts of implementation within the university. These fall-back positions need to respond to anticipated concerns over the 'ideal' model and are important because they can help keep the proposed innovation alive. Even after having undergone the scrutiny of various institutional groups prior to its presentation to the university's senior management, it may nevertheless be deemed to contain problematic, undesirable elements which could potentially lead to an out-and-out rejection of the innovation at this highest level. However, the ability to offer alternative permutations can serve to salvage a potentially fatal situation where the innovators find their proposal dead in the water and effectively have nowhere to go, and nothing else to put on the table.

Having alternatives to hand also has the advantage of demonstrating that those proposing change have had the wisdom and foresight to anticipate concerns; something which will lend them credibility and in doing so also instil confidence in those seeking reassurance that the innovation has been carefully considered and is in capable hands, and that the benefits of implementing it will outweigh the risks.

Along with an account of different permutations of the model of English language assessment and provision being proposed, a clear articulation of the resource, pedagogical and financial ramifications of each of those permutations needs to be provided. This not only serves to further demonstrate awareness and thoroughness on the part of those driving the innovation but also enables those appraising it to do so from a perspective that is well informed. In this respect, it needs to be remembered that the processes of dissemination and explanation that are part and parcel of securing support for the innovation need to be accompanied by an openness to criticism and to the possibility that there may a better way. In other words, there needs to be an element of genuine consultation which implicitly acknowledges that the innovators are certainly not infallible and that those critically appraising the proposal, and who work in different capacities within the university, bring to the process knowledge and expertise that the innovators themselves may not necessarily have, yet an awareness of which may, ultimately, prove critical to successful implementation, should the proposal be approved.

Finally, as indicated earlier, those leading the innovation need to organise the piloting of their proposed model, but not only for political reasons or what can too easily be erroneously seen as a necessary box-ticking exercise. Information gleaned from a carefully choreographed pilot can deliver important information concerning the model's overall feasibility and its strengths and weaknesses – information that cannot always be obtained merely through theorising and reflection, for reality on the ground will often throw up issues that any amount of theorising and reflection cannot always predict. Indeed, it is in the very nature of innovation, and the fact that it is breaking new ground in some way, that means it is subject to uncertainty – and thus also risk, as we have seen.

Those driving innovation should be careful not to lose sight of the fact that innovation is fundamentally developmental; it is about improving – in this case the way in which English language assessment and provision is shaped in order to improve students' language development and their academic performance and potential as graduates. Nicholls (1983) and Miles (1964) respectively have defined innovation in the following terms:

An innovation is an idea, object or practice perceived as new by an individual or individuals, which is intended to bring about improvement in relation to desired objectives, which is fundamental in nature and which is planned and deliberate. (Nicholls, 1983, p. 4)

Generally speaking, it seems useful to define an innovation as a deliberate, novel, specific change which is thought to be more efficacious in accomplishing the goals of a system ... it seems helpful to consider innovations as being planned for, rather than as occurring haphazardly. The element of novelty, implying recombination of parts or a qualitative difference from existing forms, seems quite essential. (Miles, 1964, p. 14)

Nisbet (1974, p. 2) defines innovation as 'any new policy, syllabus, method or organizational change which is intended to improve teaching and learning', and in 1969, the OECD's Centre for Educational Research and Innovation (CERI) stated the following:

We understand innovation to mean those attempts at change in an educational system which are consciously and purposefully directed with the intention of improving the present system. Innovation is not necessarily something new but it is something better and can be demonstrated as such. (CERI, 1969, p. 13)

This consistent emphasis placed on the qualitative aspect of innovation and the desire to improve on the status quo warns not only against introducing innovation for its own sake but also against losing sight of the primary purpose of innovation in the often fraught process of trying to secure its institutional approval. That is, without due diligence, the securing of approval can end up becoming an end in itself for those seeking to innovate, while the innovation and what it seeks to achieve becomes a casualty of the battle of negotiating the many political hurdles and of contending with the collateral damage in terms of personal cost (stress, pride, reputation etc.).

Conducting a pilot and listening to and responding to feedback with a truly open mind is about having the wisdom, maturity and breadth of vision to retain a focus on the ultimate goal of innovation, namely an improved learning experience for those students who are the target of the proposed change, and to recognise and be able to put aside any sense of personal quest.

In elucidating the theory of the diffusion of innovation within cultures – university culture, for current purposes – Rogers (1983) argues that, for it to self-sustain, an innovation needs to be widely adopted such that it reaches a critical mass. For this to happen, there are five stages through which the innovation needs to pass: awareness, interest, evaluation, trial and adoption. He speaks of adopters of the innovation gaining knowledge about it, being persuaded of its value, making a preliminary decision to adopt it, implementing their decision to adopt it, and confirming their decision to continue using the innovation. Other writers have articulated similar sequences somewhat differently. Fullan (1982), for example, refers to initiation, implementation, continuation and outcome. Whatever the terminology employed, what is critical to the innovation's ultimate success is the extent to which it beds in and becomes part of the institutional culture – what Fullan terms 'institutionalization' (2001, p. 51). Much of the discussion so far in this chapter has focused on navigating a successful passage through the university's approval process by garnishing broad support for the innovation. It is now time to turn to some of the issues that bear on the practicalities of implementation and securing its long-term viability, for without that any such passage through the preliminary phases of implementation is, for all intents and purposes, meaningless.

7.3   Developmental needs: ensuring innovation sticks

In 1993, Markee advised:

It is salutary to remember that all innovation is a risky business and that close to three quarters of educational innovations are likely to fail over time (Adams and Chen, 1981), either because they are never fully adopted or else do not survive the confirmation stage posited by Rogers (1983). (1993, p. 231)

To underline his point, he cites a study by Beretta (1990) which looked at the extent to which teachers implemented the kind of task-based methodology associated with Prabhu's procedural syllabus (1987) and which found that only forty-seven per cent of the teachers involved in implementing the procedural syllabus reached an 'adequate' level of implementation, and only thirteen per cent an 'expert' level. As Markee observes, this indicates 'how difficult it is to promote innovation at a fundamental level' (ibid. p. 231).

7.3.1   Cultural change

We have seen the way in which institutional culture, and in particular its approach to risk, can shape the fortunes of attempts to get the kind of initial ratification of concept from senior management that is a prerequisite to implementation. I have also drawn attention to the importance of convincing the broader community of stakeholders, and most especially those tasked with implementing the innovation, of its legitimacy in terms of making sense as a solution to a recognised and keenly-felt problem. Having these pieces of the jigsaw positioned such that implementation is able to proceed is a necessary but not sufficient condition for its ultimate success. For ultimate success, the actual process of implementation and the need to engage fully with the planned change will likely require a change of culture and practices. Achieving such change can often be considerably more challenging than getting users to subscribe to it in principle. That is, while stakeholders may recognise the need for change, and understand and agree with the rationale for the proposed innovation, this does not – in and of itself – guarantee absolute commitment to its practical implications, which often remain largely unappreciated until such time as users really begin to implement the new practices it entails. When the logistical and workload implications begin to make themselves felt, there will often be resistance – or at least a dragging of feet – which can ultimately prove fatal to the innovation, the diffusion of which, Markee notes (echoing Rogers), needs to reach a critical mass if it is to take off:

> Diffusion may be expressed as the percentage of adopters who implement an innovation over a given period of time (Rogers, 1983). Figure 2 shows a typically S-shaped diffusion curve. The lazy slope of the toe of the curve shows that adoption at first occurs very slowly; if a critical mass of approximately 25 percent of potential adopters accept the innovation, it may take off. At this point, the slope in the mid-section of the curve becomes steeper (i.e., the rate of adoption accelerates) as people 'jump on the bandwagon'. Finally, the curve plateaus as diffusion slows down and eventually tapers off, either because every potential adopter has adopted or else because the innovation stalls. (1993, p. 235)

The reality is that, while a university's senior management may sanction change, if resistance is of an extent and duration that suggests the innovation is unlikely to gain traction and bed in, it may lose confidence and patience and withdraw its support or simply leave the innovation to die a natural death. This is especially likely to happen where there is a growing feeling of ill-will towards it by stakeholders generally, a growing sense of struggle in coming to terms with the challenges of implementation, or where there exist other initiatives which senior management see as more pressing and thus a more productive use of their time and energy. This final point is important: senior management will often be attuned to the mood of academic staff, and if they sense that staff are feeling disgruntled, this can be seen by senior management as creating an undesirable climate for the introduction of other changes, the implementation of which are considered a higher priority.

The embedding of academic literacies within the curriculum, as described in Chapter 6, is a good example of an innovation which is seen by those tasked with implementing it as an appropriate response to students' language needs. However, for academic staff who will need to identify the academic literacies of their discipline, re-work the curriculum in order to encompass them, and eventually teach them, this can be threatening not only in terms of the added workload it will involve but also of their perceived – and in many cases actual – lack of the knowledge and pedagogical skills needed to furnish students with an understanding and working knowledge of academic literacies. This point brings me to another factor that will influence the extent to which an innovation really takes hold or not, namely professional development.

7.3.2   Professional development

Almost any innovation, whether within the education field or otherwise, is likely to require professional development for those implementing it. Failure to identify areas in which this is required and to ensure that, once identified, training needs are met, is short-sighted, for no matter how timely and appropriate the innovation is, it will ultimately fail if those tasked with implementing it do not have the skills and confidence needed to do so effectively. Any such skills deficit will ultimately mean that the end-users of the innovation – the students – will fail to benefit from it and will likely react negatively as a result. And once those at the coalface begin to struggle with the innovation, traction can quickly be lost as demoralisation creeps in and faith in the idea and its feasibility dissipates. This is inclined to happen all the more quickly when changes implicated in the innovation are significant and demanding of those required to implement them. Drawing on the work of Maslow, 1970, Fullan, 1991 and Hersey and Blanchard, 1993, Waters and Vilches acknowledge the importance of professional development to successful innovation, citing *application* as one of the four levels of innovation implementation need. This, they say, 'is to do with ensuring that the process by which the users actually test the worked-out innovations is monitored and supported in such a way that the necessary level of personal, practical understanding and expertise is built up' (Waters and Vilches, 2001, p. 134).

Embedding academic literacies in the curriculum in the manner described in Chapter 6 can certainly be regarded as 'significant and demanding' – what

Markee (1993, p. 232) describes as 'fundamental change' that involves 'a modification of pedagogical values' – and laying the necessary groundwork in terms of spelling out clearly and precisely what needs to be done and why, and ensuring that appropriate professional development opportunities are forthcoming, is therefore crucial. In this case, academic teaching staff need to fully comprehend what is meant by academic literacies and how they are related to but distinct from general language proficiency. An understanding of this distinction is, in turn, important to their understanding of what the requirements are of them with respect to the innovation; namely that they will not be expected to be English language specialists and to impart linguistic knowledge to students that they do not and cannot be expected to have, but rather will need to impart to them the academic literacies of their discipline. In order to do this, and with the help of the help of English language specialists and academic developers, they will need to articulate those literacies as well as develop the pedagogical skills to teach them effectively. And, as I have indicated previously (6.3.2), this is where training enters the equation: training which may consist of workshops, the modelling of lessons, observations with feedback sessions etc., conducted by English language specialists and, where they exist, academic developers responsible for supporting curriculum development. Academic teaching staff and those supporting them in the process will also need to be able to think about the curriculum and assessment practices and consider how and where to embed academic literacies so that they are taught within contexts where they are most relevant and the need to understand them naturally arises.[1] Finally, they may be required to upskill in terms of their technological competence if they are to create online resources, download applications and materials, moderate and engage in blogs and forums, create podcasts, provide electronic English language feedback on and upload students' assignments, and process post-enrolment language tests administered, marked and recorded electronically.

7.3.3   Technological requirements

Professional development requirements involving technological literacy presuppose the existence of the relevant technology. Certainly, in an increasingly technologically-driven world the implications of innovation are likely to extend to technology. That is, the existence of particular hardware and software may be either an essential prerequisite for the innovation to be implemented or an important element in making certain that its implementation is enacted to greatest effect. This would be the case, for example, where the kind of electronically-administered post-enrolment English language test referred to above (and discussed in Chapters

---

[1] See Chapter 6 for a more detailed discussion of this.

5 and 8) is adopted. Here, there would need to be a suitable platform for the delivery of the test as well as for its automatic marking, where possible and practicable. In cases where students are able to take the test as and when they choose and/or when there are restrictions on how often they can take the test within a given period, the technology would need to be able to alert English language staff when a test submission has been made, as well as keep a record of students who have taken the test and the frequency with which they have done so.

Similarly, technology would need to be able to support the provision of electronic feedback on students' assignments in respect of English, where available, as well as the development of online resources.

7.3.4   Other resources

Other resources may include:
- Pedagogical materials – for example, textbooks, sample texts, examples of student writing, and sample assessment tasks that relate to students' disciplines. In the teaching of general proficiency, such texts would allow for the embedding of points of learning within contexts of immediate relevance to students, while in relation to academic literacy, they would (a) support academic content tutors' efforts to impart academic literacies to their students, and (b) provide English language tutors with a set of resources through which to support academic content tutors' efforts to teach academic literacies.
- A bank of tests – for the purposes of post-enrolment language assessment and/or self-assessment, where this option is selected over an assessed piece of coursework (see sections 5.4.4 and 5.4.5).
- Additional staff – where needed, to ensure that the innovation can be implemented effectively as originally envisaged. In the case of the decentralised model of English language provision proposed in Chapter 6, it is likely that individual, faculty-based English language teams would necessitate the recruitment of additional English language teaching staff.

7.3.5   Personal ownership of the innovation

The topmost level of Waters and Vilches' hierarchy of innovation implementation needs is that of integration. Here, they say, 'scope should be given for the innovation to become the personal "property" of the users, through its personal development, in ways determined as far as possible by the users' individual priorities' (2001, p. 134). As we have already seen in this chapter, the process of securing from users and other stakeholders initial buy-in to the innovation is crucial if the point of implementation is to be reached. It is also almost certainly a prerequisite to users feeling a sense of personal ownership of it. However, the two things are not one and the same. Having agreed *in principle* with the need for the innovation, that agreement subsequently needs to be translated into vigorous engagement in the implementation process if the change envisaged is to come to fruition and be sustained. Such engagement will both thrive from and promote feelings of personal ownership and, consequently, those driving innovation need to think strategically about how best to engage and gain the commitment of users. This means allowing them rein to grow and adapt the innovation in ways that reflect their particular contexts and ideas about learning without compromising its essential integrity. This allows for personalisation of the innovation and gives it meaning for them. Once this has been achieved, the chances of the innovation bedding into the culture increase dramatically.

The kind of decentralised model of language provision advocated in Chapter 6 exemplifies this idea. Here, although there is a common vision for English language provision across the various university faculties, the way in which that vision is realised by the different faculty English language teams is open to local interpretation and negotiation. This might, for example, be felt in the way in which they organise workshops and the basis on which they establish credit-bearing courses in light of consultations with academic staff within the faculty. Similarly, while a basic template defining the format of each faculty English language website may be non-negotiable on the grounds that it needs to be familiar to and easily navigated by students studying across different faculties, within that template there can be flexibility that gives each faculty English language team the freedom to adjust the content and sub-categories according to their own preferences and what they think will best meet the needs of the students in their faculty, and what will have greatest meaning and relevance for them.

Ultimately, of course, despite the best intentions and no matter how well rationalised and implemented it may be, an innovation can fail simply because it does not succeed in producing the degree of student learning anticipated due to the principles of learning on which it is based proving to be unsound and/or because students simply do not engage with it to the extent expected and needed for significant learning to take place. Particularly with regard to innovations that directly impact on pedagogy and to which learners are therefore directly exposed, it is possible to rationalise an innovation yet end up with something that is simply unappealing and unengaging to those it targets, and this again makes the argument for piloting innovations on a limited scale in the first instance a cogent one.

7.3.6   *Keeping stakeholders informed*

The importance of communicating developments concerning the implementation and diffusion of the innovation cannot be underestimated. Maintaining an ongoing dialogue with all those involved helps sustain project momentum and keeps the innovation alive in the sense of being in stakeholders' consciousness, a focus or centre-point of activity, and a reminder of what is being done and what needs to be done, and its significance. It also helps to ensure that experiences, both positive and negative, are shared. In the case of the model of assessment and provision I have proposed in Chapter 6, this kind of sharing of experience would, for example, take place between the different faculty-based English language teams who, within the essential parameters of the model, would be encouraged to exercise their collective creativity and realise its implementation in any way they deem most appropriate and effective. Some initiatives will meet with success, while others will not, and although there may be contextual differences between the different faculties, sharing experiences nonetheless allows other teams to benefit and avoids inefficiencies that can result from failure to communicate the results they achieve: it's better to use the time that would otherwise have been spent on adopting an implementation strategy that had already proven to be ineffectual elsewhere, on devising and implementing an alternative strategy.

The importance of good communication and the effective dissemination of progress and experiences during the implementation phase of innovation, until such time as it has bedded into the culture, also lies in the fact that rates of staff turnover can be very high in university contexts, among both academic and English language staff and, particularly, administrative staff. The latter frequently switch roles or undertake secondments and will, in all probability, be involved in English language innovation, if only to provide advice and guidance to students on what language development opportunities are available and how to access them, as well as on processes and procedures such as those associated with post-enrolment English language assessment.

7.3.7   *Reviewing, evaluating and fine-tuning*

Finally, the ultimate success of any innovation requires that the process of implementation be monitored, regardless of whether or not the innovation has undergone trialling. Innovators and those tasked with implementation need to be responsive to feedback and also sensitive to issues that arise during the course of rolling out the innovation, for any significant change process, no matter how well conceived and despite having run the gauntlet of the organisation's approval process and been subject to detailed scrutiny, will have fragilities and come up against unforeseen obstacles requiring modifications and adaptations. By having feedback mechanisms in place that enable them to be responsive, those driving change are seen as being in touch with the real world and their willingness to listen both further enhances their credibility and helps to maintain the support of those upon whose shoulders the success of the innovation ultimately rests. As such, innovators need to accept that the adjustment of their ideas 'in practice' is an almost inevitable consequence of change that is significant enough to constitute innovation. They need to be prepared and willing to accept change where necessary but also astute enough to judge whether calls for change by those implementing the innovation are well-reasoned and thus justified, and not simply a means of avoiding the kind of discomfort associated with disturbance of the status quo.

7.4   Summary

This chapter has focused on some of the critical factors that determine whether or not an innovation succeeds, firstly, in terms of securing the approval and support of the institution, including management and those tasked with implementation, and secondly, in terms of its becoming embedded in the institutional culture in a way that ensures its sustainability. It has been suggested that, with regard to the former, success can be analysed according to three dimensions: the personal, the political and the organisational. The ability to manifest certain traits and behaviours in all three areas will determine the nature of the reception the proposed innovation receives, for crucially, each dimension individually constitutes a necessary but not sufficient condition for innovation to win the approval and support needed to move to the implementation phase.

Whether, ultimately, it becomes embedded in the institutional culture and prospers depends on other factors. These include a willingness to engage with efforts to change that culture where necessary; the identification of relevant professional development needs and the provision of development resources appropriate to and commensurate with those needs; an appreciation of the technological and other hardware, software and human resources required to implement the innovation; genuine commitment to the innovation and a sense of ownership of it by those tasked with its implementation; and maintaining good channels of communication with all stakeholders, both with respect to keeping them informed of developments and the sharing of experiences, as well as listening to and, where appropriate, acting on feedback from those implementing the innovation and from its end users – in this case, the students.

In the next and final chapter, I will report on an example of innovation implemented in Australia and based on the model articulated in Chapter 6. The report will give an account of the motivation behind the innovation as well as the processes and challenges with respect to securing support for the model, attempting to embed it in the culture, and addressing issues that arose during its implementation. Among other things, the report serves to highlight the fact that, regardless of the extent of the preparatory work carried out, innovation can be – and usually is – a somewhat messy and unpredictable business that requires perseverance and well-developed problem-solving skills; as such, it is most certainly not for the faint-hearted.

8   Innovation in English language provision in higher education: an Australian case study

8.1   Introduction

The purpose of this final chapter is to describe a case study which serves to illustrate, in concrete terms, many of the issues discussed in the foregoing chapters and which come into play when attempting to bring about institution-wide change in relation to the way in which the question of students' English language competence is addressed by English-medium universities. The study focuses on a university in Australia which, eight years ago, sought to develop a strategy for addressing what I have referred to as 'the English language question'; a strategy that would respond effectively to students' English language needs and thereby help ensure that they would maximally fulfil their academic potential and be well placed to meet the requirements and expectations of employers. Such a strategy, while desirable in and of itself, was also seen as a necessary response to government-driven regulatory changes, discussed in detail in Chapter 2 and concerning English language provision within institutions of higher education. Most particularly, it was a response to AUQA's document titled *Good Practice Principles for English language proficiency for international students in Australian universities*, published in 2009, and to that of its successor *English language standards for higher education*, produced and released under the auspices of TEQSA. As we saw in Chapter 2, this document was heralded as the basis for future audits in respect of the calibre and adequacy of universities' English language assessment processes and provision, with a view to ensuring that students entered their degree programmes with a level of language commensurate with the linguistic demands of their courses and with access to language development opportunities that would allow them to increase their communicative competence during their lifecycle as students. The Good Practice Principles document has been reinforced by recent revisions to the Educating Services for Overseas Students (ESOS) Act, designed to ensure that English language entry levels for commencing students are consistent and that institutions have adequate services in place to support students once enrolled.

In 2012, the university concerned finally introduced a whole-of-institution approach to English language proficiency in an effort to ensure that it succeeded in responding appropriately, creatively and systematically to students' English language needs, and in doing so to the expectations articulated in these regulatory initiatives.

It bears reiterating that, while it does represent a particular view, the case study described is certainly *not* intended as a blueprint of an ideal model that all English-medium universities should be striving to implement. To present it in that spirit would be presumptuous, for if there is one thing recent research into English language provision in higher education has shown, it is that there *is* no silver-bullet response to the English language question, and while there may be universal principles underlying good practice which should steer decision-making, each institution needs to address the question according to the characteristics of its own particular context and the constraints under which it operates.

In particular, the case study described in the following pages serves to illustrate that what finally gets implemented will almost never be a perfect reflection of what was originally envisaged by those attempting to bring about change. During the process of seeking institutional approval it will inevitably be transformed as compromises are negotiated. Furthermore, as we saw in Chapter 7, even once approval has been secured, the process of implementation will throw up unforeseen problems that will require those at the helm to generate creative and effective solutions, sometimes at very short notice. This fact is vividly illustrated through the attempt, described in the following sections, to embed academic literacies in the curriculum and assess students' English language competence post enrolment – two notions that have formed key foci for discussion in the preceding chapters. While I believe and have sought to demonstrate that there are good reasons for universities to institute these processes, they can – and certainly did – bring with them considerable challenges.

8.2   The institutional context

The institution at which the innovation described here was conceived and implemented was a large multi-campus university based in South Australia, boasting a considerable regional presence and comprising four metropolitan campuses broadly reflecting the division of the university into four 'Divisions' (or faculties): Education, Arts and Social Sciences (EASS); Health Sciences (HSC); Business and Law (BUE); and IT, Engineering and the Environment (ITEE). The institution operated on a semester-basis and its mission highlighted the educating of professionals, as well as concerns with social justice and engagement with the community, both locally and internationally. These principles were enshrined in its founding legislation and were traditionally highly valued. The University had a long-term commitment to widening participation, and as such it supported students from diverse educational and socio-economic backgrounds to attend and achieve in higher education. Around twenty-seven per cent of students were classified as 'low-socioeconomic status' (Wheelan, 2009). The total University student population was in excess of 33,000, of which approximately thirty-five per cent were international students. While the great majority of these studied in South Australia, a proportion did so in their home countries – predominantly located within Asia. Consistent with Australia's reputation as a country of immigrants, there was a significant section of the university's student population for whom English was not a first language but who were classified as home students on the basis of residency and/or citizenship.

Many of the university's international and, indeed, domestic students originated from countries within Asia and the Far East, and a high proportion of these tended to enrol in the Divisions of Health Sciences (Nursing in particular) and Business and Law, followed by rather fewer in IT, Engineering and the Environment, and considerably smaller numbers in Education, Arts and Social Sciences. Unsurprisingly, therefore, it was in Health Sciences and Business and Law that the issue of English language was most salient, for it was here that the greatest number of students struggled with English and risked either failing or underperforming in their courses and/or being unsuccessful in their bids to acquire professional accreditation, with obvious potential reputational fallout for the university. Put differently, those Divisions that were more dependent on students of non-English-speaking backgrounds were potentially – and actually – more vulnerable to the risks associated with insufficient levels of English language competence.

Traditionally, English language provision at the university was managed centrally under the auspices of the Learning and Teaching Unit (Deputy Director: Academic Learning Services), although delivered by staff based at each of the four campuses – approximately three English language teachers per campus. Among other things, this avoided excess travelling between campuses by English language teaching staff. The Learning and Teaching Unit had a suite of offices on each of its four campuses, occupied by its Campus Support Services team, which comprised Campus Support Officers, International Support Officers and Administrative Officers, whose roles consisted in part of supporting students looking for English language assistance by providing information on the provision available and booking appointments with English language teachers (called Language and Learning Advisors – a term widely used within the Australian university context).

The approach to English was very much generic EAP and study skills, although there were a number of sporadic, rather piecemeal initiatives to develop workshops that reflected the particular language demands of certain disciplines. These typically arose from negotiations that were the product of personal connections between English language teaching staff and academic staff based within the departments concerned. They certainly did not reflect any systematic effort to adopt an academic literacies approach to English language across the institution. Alongside a programme of EAP and study skills workshops, open to all students across all faculties, the main form of English language support was one-on-one consultations. These could be initiated by the students themselves, who would make appointments in person at the Learning and Teaching Unit offices located at the relevant campus, or by academic staff through an electronic referral system. A database was maintained that recorded all such consultations and, among other things, provided information on the number of consultations a given student had had and their broad focus (specified according to predefined categories of language issues). Although there was no limit placed on the number of consultations to which a student was entitled, records indicated that the vast majority of students had no more than two consultations, and in most cases only one. The were some instances of workshops that were embedded within academic content courses; however, these were, again, relatively rare and tended to be the result of personal connections between academic staff in the department concerned and a Language Learning Advisor.

The Language and Learning Advisors were employed on Level A[1] academic contracts; as such, there was a requirement for them to be research active and twenty per cent of their time (i.e. one working day) was earmarked for this activity.[2] Although many Language Learning Advisors were professionally active, and keen to develop themselves and keep abreast of developments in the field, publication outputs were sporadic and tended to be associated with a core group within the team. The majority of teachers presented quite regularly at conferences and hosted and/or organised national English language conferences, such as the biennial conference of the Association for Academic Language and Learning.

Although there had been a number of initiatives at the University designed to evaluate and improve its English language provision, for a variety of reasons – such as key personnel leaving to take up posts elsewhere – these failed to take root, and there was a sense of frustration among staff that the issue had not really been taken in hand and addressed at an institution-wide level. It was decided, therefore, that a Senior Consultant with a strong background in ELT and long experience of working within the higher education sector should be employed, with the remit to scope the institution's current provision, submit a report of findings and proposals for change, and oversee the implementation of

---

[1] Level A is the most junior level academic grade.
[2] It is notable that other 'regular' academic staff (i.e. who were not Language and Learning Advisors) had a forty per cent workload allowance for research activity.

those proposals. A Senior Consultant, seconded from the University's Research Centre for Languages and Cultures, was appointed in 2009, shortly after publication of the *Good Practice Principles*, to steer what became known as *The English Language Proficiency Project* (henceforth the ELPP). He conducted his work under the auspices of the Learning and Teaching Unit, where he worked closely with the Director of the Unit and the Deputy Vice Chancellor: Academic, whose backing and ongoing support for the model ultimately proposed would be critical in determining its success.

After approximately six months, during which the consultant acquired familiarity with the national, institutional and regulatory context, and conducted a series of interviews[3] with key individuals at the University, a report was produced and formed the basis of a paper which was subsequently tabled shortly thereafter at a meeting of the institution's Senior Management Group, chaired by the Vice-Chancellor. It received a mixed reception. While it was generally acknowledged that there was a need to reshape the approach to English language currently in place, there were concerns over the scale of the changes proposed and the impact on and reaction of staff. In particular, there was considerable trepidation over the idea, recommended in this initial report, of mandatory testing post-enrolment of students' English language proficiency. That trepidation was based on many of the issues discussed in Chapter 5, section 5.3, including stakeholder perceptions and the associated potential for damage to the University's reputation, brand and market share. As a result of these concerns, the Senior Management Group decided not to ratify the proposal but instead suggested that it be reworked and subjected to a more wide-ranging and longer period of consultation with stakeholders within the institution. This, it believed, would help ensure that the wider community felt both that they had had sufficient opportunity to engage in deliberations about the change process and that the proposal had been adequately informed by reality on the ground. This was seen as crucial if the proposed changes were to be sympathetically received. Furthermore, it was agreed that alternative approaches to post-enrolment language assessment should be investigated which did not make it compulsory for students, and thereby reduced the level of perceived risk to the institution.

The initial failure to secure ratification by the University's Senior Management Group of the proposed changes to English language provision is the point of departure for the remainder of this chapter, which concludes by

---

[3] These interviews provided a picture not only of current provision and reactions to it, but also of staff attitudes to the English language issue and views of why it needed to be more effectively addressed and how. Moreover, they served to shed light on the problems academic staff faced in the different divisions and departments as a result of weak English language skills among students and the constraints that militated against certain kinds of interventions intended to address the issue.

looking at the challenges presented during the implementation phase and includes some of the findings of a recently-conducted study which attempted to evaluate what necessarily (given its scale and ambition) remains a work in progress, and sheds light on those elements that have been well received and successfully implemented, on the one hand, and on the other, those that have met with greater resistance and less success, and why. These findings highlight the fact that the course of innovation rarely runs smoothly and that, almost inevitably, during implementation there will be a need for flexibility and well-developed problem-solving skills among those driving the innovation. They also offer insights that should help institutions looking to develop their own models of English language provision to adopt approaches that are likely to meet with success and to avoid those that are not.

8.3   Essentials of the model

The model proposed and ultimately adopted by the university as a strategic response to the context described above, and to the broader, more universal drivers identified in Chapter 1, was essentially a realisation of many of the guiding principles discussed in Chapters 3, 5 and 6 of this volume. It was designated 'L^3' (Language, Learning & Literacies) and comprised four dimensions: a conceptualisation of English language proficiency, an approach to post-enrolment English language assessment, a decentralised architecture for the management and delivery of English language services, and an account of the nature of English language provision and the mechanisms for determining access to it.

8.3.1   The conceptualisation of English language proficiency

Statements of the following kind (see section 3.1 of this volume) that appear in the literature reflect the variability in how the notion of English language proficiency is understood:

The above discussion shows that ELP in higher education is being debated but that we are still struggling with our terminology and definitions. What is clear is that ELP in higher education settings is complex and challenging to define (Barrett-Lennard et al., 2011) and also that we have no agreed definition either of the construct itself or of the level of the construct that is appropriate (Dunworth, 2010; Webb, 2012). (IEAA, 2013, p. 83)

This perception of variability was reinforced in the early stages of the ELPP, during which stakeholders' views and opinions were canvassed. As Murray and Hicks (2014) note, 'English language proficiency was prone to diverse interpretations, with people referring to study skills, academic skills, English for academic purposes, communicative competence, academic literacy, academic literacies, communication skills, and professional communication – often seeming to use some or all of these terms synonymously' (p. 4). They continue:

This was cause for concern: the importance of a common understanding of the construct cannot be over-estimated, not only in terms of a clearly conceived model that is defensible to auditors but also in terms of getting buy-in from stakeholders across the university – a key to the success of any such institution-wide initiative. (Ibid. p, 4)

With this is mind, it was determined at the outset of the project that a clear definition of English language proficiency which made sense to all stakeholders was critical to the successful design and implementation of a systematic English language strategy. Eventually, the tripartite conceptualisation of English language proficiency articulated in section 3.3 was conceived and adopted. This conceptualisation can be summarised as follows:

Component 1: General proficiency – Those skills that furnish the user with the ability to communicate for the purposes of everyday, general communication. As such, general proficiency approximates to Cummins' Basic Interpersonal Communication Skills (BICS).

Component 2: Academic literacy – Those literacy practices pertinent to individual disciplines and conversancy in which is required in order to meet the academic and, where relevant, professional demands of those disciplines and thereby lay claim to membership of their respective communities of practice.

Component 3: Professional communication skills – Those skills and strategies that bear on communicative performance in professional settings, including intercultural competence; interpersonal skills that encompass an understanding of the pragmatics of communication and associated notions of accommodation, politeness/'face', turn-taking and awareness of self and other; conversancy in the discourses and behaviours associated with particular professional domains of use; leadership skills; and non-verbal communication skills.

While these three components can be regarded as conceptually distinct – an important factor in the consideration of how to structure language provision, as will become evident later in this chapter – it was recognised that, in practice, they overlap (see section 3.3.2). Thus, for example, the acquisition of academic literacy and professional communication skills presupposes a level of general proficiency in English; and similarly, academic literacies will presuppose a conversancy in discourses frequently shared with those of contexts of professional communication.

During the process of presenting the ELPP model and its rationale to stakeholders across the university, the tripartite conceptualisation described was very positively received and it was generally felt that it added helpful clarity to the notion of language proficiency (Harper, 2013). This conceptual buy-in helped provide the model with credibility and momentum in the crucial early stages of the project.

8.3.2   Embedding academic literacies in the curriculum

As discussed in detail in section 6.3, it was established early on that it could not be assumed that any students, whether native or non-native speakers of English, would come to their studies with the necessary understanding of those academic literacies pertinent to their disciplines. In the case of non-native speakers in particular, the gatekeeping tests they had sat in order to demonstrate that their level of English language competence met the language conditions of entry stipulated by their receiving universities were designed to assess general academic English language skills and were not nuanced in such a way that they could assess students' conversancy in the specific academic literacies of particular disciplines. Thus, while some students would be entering university with some awareness of those literacies, such knowledge would, in all likelihood, be highly variable. For this reason it was decided that academic literacies needed to be imparted to students within the regular curriculum, for knowledge of those literacies was fundamental to understanding and engaging with their disciplines, and consequently the university and its constituent departments needed to feel confident that all students would stand to benefit from tuition in those literacies. Furthermore, and in line with findings reported in the literature (Bohemia, Farrell, Power and Salter, 2007; Curnow and Liddicoat, 2008; Percy and Skillen, 2000; Wingate, 2006; Wingate, Andon and Cogo, 2011), it was felt that their acquisition was best assured by embedding them in contexts that were meaningful and engaging for students and at points in the delivery of the curriculum where they naturally emerged as relevant and necessary.

The embedding process was trialled in eight programmes across the four faculties of the University – two programmes in each faculty – and required close collaboration between relevant stakeholders, including course Programme Directors, Language and Learning Coordinators, Language and Learning Advisors, Programme Directors, Academic Developers and Faculty Deans of Teaching and Learning. It was decided that initially there would be some advantage in focussing on only two or three academic literacies as a way of helping those involved gain familiarity with the embedding process and avoiding overwhelming Programme Directors and their teams. It was felt that to be overly ambitious, and seek to move too quickly in the early stages, could be counter-productive and lead to a backlash. For each course targeted in the trial, its aims, learning outcomes and assessment methods were established and the pertinent academic literacies identified and scaffolded. In doing so, experience gained previously from attempts to embed academic literacies in the

University's *Bachelor of Applied Linguistics* and *Bachelor of Aviation* programmes was drawn upon. Despite this, as I will show in my discussion of
issues that arose during the model's implementation (section 8.5), the embedding process would prove to be a very demanding one.

8.3.3 Implementing post-enrolment language assessment

Given that academic literacies were to be embedded in the curriculum as a way
of ensuring that all students had the opportunity to acquire those literacies
needed to engage sufficiently with their disciplines, it was felt that there was
little point in testing students' competence in this area. It was decided, instead,
that PELA should focus on general proficiency, for this was seen as crucial if
students of non-English-speaking backgrounds were to understand the academic literacy tuition they would be receiving within the curriculum.
Furthermore, it would also constitute an important factor in their overall
engagement with their studies as well as their social integration into the life
of the university and beyond.

After considerable discussion, it was decided that a test would be used to
assess students' level of general proficiency post-enrolment and that, in
response to the concerns of senior management and the logistical challenges
envisaged, the test would not be mandated for any students. This was in
contrast to the policy adopted in a number of other institutions where PELA,
in some form, was compulsory for all students for whom English was not a first
language or for only those students who had met minimum English language
entry requirements but fell below a specified proficiency threshold.

While the scoping of English language provision was being constructed and
a new model conceived, a test was simultaneously being jointly trialled with
Melbourne University. The test, dubbed the Academic English Screening Test
(AEST), had been designed by Melbourne University's Language Testing
Research Centre (LTRC), a specialist centre in language testing and evaluation,
and was a development of an earlier iteration, the DELA (Diagnostic English
Language Assessment) test, developed and used by the University of Auckland
(see Elder and Erlam, 2001; Elder and von Randow, 2002; Elder, 2003). As its
name suggests, the test was a screening rather than a diagnostic test, the
purpose of which Elder and Knoch describe the in the following terms:

The AEST is designed to provide a quick and efficient means of identifying those
students who are likely to experience difficulties in coping with the English language
demands of their academic study in a large and linguistically diverse student population.
It is based on the assumption of universal testing, rather than the targeting of particular
categories of student, and builds on work done at the University of Auckland and the
University of Melbourne over the past decade. (2009, p. 1)

I have described the format of the AEST as follows:

> The test comprises three components: a c-test (text completion) exercise—shown to be a good predictor of language proficiency (Eckes & Grotjahn, 2006; Klein-Braley, 1997); a cloze elide (speed reading) exercise, shown to be an efficient measure of linguistic abilities and a good predictor of scores on more time-consuming performance-based measures (Alderson, 2000; Davies, 1989, 1990; Elder & von Randow, 2008); and a written component in the form of an argumentative essay. (Murray, 2010a, p. 355)

The test was of fifty-five minutes' duration, with the three components taking fifteen, ten and thirty minutes to complete, respectively. It was adapted for delivery via the Moodle (online) platform and was thus administered electronically on the grounds that this would be less demanding of Language and Learning Advisors' time and less costly in terms of materials and human resources. Furthermore, a test delivered electronically would lend itself more readily to electronic marking and the efficiencies associated with this. Two of the three tasks that comprised the test eventually adopted (the C-test[4] and the cloze elide exercise) were marked electronically, and one (the short argumentative essay) manually. While the existence of technologies that allow for the electronic marking of written texts was recognised, the cost associated with these was deemed prohibitive and, as a relatively recent development, they were still seen as somewhat unproven. It was, however, agreed that the question of whether or not to take advantage of such technology should be reviewed at a future date as part of an ongoing evaluation of the model.

Three versions of the AEST were trialled over an eighteen-month period. Drawing on Elder and Knoch's 2009 report, I described (Murray, 2010a) the results of the initial AEST trial as follows:

> Although it will be subject to further refinement based on the ongoing trials, results obtained to date are promising, with the test proving to be a valid, reliable, and efficient measure of the full range of students' English language proficiency and able, in particular, to discriminate well between native and non-native speakers and between those born in English medium countries and those born elsewhere (see Elder & Knoch, 2009). (p. 355)

Although the university ultimately chose not opt for 'universal testing', it was decided that all students, whether native or non-native speakers of English, domestic or international, should be free to take the test and to access the English language development opportunities available. Although it was

---

[4] C-tests typically comprise a number of short texts within which the first sentence is left unchanged in order to create a meaningful context for the sentences that follow. From the second sentence onwards, every second word has the second half of its letters deliberately omitted. Test takers are required to reconstruct the original text by inserting the missing letters. As Elder and Knoch (2009) note, among the advantages of the C-test are its higher reliability indices compared to the cloze test, where every nth word is entirely omitted, and the fact that it is more broadly representative of the academic domain, as a wider variety of text-types can be sampled.

strongly felt that it was inappropriate to describe native speaker students as lacking in proficiency, it was recognised that in light of the diverse student demographic – in part the result of the University's widening participation agenda – the language of some would exhibit *dialectal* features considered not in keeping with the requirements and expectations of the academy. While, in some respects, at least, those features may be of a different order from the linguistic infelicities of non-native speaker students, it was nonetheless felt that this fact should make them no less eligible to take the test and benefit from the English language provision available. Consequently, equal access was deemed appropriate according to equity principles as well as for educational reasons. What could not be quantified at this stage, however, was the extent of student uptake of the test – something I shall return to later.

Logistical, security and timing issues   Electronic delivery of the test raised a number of concerns among the project team relating to logistics and security. Although its status as an as yet untried optional test meant that it was difficult to predict student take-up, nonetheless the security implications of a scenario where there were more students wishing to take the test than there were workstations available had to be carefully considered, for if students were not able to take the test simultaneously, then there could be security breaches between different administrations of the test. Furthermore, it would likely prove extremely difficult to schedule the test at a time suitable for all potential test-takers on all four campuses of the university.

Upon consideration, however, these potential security risks were mitigated by a number of factors. Firstly, and most importantly, the C-test and cloze–elide tasks did not lend themselves to cheating, and the essay title could easily be changed should the test be administered at different times, for different cohorts sitting the test in different locations. Secondly, it was intended that the test should, in part, function as a filtering mechanism that would determine the level of access test-takers would have to English language support. In essence, students who scored below a predetermined threshold and were thereby identi-fied as 'at risk' would not only have access to those forms of support universally available, such as electronic resources and workshops, but also to those more intensive and costly forms of support, namely one-on-one consultations with a Language and Learning Advisor and electronic language feedback on written assignments (see section 8.3.4, below). In this regard, I have reported (2014) that:

This access or 'filtering' function meant that there was little motivation for students to cheat on what was, anyway, an optional test; indeed, there was more concern expressed by some of the English language team – and other university stakeholders who were consulted – that students might be inclined to fail deliberately in order to secure such access. On reflection, however, it was considered unlikely that such an eventuality would materialise on the grounds that students confident in their language ability would tend to be more interested in successfully engaging with their coursework than in receiving language support services from which, on balance, they would be likely to derive less benefit ... this perception was reinforced somewhat in that where students did attend 1:1 consultations post-test, they seemed genuinely to be at the weaker end of the spectrum and to be in need of assistance with their language. (p. 330)

The fact of having established that concerns over security would be unlikely to have any basis in fact had implications for the scheduling of the AEST. Most significantly, it meant that students could take the test any time, in any location and on virtually any computer, provided it had minimal specification software and an internet connection. This offered a number of advantages:

- It increased the likelihood that students would sit the test, as they could do so at their own convenience and in a low-stress environment, such as their own home.
- It addressed the possible logistical problem of there being an insufficient number of workstations.
- It helped ensure that the marking of tests would be more spread out and thus less intensive.
- It addressed concerns that if the test were administered at a set time at the beginning of the year, students may be too distracted by the many other activities going on during what would be an orientation period, and, as a result, less likely to know about and sit the test.
- It allowed for the fact that different students would be motivated to sit the test by different triggers at different times. For example, while some students might feel insecure about their English from the outset and thus take the test at the first opportunity, others might be overly confident about their ability and only realise their linguistic shortcomings after a few lectures and seminars and/or receiving feedback on their first assignment.
- It provided an opportunity for students to take responsibility for their own learning – an important principle highlighted thus in the Good Practice Principles:

Students have responsibilities for further developing their English language proficiency during their study at university and are advised of these responsibilities prior to enrolment. (DEEWR, 2009, p. 3)

Although, for reasons explained above, it seemed unlikely that students would cheat on the test, there were concerns expressed during discussions early on that students may deliberately *fail* the test if in doing so they were assured access to the more labour-intensive, costly forms of provision described in section 8.3.4. However, it was felt that given the other demands their degree programmes would be placing on them, students were unlikely, on the whole, to be looking to spend time taking up English language improvement opportunities that they may not need, and as such it made sense to perform 'authentically' on the test in order for them to be able to judge more realistically how best to apportion their time according to their needs.

Another concern raised by some academic staff members during the consultation phase of the project's development was that if gaining access to certain forms of provision meant having to sit a test, many students would simply not bother, one result being that the test would effectively act as a deterrent to students pursuing opportunities for language development, despite being in need of such opportunities. This situation is described in Dunworth's research, in which a number of participants expressed the view that 'students might suffer from "test fatigue", be reluctant to take PELA and unmotivated to seek out developmental assistance if identified as appropriate' (2009, p. A-8).

It was felt that the very word 'test' was likely to further increase the probability of students opting out the AEST, and some consideration was consequently given to the name of the test and how best to present it in a non-threatening way. It was eventually decided to call the test ELSAT (English Language Self-Assessment Tool).[5] In addition, it was made clear in all publicity materials and on the L^3 website that the test was optional, that it existed solely for the benefit of the students, and that students' scores on the test would neither have any ramifications for their academic progress nor appear on their academic transcripts. Sensitivities about the presentation of ELSAT were such that even references to 'sitting ELSAT' were avoided in light of the collocation of sit with test.

As ELSAT could be taken at any time by students, it was important that completed tests were dealt with systematically. An electronic process was therefore set up whereby the Language and Learning team was alerted, via a dedicated email account (checked manually each day), to any new instances of tests having been completed. The written component of the test was manually marked,[6] a final test score calculated based on the individual's performance on all three test components (the other two having been marked electronically), and the student informed of their result, along with advice on the kinds of provision they were entitled to access. It was the intention that, in time, most of these processes should be automated, thereby increasing efficiencies.

It was decided, in consultation with the test developers, that the objectively-scored exercises (i.e. the C-test and cloze–elide) should be used to predict who was linguistically at risk in their academic studies and who was sufficiently linguistically proficient. The writing score was to serve only as a verification measure for those students who fell into a defined 'borderline' category. This

---

[5] ELSAT was a licenced version of the AEST.

[6] All members of the Language and Learning team underwent an afternoon of rater training using anchor sets and conducted by Melbourne University's Language Testing Research Centre.

would represent a cost saving to the university as it would reduce the amount of time devoted to marking. It was also the intention that the writing scripts might be used diagnostically to determine appropriate interventions for those students identified as being at risk. Elder and Knoch (2009) describe the scoring scheme as follows:

> Students scoring 100 or above on the screening component (C-test and cloze elide scores combined) would be exempt from any requirement to undertake courses to develop their academic English proficiency.
>
> Students scoring in the borderline region between ≥ 80 and below 100 would have their writing marked. If the writing score is 4.0 or below on average, students are regarded as being at risk. If the writing score is above 4.0, the students are exempt from any requirement to enrol in English language development courses.
>
> Students scoring below 80 on the screening test are regarded as linguistically at risk and need additional opportunities for academic English development (the writing scripts for these students need not be marked unless further diagnostic information is required). (p. 3)

Students could find information on ELSAT (and the language development options available to them) on the L^3 website and via the Learning and Teaching Unit's campus offices. Where they had the knowledge to do so, office staff would also assist students experiencing technical difficulties, some of which will be reported later in this chapter.

8.3.4   A decentralised delivery model

It was decided to adopt a decentralised model of English language provision on the basis of the benefits outlined in section 6.6, namely (and in summary) that:

- English language tutors aligned with particular faculties would be well placed to develop productive working relationships with academic and professional staff in their respective divisions and to build their discipline knowledge, thereby enabling them to more effectively support students through materials specifically tailored to their particular needs. This, in turn, would promote greater student engagement in the learning process.
- English language tutors would feel more integrated with their particular faculties, more in tune with the 'local' context (systems and structures, possibilities, constraints etc.) and connected with academic staff in a way that would promote their ability to operate effectively and better influence and support both academic staff and students through personal contact, faculty and departmental committees etc. Such connectedness would be especially critical to the success of the initiative to embed academic literacies in the curriculum.
- By working more closely with particular academic communities, there would be a greater likelihood of academic staff developing a deeper understanding

and appreciation of the work – and its value – undertaken by English
language tutors.

- Localising provision would emphasise the intimate relationship between
  academic literacies and disciplines, while de-emphasising the misleading
  construction of academic literacy in terms of general skills that equip students to cope with the academic demands of their studies regardless of the
  specific literacy requirements of their area of academic focus.
- Localising provision would not preclude cooperation between Faculty-
  aligned English language tutors across the University in the form of consultation, the sharing of ideas, creative initiatives, experiences and strategies,
  and collaboration in professional development activities.
- Decentralising provision would allow for the shaping of provision according
  to local circumstances rather than according to a single, one-size-fits-all
  model decided and imposed centrally and which may not be as effective.
  With this in mind, while a template was agreed for the design of each faculty
  L^3 website,[7] within that template, teams were encouraged to be creative and
  to tailor resources to local needs in the way they deemed most appropriate
  and engaging.

In addition to delivering its English language development programme, each
faculty L^3 team would also oversee the administration of ELSAT for students
within their faculty. Thus each faculty team had its own email account through
which it would receive notification of any instances of the test having been
taken; and, similarly, each team would have responsibility for marking those
students within its faculty and informing them of their ELSAT result.

It was agreed that a decentralised model of provision required each faculty to
have its own L^3 team. This comprised a number of Language and Learning
Advisors managed by a Language and Learning Coordinator who, in turn, was
line managed by a newly-appointed Head of Language and Literacy. The Head
of Language and Literacy was part of the Learning and Teaching Unit's
Management Team. Significant EAP/ESP experience was a requirement for
all appointments, and evidence of research and a desire to engage in relevant
research activity was expected of the Language and Learning Coordinators – a
fact reflected in one day a week being earmarked for this purpose. Individuals
were eventually appointed to the above positions following a change management process and would subsequently be tasked with implementing L^3.[8]

---

[7] It was felt that a template would reduce the likelihood of students studying on joint degree
courses, and therefore potentially moving between two faculty L^3 websites, having difficulty
navigating the different sites.

[8] The restructuring of posts as part of the change process meant that while the Language and
Learning Coordinators had a responsibility to be research-active, the Language and Learning
Coordinators who previously had a similar such responsibility were placed on teaching-only
contracts.

During the implementation phase, the L^3 Team would work with the existing Academic Developers,[9] Campus Support Officers (CSOs),[10] Administrative officers, and International Student Officers (ISOs),[11] all of whom were already historically aligned with the four University Campuses, having a presence on each. It was envisaged that the Language and Learning team would work particularly closely with the Academic Developers in the process of embedding academic literacies in the curriculum.

8.3.5   English language provision: design and means of access

While each faculty Language and Learning team was given responsibility for developing the exact shape of its English language provision and associated resources, based on the particularities and requirements of the context in which it was operating, there were a number of overarching principles governing all faculty teams:

• **One-on-one appointments** – Although, previously, students were free to make one-on-one appointments with Language and Learning Advisors and academic staff were at liberty to refer them whenever they deemed it appropriate, the resource-intensive nature of this form of provision and the increase in initiatives concerning other forms of provision that were part of the new model led to the decision that access to one-on-one appointments should be restricted and linked to the ELSAT. That is, only those students who had sat ELSAT and been identified as 'at risk' would have access to this particular form of language support. The idea motivating this decision was not simply to reduce the potential draw on limited resources but also to encourage students to sit ELSAT and take responsibility for their own learning. It was envisaged that, in light of the fact that ELSAT tested general proficiency and

[9] Academic Developers made up a nine-person team that provided academic staff with a range of services and resources in relation to the implementation of the University's Teaching and Learning framework. The team developed teaching and supervision practice, as well as internal and external grants and awards, and fostered the scholarship of teaching and learning. It offered assistance in the form of online resources, one-on-one and small group meetings, seminars, workshops and project-based work concerning curriculum development, assessment, group work, feedback, internationalising the curriculum, supervision of Higher Degree by Research students, technology-enhanced teaching and learning, and embedding Graduate Qualities.

[10] CSOs and the Administrative Officers they line managed operated front desks at each of the four LTU campus offices and were frequently the first port of call for students looking for English language (and other) support services. As such, they had their finger very much on the pulse and were often the first to be aware of problems in implementation, fronting students' questions, complaints etc. where necessary.

[11] International Support Officers (ISOs) assisted students with their transition to the University and provided information and advice about such matters as life in the city, orientating to and studying at the University, community and government services, support for spouses, partners and families, academic policies and procedures, and other University support services such as Learning Advice, Careers and Counselling.

determined access to one-on-one appointments, those appointments should have as their primary focus aspects of general proficiency. For those students who were eligible for one-on-one appointments, it was decided that they would have access to eight such appointments during the course of the twelve months following the time access was granted, each of thirty minutes' duration (up from the twenty minutes previously assigned under the old model). This number was considered generous in light of the fact that, according to records held on a database maintained by the Language and Learning team, even when they had free access to Language and Learning Advisors students rarely requested more than two appointments. It was envisaged that, in time, one-on-one appointments might be conducted at a distance with the use of real-time communication applications such as *Skype* and Adobe *Connect*.

- **Written feedback on assignments** – Where students sat ELSAT and were identified as being at risk, they would be entitled to written feedback on two assignments. That feedback would be provided electronically by a Language and Learning Advisor only once the students had been awarded a grade for the assignment by the academic tutor concerned, and it would focus on the quality of the language produced rather than the content, the latter being the concern of the academic tutor. While the language feedback was to focus on general proficiency – the focus of the test (ELSAT) through which they had acquired access to this form of provision – it was acknowledged that the separation of language and content was somewhat problematic, even con-tentious, and was at the very heart of the notion of academic literacy. Nonetheless, in keeping with the rationale behind the tripartite distinction of competencies underpinning the model, it was determined that feedback could reasonably and usefully focus on grammatical accuracy, vocabulary and general organisational principles. Advisors were encouraged to embed hyperlinks into their feedback, directing students to online support materials that would help them address language problems apparent in their written work. It was intended that the number of hits individual resources received should be tracked and that the resulting records be used to help determine the focus of workshops (see below). The thinking here was that those links receiving the greatest number of hits were likely providing information on areas of greatest weakness or uncertainty among students. Where students had received a lower grade than would otherwise have been the case, due to weak language, academic tutors were to be encouraged to make this clear to students in the hope that it would encourage them to take on board the language feedback received from Language and Learning Advisors and follow the embedded hyperlinks.
- **Workshops** – In consultation with staff and students, and so as to respond to students' needs, each faculty team would develop a series of workshops

focusing on general proficiency and academic literacy in relation to the disciplines of their particular faculty, but with a primary emphasis on academic literacy to support the teaching of academic literacies within the regular curriculum. These would be delivered on a cyclical basis during the University semesters and be available to all students of the faculty regardless of whether or not they had sat ELSAT. In addition, a separate programme of more generic workshops, the Academic English Language Development Programme (AELDP), would be developed and delivered collaboratively by the four faculty teams, and offered centrally during semester breaks. 278 such workshops would be delivered across the four University faculties – each typically attracting enrolments of between ten and thirty students once up and running. In addition, twenty general proficiency-focused workshops, with similar attendance, would be delivered during mid-semester breaks. These would be open to all students across the University and be advertised around the campuses on electronic notice boards.

- **Online resources** – Online resources were to be further developed and reorganised by each faculty L^3 team so as to make them more engaging and responsive to the language needs of students within their faculty, while remaining faithful to the agreed design template discussed earlier. This meant that the Business Faculty L^3 website, for example, would end up having links to *Studying at University, Upcoming Workshops* and online registration, *Assignments and Exams for Business, Writing for Business, Reading for Business, Listening for Business, Speaking for Business, Referencing for Business Studies, English Language Tools, IELTS Preparation, and Course-Specific Resources.* Even points of grammar were to be contextualised within discipline-based content that was broadly relevant to students. There would be a new emphasis on minimising the use of heavily text-based resources in favour of more interactive multimedia materials and the use of models and tasks with accompanying answer keys that would promote autonomous learning. These faculty L^3 websites were seen very much as a work in progress and it was envisaged that they would therefore be subject to an ongoing process of refinement and become increasingly responsive to the needs of particular departments/disciplines within the respective faculties. In order for that development to occur, a series of IT training sessions was held for the L^3 teams in order to provide them with the technical ability to design and edit webpages and to create and post engaging online materials. All faculty L^3 websites included links to apps and social media websites, such as YouTube, Facebook, Twitter and Flickr, along with *Referencing* and *Exams* forums. The L^3 homepage was the landing page for entry to the four individual faculty L^3 homepages. It also contained three ELSAT related links: *What is ELSAT?, ELSAT Instructions, ELSAT FAQs,* and *Take ELSAT here.* To help navigation, materials were colour-coded to reflect the faculty to which they related. As with workshops, all students would have access to online resources regardless of whether or not they had sat ELSAT. Finally, it was decided that a team should be nominated to vet all materials intended for posting on the L^3 website in order to ensure appropriateness, quality and consistency in terms of their format and remaining faithful to the agreed template.

- Credit-bearing and non-credit-bearing proficiency courses could be available to students during and/or between semesters, although such courses would be subject to negotiation, on a case-by-case basis, between faculty Language and Learning Coordinators and individual faculties/departments.

Information on English language provision and how to access it was made available to students and staff electronically, via the L^3 website, as well as in hard copy form through Learning and Teaching Unit campus offices. That information is summarised in Figure 8.1.

8.4 Establishing a governance structure

In preparation for the implementation phase of the project, and in addition to the appointment of Language and Learning Coordinators and Advisors following a change management process (see section 8.3.3, above), two key actions were taken. Firstly, a new *IT and Project Administrator* post was created and filled. The individual appointed to the role came with a rich history of project management and programme development/implementation experience, as well as a strong background in IT, particularly in the creative utilisation of the web, multimedia, digital content development and online communications/real-time interactions.

Secondly, it was decided that an L^3 governance structure should be formed and that the pre-existing *English Language Steering Committee* be disbanded and replaced by a newly-established *L³ Advisory Implementation Group* that included better representation from key stakeholder groups within the University. This new Group would be responsible to the Deputy Vice Chancellor: Academic and also report to the University Teaching and Learning Committee. It would meet on a monthly basis and comprised:

- the Director of the Learning & Teaching Unit (Chair);
- the Deputy Director of the Learning & Teaching Unit (responsible for Academic Learning Services);
- the Head of Language and Literacy (formerly Senior Consultant: English Language Proficiency);
- one Dean of Teaching and Learning[12] (Division of Business and Law);

---

[12] Each Division of the University had appointed to it a Dean of Teaching and Learning responsible for overseeing teaching and learning initiatives within the Division and reporting to the University Teaching and Learning Committee.

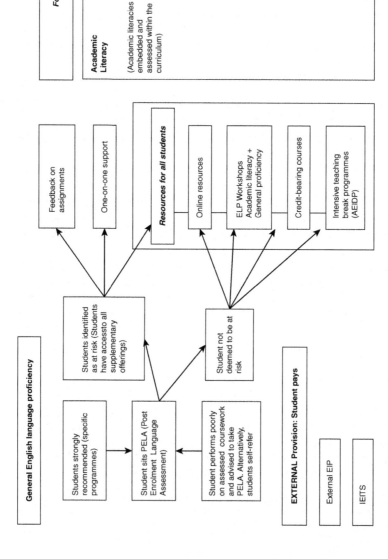

Figure 8.1 A framework for the provision of English Language Proficiency (Murray and Hicks, 2014)

- one Programme Director;
- one Academic Developer;
- one Language and Learning Coordinator;
- one Language and Learning Advisor;
- the Head of the University's College – a newly-formed College established as a pathway into the University, particularly for non-traditional students and
- one member of the Centre for Regional Engagement (CRE).[13]

In addition to the L^3 Advisory Implementation Group, five Operational Groups were established, one Learning & Teaching Unit (LTU) L^3 Operational Group, and one further L^3 Operational Group for each of the Divisions: the BUE L^3 Operational Group, the EASS Division L^3 Operational Group, the ITEE Division L^3 Operational Group, and the HSC L^3 Operational Group. These groups met fortnightly to reflect on progress and address any issues that had arisen in the intervening period.

The LTU Operational Group comprised:

- the Head of Language and Literacy (formerly Senior Consultant: English Language Proficiency);
- the Deputy Director of the Learning & Teaching Unit (responsible for Academic Learning Services);
- the L^3 IT and Project Administrator;
- the four Language and Learning Coordinators (one per Division);
- one Central Services Officer[14] (CSO) (to represent the CSOs across the four University Campuses);
- two Administrative Officers (AOs) (to represent the AOs across the four University Campuses) explain role and
- one representative from the Centre for Regional Engagement.

Each Divisional Operational Group comprised:

- the Head of Language and Literacy;
- the Dean of Teaching and Learning for the Division;
- the Academic Developer assigned to the Division;
- two to three Programme Directors from within the Division and
- the Language and Learning Coordinator for the Division.

The idea was that each Divisional Operational Group should agree a strategy they believed would be most efficacious in implementing the approved model, given the characteristics of their particular Divisional context.

The Head of Language of Literacy would move between the four Divisional Groups, acting as a hub, sharing information and experience between them and

---

[13] The Centre for Regional Engagement worked towards the active development and growth of regional communities at an intellectual, social and economic level, largely through its regional campuses and programme offerings.

[14] CSOs were key to deliberations, for they fed back to the LTU Operational Group – and by extension the Advisory Implementation Group – the state of play on the ground during the implementation phase.

reporting to the L^3 Advisory Implementation Group. One of the particularly challenging elements of the Divisional Group discussions, for example, was where to begin with the process of embedding academic literacies in the curriculum. Because of its significant implications for changes to the curriculum and the increased workload associated with it, this was viewed with trepidation by many academic staff and it was felt that in order to instil confidence in the model, encourage maximum engagement and help bed down the process, the initial focus should be on one or two courses within each Division where the Programme Directors – and ideally their staff – were particularly sympathetic to the notion of embedding and/or where other factors made certain courses particularly fertile territory for rolling out the process. This was true, for example, within the Division of EASS, where the School of Education was, independently of the English Language Proficiency Project, about to embark on a process of curriculum renewal and where the embedding of academic literacies was therefore especially timely and would represent less of an upheaval and disruption to the status quo.

The sharing of experience between the four groups had one noteworthy advantage of creating a competitive edge to the implementation process. Not only did those implementing the model want to demonstrate that their particular Division was making exceptional progress, but equally, no Divisional Group wanted to feel that they were getting left behind in the process and not keeping up with the pace. This was true, for example, with the development of the L^3 Divisional websites, where there was a strong sense of competition motivating the respective Divisional Language and Learning teams. This led to considerable achievements in a remarkably short space of time.

Being comprised exclusively of members of the Learning and Teaching Unit, the LTU Operational Group was concerned particularly with the implications and effects of implementation on LTU services and some of the unforeseen challenges it was to throw up, particularly in relation to ELSAT (for example, some of the technical difficulties experienced) and student access to individual consultations with Language and Learning Advisors – issues to which I shall return later.

The progress and insights gleaned by Operational Groups informed the discussions and decision-making of the L^3 *Advisory Implementation Group*.

8.5   Issues arising

8.5.1   *Embedding academic literacies in the curriculum*

Various challenges were experienced during implementation of the embedding process (see Murray and Nallaya, 2014). There was a realisation, for example, that despite efforts to raise awareness among academic content staff of what academic literacies were, there remained a lack of clarity that needed addressing through repetition and example. Furthermore, in order to assist faculty staff with identifying and mapping academic literacies onto the curriculum, English language teams needed to glean as much information as possible about the programmes and courses with which they were working and to meet regularly with Programme Directors and the Deans and Departmental Associate Heads of Teaching and Learning.

Achieving the level of collaboration required to achieve the momentum necessary to bring about implementation within a reasonable timescale was often difficult, and for a number of reasons including:

- Insufficient understanding of the project.
- Reluctance, quite characteristic of innovation, to engage with a process that spelt change and a shift away from academics' comfort zone.
- Political motivations both at an individual and departmental level.
- Lack of belief in the efficacy of embedding academic literacies in the curriculum.
- A feeling among some academic staff that they were content specialists, *not* language specialists.
- A sense, on the part of some Course Coordinators, of being overwhelmed by their other course commitments and having neither the time nor the expertise to focus on this 'additional' endeavour. This was important, for Coordinators were key to driving change.
- A belief on the part of some academic staff that they were already teaching certain academic literacies. It was 'difficult to verify such claims or establish how effectively they were doing so and whether they were scaffolding the teaching and learning process in the way intended within the proposed model' (Murray and Nallaya, 2014).

Another problem encountered concerned the training that academics had undergone in the past and previous knowledge they had acquired. In a few cases, there was evidence that these things both dictated and constrained their understanding of academic literacies and how they should be taught. Thus, for example, and as reported elsewhere:

some Course Coordinators insisted that the framework adopted failed to address the learning needs of the students ... and expressed a desire to adopt an alternative approach that drew on Willison and O'Regan's (2007) Research Development Framework (RDF) – a framework with which they were familiar but which does not address discipline-specific academic literacies. Changing the views of these Coordinators, for whom the familiar was more reassuring and less daunting, proved difficult. (Murray and Nallaya, 2014)

Academic staff also tended to see academic literacies as the same thing as study skills and/or generic English for academic purposes; as such, they regarded it as something that could be taught outside of the curriculum. This perception could, in part, have been the result of previous attitudes and practices – still quite prevalent in the sector – concerning the construction of English language proficiency and the organisation of its delivery. It could also have been indicative of a reluctance to discern and/or acknowledge any distinction between these facets of language development and support as result of an adversity to change.

In other cases, there was 'scepticism regarding the fundamental inseparability of academic literacies and content knowledge and the notion that academic literacies could be embedded in the curriculum and thereby contribute toward better learning outcomes through careful scaffolding' (Murray and Nallaya, 2014).

Most critical, however, was the issue of compliance. Although approved and subsequently mandated by the senior management of the university, there were no punitive measures put in place in the event that those responsible for implementation should fail to bring about – or at least attempt to bring about – the expected changes to practices:

Given the scale and ambition of this institution-wide innovation, clear directives from senior management regarding the significance of undertaking the embedding process, deadlines for compliance, and the consequences of failure to implement would have provided the project with greater credibility and momentum. In the event, it was left almost exclusively to the Language and Learning team within the identified schools to oversee the embedding process and the impression created was that it was the sole responsibility of the English language tutors to facilitate that process. The consequence of this was that Course Coordinators perceived the initiative as unimportant and unnecessary. This in turn had a somewhat demoralising effect on language tutors who at times felt as though they were swimming against the tide and that attempts to bring about change were futile'. (Murray and Nallaya, 2014)

Ultimately, the effect of these and other factors was to make more arduous, and ultimately retard, the embedding process, for the mapping and scaffolding of academic literacies was sporadic as a result, as were the setting of clear assessment tasks and the provision of models for students to emulate.

8.5.2   ELSAT

One problem with ELSAT, flagged early on in its life, was that, despite efforts to ensure the widest possible dissemination of information on the test and related forms of provision, ignorance of the test in particular, and its purpose as purely a supportive mechanism for their benefit, was quite widespread and the number of students opting to sit ELSAT (four hundred in an eighteen-month period) was modest in relation to the number of students enrolled at the University (see Harper, 2013, pp. 153–6). Furthermore, there was evidence that information was not always being presented accurately and sympathetically to students and that this was, in part, responsible for students misunderstanding and feeling threatened by the test. I have remarked on this in the following terms:

This underlines the criticality, in any institution-wide initiative of this kind, of good communication across the institution and the need to continually regurgitate and reinforce information at every opportunity and in every form available. Equally, it is important to be aware of the fact that while applied linguists and language teachers may be especially sensitive to language and to presentation, and their effect on audience, this is not necessarily shared by all academic and administrative staff. While it is difficult to control for this, being aware of the fact can, nevertheless, help ensure that dissemination is as thorough and information as comprehensive and precise as possible, and that those tasked with passing on information to students are aware of the sensitivities involved and the need to convey that information accordingly. (Murray, 2014, p. 332)

Of those students who *did* sit ELSAT, ninety per cent were identified as being at risk and potentially benefiting from the language development opportunities on offer. This suggested that it was not the assessment tool per se that was 'depriving' students of these opportunities, but rather that fact that they were opting out of ELSAT and thereby simply not giving themselves the option to access the provision that might otherwise be available to them. This tallies with an observation made in Dunworth's 2009 study, cited earlier, in which a number of her participants expressed the view that 'students might suffer from "test fatigue", be reluctant to take PELA and unmotivated to seek out developmental assistance if identified as appropriate' (2009, p. 8). The ninety per cent figure was also seen as possibly reflecting the fact that, while at an intellectual level there was little sense in deliberately failing a test in order to get access to provision that the test may, if taken in good faith, determine as unnecessary for any given individual, some academic staff who disliked the idea of ELSAT as a mechanism were nonetheless advising students to deliberately fail it (Harper, 2013, p. 156). This threatened to undermine the validity of ELSAT, not as a test per se (which had undergone appropriate development) but as a result of its application within the model. Harper (ibid.) reflects on this in the following terms:

[ELSAT's] position ... – as a tool that managed access to individual teaching [one-on-one consultations] – created a strong incentive to fail which has led to validity problems in practice. The role of ELSAT must be rethought to ensure it is fulfilling its potential to identify students at-risk and facilitate access to language development. (p. 159)

For those students who opted into ELSAT, a number of problems arose that can broadly be divided into two categories, the first being student-driven and the second technology-driven. In terms of student-driven problems, the majority of these consisted of students failing to complete ELSAT as a result of not having read or read carefully enough the online instructions accompanying the test, or of failing to comprehend them despite efforts to make the instructions as comprehensible and transparent as possible. One issue that arose repeatedly was a product of students' failure either to click Moodle's 'save without submitting' and 'submit all and finish' buttons at the end of each online test page and/or to attempt every exercise. In cases where this occurred, the system was unable to generate a score, which in turn meant that the process of communicating with students would not be triggered.

A further issue that arose had to do with some students misinterpreting the speed reading task. These students incorrectly understood that the three lengthy texts of which the task was composed constituted the three parts of ELSAT (C-test, cloze–elide, argumentative essay), rather than collectively constituting only one part. Having finished the speed reading exercise, they consequently clicked 'submit all and finish', unaware that they had only completed one part of the three-part test. In order to address this, the positioning, formatting and wording of instructions underwent modifications, and a PDF document and video were produced explaining the test and providing instructions. These were located on the Language and Learning website for students to read/watch without needing to enter the test site. This improved the situation, and instances of non-completions decreased markedly. Although the ideal would have been to present the entire test on a single page that students would simply scroll down – thereby avoiding any confusion caused by the 'save without submitting' and 'submit all and finish' buttons – the constraints imposed by the Moodle platform did not permit this design feature.

In terms of technical issues, idiosyncratic computer configurations presented some test-takers with problems and technicians with diagnostic challenges. Where students were having problems completing the test on their own computers, they were advised to do ELSAT on one of the University's own machines, and in every case completed the test successfully. Although the possibility of technical issues interfering with the delivery of the test for a proportion of test-takers was recognised at the outset as being almost inevitable, given the enormous potential variation in the hardware and software configurations of different machines, and while it was understood that the risk here could never be fully mitigated, nonetheless, it was agreed that some attempt should be made to reduce the incidence of such instances. Thus, in an effort to minimise glitches, or at least understand under what circumstance they could be expected to arise, it was decided that information should be collected on the particular configurations of those computers involved in problem cases in order to ascertain whether there were any commonalities that might provide insights into causes and solutions.

Working with the Moodle environment (the institution's preferred platform) presented significant challenges to the project team, the most severe of which was presented by the speed-reading task (see also above). Here, students were required to identify redundant words in an extended piece of text and it was critical that the exercise was presented in such a way that they could do this in a manner that would not invalidate the test. Eventually, it was determined that dragging a red cross over redundant words was the only viable way of implementing this particular task. In order not to assist students inadvertently, the same number of crosses was available to students on each page of the task regardless of how many were actually required. Other challenges included getting Moodle to add the scores of the different tasks and making more efficient the process by which students would be informed of their results. Attempts were initiated to automate this process and thereby increase efficiencies.

8.5.3   One-on-one appointments

Within a few weeks of implementing the model, it became evident that approximately thirty per cent fewer students were registering for one-on-one consultations and that this equated to a reduction in the (fluctuating) annual figure of approximately 1400 consultations. A percentage drop of this magnitude had been anticipated and, indeed, factored into the model's conceptualisation, resulting in a considerably more comprehensive programme of workshops than had hitherto been the case, bolstered by the embedding of academic literacy tuition within all programme curricula. It was felt that a new and stronger emphasis on workshops and embedded academic literacies represented a more efficient, utilitarian approach than one-on-one appointments.

The reduced access to one-on-one appointments brought with it a sense of dissatisfaction among some academic staff, who felt uneasy about students having to sit a test in order to access certain supports. This was in part a product of their no longer being able to send students directly to Language and Learning Advisors for one-on-one appointments, as and when they chose. In reference to this, I have stated:

The ability, hitherto, to do so had provided academic staff with a quick-fix option that they were reluctant to relinquish, and it is interesting to surmise whether or not this has coloured the way in which the test has been presented to students by these individuals – with obvious potential implications for take-up. With this in mind, a recent decision was taken to allow all students an initial one-on-one appointment. This was seen as a sensible adjustment to and evolution of the model for the following reasons:

• It would help appease academic staff by giving them back the ability to refer students, although on a much more limited scale.
• It would allow Language and Learning Advisors to assist students with relatively simple problems, present the model and its rationale sympathetically, direct them to resources, encourage them to take ELSAT where advisable, and provide them with strategies for becoming more autonomous learners.

- It would reduce some of the frustration felt by a proportion of students who may feel 'locked out' and simply want quick advice or an answer to a relatively simple question.
- It would alleviate some of the stress faced by front-desk administrative staff who are the first port of call for students and upon whom they tend to vent their frustration.
- It would place less onus on front-desk staff to understand in detail and explain the model of language provision and its underlying rationale. (Murray, 2014, p. 331)

This adaption of the model was generally well received and helped allay the concerns and anxieties of both students and staff. Furthermore, it did not, as some had feared, result in Language and Learning Advisors being inundated with requests for one-on-one appointments. Equally, while the number of students doing ELSAT increased, that increase proved manageable in terms of the Language and Learning teams' workloads. However, the beneficial effects were short-lived and in the longer term did not significantly increase instances of students sitting the test. This was a phenomenon experienced by other universities, as Ransom (2009) notes in her discussion of DELNA and the rationale behind Melbourne University's post-enrolment English language assessment strategy:

Contrary to the general principle of 'personal choice' initially advocated at the University of Auckland (Read, 2008), which shares a history of post-entry language assessment in the form of the Diagnostic English Language Needs Assessment (DELNA), the Task Force recommended compulsory as opposed to voluntary testing. The reason for this was twofold: the low take up rate of DELA [the predecessor to DELNA and of which the latter was a development] in its voluntary form, and the belief that mandatory testing would ensure targeted students were channelled into appropriate academic language programs. Despite funding being available to assess 1200 students, this figure was never attained, with the largest participation rate at 66% (of the 1200 places allocated under the funding model) in 2006. Under the previous voluntary testing regime, many students avoided DELA, despite a faculty recommendation that they attend. Consequently, intervention did not occur for targeted linguistically at risk students. Similarly, participation rates in the DELNA screening (the first part of a two-tiered testing system) at Auckland University were also low in the beginning, but increased to around 70% in 2007 when the screening 'officially became a requirement for almost all first-year students, regardless of their language background' (Read, 2008, p. 186). (p. A-16; my parenthetic insertion)

Whether the University eventually decides to change its current stance on ELSAT and make it mandatory in the way that the DELA and DELNA are remains to be seen. What is certain is that there would appear to be little point in mandating it except for those who are identified as at-risk and also required to engage in structured language development activities; and, as we have seen, there can be major logistical and other challenges associated with this. Furthermore, mandating the test is no guarantee that students will not continue to deliberately fail it, except in so far as it will discourage students from failing if they are averse to the idea of engaging in mandated language development activities.

Despite the idea that one-on-one consultations should have general proficiency as their main focus, records suggested that, in reality, Language and Learning Advisors were dealing with a mix of general proficiency and academic literacy and as such these sessions closely resembled the character of consultations prior to implementation of the model. Yet they appeared to be almost universally well received by students: of the 2,578 appointments that took place in 2012, 98.3% of students said that they would recommend the service to other students (Harper, 2013).

8.5.4   *Language feedback on assessed coursework*

As with ELSAT, there was some evidence that staff were either not aware of or did not fully understand the nature of this form of provision, and as a result its uptake by students was minimal. While there may be other reasons for this that warrant investigation, there is nonetheless a suggestion here that any innovation requires an ongoing and systematic programme of awareness-raising across the institution, especially given the quite high turnover of academic and administrative personnel that is commonplace in universities.

It is interesting to note that in Harper's 2013 study, staff both within and outside the Academic Language & Learning Team felt disempowered 'because they could no longer use their own professional judgement to identify students who might benefit from talking to an Academic Language & Learning Advisor' and were instead dependent on the result of a test (ELSAT) (p. 156). Yet in the same study, it is reported that a number of participants also desired 'greater support in marking assignments, particularly those affected by grammar and sentence structure' and were 'unsure how to handle such assignments' (p. 157). There appears to be something of a contradiction here in relation to their perceived expertise which may, again, reflect the frustration felt by some staff at not being able to refer students as and when they desired.

8.6   Summary

The case study described in this final chapter offers a glimpse into one way in which many of the ideas and principles discussed in the foregoing chapters, in particular the conceptualisation of language proficiency articulated in Chapter 3, have been realised in one specific institutional context, within an English-medium higher education system where regulation has forced universities to reflect critically on how they deal with the increasingly prominent – many would say problematic – issue of English language.

As I suggested out at the outset of this book, it would be foolhardy of me to presume that the model as a whole outlined in this chapter is in any way an ideal to be aspired to, or that those many individual ideas and principles that together constitute its rationale are unquestionable and not contentious and subject to disagreement. They most assuredly are, not least because of the contextual variation that exists between different universities and higher education systems and what this means for the constraints that govern what is and is not possible. Such variation means that there can be no ideal response (or solution) to the 'English language question'. What the case study described here does is to serve to highlight the fact that, with any innovation, there is likely to be a degree of disparity between ideas in principle and ideas in practice: between conceptualisation and implementation. In anticipating and responding to such disparity, those driving change need to be cognisant of potential pitfalls and some of the strategies for avoiding them, and of the importance of being able to adapt swiftly and elegantly when unforeseen obstacles arise during implementation. Failure to do so can ultimately sound the death knell for the innovation concerned.

Whatever the benefits and challenges that accompany innovation, one thing is certain: in the fast-changing, increasingly regulated context of higher education, the need for innovation and an understanding of and ability to effectively plan and implement significant change is greater than ever; and this is no more so than in the field of English language assessment and provision. Universities need to give substance to their claims of internationalisation via robust mechanisms for assessing their students and providing high quality and relevant language development opportunities which ensure, as far as is practicably possible, that every individual they enrol has the best opportunity to succeed to their full potential and that the standard of education delivered by the institution is not merely maintained by diversifying the student body, but enhanced. Students need to exit their programmes of study academically, socially and culturally richer, and with a skills set and the ability to observe, reflect and adapt that prepares them sufficiently for a changing world and, in particular, a workplace that is increasingly diverse. That must surely be the primary goal and benefit of internationalisation, and language and communication lie at its very heart.

References

Adams, R. (2013). Number of students going on to higher education almost reaches 50%. *The Guardian*, Wednesday, 24 April 2013. www.theguardian.com/educa tion/2013/apr/24/students-higher-education-almost-50-per-cent Retrieved 30 May 2014

Adler, R., Rosenfeld, L. and Proctor, R. F., II. (2013). *Interplay: The Process of Interpersonal Communication.* Oxford University Press

Advisory Committee on Student Financial Assistance. (2012). *Pathways to Success. Integrating Learning with Life and Work to Increase National College Completion: A Report to the U.S. Congress and Secretary of Education.* Washington, DC: U.S. Government. www2.ed.gov/about/bdscomm/list/acsfa/ptsreport2.pdf Retrieved 24 October 2014

Alderman, G. (2010). Why university standards have fallen. *The Guardian*, Wednesday 10 March 2010. www.theguardian.com/commentisfree/2010/mar/10/universi ties-standards-blair-target Retrieved 6 June 2014

Allen, J. P. (1975). Some basic concepts in linguistics, in Allen, J. P. and Corder, S. Pit (eds.), *Papers in Applied Linguistics.* London: Oxford University Press

Allwright, J. and Banerjee, J. (1997). *Investigating the Accuracy of Admissions Criteria: A Case Study in a British University.* Lancaster: Centre for Research in Language Education, Lancaster University

Alptekin, C. (2002). Toward intercultural communicative competence in ELT. *ELT Journal*, 1(1), 57–64

Anderson, J. R. (1983). *The Architecture of Cognition.* Cambridge, MA: Harvard University Press

Anderson, J. R. (1995). *Learning and Memory: An Integrated Approach.* New York: Wiley

Arkoudis, S. and Tran, L. (2010). Writing blah, blah, blah: Lecturers' approaches and challenges in supporting international students. *International Journal of Teaching and Learning in Higher Education*, 22(2), 169–178

Arkoudis, S., Baik, C. and Richardson, S. (2012). *English Language Standards in Higher Education.* Camberwell, Victoria: ACER (Australian Council for Educational Research) Press

Aschaffenburg, K. and Mass, I. (1997). Cultural and educational careers: The dynamics of social reproduction. *American Sociological Review*, 62: 573–87

Association of Academic Language and Learning. Degrees of Proficiency (2014). (Website designed as part of the Office of Learning and Teaching project titled Degrees of Proficiency: Building a strategic approach to university students' English language assessment and development, 2011–13. [Dunworth, K., Drury,

H., Kralik, C. and Moore, T.]). www.degreesofproficiency.aall.org.au Retrieved 28 June 2014

Attwood, R. (2009). QAA reveals guidelines to counter 'dumbing-down' fears. *Times Higher Education*, 11 May 2009. www.timeshighereducation.co.uk/news/qaa-re veals-guidelines-to-counter-dumbing-down-fears/406498.article Retrieved 14 July 2013

Austin, J. L. (1962). *How to Do Things with Words*. Oxford: Clarendon Press

Australian Bureau of Statistics (2013). *3412.0 – Migration, Australia, 2011–12 and 2012– 13: Australia's Population by Country of Birth*. www.abs.gov.au/ausstats/abs@.nsf/ Lookup/3412.0Chapter12011-12%20and%202012–13 Retrieved 22 June 2014

Australian Bureau of Statistics. (2013). *4102.0 – Australian Social Trends, Dec 2011*. www.abs.gov.au/AUSSTATS/abs@.nsf/Lookup/4102.0Main+Features20Dec+20 11 Retrieved 6 June 2014

Australian Government: Department of Immigration and Border Protection. www.im mi.gov.au/skilled/general-skilled-migration/skilled-occupations/skills-assessed. htm Retrieved 7 June 2014

Bachman, L. (1990). *Fundamental Considerations in Language Testing*. Oxford: Oxford University Press

Bachman, L. and Palmer, A. (1996). *Language Testing in Practice*. Oxford: Oxford University Press

Baik, C. and Greig, J. (2009). Improving the academic outcomes of undergraduate ESL students: The case for discipline-based academic skills programs. *Higher Education Research & Development*, 28(4), 401–16

Baker, C. (2011). *Foundations of Bilingual Education and Bilingualism* (5th Edition). Multilingual Matters

Baker, S. (2013). London Met visa ban lifted. *Times Higher Education*, 9 April 2013. www.timeshighereducation.co.uk/news/london-met-visa-ban-lifted/2003073.arti cle Retrieved 18 October 2014

Banks, M. and Lawrence, R. (2008). Outcomes for graduates, in Banks, M. and Olsen, A. (eds.), *Outcomes and Impacts of International Education: From International Student to Australian Graduate, the Journey of a Lifetime*, pp. 23–48. IDP Education

Barker, M., Hibbins, R. and Farrelly, B. (2011). Walking the talk: Fostering a sense of global citizenry amongst staff in higher education, in Clifford, V. and Montgomery, C. (eds.), *Moving Towards Internationalisation of the Curriculum for Global Citizenship in Higher Education*, pp. 47–68. Oxford: Oxford Brookes University

Baron, R. S., Kerr, N. L. and Miller, N. (1996). *Group Process, Group Decision, Group Action*. Buckingham: Open University Press

Barrett-Lennard, S., Dunworth, K. and Harris, A. (2011). The Good Practice Principles: Silver bullet or starter gun? *Journal of Academic Language and Learning*, 5(2), A99–106. Wellington, New Zealand: International First Year in Higher Education Conference

Bassnett, S. (2012). Speed trap sprung. *Times Higher Education*, 20 September 2012. www.timeshighereducation.co.uk/comment/columnists/speed-trap-sprung/42118 7.article Retrieved 7 June 2014

Baty, P. (2004). Caught in vicious cycle of declining standards. *The Times Higher Education*, 19 November 2004. www.timeshighereducation.co.uk/news/caught-in-vicious-cycle-of-declining-standards/192504.article Retrieved 2 February 2014

Bayless, A. and Ingram, D. E. (2006). IELTS as a predictor of academic language performance. *Australian International Education Conference 2006*. aiec.idp.com /uploads/pdf/BaylissIngram%20(Paper)%20Wed%201630%20MR5.pdf Retrieved 15 June 2013

BBC News. (2010). Foreign students not 'cash cows', says British Council. *BBC News*, 26 March 2010. news.bbc.co.uk/1/hi/education/8584819.stm Retrieved 8 July 2014

BBC News: Wales. (2012). Lecturer claims pressure to accept substandard work from overseas students. *BBC News: Wales*, 16 October 2012. www.bbc.co.uk/news/uk -wales-19945919 Retrieved 8 June 2014

Bellingham, L. (1993). The relationship of language proficiency to academic success for international students. *New Zealand Journal of Educational Studies*, 30(2), 229–32

Bennett, N., Dunne, E. and Carré, B. (2000). *Skills Development in Higher Education and Employment*. Buckingham: The Society for Research into Higher Education

Benoit, P. and Graham, S. (2005). Leadership excellence: Constructing the role of department chair. *Academic Leadership: The Online Journal*. 3(1). www.academic leadership.org/volume3/issue1/articles/5/5_full Retrieved 19 February 2015

Beretta, A. (1990). Implementation of the Bangalore project. *Applied Linguistics*, 11(4), 321–337

Berko, R. M., Wolvin, A. D. and Wolvin, D. R. (eds.) (2007). *Communicating: A Social and Career Focus*. New York: Pearson

Berns, M. (1990). *Contexts of Competence: Social and Cultural Considerations in Communicative Language Teaching*. New York: Plenum Press

Berry, B. and Lewkowicz, J. (2000). Exit-tests: Is there an alternative? *Hong Kong Journal of Applied Linguistics*, 5(1), 19–49

Bhatt, R. M. (2002). Experts, dialects, and discourse. *International Journal of Applied Linguistics*, 12(1), 74–109

Billig, M. (2013). *Learn to Write Badly*. Cambridge: Cambridge University Press

Birdwhistell, R. L. (1952). *Introduction to Kinesics*. Louisville: University of Louisville Press

Birdwhistell, R. (1970). *Kinesics and Context*. Philadelphia, PA: University of Pennsylvania Press

Birrell, B. (2006). Implications of low English standards among overseas students at Australian universities. *People and Place*, 14 (4), 53–64

Birrell, B. and Hawthorne, L. (1996). Immigrants and the professions. *People and Place*, 4(4), 1–11

Bizzell, P. (1982). *Cognition, Convention, and Certainty: What We Need to Know about Writing. PRE-TEXT 3*, 213–241

Bizzell, P. (1992). *Academic Discourse and Critical Consciousness*. Pittsburgh, PA: University of Pittsburgh Press

Bohemia, E., Farrell, H., Power, C. and Salter, C. (2007). Embedding literacy skills in design curriculum. Conference paper proceedings: *ConnectED 2007: International Conference on Design Education, Sydney* [Online]. Available from: nrl.northumbria.ac.uk/25/ Retrieved 19 June 2014

Bool, H., Dunmore, D., Tonkyn, A., Schmitt, D. and Ward-Goodbody, M. (2003). *The BALEAP Guidelines on English Language Proficiency Levels for International Applicants to UK Universities*, London: British Association of Lecturers in English for Academic Purposes

Bonanno, H. and Jones, J. (2007). *The MASUS Procedure: Measuring the Academic Skills of University Students. A Diagnostic Assessment.* Sydney: Learning Centre, University of Sydney, sydney.edu.au/stuserv/documents/learning_centre/MASUS.pdf Retrieved 23 March 2014

Bourdieu, P. (1977). Cultural reproduction and social reproduction in J. Karabel and A. H. Halsey (eds), *Power and Ideology in Education.* New York: Oxford University Press, pp. 487–551

Bourdieu, P. (1984). *Distinction: A Social Critique of the Judgment of Taste.* Cambridge, MA: Harvard University Press

Bourdieu, P. (1986). The forms of capital in J. E. Richardson (ed.), *Handbook of Theory of Research for the Sociology of Education.* New York: Green word Press, pp. 241–258

Bourdieu, P. (1989). Social space and symbolic power. *Sociological Theory*, 7(1), 14–25

Bradley, D. (2008). *Review of Australian Higher Education: Final Report*, Canberra: Department of Education, Employment and Workplace Relations

Brady, K. (2013). Towards a university-wide approach to developing first-year students' academic literacy and professional communication skills. Paper presented at the 16th International First Year in Higher Education Conference. Wellington: New Zealand

Bretag, T. (2007). The Emperor's new clothes: Yes, there is a link between English language competence and academic standards. *People and Place*, 15 (1), 13–21

Bright, C. and von Randow, J. (2004). Tracking language test consequences: The student perspective. *Proceedings of the 18th IDP Australian International Educational Conference, Sydney, Australia, October 7.* www.aiec.idp.com/pdf/thur%20-%20Bright%20&%20Randow.pdf Retrieved 3 January 2012

Briguglio, C. (2005). Assessing the writing skills of entry-level undergraduate business students to enhance their writing ability during tertiary studies. *Unpublished research report*, Perth: Curtin University of Technology

British Council (2012). *Accreditation UK: Handbook 2012 and 2013.* www.britishcouncil.org/2012–13_accreditation_uk_handbook.pdf Retrieved 14 July 2013

Brooks, G. and Adams, M. (1999). Spoken English proficiency and academic performance: Is there a relationship, and if so how do we teach? Macquarie University Research Online, Retrieved April 25, 2010, from http://www.researchonline.mq.edu.au/vital/access/manager/Repository/mq:1579;jsessionid=155CA4E69BCA51DAEF8852C2A8BBE822?f0=sm_creator%3A%22Adams%2C+Moya%22

Broughan, L. and Hunt, L. (2013). Inclusive teaching in L. Hunt and D. Chalmers (eds), *University Teaching in Focus: A Learning-centred Approach.* Camberwell, Victoria: ACER (Australian Council for Educational Research) Press, pp. 182–98

Brown, P. and Levinson, S. (1978). Universals in language usage: Politeness phenomena in E. N. Goody (ed.), *Question and Politeness.* Cambridge: Cambridge University Press

Brown, P. and Levinson, S. (1987). *Politeness: Some Universals of Language Use.* Cambridge: Cambridge University Press

Buchanan, R. (2013). University fees for 'cash cow' overseas students attacked. *The Times Education*, 9 August 2013 www.thetimes.co.uk/tto/education/article3838078.ece. Retrieved 7 June 2014

Burgess, R. (2010), April. Australia's language climate. *Guardian Weekly.* www.guardianweekly.co.uk/?page=editorial&id=1532&catID=18 Retrieved 20 April 2010

Burgoon, J. K. (ed.) (1994). *Nonverbal Signals. Handbook of Interpersonal Communication*. Beverly Hills, CA: Sage

Burgoon, J. K., Jensen, M. L., Meservy, T. O., Kruse, J. and Nunamaker, J. F. (2005). *Augmenting Human Identification of Emotional States in Video. Intelligence Analysis Conference*, McClean, VA

Business Forums International (2013). Document Verification Workshop for Overseas Students & Staff – Universities, Schools & Colleges. www.bfi.co.uk/event-detail .asp?eventid=210 Retrieved 17 March 2014

Byram, M., Nichols, A. and Stevens, D. (2001). Introduction in M. Byram, A. Nichols and D. Stevens (eds), *Developing Intercultural Competence in Practice*. Multilingual Matters

Calderon, A. (2012). Massification continues to transform higher education. *University World News* No. 237. www.universityworldnews.com/article.php? story=20120831155341147 Retrieved 30 June 2014

Canagarajah, A. S. (ed.) (1999). *Resisting Linguistic Imperialism in English Teaching*. Oxford: Oxford University Press

Canagarajah, A. S. (ed.) (2005). *Reclaiming the Local in Language Policy and Practice*. Mahwah, NJ: Lawrence Erlbaum

Canale, M. and Swain, M. (1980). Theoretical bases of communicative approaches to second language teaching and testing. *Applied Linguistics 1*, 1–47

Canale, M. (1983). From communicative competence to communicative language pedagogy in J. Richards and R. Schmidt (eds), *Language and Communication*. London: Longman

Carroll, J. and Ryan, J. (eds) (2005). *Teaching International Students: Improving Learning for All*. Abingdon: Routledge

CBC News. (2014). International students used as 'cash cows', prof says. *CBC News* 14 March 2014. www.cbc.ca/news/canada/windsor/international-students-used-as -cash-cows- prof-says-1.2572663 Retrieved 16 May 2014

Centre for Teaching Excellence (n.d.) Teamwork skills: Being an effective group member. uwaterloo.ca/centre-for-teaching-excellence/teaching-resources/teach ing-tips/tips-students/being-part-team/teamwork-skills-being-effective-group -member Retrieved 2 May 2014

CERI (1969). *The Management of Innovation in Education*. Paris: Organisation for Economic Co-operation and Development

Chang, J. (2006). A transcultural wisdom bank in the classroom: Making cultural diversity key resource in teaching and learning. *Journal of Studies in International Education*, 10(4), 369–77

Chomsky, N. (1965). *Aspects of the Theory of Syntax*. Cambridge, MA: MIT Press

Christie, H., Tett, L., Cree, V. E., Hounsell, J. and McCune, V. (2008). 'A real roll-ercoaster of confidence and emotions': Learning to be a university student. *Studies in Higher Education*, 33(5), 567–81

Clapham, C. (2001). Discipline specificity and EAP in M. Peacock and J. Flowerdew (eds), *Issues in English for Academic Purposes*. Cambridge: Cambridge University Press, pp. 84–100

Clerehan, R. (2003). Transition to tertiary education in the arts and humanities: Some academic initiatives from Australia. *Arts and Humanities in Higher Education*, 2(1), 72–89

Coates, A. J. S. (2012). Monash–Warwick: What does a global university partnership look like?, *The Guardian*. www.guardian.co.uk/higher-education-network/blog/2 012/oct/29/monash-warwick-alliance-global- education Retrieved 23 June 2013

Cochran-Smith, M. (2004). *Walking the Road: Race, Diversity, and Social Justice in Teacher Education*. New York: Teachers College Press

Coffey, B. (1984). ESP – English for Specific Purposes. *Language Teaching*, 17(1), 2–16

Coffin, C., Curry, M. J., Goodmann, S., Hewings, A. Lillis, T. and Swann, J. (2003). *Teaching Academic Writing: A Toolkit for Higher Education*. London: Routledge

Coleman, J. A. (2006). English-medium teaching in European higher education. *Language Teaching*, 39(1), 1–14

Coley, M. (1999). The English language entry requirements of Australian universities for students of non-English-speaking background. *Higher Education Research & Development*, 18(1), 7–17

Collier, P. J. and Morgan, D. L. (2008). 'Is that paper really due today?': Differences in first generation and traditional college students' understandings of faculty expectations. *Higher Education*, 55(4), 425–46

Conger, J. A. (1998). The necessary art of persuasion. *Harvard Business Review*, 76(3), 84–95

Conrad, S. and Mauranen, A. (2003). The Corpus of English as a Lingua Franca in Academic Settings. *TESOL Quarterly*, 37(3), 513–27

Cook, H. (2008). Impacts add outcomes for providers in M. Banks and A. Olsen (eds), *Outcomes and Impacts of International Education: From International Student to Australian Graduate, the Journey of a Lifetime*. IDP Education, pp. 62–95

Cooper, M. (ed.) (2010). From access to success: Closing the knowledge divide. Higher education for under-represented groups in the market economy. *Papers from the 19th EAN Annual Conference of the European Access Network, Södertörn University, Stockholm, Sweden, 14–16 June 2010*

Cooper, R. L. (1989). *Language Planning and Social Change*. Cambridge: Cambridge University Press

Cotton, F. and Conrow, F. (1998). An Investigation of the Predictive Validity of IELTS amongst a Group of International Students studying at the University of Tasmania. *IELTS Research Reports* 1998, Vol. *1*, pp. 72–115

Cotton, D. R. E., George, R. and Joyner, M. (2013). Interaction and influence in culturally mixed groups. *Innovations in Education and Teaching International*, 50(3), 272–83

Council of Europe (2001). *Common European Framework of Reference for Languages: Learning, Teaching, Assessment* [CEFR]. Cambridge: Cambridge University Press

Cownie, F. and Addison, W. (1996). International students and language support: A new survey. *Studies in Higher Education*, 21(2), 221–31

Crichton, J. and Murray, N. (2014). Plurilithic and ecological perspectives on English: Some conceptual and practical implications in N. Murray and A. Scarino (eds), *Dynamic ecologies of languages education in the Asia-Pacific Region: Developments, Issues and Challenges*. Dordrecht: Springer

Crichton, J. and Scarino, A. (2007). How are we to understand the 'intercultural dimension?': An examination of the intercultural dimension of internationalisation in the context of higher education in Australia. *Australian Review of Applied Linguistics*, 30(1), 4.1–4.21

Criper, C. and Davies, A. (1988). *Research Report 1 (i)*. ELTS Validation Project Report Cambridge: British Council/UCLES

Crose, B. (2011). Internationalization of the higher education classroom: Strategies to facilitate intercultural learning and academic success. *International Journal of Teaching and Learning in Higher Education*, 23(3), 388–95

Crowley, S. (1998). *Composition in the University: Historical and Polemical Essays*. Pittsburgh: University of Pittsburgh Press

Cummins, J. (1979). Cognitive/academic language proficiency, linguistic interdependence, the optimum age question and some other matters. *Working Papers on Bilingualism*, *19*, 121–129

Cummins, J. (1980a). The construct of language proficiency in bilingual education in J. E. Alatis (ed.), *Current Issues in Bilingual Education. Georgetown University Round Table on Languages and Linguistics (GURT) 1980*. Washington, DC: Georgetown University Press, pp. 81–103

Cummins, J. (1980b). The cross-lingual dimensions of language proficiency: Implications for bilingual education and the optimal age issue. *TESOL Quarterly*, 14, 175–187

Cummins, J. (2000). *Language, Power and Pedagogy: Bilingual Children in the Crossfire*. Clevedon: Multilingual Matters

Cummins, J. (2000). Putting language proficiency in its place: Responding to critiques of the conversational/academic language distinction in J. Cenoz and U. Jessner (eds), *English in Europe: The Acquisition of a Third Language*. Multilingual Matters Ltd, pp.54–83

Cummins. J. (2008). BICS and CALP: Empirical and theoretical status of the distinction in B. Street and N. H. Hornberger (eds), *Encyclopedia of Language and Education, 2nd edition, volume 2: Literacy*. New York: Springer Science + Business Media LLC, pp. 71–83

Curnow, T. J. and Liddicoat, A. J. (2008). Assessment as learning: Engaging students in academic literacy in their first semester in A. Duff, D. Quinn, M. Green, K. Andre, T. Ferris and S. Copland (eds), *Proceedings of the ATN Assessment Conference 2008: Engaging Students in Assessment*, [Online]. www.ojs.unisa.edu.au/index. php/atna/issue/view/ISBN%20978-0-646-504421/showToc   Retrieved   30 October 2013

Curry, M. J. and Lillis, T. M. (2003). Issues in academic writing in higher education in C. Coffin, M. J. Curry, S. Goodmann, A. Hewings, T. Lillis and J. Swann (eds), *Teaching Academic Writing: A Toolkit for Higher Education*. London: Routledge, 1–18

Daily Telegraph. (2014). The top 10 most popular degree courses., *The Daily Telegraph*, 14 February 2014 www.telegraph.co.uk/education/universityeducation/8695883 /The-top-10-most-popular-degree-courses.html Retrieved 1 June 2014

Davies, A., Brown, A., Elder, C., Hill, K., Lumley, T. and McNamara, T. (1999). *Dictionary of Language Testing. Studies in Language Testing, Volume 7*. Cambridge, UK: UCLES/Cambridge University Press

Davies, A. (2008). Textbook trends in teaching language testing. *Language Testing*, 25(3), 327–347

Dawson, J. (2011). Implementing good practice principles for English language proficiency: A case study. *English Australia Journal*, 26(2), 4–14

Deardorff, D. K. (2006). Identification and assessment of intercultural competence as a student outcome of internationalization. *Journal of Studies in International Education*, 10(3), 241–266

De Lano, L., Riley, L. and Crookes, G. (1994). The meaning of innovation for ESL teachers. *System*, 22(4), 487–496

Department of Education, Employment and Workplace Relations (DEEWR) (Good Practice Principles steering committee). (2010). English language standards for Higher Education. www.aall.org.au/sites/default/files/FinalEnglishLanguageStan dardsMay2012.pdf Retrieved 1 July 2015

Department of Education, Employment and Workplace Relations (DEEWR). (2009). Good Practice Principles for English language proficiency for international students in Australian universities. pandora.nla.gov.au/pan/127066/20110826-00 04/www.auqa.edu.au/files/otherpublications/good%20practice%20principles%20 for%20english%20language%20proficiency%20report.pdf Retrieved 30 June 2015

Department of Immigration and Citizenship. Fact Sheet 4 – More than 60 Years of Post-war Migration. www.immi.gov.au/media/fact-sheets/04fifty.htm Retrieved 25 April 2010

de Vita, J. (2002). Does assessed multicultural group work really pull UK students' average down? *Assessment & Evaluation in Higher Education*, 27(2), 153–61

Dooey, P. and Oliver, R. (2002). An investigation into the predictive validity of the IELTS test as an indicator of future academic success. *Prospect*, 17(1), 36–54

Drennan, L. T. and Beck, M. (2000). Teaching and research: Equal partners or poor relations? Paper presented at the Qualitative Evidence-based Practice Conference, Coventry University, 15–17 May 2000. Education-Line. www.leeds.ac.uk/edu col/documents/00001405.htm Retrieved 8 February 2015

Drennan, L. T. (2001). Quality assessment and the tension between teaching and research. *Quality in Higher Education*, 7, (3), 167–78

Drummond, I., Alderson, K., Nixon, I. and Wiltshire, J. (1999) *Managing Curriculum Change in Higher Education*. Newcastle: University of Newcastle-Upon-Tyne

Ducasse, A. M. and Brown, A. (2009). Assessing paired orals: Raters' orientation to interaction. *Language Testing*, 26(3), 423–43

Ducasse, A. M. (2010), *Interaction in Paired Oral Proficiency Assessment in Spanish (Language Testing and Evaluation)*. Peter Lang

Dunne, C. (2009). Host students' perspectives of intercultural contact in an Irish university. *Journal of Studies in International Education*, 13, 229–39

Dunne, C. (2013). Exploring motivations for intercultural contact among host country university students: An Irish case study. *International Journal of Intercultural Relations*, 37, 567–78

Dunworth, K. (2009). An investigation into post-entry English language assessment in Australian universities. *Journal of Academic Language and Learning*, 3(1), A1–A13

Dunworth, K. (2010). Clothing the Emperor: Addressing the Issue of English Language Proficiency in Australian Universities. *The Australian Universities' Review*, 52(2), 5–10

Dunworth, K., Drury, H., Kralik, C. and Moore, T. (2013). *Degrees of Proficiency: Building a Strategic Approach to University Students' English Language Assessment and Development. Final Report*. Sydney: Australian Government, Office of Learning and Teaching. www.olt.gov.au/project-degrees-proficiency-bu

ilding-strategic-approach-university-studentsapos-english-language-ass Retrieved 23 May 2014

Dunworth, K. (2013). Discussion paper 2: In-course student English language development. *Five Years On: English Language Competence of International Students Discussion Papers*. Melbourne: International Education Association of Australia, pp. 39–67

Edelsky, C., Hudelson, S., Altwerger, B., Flores, B., Barkin, F. and Jilbert, K. (1983). Semilingualism and language deficit. *Applied Linguistics*, 4(1), 1–22

Egbert, J. L. (2005). Conducting research on CALL in J. L Egbert and G. M. Petrie (eds), *CALL Research Perspectives*. Mahwah, NJ: Lawrence Erlbaum, pp. 4–8

Elder, C. (1993). Language proficiency as a predictor of performance in teacher education. *Melbourne Papers in Language Testing*, 2, 68–85

Elder, C. and Davis, A. (2006). Assessing English as a lingua franca. *Annual Review of Applied Linguistics*, 26, 282–301

Elder, C. and Erlam, R. (2001). *Development and Validation of the Diagnostic English Language Needs Assessment (DELNA): Final Report*. Auckland: University of Auckland, Department of Applied Language Studies and Linguistics

Elder, C. and von Randow, J. (2002). *Report on the 2002 Pilot of DELNA at the University of Auckland*. Auckland: University of Auckland, Department of Applied Language Studies and Linguistics

Elder, C. (2003). The DELNA initiative at the University of Auckland. *TESOLANZ Newsletter*, 12(1), 15–16

Elder, C., Bright, C. and Bennett, S. (2007). The role of language proficiency in academic success: Perspectives from a New Zealand university. *Melbourne Papers in Language Testing*, 12(1), 24–58

Elder, C. and Von Randow, J. (2008). Exploring the utility of a web-based English language screening tool. *Language Assessment Quarterly*, 5(3), 173–94

Elder, C. and Knoch, U. (2009). *Report on the development and trial of the Academic English Screening Test (AEST)*. Melbourne: The University of Melbourne

Engle, J. and Tinto, V. (2008). Moving beyond access: College success for low-income, first- generation students. Washington: The Pell Institute for the Study of Opportunity in Higher Education. eric.ed.gov/?id=ED504448 Retrieved 2 March 2014

Entwistle, N. and Tait, H. (1995). Approaches to studying and perceptions of the learning environment across disciplines. *New Directions for Teaching and Learning*, 64 (Winter), 93–103

Everard, K. B. and Morris, G. (1985). *Effective School Management*. London: Harper & Row

Fantini, A. E. and Tirmizi, A. (2006). *Exploring and Assessing Intercultural Competence: Final Report*. World Learning Publications. digitalcollections.sit.edu /cgi/viewcontent.cgi?article=1001&context=worldlearning_publications Retrieved 22 August 2014

Fiocco, M. (1992). *English Proficiency Levels of Students from a Non-English Speaking Background: A Study of IELTS as an Indicator of Tertiary Success*. Unpublished research report. Perth: Curtin University of Technology

Firth, J. R. (1957a). *Papers in Linguistics 1934 – 1951*. London: Oxford University Press

Firth, J. R. (1950). Personality and language in society in J. R. Firth (1957): *Papers in Linguistics 1934–1951*. London: Oxford University Press

Fischer, K. (2012). Fess up: Foreign students are cash cows. *The Chronicle of Higher Education*, 16 October 2012. chronicle.com/article/What-If-Colleges-Acknowledged/135080/ Retrieved 7 June 2014

Foot, M. C. (1999). Relaxing in pairs. *English Language Teaching Journal*, 53(1), 36–41

Freeman, R. and Lewis, R. (1998). *Planning and Implementing Assessment*. Psychology Press

Fox, J. (2005). Test decisions over time: Tracking validity. *Language Testing*, 21, 437–65

Fraser, B. and Nolan, W. (1981). The association of deference with linguistic form. *International Journal of the Sociology of Language*, *27*, 93–109

Fullan, M. (1982). *The Meaning of Educational Change*. New York: Teachers College Press

Fullan, M. (1991). *The New Meaning of Educational Change*. London: Cassell

Fullan, M. (2001). *The New Meaning of Educational Change* (3rd edn). London: Routledge Falmer

Gabris, G. T., Golembiewski, R. T. and Ihrkw, D. M. (2001). Leadership credibility, board relations and administrative innovation at the local government level. *Journal of Public Administration Research and Theory*, 11(1), 89–108

Gardner, S. and Nesi, H. (2013). A classification of genre families in university student writing. *Applied Linguistics*, *34* (1), 1–29

Gelb, C. (2012). Cultural issues in the higher education classroom. *Student Pulse*, 4(7), 1–3. www.studentpulse.com/articles/661/cultural-issues-in-the-higher-education-classroom Retrieved 13 July 2014

General Dental Council. Before you apply for ORE [Overseas Registration Exam]. www.gdc-uk.org/Dentalprofessionals/ORE/Pages/Before-you-apply.aspx Retrieved 30 November 2014

Gibson, C. and Rusek, W. (1992) The validity of an overall band score of 6.0 on the IELTS test as a predictor of adequate English language level appropriate for successful academic study. Unpublished Masters of Arts (Applied Linguistics) thesis, New South Wales: Macquarie University,

Gidley, J. M., Hampson, G. P., Wheeler, L. and Bereded-Samuel, E. (2010). From access to success: An integrated approach to quality higher education informed by social inclusion theory and practice. *Higher Education Policy*, 23, 123–47

Gielis, I. (2010). The students' perspective on access, retention and diversity in *Access to Success: Project Compendium*, European University Association. www.accesstosuccess-africa.eu/reports/116.html Retrieved 3 September 2013

Ginns, P., Kitay, J. and Prosser, M. (2008). Developing conceptions of teaching and the scholarship of teaching through a Graduate Certificate of Higher Education. *International Journal for Academic Development*, 13(3), 75–85

Goffman, E. (1955). On face-work: An analysis of ritual elements in social interaction. *Psychiatry: Journal of the Study of Interpersonal Processes*, 18(2), 213–231

Goffman, E. (1967). *Interaction Ritual: Essays in Face-to-Face Behaviour*. Garden City, NY: Doubleday

Goldsmith, W. and Clutterbuck, D. (1984). *The Winning Streak*. Harmondsworth: Penguin

Goleman, D. (1995). *Emotional Intelligence*. Bantam Books

Goleman, D., Boyatzis, R. and McKee, A. (2013). *Primal Leadership: Unleashing the Power of Emotional Intelligence*. Harvard Business Review Press

Great Britain. (1992). Further and Higher Education Act 1992: Elizabeth II. *Chapter 13.* (1992) [Online]. www.legislation.gov.uk/ukpga/1992/13/contents Retrieved 2 June 2014

Grice, H. P. (1975). Logic and conversation in P. Cole and J. Morgan (eds), *Syntax and Semantics, 3: Speech Acts,* New York: Academic Press, pp. 41–58. Reprinted in H. P. Grice (ed.), *Studies in the Way of Words,* Cambridge, MA: Harvard University Press, 1989, pp. 22–40

Hakuta, K., Butler, Y. G. and Witt, D. (2000). *How Long Does It Take English Learners to Attain Proficiency?* Santa Barbara: University of California Linguistic Minority Research Institute

Halliday, M. A. K. (1975). *Learning How to Mean.* Edward Arnold

Harper, R., Prentice, S. and Wilson, K. (2011). English language perplexity: Articulating the tensions in the DEEWR 'Good Practice Principles'. *The International Journal of the First Year in Higher Education,* 2(1), 36–48. fyhejournal.com/article/viewFile/51/82

Harper, R. (2013). From principles to practice: Implementing an English language proficiency model at UniSA. *Journal of Academic Language & Learning,* 7(2): A150–A164

Harris, A. (2009). Addressing English language proficiency in a business faculty. *eCulture,* 2, 92–8. otl.curtin.edu.au/professional_development/conferences/tlf/tlf2010/refereed/harris.html Retrieved 9 May 2014

Harris, A. (2009). Creative leadership: developing future leaders. *Management in Education,* 23(1), 9–11

Harrison, N. and Peacock, N. (2010). Cultural difference, mindfulness and passive xenophobia: Using Integrated Threat Theory to explore home higher education students' perspectives on 'internationalisation at home'. *British Educational Research Journal,* 36(6), 877–902

Havelock, R. G. (1970). *A Guide to Innovation in Education,* Ann Arbor: University of Michigan

Havelock, R. G. (1971). The Utilization of Education Research and Development. *British Journal of Educational Technology,* 2 (2), 84–98

Health and Care Professions Council. What to do before you make an international application. www.hcpc-uk.org.uk/apply/international/ Retrieved 24 November 2014

Henderson, R. and Hirst, E. (2006, November). *How Sufficient Is Academic Literacy? Re- examining a Short Course for 'disadvantaged' Tertiary Students.* Paper presented at the AARE Conference, Adelaide, Australia

Henderson, R. and Hirst, E. (2007). Reframing academic literacy: Re-examining a short- course for 'disadvantaged' tertiary students. *English Teaching: Practice and Critique,* 6(2), 25–38

Hersey, P. and Blanchard, K. (1993). *Management of Organisational Behaviour* (6th edn), Upper Saddle River, NJ: Prentice-Hall

Higher Education Statistics Agency (HESA). (2014). *Statistical First Release (SFR)* 197, 2014 (Table 1). www.hesa.ac.uk/sfr197 Retrieved 23 July 2014

Higher Education Funding Council for England (HEFCE). (2010). *Recession to Recovery: Changes in Student Choices and Graduate Employment.* Universities UK. www.universitiesuk.ac.uk/highereducation/Documents/2010/ChangesInStudentChoices.pdf Retrieved 1 June 2014

Hirst, E., Henderson, R., Allan, M., Bode, J. and Kocatepe, M. (2004). Repositioning academic literacy: Charting the emergence of a community of practice. *Australian Journal of Language and Literacy*, 27(1), 66–80

Hockings, C. (2010). Inclusive learning and teaching in higher education: A synthesis of research. *EvidenceNet*, Higher Education Academy. www.heacademy.ac.uk/resour ces/detail/ourwork/evidencenet/Inclusive_ learning_and_teaching_in_higher_edu cation_synthesis Retrieved 4 August 2012

Hofstede, G. (1991). *Cultures and Organizations: Software of the Mind*. London: McGraw-Hill

Horton, P. B. and Hunt, C. L. (1976). *Sociology*. London: McGraw-Hill

House, J. (2003). English as a lingua franca: A threat to multilingualism? *Journal of Sociolinguistics*, 7(4), 556–78

House, J. (2009). The pragmatics of English as a lingua franca. *Intercultural Pragmatics*, 6(2), 141–5

Huchinson, T. and Waters, A. (1987). *English for Specific Purposes: A Learning-Centred Approach*. Cambridge: Cambridge University Press

Hughes, K. L., Karp, M. M., Fermin, B. J. and Bailey, T. R. (2005). *Pathways to college access and success*. Washington, DC: U.S. Department of Education Office of Vocational and Adult Education

Hulstijn, J. H. (2011). Language Proficiency in Native and Nonnative Speakers: An Agenda for Research and Suggestions for Second-Language Assessment. *Language Assessment Quarterly*, 8(3), 229–49

Humphreys, P. and Gribble, C. (2013). Discussion paper 3: Outcomes – English language and the transition to work or further study. *Five Years On: English Language Competence of International Students Discussion Papers*. Melbourne: International Education Association of Australia, pp. 69–103

Hyland, K. (2000). *Disciplinary Discourses: Social Interactions in Academic Writing*. Harlow, UK: Longman

Hyland, K. (2006). Disciplinary differences: Language variation in academic discourses in K. Hyland and M. Bondi (eds), *Academic Discourse Across Disciplines*. Frankfurt: Peter Lang, pp. 17–45

Hyland, K. (2007). Different strokes for different folks: Disciplinary variation in academic writing in K. Flottem (ed.), *Language and Discipline Perspectives on Academic Discourse*. Newcastle: Cambridge Scholars Press, pp. 89–108

Hyland, K. (2008). Genre and academic writing in the disciplines. *Language Teaching*, 41(4), 543–62

Hyland, P. W. and Beckett, R. C. (2009). Effective communication in innovation processes. *10th Proc International CINet Conference*, 6–8 September, Brisbane, Australia

Hymes, D. (1971). Competence and performance in linguistic theory in R. Huxley and E. Ingram (eds), *Language Acquisition: Models and Methods*. London: Academic Press

Hymes, D. (1972). On communicative competence in J. B. Pride and J. Holmes (eds), *Sociolinguistics*. Harmondsworth: Penguin

Ingram, D. E. and Bayliss, A. (2007). IELTS as a predictor of academic language performance. Part 1: The view from participants. *IELTS Impact Studies Vol. 7* (IELTS Joint-funded research programme). IELTS Australia and the British Council

Institute of International Education. (2013). Open Doors 2013: International Students in the United States and Study Abroad by American Students are at All-Time

High.*Press Release*, 11 Nov 2013. www.iie.org/Who-We-Are/News-and-Events/ Press-Center/Press-releases/2013/2013-11-11-Open-Doors-Data Retrieved 3 April 2013

International Education Association of Australia [IEAA] (2013). Good practice principles in practice: Teaching across cultures. IEAA. www.ieaa.org.au/documents/item/125. Retrieved 2 March 2014

Irish Higher Education Quality Network (Subcommittee). (2009). Provision of education to international students. www.icosirl.ie/eng/content/download/872/5346/file /Provision_of_Education_to_International_Students.pdf Retrieved 30 June 2015

Jamieson, J., Jones, S., Kirsch, I., Mosenthal, P. and Taylor, C. (2000). *TOEFL 2000 Framework: A Working Paper*. Princeton, NJ: Educational Testing Service

Jenkins, J., A. Cogo and M. Dewey. (2011). Review of developments in research into English as a lingua franca. *Language Teaching*, 44(3), 281–315

Jenkins, J. (2012). English as a lingua francafrom the classroom to the classroom. *English Language Teaching Journal*, 66(4), 486–94

Jenkins, J. (2013). *English as a Lingua Franca in the International University: The Politics of Academic English Language Policy*. Abingdon: Routledge

Jiang, X. (2011). Why interculturisation? A neo-Marxist approach to accommodate cultural diversity in higher education. *Educational Philosophy and Theory*, 43(4), 387–99

Johnson, M. E. (2008). An investigation into pedagogical challenges facing international tertiary-level students in New Zealand. *Higher Education Research and Development*, 27(3), 231–43

Joy, S. and Kolb, D. A. (2009). Are there cultural differences in learning style? *International Journal of Intercultural Relations*, 33(1), 69–85

Kachru, B. B. (1985). Standards, codification and sociolinguistic realism: The English language in the outer circle in R. Quirk and H. G. Widdowson (eds), *English in the World: Teaching and Learning the Language and Literatures*. Cambridge: Cambridge University Press, pp. 11–30

Katz, A., Low, P., Stack, J. and Tsang, S. (2004). A Study Of Content Area Assessment For English Language. U.S. Department of Education: Office of English Language Acquisition and Academic Achievement for Limited English Proficient Students, Learners. www.arcassociates.org/files/CAELLRpt9-04.pdf Retrieved 24 July 2013

Kennedy, C. (1999). Introduction – learning to change in C. Kennedy, P. Doyle and C. M. Goh (eds), *Exploring Change in English Language Teaching*. Oxford: Macmillan, pp. iv–viii

Kennelly, R., Maldoni, A. and Davies, D. (2010). A case study: Do discipline-based programmes improve student learning outcomes? *International Journal for Educational Integrity*, 6(1), 61–73

Kerstjens, M and Nery, C. (2000). Predictive validity in the IELTS test: A study of the relationship between IELTS scores and students' subsequent academic performance. *English Language Testing System research reports*, *3*, 85–108

Kirkness, A. (2006). Critical reflections on an academic literacies policy five years on in *Critical Visions, Proceedings of the 29th HERDSA Annual Conference, Western Australia, 10–12 July*. Higher Education Research and Development Society of Australasia, Inc., pp. 167–74 www.herdsa.org.au/wp-content/uploads/conference /2006/papers/Kirkness.pdf Retrieved 7 September 2012

Klesmer, H. (1994). Assessment and teacher perceptions of ESL student achievement. *English Quarterly*, 26(3), 8–11

Klinger, C. M. and Murray, N. (2012). Tensions in higher education: Widening participation, student diversity and the challenge of academic language/literacy. *Journal of Widening Participation and Lifelong Learning*, 14(1), 27–44

Knight, M. (2011). *Strategic Review of the Student Visa Programme*. Canberra: Department of Immigration and Border Protection. www.immi.gov.au/students /_pdf/2011-knight-review.pdf Retrieved 23 November 2013

Kramsch, C. (1993). *Context and Culture in Language Teaching*. Oxford, UK: Oxford University Press

Kuo, I. (2006). Addressing the issue of teaching English as a lingua franca. *ELT Journal*, 60(3), 213–221

Lakoff, R. (1973). *The Logic of Politeness: Minding Your P's and Q's. Papers from the 9th Regional Meeting*, Chicago Linguistics Society, 292–305

Larcombe, W. and Malkin, I. (2008). Identifying students likely to benefit from language support in first-year law. *Higher Education Research and Development*, 27 (4), 319–29

Lave, J. and Wenger, E. (1991). *Situated Learning: Legitimate Peripheral Participation*. Cambridge: Cambridge University Press

Lea, M. R. and Street, B. V. (1998). Student writing in higher education: An academic literacies approach. *Studies in Higher Education*, 23(2), 157–72

Lea, M. R. (1999). Academic literacies and learning in higher education: Constructing knowledge through texts and experiences in C. Jones, J. Turner and B. Street (eds), *Students' Writing in the University: Cultural and Epistemological Issues*. Amsterdam: John Benjamins, pp. 103–24

Lea, M. R. and Street, B. (2000). Student writing and staff feedback in higher education: An academic literacies approach. In *Student Writing in Higher Education: New Contexts*, ed. M. Lea and B. Stierer. Buckingham, UK: The Society for Research into Higher Education and Open University Press, pp. 32–46

Lea, M. R. and Street, B. V. (2006). The 'academic literacies' model: Theory and applications. *Theory into Practice*, 45(4), 368–377

Leask, B. (2011), Assessment, learning, teaching and internationalisation: Engaging for the future. *Assessment, Teaching and Learning Journal*, 11, 5–20

Leeuwis, C. and Aarts, N. (2011). Rethinking communication in innovation processes: Creating space for change in complex systems. *Journal of Agricultural Education and Extension*, 17(1), 21–36

Legal Profession Admission Board. English language proficiency requirements. www .lpab.justice.nsw.gov.au/lpab/legalprofession_overseas_practitioners/legalprofes sion_overseas_practitioners_english_req.html Retrieved 30 November 2014

LeVine, R. A. and Campbell, D. T. (1972). *Ethnocentrism*. New York: John Wiley

Levy M. (1997). *CALL: Context and Conceptualisation*. Oxford: Oxford University Press

Lewicki, R. J. and Bailey, J. R. (2009). The research-teaching nexus: Tensions and opportunities in S. J. Armstrong and C. V. Fukami (eds), *The SAGE Handbook of Management Learning, Education and Development*. Sage, pp. 385–402

Liddicoat, A. J. (2009). Evolving ideologies of the intercultural in Australian multicultural and language education policy *Journal of Multilingual and Multicultural Development* 31(3), 189–203

Liddicoat, A. J. and Scarino, A. (2010). Eliciting the intercultural in foreign language education in A. Paran and L. Sercu (eds), *Testing the Untestable in Foreign Language Education*. Clevedon: Multilingual Matters, pp. 52–73

Liddicoat, A. J. and Scarino, A. (2013). *Intercultural Language Teaching and Learning*. New York: Wiley & Sons

Light, R. L., Xu, M. and Mossop, J. (1987). English proficiency and academic performance of international students. *TESOL Quarterly*, *21*(2), 251–61

Lillis, T. (1997). New voices in academia? The regulative nature of academic writing conventions. *Language and Education*, 11(3), 182–199

Lillis, T. (2001). *Student Writing: Access, Regulation, Desire*. London: Routledge

Lyons, J. (1981). *Language and Linguistics*. Cambridge: Cambridge University Press

Lo Bianco, J., Crozet, C. and Liddicoat, A. J. (eds) (1999). *Striving for the Third Place: Intercultural Competence through Language Education*. Canberra, Language Australia

Lo Bianco, J. (2010). The importance of language politics and multilingualism for cultural diversity. *International Social Science Journal*, 61, 37–67

Lobo, A. and Gurney, L. (2014). What did they expect? Exploring a link between students' expectations, attendance and attrition on English language enhancement courses. *Journal of Further and Higher Education*, 38(5), 730–54

Lovegrove, B. and Clarke, J. (2008). The dilemma of the modern university in balancing competitive agendas: The USQ experience. *Higher Education Management and Policy* 20(2), 139–51

Lumsden, G. and Lumsden, D. (1997). *Communicating in Groups and Teams: Sharing Leadership*. Belmont, CA: Wadsworth

Mackay, R. and Moutford, A. (1978). *English for specific purposes*. London: Longman

Maes, R., Sztalberb, C. and Sylin, M. (2011). Acknowledgement of prior experiential learning to widen participation at the Universite Libre des Bruxelles: The challenge of the institutional message in L. Thomas and M. Tight (eds), *Institutional Transformation to Engage a Diverse Student Body (International perspectives on higher education research, Volume 6)*. Emerald Group Publishing Limited, pp. 187–98

Malinowski, B. (1923). The problem of meaning in primitive languages in C. K. Ogden and I. A . Richards (eds), *The Meaning of Meaning*. New York: Harcourt, Brace and World, Inc, pp. 296–336

Marginson, S. and Considine, M. (2000). *The Enterprise University: Power, Governance and Reinvention in Australia*. Cambridge: Cambridge University Press

Markee, N. (1986). The importance of sociopolitical factors to communicative course design. *English for Specific Purposes*, 5(*1*), 3–16

Markee, N. (1993). The diffusion of innovation in language teaching. *Annual Review of Applied Linguistics*, 13, 229–243

Maslow, A. H. (1970). *Motivation and Personality* (2nd edn). New York: Harper & Row

Matsuda, A. (2003). Incorporating world Englishes in teaching English as an international language. *TESOL Quarterly*, 37(4), 719–29

Mauranen, A. (2013). *Exploring ELF: Academic English Shaped by Non-Native Speakers*. Cambridge: Cambridge University Press

Mauranen, A., Hynninen, N. and Ranta, E. (2010). English as a lingua franca: The ELFA Project. *English for Specific Purposes*, 29(3), 183–190

Medical Board of Australia. (2010). *English Language Skills Registration Standard*. Medical Board of Australia. www.medicalboard.gov.au/Registration-Standards. aspx Retrieved 30 November 2014

Miles, M. B. (1964). Education Innovation: The Nature of the Problem in M. B. Miles (ed.), *Innovation in Education*, N. Y. Teachers College Press

Martin-Jones, M. and Romaine, S. (1986). Semilingualism: A half-baked theory of communicative competence. *Applied Linguistics*, 7(1), 26–38

MASUS Project Reports (1993–1995). Learning Centre, University of Sydney

Matthews, D. (2012). English language standards being set below recommended levels. *Times Higher Education*. www.timeshighereducation.co.uk/news/english-stan dards-being-set-below-recommended-levels/420938.article Retrieved 23 May 2014

Matthews, R. (n.d.). Exploring the development of discipline-specific language skills with increasingly diverse art and design student groups. The Higher Education Academy. www.heacademy.ac.uk/node/3489 Retrieved 20 August 2014

McDowell, C. and Merrylees, B. (1998). Survey of receiving institutions' use and attitude to IELTS in S. Wood (ed.), *EA Journal, Occasional Paper 1998* (Vol. *1*) pp. 116–39. Sydney: ELICOS Association Ltd

Merisotis, J. P. (2013). Meeting the U.S. demand for talent: The imperative of increasing attainment for underserved populations in N. Murray and C. M. Klinger (eds), *Aspirations, Access and Attainment in Widening Participation: International Perspectives on Widening Participation and an Agenda for Change*. Oxford: Routledge

Messick, S. (1996). Validity and washback in language testing. *Language Testing*, 13(3), 241–56

Molesworth, M, Scullion, R. and Nixon, E. (2010). *The Marketisation of Higher Education and the Student as Consumer*. Routledge

Moore, T. and Hough, B. (2007). The perils of skills: Towards a model of integrating graduate attributes into the disciplines in H. Marriott, T. Moore and R. Spence-Brown (eds), *Learning Discourses and the Discourses of Learning* (pp. 2.01–02.12). Melbourne: Monash E-press

Morgan, J. (2010). Overseas students 'are not cash cows'. *Times Higher Education*, 26 March 2010. www.timeshighereducation.co.uk/news/overseas-students-are-not -cash-cows/411001.article Retrieved June 8, 2014

Mort, P. and Drury, H. (2012). Supporting student academic literacy in the disciplines using genre based online pedagogy. *Journal of Academic Language and Learning*, 6(3), A1–A15

Mortenson, T. (2013). Regressive social policy and its consequences for opportunity for higher education in the United States, 1980-present in N. Murray and C. M. Klinger (eds), *Aspirations, Access and Attainment in Widening Participation: International Perspectives on Widening Participation and an Agenda for Change*. Oxford: Routledge, pp. 20–40

Munby, J. (1978). *Communicative Syllabus Design*. Cambridge: Cambridge University Press

Murray D. E. (ed.) (2008). *Planning Change, Changing Plans: Innovations in Second Language teaching*. Ann Arbor, MI: University of Michigan Press

Murray, D. and Arkoudis, S. (2013). Discussion paper 1: Preparation and selection. In *Five Years On: English Language Competence of International Students*, International Education Association of Australia, pp. 23–51

Murray, N. (2010a). Considerations in the post-enrolment assessment of English language proficiency: Reflections from the Australian context. *Language Assessment Quarterly*, 7(4), 343–58

Murray, N. (2010b). Conceptualising the English language needs of first year university students. *The International Journal of the First Year in Higher Education*, 1(1), 55–64

Murray, N. (2010c). Pragmatics, awareness-raising, and the Cooperative Principle. *English Language Teaching Journal*, 64(3), 293–301

Murray, N. (2012). Ten 'Good Practice Principles' . . . ten key questions: Considerations in addressing the English language needs of higher education students. *Higher Education Research & Development*, 31(2), 233–46

Murray, N. (2013). Widening participation and English language proficiency: A convergence with implications for assessment practices in higher education. *Studies in Higher Education*, 38(2), 299–311

Murray, N. (2014). Reflections on the implementation of post-enrolment English language assessment. *Language Assessment Quarterly*, 11(3), 325–37

Murray, N. and Hicks, M. (2014). An institutional approach to English language proficiency. *Journal of Further and Higher Education*, DOI: 10.1080/0309877X.2014.938261

Murray, N. and Klinger, C. M. (2012). Dimensions of conflict: Reflections on the first year higher education experience from an access education perspective. *International Journal of Lifelong Education*, 31(2), 117–33

Murray, N. and Nallaya, S. (2014). Embedding academic literacies in university programme curricula: A case study. *Studies in Higher Education*, DOI: 10.1080/03075079.2014.981150

Murray, N. and Scarino, A. (eds) (2014). Dynamic ecologies: A relational perspective on languages education in the Asia-Pacific region. *Multilingual Education* Vol. 9. Dordrecht: Springer

Narushima, Y. (2008). Overseas students exploited as cash cows. *Sydney Morning Herald*, 17 December 2008. www.smh.com.au/news/national/overseas-students-exploited-as-cash-cows/2008/12/16/1229189622969.html Retrieved 8 June 2014

Nesi, H. and Gardner, S. F. (2006). Variation in disciplinary culture: University tutors' views on assessed writing tasks in R. Kiely, G. Clibbon, P. Rea-Dickins and H. Woodfield (eds), *Language, Culture and Identity in Applied Linguistics*. London: Equinox Publishing, pp. 99–117

Nesi, H. and Gardner, S. (2012). *Genres Across the Disciplines: Student Writing in Higher Education*. Cambridge: Cambridge University Press

Neuliep, J. W. (2006). *Intercultural Communication: A Contextual Approach* (3rd edn). New York, NY: Houghton Mifflin

Neumann, R. (2001). Disciplinary differences and university teaching. *Studies in Higher Education*, 26(2), 135–146

Newman, M., Trenchs-Parera, M. and Pujol, M. (2003). Core academic literacy principles versus culture-specific practices: a multi-case study of academic achievement. *English for Specific Purposes*, 22(2), 45–71

New Zealand Quality Agency (2010). *Code of Practice for the Pastoral Care of International Students*. New Zealand Quality Agency. www.nzqa.govt.nz/assets /Providers-and-partners/Code-of-Practice-NZQA.pdf Retrieved 12 December 2011

Nicholls, A. (1983). *Managing Educational Innovations*. London: Allen and Unwin

Nisbet, J. (1974). Innovation – Bandwagon or Hearse? (Frank Tate Memorial Lecture)

North, B. (2000). *The Development of a Common Framework Scale of Language Proficiency*. New York: Peter Lang Publishing

Now Learning. (2013). The most popular degree programs in Australia. nowlearning.com. au/resources/the-most-popular-degree-programs-in-australia Retrieved 1 June 2014

Nursing and Midwifery Board of South Australia. (2009). Evidence supporting the changes to the English language proficiency requirements for students with English as a second language undertaking nmbSA approved courses leading to Registration or Enrolment. www.ahpra.gov.au/documents/default.aspx?record= WD10%2F4005&dbid=AP&chksum=zubVdFJwm%2BpAHLemsLVk9A%3D %3D Retrieved 6 July 2013

Nursing and Midwifery Council. International English Language Testing (IELTS). w ww.nmc-uk.org/registration/joining-the-register/trained-outside-the-eu–eea/inter national-english-language-testing-ielts/ Retrieved 30 November 2014

O'Loughlin, K. and Arkoudis, S. (2009). Investigating IELTS score gains in higher education. *IELTS Research Reports Volume* 10, 95–180

Organisation for Economic Co-operation and Development (OECD). (2013). Education indicators in focus. OECD Publishing. www.oecd.org/education/skills-beyond -school/EDIF%202013–N%C2%B014%20(eng)-Final.pdf Retrieved 5 May 2014

Organisation for Economic Co-operation and Development (OECD). (2013). Organisation For Economic Co-operation and Development indicators: Education at a Glance 2013, Table C4.1. OECD Publishing. dx.doi.org/10.1787/ eag-2013-en Retrieved 3 April 2014

Office for Fair Access (OFFA). (2013). How to produce an access agreement for 2014–15. Office for Fair Access. www.offa.org.uk/wp- content/uploads/2013/01/ How-to-produce-an-access-agreement-for-2014–15.pdf Retrieved 21 June 2013

Organisation for Economic Cooperation and Development (OECD). (2007). Education at a glance 2007: OECD indicators. OECD Paris

Organisation for Economic Cooperation and Development (OECD). (2013). Education at a glance 2013: OECD indicators. OECD Paris

Park, C. (2003). In Other (People's) Words: plagiarism by university students – literature and lessons. *Assessment and Evaluation in Higher Education*, 38(5), 471–88

Paton, G. (2012). Universities 'using foreign students as "cash cows". *The Daily Telegraph*, 20 September 2012. www.telegraph.co.uk/education/universityeduca tion/9556080/Universities-using-foreign-students-as-cash-cows.html Retrieved 3 April 2014

Paul, A. (2007). IELTS as a predictor of academic language performance. Part 2: Case studies of learner language. *IELTS Impact Studies Vol. 7* (IELTS Joint-funded research programme). IELTS Australia and the British Council

Pennycook, A. D. (1994). *The Cultural Politics of English as an International Language*. New York: Longman

Pennycook, A. D. (1998). *English and the Discourses of Colonialism*. New York: Routledge

Percy, A. and Skillen, J. (2000). A systemic approach to working with academic staff: Addressing the confusion at the source in K. Chanock (ed.), *Sources of Confusion: Proceedings of the 2000 Language and Academic Skills Conference*, La Trobe University, Melbourne, pp. 244–54

Perry, L. B. and Southwell, L. (2011). Developing intercultural understanding and skills: Models and approaches. *Intercultural Education*, 22(6), 453–66

Peters, H., Pokorny, H. and Sheibani, A. (1999). Fitting in: What place is accorded to the experiential learning mature students bring with them to higher education. Paper presented at *SCUTREA, 29th Annual Conference (University of Warwick, UK, 5–7 July)*. www.leeds.ac.uk/educol/documents/000001015.htm Retrieved 9 June 2013

Pfeffermann, N., Minshall, T. and Mortara, L. (2013). *Strategy and Communication for Innovation*. Springer

Phillipson, R. (1992). *Linguistic Imperialism*. Oxford: Oxford University Press

Phillipson, R. (2009). *Linguistic Imperialism Revisited*. Hyderabad: Black Swan

Pill. J. and Harding, L. (2013). Defining the language assessment literacy gap: Evidence from a parliamentary inquiry. *Language Testing*, 30(3), 381–402

Plant, R. (1987). *Managing Change and Making it Stick*. London: Fontana/Collins

Pokorny, M. and Pokorny, H. (2005). Widening participation in higher education: Student quantitative skills and independent learning as impediments to progression. *International Journal of Mathematical Education in Science and Technology*, 36(5), 445–67

Prabhu, N. S. (1987). *Second Language Pedagogy*. New York: Oxford University Press

Preece, S. and Godfrey, J. (2004). Academic literacy practices and widening participation: First year undergraduates on an academic writing programme. *Widening Participation and Lifelong Learning*, 6(1), 6–14

Premier, J. A. and Miller, J. (2010). Preparing pre-service teachers for multicultural classrooms. *Australian Journal of Teacher Education*, 35(2), 35–48

Pütz, M. and Neff-van Aertselaer, J. (2008). Developing contrastive pragmatics: Interlanguage and cross-cultural perspectives. *Studies on Language Acquisition*, 31. Berlin: Mouton de Gruyter

Qian, D. (2007). Assessing university students: Searching for an English language exit test. *RELC Journal*, 38(1), 18–37

Quality Assurance Agency for Higher Education (QAA), (2009). *Thematic Enquiries into Concerns about Academic Quality and Standards in Higher Education in England*. Gloucester: Quality Assurance Agency for Higher Education. dera.ioe.ac.uk/445/2/FinalReportApril09.pdf Retrieved 30 June 2015

Queen Mary, University of London. *Entry requirements: Study Abroad with English – Academic Requirements*. www.qmul.ac.uk/international/international-students/studyabroadenglish/entryreq/24762.html Retrieved 30 November 2014

Quinn, L. and Vorster, J. (2004). Transforming teachers' conceptions of teaching and learning in a post graduate certificate in higher education and training course. *South African Journal of Higher Education*, 18(1), 364–81

Raisman, N. (2001). *Embrace the Oxymoron: Customer Service in Higher Education*. LRP Publications

Rajagopalan, K. (2004). The concept of 'World English' and its implications for ELT. *ELT Journal*, 58(2), 111–117

Ransom, L. (2009). Implementing the post-entry English language assessment policy at the University of Melbourne: Rationale, processes and outcomes. *Journal of Academic Language & Learning*, 3(2), A13–A25

Read, J. (2008). Identifying English language needs through diagnostic assessment. *Journal of English for Academic Purposes*, 7(3), 180–190

Read, J. and Wette, R. (2009). Achieving English proficiency for professional registration: The experience of overseas-qualified health professionals in the New Zealand Context. *IELTS Research Reports*, Vol. *10*, pp. 1–42. www.ielts.org/pdf/vol10_re port4.pdf Retrieved 30 November 2014

Read, J. (2013). Issues in post-entry language assessment in English-medium universities. *Language Teaching*. DOI: 10.1017/S0261444813000190

Read, J. (2015). *Assessing English Proficiency for University Study*. London: Palgrave Macmillan

Read, J. and von Randow, J. (2013). A university post-entry English language assessment: Charting the changes. *English Language Studies*, 13(2), 89–110

Rea-Dickins, P., Kiely, R. and Yu, G. (2007). Student Identity, Learning and Progression: with specific reference to the affective and academic impact of IELTS on 'successful' candidates. *IELTS Impact Studies Vol. 7* (IELTS Joint-funded research programme). IELTS Australia & the British Council

Rex, L. A. and McEachen, D. (1999). If anything is odd, inappropriate, confusing, or boring, it's probably important: The emergence of inclusive academic literacy through English classroom discussion practices. *Research in the Teaching of English*, 24, 65–129

Richardson, H. (2012). London Metropolitan students fear deportation. *BBC News: Education and Family*, 30 August 2012. www.bbc.co.uk/news/education-194193 95 Retrieved 18 August 2013

Richardson, J. (1994). Mature students in higher education: II. Academic performance and intellectual ability. *Higher Education*, 28, 373–86

Robbins Report. (1963). *Report of the Committee Appointed by the Prime Minister under the Chairmanship of Lord Robbins, 1961–1963, Higher Education. Cmnd. 2154*, London: HMSO

Robbins, S. P. and DeCenzo, D. A. (2001). *Management*. Prentice-Hall

Rogers, E. M. and Shoemaker, F. (1971). *Communication of Innovations: A Cross-Cultural Approach*, 2nd ed. New York: Free Press

Rogers, E. M. (1983). *The Diffusion of Innovations*, 3rd ed. London and New York: MacMillan and Free Press

Rogers, E. M. (2010). *Diffusion of Innovations*, 4th ed. New York: The Free Press

Romaine, S. (1989). *Bilingualism*. Oxford: Wiley-Blackwell

Ryan, J. and Hellmundt, S. (2005). Maximising students' 'cultural capital' in J. Carroll and J. Ryan (eds), *Teaching international students: Improving Learning for All*, Abingdon: Routledge, pp. 13–16

Samovar, L., Porter, R. and McDaniel, E. (2006). *Intercultural Communication: A Reader*. Belmont, CA: Thomas Wadsworth

Saville, N. and Hargreaves, P. (1999). Assessing speaking in the revised FCE. *English Language Teaching Journal*, 53(1), 42–51

Scarino, A. (2009). Assessing intercultural competence in language learning: Some issues and considerations. *Language Teaching*, 42(1), 67–80

Scevak, J. and Cantwell, R. H. (2001). Adjusting to university study: The experiences of students from a manufacturing background undertaking university level study in P. L. Jeffery (ed.), *Proceedings of the Annual Conference of the Australian Association for Research in Education* Perth: December. www.aare.edu.au/01pap/can01525.htm Retrieved 9 April 2010

Scollon, R. and Scollon, S. (2001). *Intercultural Communication, A Discourse Approach*. Malden, MA: Blackwell Publishing

Scott, I. (2013). Inequality as the key obstacle to widening successful participation in South Africa – and why higher education is obliged to address it in N. Murray and C. M. Klinger (eds), *Aspirations, Access and Attainment in Widening Participation: International perspectives on widening participation and an agenda for change*. Oxford: Routledge

Searle, J. R. (1969). *Speech Acts*. Cambridge University Press

Seidlhofer, B. (2005). Key concepts: English as a lingua franca. *ELT Journal*, 59(4), 339–41

Shah, M., Lewis, I. and Fitzgerald, R. (2011). The renewal of quality assurance in Australian higher education: the challenge of balancing academic rigour, equity and quality outcomes. *Quality in Higher Education*, 17(3), 265–78

Shanahan, M. (2000) Being that bit older: mature students' experience of university and healthcare education. *Occupational Therapy International*, 7(3), 153–62

Shen, Y. (2008). The effect of changes and innovation on educational improvement. *International Education Studies*, 1(3), 73–7

Shepherd, J. (2012). UK university applications in 'steepest fall for 30 years'. *The Guardian*, Monday, 30 January 2012. www.theguardian.com/education/2012/jan/30/uk-univeristy-applications-fall Retrieved 6 June 2014

Sheridan, V. (2011). A holistic approach to international students, institutional habitus and academic literacies in an Irish third level institution. *Higher Education*, 62, 129–40

Shohamy, E., Levine, T., Spolsky, B., Kere-Levy, M., Inbar, O. and Shemesh, M. (2002). *The Academic Achievements of Immigrant Children from the Former USSR and Ethiopia*. Report (in Hebrew) submitted to the Ministry of Education, Israel

Simonds, B., Lippert, L., Hunt, S., Angell, M. and Moore, M. (2008). Communication and diversity: Innovations in teacher education. *Communication Teacher*, 22(2), 56–65

Spolsky, B. (1968). *Some Psycholinguistic and Sociolinguistic Aspects of Bilingual Education*. New Mexico: University of New Mexico

Spolsky, B. (1978). *Educational Linguistics: An Introduction*. Rowley, MA: Newbury House

Spolsky, B. (1989). Communicative competence, language proficiency, and beyond. *Applied Linguistics*, 10(2), 138–55

Spolsky, B. (2008). Introduction. Language testing at 25: Maturity and responsibility? *Language Testing*, 25(3), 297–305

Stanley, P. and N. Murray. (2013). What do we mean by 'qualified' teacher? A comparison of teacher preparation course types in English language teaching. *Australian Review of Applied Linguistics*, 36(1), 102–15

Stappenbelt, B. and Barrett-Lennard, S. (2008). Teaching smarter to improve the English communication proficiency of international engineering students – Collaborations between content and language specialists at the University of Western Australia. *Journal of English for Academic Purposes* 9, 198–210

Stephan, W. and Stephan, C. (2000). An Integrated Threat Theory of prejudice in S. Oskamp (ed.) *Reducing prejudice and discrimination*. Mahwah, NJ: Lawrence Erlbaum Associates

Stier, J. (2003). Internationalisation, ethnic diversity and the acquisition of intercultural competencies. *Intercultural Education* 14(1), 77–91

Stier, J. (2006). Internationalisation, intercultural communication, and intercultural competence. *Journal of Intercultural Communication, 11*, 1–12

Stier, J. (2010). The blindspots and biases of intercultural communication studies: A discussion on episteme and doxa in the field. *Journal of Intercultural Communication*, 20(24), 1–8

Stoller, F. L. (2009). Innovation as the hallmark of effective leadership in M. A. Christison and D. Murray (eds), *Leadership in English Language Education: Theoretical Foundations and Practical Skills for Changing Times*. New York: Routledge, pp. 73–84

Stuart, M. (2002). *Managing Widening Participation in Further and Higher Education*. National Institute of Adult Continuing Education (NIACE)

Summers, M. and Volet, S. (2008). Students' attitudes towards culturally mixed groups on international campuses: impact of participation in diverse and non-diverse groups. *Studies in Higher Education*, 33(4), 357–70

Sumner, W. G. (1906). *Folkways*. Boston: Ginn

Sumner, W. G. and Keller, A. G. (1906). *Folkways: A Study of the Sociological Importance of Usages, Manners, Customs, Mores, and Morals*. New York: Ginn

Swales, J. (1990). *Genre Analysis: English in Academic and Research Settings*. Cambridge: Cambridge University Press

Tajfel, H. and Turner, J. C. (1979). An integrative theory of intergroup conflict in W. G. Austin and S. Worchel (eds), *The Social Psychology of Intergroup Relations*, Monterey, CA: Brooks-Cole, pp. 33–47

Tan, L. (2010). Benefits of foreign students overlooked. *New Zealand Herald*, 9 March 2010. www.nzherald.co.nz/nz/news/article.cfm?c_id=1&objectid=10630745 Retrieved 27 October 2012

Taylor, L. (2004). Issues of test comparability. *Research Notes 15*. Cambridge, UK: Cambridge ESOL

Taylor, L. (2009). Developing assessment literacy. *Annual Review of Applied Linguistics, 29*, 21–6

Tellez, K. (2007). Have conceptual reforms (and one anti-reform) in pre-service teacher education improved the education of multicultural, multilingual children and youth? *Teachers and Teaching: Theory and Practice*, 13(6), 543–64

Thomas, W. P. and Collier, V. P. (2002). *A National Study of School Effectiveness for Language Minority Students' Long-Term Academic Achievement*. Santa Cruz, CA: Center for Research on Education, Diversity and Excellence, University of California-Santa Cruz. www.usc.edu/dept/education/CMMR/CollierThomasEx Report.pdf Retrieved 18 July 2014

Thomas, L. (2002). Student retention in higher education: The role of institutional habitus. *Journal of Education Policy*, 17(4), 423–42

Tight, M. (2013). Widening participation in UK Higher Education: the institutional performance in N. Murray and C. M. Klinger (eds), *Aspirations, Access and*

Attainment in Widening Participation: International Perspectives on Widening Participation and an Agenda for Change. Oxford: Routledge

Tinto, V. (2008). Access without support is not opportunity. Keynote address at the 36th Annual Institute for Chief Academic Officers, The Council of Independent Colleges, 1 November 2008, Seattle, Washington. www.cic.edu/conferences _events/caos/2008_cao_resources/2008cao_tinto.pdf Retrieved 28 August 2009

Tollefson, J. W. (1991). *Planning Language, Planning Inequality: Language Policy in the Community.* London: Longman

Tollefson, J. W. (1995). *Power and Inequality in Language Education.* Cambridge: Cambridge University Press

Turner, Y. (2009). Challenges in using group work to create an intercultural learning space: 'Knowing Me, Knowing You, Is There Nothing We Can Do?': Pedagogic challenges in using group work to create an intercultural learning space. *Journal of Studies in International Education,* 13(2), 240–55

UK Government, Department for Business Innovation and Skills, (June, 2011). Estimating the value to the UK of education exports. www.gov.uk/government/ uploads/system/uploads/attachment_data/file/32395/11-980-estimating-value-of-education-exports.pdf Retrieved 3 July 2015

Universities UK. (2013). *Patterns and trends in higher education.* Universities UK. w ww.universitiesuk.ac.uk/highereducation/Pages/PatternsAndTrendsInUKHigherE ducation2013.aspx#.U5G6G01OWM8 Retrieved 23 March 2014

University of Sydney. (n.d.). *Good Practice Principles for the Development of Students' Academic and Professional Communication Skills at the University of Sydney.* University of Sydney

US Department of Education, National Center for Education Statistics. (2013). Digest of Education Statistics, 2012 (NCES 2014–015). nces.ed.gov/fastfacts/display.asp? id=37 Retrieved 1 June 2014

Vachek, J. (1966). *The Linguistic School of Prague.* Bloomington, IN: Indiana University

van Schalkwyk, S., Bitzer, E. and van der Walt, C. (2009). Acquiring academic literacy: a case of first-year extended degree programme students, *Southern African Linguistics and Applied Language Studies,* 27(2), 189–201

Vertovec, S. (2010). *Towards Post-Multiculturalism: Changing Communities, Conditions and Contexts of Diversity.* UNESCO

Victorian Institute of Teaching. English language requirements. www.vit.vic.edu.au/re gistration/apply-for-registration/all-other-applicants/Pages/english-require ments.aspx Retrieved 30 November 2014

Volet, S. E. and Ang, G. (2012). Culturally mixed groups on international campuses: an opportunity for inter-cultural learning, *Higher Education Research & Development,* 31(1), 21–37

Wallis, D. (1995). Testing in twos—the paired format in oral examinations. *UCLES Presentation,* IATEFL Annual Conference, York

Warren, D. (2002). Curriculum design in a context of widening participation in higher education. *Arts and Humanities in Higher Education,* 1(1), 85–99

Waters, A. (2009). Managing innovation in English language education. *Language Teaching,* 42(4), 421–58

Waters, A. and Vilches, M. L. C. (2001). Implementing ELT innovations: A needs analysis framework. *ELT Journal,* 55(2), 133–41

Watson, K. W. (1996). Listening and feedback in L. Barker and D. Barker (eds), *Communication*. Boston, MA: Allyn & Bacon, pp. 49–77

Watts, R. (2003). *Politeness*. Cambridge: Cambridge University Press

Webb C. and Bonanno, H. (1994). Systematic measurement of students' academic literacy Skills. *Research and Development in Higher Education*, 16, 577–81

Webb C. and Bonanno, H. (1995). Assessing the Literacy Skills of an increasingly diverse Student Population, *Research and Development in Higher Education*, Higher Education Research and Development Society of Australasia, 17 (electronic version)

Webb C., English, L. and Bonanno, H. (1995). Collaboration in Subject Design: integration of the teaching and assessment of literacy skills into a first-year Accounting course. *Accounting Education*, 4(4), 335–50

Wedell, M. (2009). *Planning for Educational Change – Putting People and Their Contexts First*. London: Continuum

Wheelahan, L. (2009). What kind of access does VET provide to higher education for low SES students? Not a lot. *'Student Equity in Higher Education: What we know. What we need to know'* National Centre for Student Equity in Higher Education Launch & Forum, University of South Australia, 25–26 February 2009. w3.unisa.edu.au/hawkeinstitute/ncsehe/student-equity-forum-2009/wheel ahan-what-kind-of-access.pdf

White, R. V. (1987). Managing innovation. *ELT Journal*, 41(3), 211–18

White-Clark, R. (2005). Training teachers to succeed in a multicultural classroom. *Education Digest: Essential Readings Condensed for Quick Review*, 70(8), 23–6

White House Briefing. (2009). *Remarks of President Barrack Obama – as Prepared for Delivery Address to Joint Sessions of Congress Tuesday, Februray 24th, 2009*. Washington DC: U.S. Government. www.whitehouse.gov/the_press_of fice/Remarks-of-President-Barack-Obama-Address-to-Joint-Session-of-Congre ss Retrieved 24 October 2014

Widdowson, H. G. (1990). *Aspects of Language Teaching*. Oxford: Oxford University Press

Widdowson, H. G. (1994). The ownership of English. *TESOL Quarterly*, 28(2), 377–89

Widdowson, H. G. (2003). *Defining Issues in English Language Teaching*. Oxford University Press

Wiley, T. G. (1996). *Literacy and Language Diversity in the United States*. Washington, DC: Center for Applied Linguistics and Delta Systems

Wilkins, D. (1976). *Notional Syllabuses*. Oxford University Press

Wingate, U. (2006). Doing away with 'study skills'. *Teaching in Higher Education*, 11(4), 457–69

Wingate, U. (2007). A framework for transition: supporting 'learning to learn' in higher education. *Higher Education Quarterly*, 61(3), 391–405

Wingate, U., Andon, N. and Cogo, A. (2011). Embedding academic writing instruction into subject teaching: A case study. *Active Learning in Higher Education*, 12(1), 69–81

Woodrow, L. (2006). Academic success of international postgraduate education students and the role of English proficiency. *University of Sydney Papers in TESOL*, 1, 51–70

Zhengdong, G. (2009). IELTS preparation course and student IELTS performance: A case study in Hong Kong. *RELC Journal*, 40(1), 23–41

Appendix A Good Practice Principles for English language proficiency for international students in Australian universities

Introduction

The project

The Department of Education, Employment and Workplace Relations (DEEWR) in 2008 funded a project to develop a set of good practice principles for English language proficiency in academic studies.

This project's focus is international students studying in universities in Australia. However, the Principles can be applied more generally to learning and teaching of all higher education students and they can be used by other post-secondary educational institutions.

The project was undertaken by a Steering Committee convened by the Australian Universities Quality Agency (AUQA). A list of Steering Committee members is given on the last page of this document.

The project is a quality enhancement activity for the Australian university sector and reflects extensive work being undertaken in many Australian universities. It builds on the outcomes of a 2007 National Symposium commissioned by the Department of Education, Science and Training. (The outcomes from this Symposium, and the evidence-based background papers that informed discussions at the Symposium, are available from the Australian Education International website at www.aei.dest.gov.au.)

Definition of English language proficiency

For this project, 'English language proficiency' has been defined as the ability of students to use the English language to make and communicate meaning in spoken and written contexts while completing their university studies. Such uses may range from a simple task such as discussing work with fellow students, to complex tasks such as writing an academic paper or delivering a

255

speech to a professional audience. This view of proficiency as the ability to organise language to carry out a variety of communication tasks distinguishes the use of 'English language proficiency' from a narrow focus on language as a formal system concerned only with correct use of grammar and sentence structure. The project Steering Committee recognises that in many contexts the terms 'English language proficiency' and 'English language competence' are used interchangeably.

Context

English language proficiency has become an important issue in Australian higher education due in part to a heightened awareness of the role of English language ability in employment outcomes and the role of international graduates in meeting skill shortages in the Australian workforce. There is also an increased recognition within universities of the fundamental nature of language in learning and academic achievement for all students.

The rapid progress of global higher education is prompting universities in other countries to address the complex issues of learning and teaching in multilingual environments. Given the current prevalence of English in work and professional fields internationally, many universities are seeking better ways for students whose first language is not English to develop their disciplinary English language proficiency through academic studies.

For the retention and academic success of international students in Australian universities, a range of skills and strategies (in particular, written and oral communication) need to be made visible, explicit, and accessible and, importantly, integrated within specific disciplinary contexts. The Good Practice Principles are one way to demonstrate the commitment and leadership of Australian universities in the area of English language proficiency for international students with English as an additional language.

While attending to university entry requirements, the Steering Committee has emphasised the development of English language proficiency throughout students' studies. In doing so, the Steering Committee has been guided by a number of key ideas, as follows:

- With widening participation across tertiary education and the increasing numbers of international students, it can no longer be assumed that students enter their university study with the level of academic language proficiency required to participate effectively in their studies.
- Irrespective of the English language entry requirements of the university, most students, in particular those from language backgrounds other than English, will require English language development throughout the course of their studies.
- Different disciplines have different discourses of academic inquiry.

- Students' English language proficiency can be developed through appropriate course design, supplemented where necessary by other developmental activity.
- Development of academic language and learning is more likely to occur when it is linked to need (e.g. academic activities, assessment tasks).
- English language proficiency is one part of the wider graduate attribute agenda since English language communication skills are crucial for graduate employment.

How will the Good Practice Principles be used?

The Good Practice Principles have been developed in consultation with Australian universities and other stakeholders. They aim to describe what is known about current good practice, taking into account the diversity of Australian universities.

The Principles are general statements for individual universities to address in the context of their own operations and environment.

As one university stated in its response to the consultation draft: 'Because the missions, pedagogical approaches, and student populations at and within each university are increasingly diverse, the principles must be broad enough to allow for institutions to respond in ways appropriate to their particular situation'.

The expectation of the project Steering Committee is that universities will consider the Principles as they would consider other guidelines on good practice. As part of AUQA quality audits universities can expect to be asked about the way they have addressed the Principles, just as they are likely to be asked by AUQA auditors about their application of a range of other external reference documents for the university sector.

The examples of good practices given in the thematic guide are examples only and not intended to be prescriptive. They are provided to assist universities and other institutions in reviewing and improving their own activities.

Good Practice Principles

1. Universities are responsible for ensuring that their students are sufficiently competent in the English language to participate effectively in their university studies.[*]

---

[*] For international students studying in Australia, it is a requirement of the National Code's standard 2 under the *Education Services for Overseas Students Act 2000* that 'registered providers ensure students' qualifications, experience and English language proficiency are appropriate for the course for which enrolment is sought'. This requirement is also relevant to Principle 4.

2. Resourcing for English language development is adequate to meet students' needs throughout their studies.
3. Students have responsibilities for further developing their English language proficiency during their study at university and are advised of these responsibilities prior to enrolment.
4. Universities ensure that the English language entry pathways they approve for the admission of students enable these students to participate effectively in their studies.
5. English language proficiency and communication skills are important graduate attributes for all students.
6. Development of English language proficiency is integrated with curriculum design, assessment practices and course delivery through a variety of methods.
7. Students' English language development needs are diagnosed early in their studies and addressed, with ongoing opportunities for self-assessment.
8. International students are supported from the outset to adapt to their academic, sociocultural and linguistic environments.
9. International students are encouraged and supported to enhance their English language development through effective social interaction on and off campus.
10. Universities use evidence from a variety of sources to monitor and improve their English language development activities.

Thematic Guide with Explanation and Examples

Examples of good practices in relation to each of the ten Principles are provided below under the following thematic areas:
1. University-wide Strategy, Policy and Resourcing
2. Prospective Students and Entry Standards
3. Curriculum Design and Delivery
4. Transition and Social and Academic Interaction
5. Quality Assurance

Theme 1: University-wide Strategy, Policy and Resourcing

Relevant Principles

Principle 1
Universities are responsible for ensuring that their students are sufficiently competent in the English language to participate effectively in their university studies.

Principle 2
Resourcing for English language development is adequate to meet students' needs throughout their studies.

Explanation

The first Good Practice Principle is an overarching general statement reflective of the fact that universities themselves set entry standards for admission to their courses (programs). Entry standards are designed to allow most students to graduate, if the students engage diligently with their studies. English language entry standards form part of admission criteria.

Universities also make decisions about the nature and extent of learning that students must demonstrate and therefore about the nature and extent of teaching and other learning activities to be provided. For students to be able to engage effectively in their academic studies in Australia, they must be able to communicate in English in a manner appropriate to these studies. It is assumed that academic studies in Australia necessarily involve ongoing development of students' discipline-specific English language proficiency. If some or many students are not able to participate at an appropriate level in their studies for reasons associated with their English language proficiency, a university will need to consider how to change its practices to better develop this proficiency. No university can guarantee that each and every student will participate effectively in their academic studies but every university should take responsibility for ensuring that the students it admits do not face unreasonable expectations of English language proficiency.

The second Good Practice Principle reflects the view that, having taken decisions on the extent of development of discipline-specific (and more general) English language proficiency its student population requires, a university should provide sufficient resources for development of this proficiency. A university should be able to demonstrate how resources for English language development are allocated and how it knows whether or not these resources are adequate to meet requirements. This resourcing needs to consider the needs of research students as well as coursework students and take into account funding for data collection and analysis.

Examples of Good Practices

- The university acknowledges significant responsibility for the ongoing development of its students' English language proficiency, while recognising that students play an active role developing their proficiency during their studies.
- The university has a policy that includes its goals for the development of English language proficiency for all students.
- The university has comprehensive plans to develop and monitor students' English language proficiency throughout their studies up to the time of

graduation and recognises that implementation of these plans involves a range of groups within the university.

- The university ensures there are adequate resources for qualified academic language and learning staff to assist academics to integrate language development into curricula and to provide other forms of individual and group support to students.
- The university is able to demonstrate an objective basis for the allocation of resources for English language development commensurate with need.
- The university provides professional development assistance for staff to increase their understanding of, or expertise in, the development of English language proficiency.

Theme 2: Prospective Students and Entry Standards

Relevant Principles

Principle 3
Students have responsibilities for further developing their English language proficiency during their study at university and are advised of these responsibilities prior to enrolment.

Principle 4
Universities ensure that the English language entry pathways they approve for the admission of students enable these students to participate effectively in their studies.

Explanation
The third Good Practice Principle reflects mutuality in development of English language proficiency. While universities have responsibilities to set entry standards and provide means for students to develop their English language proficiency during their studies, students must also take responsibility for their own language development while at university, as part of taking responsibility for their learning. It is important that students are aware of this expectation before they commit to a course of study, so universities need to advise prospective students of their responsibilities while at university. Many Australian universities have charters of student rights and responsibilities but these may need to make more explicit reference to development of English language proficiency than at present.

The fourth Good Practice Principle refers back to Principle 1 and the fact that universities are able to determine their own requirements for admission*. Most universities provide for English language entry standards to be met by students through a variety of means, so many students with English as an additional language do not need to take a recognised test of English language *proficiency to meet English language entry requirements. Given the practical impossibility of equating these other means with English language test scores, universities need to find other means to assure themselves that students entering through pathways (including articulation from other studies, completion of English language courses and foundation programs) are equipped to participate effectively in their studies. In practice, this means that universities need to monitor how well students from different entry pathways are able to deal with the language requirements of their discipline at various levels of study and further develop their proficiency. (Simple measures of aggregate academic performance by cohort may not provide sufficient information.) Universities need to ensure that their expectations are conveyed clearly to pathway providers. They need to manage their relationships with pathway providers effectively, including giving providers feedback on their performance and drawing attention to problems.*

* While there may be limitations on the extent to which universities feel able to change their English language admission requirements for some groups, e.g. school leavers and students articulating from vocational education and training (VET) providers, universities should make known any concerns about the English language proficiency of students admitted through these pathways.

Examples of Good Practices

- The university provides information for prospective and admitted students about the need for further development of their English language proficiency and advises students about the ways in which this development is supported by the university.
- All students are advised of the nature and level of support that will be given to help them meet the expectations that are placed on them.
- There is clear communication of the university's expectations for further development of students' English language proficiency to onshore and offshore educational partners and agents.
- The university has formal English language entry standards that reflect the particular needs of each discipline. In setting such entry standards, the university has given consideration to international norms. The university regularly reviews its standards, taking into account external reference points, and makes changes as appropriate.
- English language entry standards are not considered in isolation but in the context of the developmental support that the university will provide, so that entry standards, the needs of the course and the support that is provided form a coherent whole.
- The university has explicit statements of the English language qualifications that it accepts as equivalent to particular test scores (e.g. IELTS, TOEFL).

- There are defined academic responsibilities for setting and reviewing entry standards.
- Staff and students understand what is signified by IELTS or TOEFL or similar language test results, including the strengths and limitations of these tests.
- The university systematically reviews the academic performance of students entering through different pathways or channels.
- The university has secure and documented processes to allow it to check and approve that entering students meet English language entry requirements, including the use of precedent databases. These processes are controlled by the university, involve more than a single individual and are subject to internal audit. Exemptions are given rarely and follow documented procedures.
- The university has clarified its expectations with direct entry pathway providers and there are formal contracts between the university and direct entry pathway providers.
- The university provides feedback to direct entry providers on the performance of student cohorts.
- The university has mechanisms to assure itself of the quality and relevance of pathway programs and the adequacy of assessment practices of pathway providers.

Theme 3: Curriculum Design and Delivery

Relevant Principles

Principle 5
English language proficiency and communication skills are important graduate attributes for all students.

Principle 6
Development of English language proficiency is integrated with curriculum design, assessment practices and course delivery through a variety of methods.

Principle 7
Students' English language development needs are diagnosed early in their studies and addressed, with ongoing opportunities for self-assessment.

Explanation
The fifth Good Practice Principle recognises that when students graduate from an Australian university, they should possess the English language proficiency and communication skills to perform effectively in subsequent employment and

professional activities and to engage in society more generally. The Principle holds equally for international students as for domestic students, especially as many graduates can expect to live and work in more than one country. This Principle is consistent with Australian universities' statements of graduate attributes, which almost without exception mention communication skills as a desired attribute, and one that research shows is crucial for employment on graduation. English language proficiency is sometimes treated as a 'taken for granted' element in communication skills. By highlighting it in this Principle, the implications for university studies become clear.

The sixth Good Practice Principle acknowledges that different disciplines have different English language requirements and discourses and that most students do not enter university with 'ready-made' proficiency in the academic language of their discipline(s). It is based on a view that development of appropriate English language proficiency is more likely to occur when it is linked to need (e.g. discipline-specific academic activities, assessment tasks, practica).

This Principle draws on expert advice, emerging practice and the available evidence on how to develop students' English language proficiency during their studies, taking account of the varying needs of students, especially students with English as an additional language. These sources indicate that while there is no single 'best' way to develop students' English language proficiency, contextualisation within disciplines and integration of language development across the curriculum seem likely to be effective approaches. 'Integration' in this context means taking a holistic view across a discipline to address needs through a variety of means, including: embedding language development through curriculum design and assessment; workshops or credit-bearing units within a course; 'adjunct' workshops or sessions within a course; developing workplace communication through preparation for work placements and practica; and targeted individual or group support provided by academic language and learning experts. Similar ideas can be applied to support research students.

The seventh Good Practice Principle recognises that, irrespective of universities' English language entry requirements, students now enter university with quite widely varying degrees of English language proficiency. Early assessment of students' English language development needs means that students and staff identify these needs at a time when they can start to be addressed, rather than at a point when the stakes are much higher. At least 18 Australian universities are now adopting or examining tools for early diagnosis of students' English language development needs. Consistent with Principle 3, this Principle also recognises that providing students with ongoing opportunities to self-assess their English language development needs encourages students to take responsibility for this development.

Examples of Good Practices

- Curricula, teaching and assessment practices are designed to develop discipline-specific English language proficiency as part of the standard learning expected within a course.
- English language proficiency and course learning outcomes are aligned.
- The university gives attention to all aspects of language proficiency in assessment methods, e.g. attention to listening, speaking, reading and writing.
- The university encourages and supports international students (and others) to undertake a diagnostic assessment of their development needs for English language proficiency at a very early stage of their studies.
- The university offers students opportunities to self-assess their language skills throughout their studies and to undertake developmental activities in response to the needs they identify.
- The university has a clear statement of the respective responsibilities of individual academics, course and unit coordinators and academic language staff for developing students' English language proficiency.
- The university ensures that academic staff know how to access professional assistance for the development of curricula, assessment tasks and teaching to develop English language proficiency.
- The curriculum takes into account time for students to develop their English language capacity within overall expected student workloads.
- The university has considered how best to use work placements or practica to assist students to develop their English language proficiency in professional or employment settings.
- The university has considered ways for domestic and international students to demonstrate their English language proficiency to prospective employers, referees and other institutions.

Theme 4: Transition and Social and Academic Interaction

Relevant Principles

> Principle 8
> International students are supported from the outset to adapt to their academic, sociocultural and linguistic environments.

> Principle 9
> International students are encouraged and supported to enhance their English language development through effective social interaction on and off campus.

Explanation

The eighth Good Practice Principle aims to emphasise the role that effective academic and social acculturation can play in the development of international students' English language proficiency. In particular, it is important for international students with English as an additional language to enter an environment where they have opportunities and encouragement to develop their English language skills in ways that boost their confidence and willingness to experiment with the use of language while also contributing to their socialisation to their chosen discipline. This Principle recognises the growing emphasis placed by Australian universities on transition and orientation to academic language and skills for entering students. While there are substantial orientation programs for international students entering Australian universities, these are less commonly discipline-specific and may not provide support for international students to plan for the development of their English language proficiency. Universities might consider how best to introduce international students to supportive and competent English language speakers at orientation, e.g. through 'buddy' or peer mentor schemes.

The ninth Good Practice Principle builds on the eighth Principle but focuses on the need for universities to develop effective strategies (not only 'opportunities') to ensure that international students have experience of a wide range of contexts where English is used and thus are able to extend the breadth and depth of their skills in using English appropriate to the sociocultural or academic circumstances. One element in these strategies is supporting international students to feel that they are able to enrich the experience and cultural knowledge of others. Certainly, universities can consider ways to demonstrate that they genuinely value multilateral exchanges of experience and ideas among people from differing language backgrounds. Although universities cannot 'ensure' that international students have effective social interaction that develops their English language proficiency off campus they can develop strategies to assist international students to have these experiences.

Examples of Good Practices

- The university provides discipline-specific academic and learning skills acculturation, which includes consideration of language proficiency and communication skills.
- The university has implemented plans to ensure academic and social inclusion for its international students from the commencement of their stay in Australia.
- The university demonstrates that it values the role played by international students in enhancing the learning experiences for all its students.

- The university ensures effective interaction of students from differing cultural backgrounds in regular academic activities.
- The university creates opportunities for students to form intercultural social networks in their learning settings and to engage in cross-cultural discussion in the discipline area.
- The university ensures international students in Australia are supported to have social interaction with a range of people in Australian communities, as well as opportunities for sharing their own culture.
- The university's community engagement strategies include intercultural experiences for international students.
- The university supports faculties or other groups (alumni) to provide intercultural interaction in a professional or disciplinary context.

Theme 5: Quality Assurance

Relevant Principles

Principle 10
Universities use evidence from a variety of sources to monitor and improve their English language development activities.

Explanation

The tenth Good Practice Principle is derived from continuous quality improvement models, which entail the monitoring of outcomes and identification of ways to improve one or more elements of current practices. These elements include policies, procedures, projects and activities, curricula, resourcing and the ways in which 'results' are defined and assessed. Identification of improvements can occur through internal reflection, benchmarking and comparisons, research findings, or considering the views of students and other stakeholders.

Examples of Good Practices

- The university regularly compares its policies and practices for English language development against those of comparable institutions nationally and internationally and considers these in developing policies and practices that reflect the specific needs of its students and the requirements of specific discipline areas.
- Course reviews consider the extent to which development of English language proficiency and communication are taken into account in curriculum design and delivery.
- The university obtains regular information from students on the extent to which they consider their English language proficiency is improving.

- The university knows the extent to which its graduates are satisfied with the development of their English language proficiency through their time at university.
- The university knows the extent to which academics consider students' English language proficiency on entry is appropriate and is developed through their studies.
- The university knows the extent to which employers are satisfied with the English language proficiency and communication skills of its graduates.
- The university has ongoing dialogue with professional accreditation and registration bodies about their expectations regarding English language proficiency and the English language proficiency of the university's graduates.
- The university uses research findings, including its own, to inform its strategies for the development of students' English language proficiency.

Steering Committee Membership

Dr Sophie Arkoudis
Deputy Director, Centre for the Study of Higher Education
Melbourne Graduate School of Education
University of Melbourne

Dr Claire Atkinson
Acting Director
Quality Assurance Framework Unit
Higher Education Group
Department of Education, Employment and Workplace Relations
    (DEEWR)

Dr Jeanette Baird (*Convenor*)
Audit Director
Australian Universities Quality Agency

Mr Alex Barthel
Director, ELSSA Centre, UTS and
President, Association for Academic Language and Learning (AALL)

Dr Anna Ciccarelli
Pro Vice Chancellor & Vice President, International & Development
University of South Australia

Professor David Ingram
Honorary Professorial Fellow, Faculty of Education
University of Melbourne

Mr Dennis Murray
Executive Director, International Education Association of Australia
  (IEAA)

Mr Patrick Willix (representing Mr Stephen Trengove-Jones)
Assistant Director, Strategic Policy
Australian Education International, DEEWR

Appendix B English language standards for Higher Education

In 2008/2009, the Department of Education, Employment and Workplace Relations (DEEWR) funded a project to develop a set of *Good Practice Principles for English language proficiency for international students in Australian universities* (GPP). This project's focus was **international** students studying in Australian **universities**.

The project was undertaken by a steering committee convened by the Australian Universities Quality Agency (AUQA). The project was a quality enhancement activity for the Australian university sector and reflected extensive work being undertaken in many Australian universities. It built on the outcomes of a 2007 National Symposium commissioned by the Department of Education, Science and Training.

Following extensive consultations with the Australian higher education sector, the DEEWR reconvened the Good Practice Principles steering committee in 2010 (p. 12) and asked it to develop the principles into English standards that would apply to **all** students in the Australian **Higher Education sector**. The draft standards were submitted to the DEEWR in July 2010.

This document is the outcome of the work of the reconvened steering committee.

The inclusion of the *English language standards for Higher Education* (ELSHE) in a global standards framework is essential in the current context of developing a national framework for academic standards that would assist the higher education sector in setting up quality systems, in particular, to respond to recent government regulations and initiatives, such as the Knight recommendations and the Bradley Social Inclusion agenda.

Alex Barthel

Member, ELSHE Steering Committee

Public Officer, Association for Academic Language & Learning

May 2012

final version 5 JULY 2010

English Language Standards for Higher Education

Introduction

The project

This document provides standards for successful academic study in English in Australian higher education. The standards apply to **all higher education providers** operating in Australia.

This project was undertaken by a Steering Committee convened by the Australian Universities

Quality Agency (AUQA). **Appendix B1** lists members of the Steering Committee.

How should these standards be used?

In the first instance, the standards provide a set of external reference points for higher education providers. The standards are general statements for individual higher education providers to address in the context of their own operations and environment. The standards do not require and are not intended to produce a standardisation of approaches among providers. They are broad enough to allow for institutions to respond in ways appropriate to their particular situation.

These standards for providers are intended to complement the academic disciplinary outcome standards being developed through the ALTC Learning and Teaching Academic Standards project.

The Australian Government is introducing legislation to ensure that all higher education providers meet requirements in a new Higher Education Standards Framework, with providers to be subject to evaluations as determined by the Tertiary Education Quality and Standards Agency (TEQSA). The English language standards in future may be used by TEQSA in assessing higher education providers' performance against the Framework.

Definition of English language proficiency

For this project, 'English language proficiency' has been defined as the ability of students to use the English language to make and communicate meaning appropriately in spoken and written contexts while completing their higher education studies and after they graduate. Such uses may range from a simple task such as discussing work with fellow students, to complex tasks such as writing an academic paper or delivering a speech to a professional audience.

While some students will enter higher education with a very high level of general English language proficiency, all students will need to acquire specific academic literacy skills during their studies, and the acquisition of these skills is part of improving English language proficiency. English language standards on entry are not adequate to ensure students' English language proficiency on graduation.

However, some students will require greater assistance than others in developing specific aspects of their English language proficiency. It is for this reason that higher education providers should identify the developmental needs of individual students at an early stage of their studies.

Structure of the standards

There are six standards, which are listed on the next page. Succeeding pages provide:

- The standard
- An account of the expectations, i.e. actions that providers are expected to have implemented to meet the standard
- Examples of good practice, which are not intended to be prescriptive
- A brief explanation of the reasons for the standard.

The *English Language Standards for Higher Education*

1. The provider ensures that its students are sufficiently proficient in English to participate effectively in their higher education studies on entry.
2. The provider ensures that prospective and current students are informed about their responsibilities for further developing their English language proficiency during their higher education studies.
3. The provider ensures that resourcing for English language development meets students' needs throughout their studies.
4. The provider actively develops students' English language proficiency during their studies.
5. The provider ensures that students are appropriately proficient in English when they graduate.
6. The provider uses evidence from a variety of sources to monitor and improve its support for the development of students' English language proficiency.

Standard 1

The provider ensures that its students are sufficiently proficient in the English language to participate effectively in their higher education studies on entry.

Expectations
- The provider recognises that appropriate English language standards on entry are not of themselves adequate to ensure students' English language

proficiency on graduation, and considers entry standards, the needs of the course of study and the support that is provided as a coherent whole.

- The higher education provider adheres to a formal policy that specifies English language entry criteria, including criteria for direct entry pathways, which are appropriate for the level of studies and the discipline and which are consistent with research evidence, including the recommendations of relevant testing organisations.
- The provider verifies the accuracy and authenticity of the evidence provided by prospective students to satisfy its English language entry criteria.
- The provider systematically monitors the performance of students by entry pathway or by cohort and makes appropriate changes to entry criteria to ensure that it admits only those students who are able to participate effectively on entry.
- The higher education provider gives feedback to direct entry pathway providers on the comparative academic performance of students who have entered through pathway provisions and on the provider's satisfaction with the English language proficiency of entering students from the pathway provider.
- If the provider uses a test of English language proficiency to determine student entry, the provider is able to demonstrate the security, reliability and validity of the test that is applied.

Examples of Good Practice

- The provider has detailed and explicit statements of the measures of English language proficiency that it accepts for admission of students to a course of study, not limited to a list of particular standardised test scores.
- There are defined academic responsibilities for setting and reviewing entry standards.
- The provider's staff and students understand what is signified by English language test results, including the strengths and limitations of these tests.
- The provider has secure and documented processes to allow it to check and approve that entering students meet English language entry requirements, including the use of precedent databases. These processes are controlled by the provider, involve more than a single individual and are subject to internal audit. Exemptions are given rarely and follow documented procedures.
- The provider has clarified its expectations with direct entry pathway providers and there are formal agreements between the provider and direct entry pathway providers.
- In determining entry criteria, the provider takes advice from people with expertise in the development and assessment of English language proficiency.

Explanation

This standard is an overarching general statement reflective of the fact that higher education providers set entry standards for admission to their courses of study. Entry standards are designed to allow most students to graduate, if the students engage diligently with their studies and are provided with appropriate opportunities for development during their studies. English language entry standards form part of admission criteria.

The standard assumes that students will complete their studies with greater English language proficiency than when they enter a course of study but recognises that a reasonable level of proficiency is needed for students to participate effectively in their studies from the commencement of the course.

Most providers allow English language entry standards to be met by students through a variety of means, so many students do not need to take a recognised test of English language proficiency to meet English language entry requirements. Given the practical impossibility of equating these other means with English language test scores, higher education providers need to find other means to assure themselves that students entering through pathways (including articulation from other studies, completion of English language courses and foundation programs) are equipped to participate effectively in their studies. In practice, this means at a minimum that providers need to monitor how well students from different entry pathways are able to deal with the language requirements of their discipline at various levels of study and further develop their proficiency. (Simple measures of aggregate academic performance by cohort may not provide sufficient information.) Higher education providers need to satisfy themselves that their pathway providers' programs are likely to be appropriate and to convey their expectations clearly to providers of pathway programs. Higher education providers need to manage their relationships with pathway providers effectively, including giving feedback on their performance and drawing attention to problems. While there may be limitations on the extent to which higher education providers feel able to change their English language admission requirements for some groups, e.g. school leavers and students articulating from vocational education and training (VET) providers, providers should make known to relevant authorities any concerns about the entry-level English language proficiency of students admitted through these pathways.

Standard 2

The provider ensures that prospective and current students are informed about their responsibilities for further developing their English language proficiency during their higher education studies.

Expectations

- The provider formally acknowledges significant responsibility for the ongoing development of its students' English language proficiency and provides explicit advice to students of the nature and level of support that will be given to help them meet expectations of graduate English language proficiency.
- The provider ensures that students know they must play an active role in developing their English language proficiency during their studies.
- The provider's education agents understand the provider's expectations for further development of students' English language proficiency.
- The provider's onshore and offshore educational partners understand the provider's expectations for further development of students' English language proficiency.

Examples of Good Practice

- The provider has a policy that includes its goals for the development of English language proficiency for all students.
- The provider has a charter of student rights and responsibilities which makes explicit reference to development of students' English language proficiency.
- As part of its orientation and transition programs, the provider ensures that students understand the English language proficiency required for their studies, the importance of further developing this proficiency, and how early identification of language development needs can assist them.
- The provider explains to new students how they will have opportunities during their studies to improve their intercultural competence and understanding of a range of English communication styles and why these opportunities are important.

Explanation

This standard reflects mutuality in the development of English language proficiency. While higher education providers have responsibilities to set entry standards and provide means for students to develop their English language proficiency during their studies, students must also take responsibility for their own language development during their studies, as part of taking responsibility for their learning. It is important that students are aware of this expectation before they commit to a course of study, so providers need to advise prospective students of their responsibilities. Students also need to be aware of the importance of taking opportunities to develop their intercultural competence and capacities.

Standard 3

The provider ensures that resourcing for English language development meets students' needs throughout their studies.

Expectations
- The higher education provider identifies students' individual English language development needs early in their studies and addresses these needs.
- The provider ensures there are adequate resources for appropriately-qualified academic language and learning staff to meet the language and learning needs of students.
- The provider ensures there is adequate expertise available to assist academic staff to integrate English language proficiency into curricula and teaching.
- The provider ensures that academic staff know how to and are able to access professional assistance for the development of curricula, assessment tasks and teaching to develop English language proficiency in specific academic disciplinary contexts.
- The provider ensures that academic staff have opportunities to revise curricula and teaching to integrate English language proficiency with discipline-specific learning.

Examples of Good Practice
- The provider offers students opportunities to self-assess their language skills throughout their studies and to undertake developmental activities in response to the needs they identify.
- The provider has considered and addresses how best to meet the English language development needs of students studying online or remotely.
- The provider is able to demonstrate that its allocation of resources for English language development is commensurate with need.
- The provider has a clear statement of the responsibilities of various staff positions for developing students' English language proficiency.
- The provider offers professional development activities to develop the expertise of academic staff in understanding, promoting and integrating English language proficiency in differing disciplinary contexts.

Explanation
The standard recognises that, having identified the development of English language proficiency its students require, the provider needs to provide sufficient resources for development of proficiency. A provider should be able to demonstrate how resources for English language development are allocated and how it knows whether or not these resources are adequate to meet students' needs. Resourcing must ensure that adequate numbers of appropriately-qualified language and learning staff are engaged. (The Association for Academic Language and Learning (AALL) is developing in consultation with the Australian higher education sector, a statement on appropriate qualifications for academic language and learning professionals.) Further, resourcing needs to be provided to support academic staff to improve and revise curricula and their teaching to integrate English language proficiency with discipline-specific learning.

Standard 4

The provider actively develops students' English language proficiency during their studies.

Expectations
- The provider ensures that development by students of their English language proficiency is integrated into curriculum design, assessment practices and course delivery.
- Course learning outcomes include English language proficiency outcomes that are taught and assessed during the course and take account of the proficiency that is required of graduates in the discipline for employment or further study.
- The provider gives attention to all aspects of English language proficiency in assessment methods, e.g. attention to listening, speaking, reading and writing.
- The curriculum takes into account time for students to develop their English language proficiency within overall expected student workloads.
- The provider has considered how best to use work placements or practica to assist students to develop their English language proficiency in professional or employment settings.
- Course approvals and reviews consider the extent to which English language proficiency outcomes are designed into curricula, assessment and teaching.
- The provider ensures effective interaction of students from differing cultural and language backgrounds in regular academic activities.
- The provider ensures that students are encouraged and supported to enhance their English language development through effective intercultural social interaction in a range of formal and informal settings.

Examples of Good Practice
- As part of its orientation and induction programs for staff, the provider ensures that all its academics, including contract staff, understand the importance of further developing students' English language proficiency throughout the course.
- The provider offers fully contextualised, discipline-specific English language proficiency development within the course of study, for example through dedicated credit-bearing units or through specific learning activities.
- The provider has specific activities to assist online or distance education students to improve their spoken as well as their written English.
- The provider undertakes course mapping activities to identify and improve the ways in which appropriate English language proficiency will be achieved throughout the course of study.

Explanation

This standard acknowledges that different disciplines have different English language requirements and discourses and that most students do not enter higher education with 'ready-made' proficiency in the academic language of their discipline(s). It is based on a view that development of appropriate English language proficiency is more likely to occur when it is linked to need (e.g. discipline-specific academic activities, assessment tasks, practica).

The standard draws on expert advice, emerging practice and the available evidence on how to develop students' English language proficiency during their studies, taking account of the varying needs of students, especially students with English as an additional language. These sources indicate that while there is no single 'best' way to develop students' English language proficiency, contextualisation within disciplines and integration of language development across the curriculum seem likely to be effective approaches. 'Integration' in this context means taking a holistic view across a discipline to address needs through a variety of means, including: embedding language development through curriculum design and assessment; workshops or credit-bearing units within a course; 'adjunct' workshops or sessions within a course; developing workplace communication through preparation for work place-ments and practica; and targeted individual or group support provided by academic language and learning experts. Similar ideas can be applied to support research students. Particular strategies may be needed to support online or distance education students.

The standard also addresses the need for providers to develop effective strategies to ensure that all students have experience of a wide range of contexts where English is used and thus are able to extend the breadth and depth of their skills in using English appropriate to particular sociocultural or academic contexts.

Standard 5

The provider ensures that students are appropriately proficient in English when they graduate.

Expectations

- The higher education provider states clearly to students and other stake-holders its expectations of its graduates, including its expectations regarding English language proficiency encompassing a range of communication skills.
- English language proficiency is an explicit component of academic standards for the course of study and is aligned to disciplinary standards.
- The provider obtains regular information from students on the extent to which they consider their English language proficiency is improving.

• The provider has ongoing dialogue with industry and with professional accreditation and registration bodies about their expectations regarding English language proficiency and the English language proficiency of the provider's graduates.

Examples of Good Practice

• The provider has comprehensive plans to develop and monitor students' English language proficiency throughout their studies up to the time of graduation.
• The provider uses stated criteria to assess students' English language proficiency within assessment of course units.
• The course allows students to demonstrate the range of abilities and skills they have acquired throughout the course including appropriate English language proficiency, for example through capstone experiences.
• The provider has implemented ways for students to demonstrate their English language proficiency to prospective employers, professional referees, academics and others.

Explanation

This standard recognises that when students graduate with an Australian higher education qualification, they should possess the English language proficiency skills to communicate effectively in subsequent employment and professional activities or further study, and to engage in society more generally. This standard is consistent with most Australian universities' statements of graduate attributes, which mention high level communication skills as a desired attribute, and one that research shows is crucial for employment in Australia on graduation.

The standard focuses on student learning outcomes and how providers know that students have an appropriate level of English language proficiency when they graduate. The standard does not suggest that providers offer students an external test of English language proficiency. Currently-available tests of English language proficiency for entry to higher education studies are not designed to assess proficiency on exit. Consistent with the principles of quality assurance, the standard asks providers to develop means to assure themselves that graduating students have appropriate English language proficiency. If providers have addressed all the other standards, they will have considerable evidence to demonstrate how this standard is being met.

Standard 6

The provider uses evidence from a variety of sources to monitor and improve its support for the development of students' English language proficiency.

Expectations
- The provider regularly compares its policies and practices for English language development against those of comparable institutions nationally and internationally and considers these in developing policies and practices that reflect the specific needs of its students and the requirements of specific discipline areas.
- The provider systematically monitors the extent to which its academics consider students' English language proficiency on entry is appropriate and is developed through their studies.
- The provider systematically monitors the extent to which its graduates believe their English language proficiency was developed throughout their higher education studies.
- The provider makes adjustments as appropriate to its entry standards, resourcing, curricula, assessment practices or teaching to better meet students' needs for development of their English language proficiency.

Examples of Good Practice
- The provider uses research findings, including its own, to inform its strategies for the development of students' English language proficiency.
- The provider systematically monitors the extent to which employers are satisfied with the English language proficiency and communication skills of its graduates.
- The provider obtains comparative feedback from students on the forms of English language development support that they believe meet their needs most effectively.

Explanation
This standard uses the principle of continuous quality improvement, which entails the monitoring of outcomes and identification of ways to improve one or more elements of current practice. These elements include policies, procedures, projects and activities, curricula, resourcing and the ways in which 'results' are defined and assessed. Identification of improvements can occur through internal reflection, benchmarking and comparisons, research findings, or considering the views of students and other stakeholders.

Appendix B1   Steering Committee Membership

Associate Professor Sophie Arkoudis
Deputy Director, Centre for the Study of Higher Education
Melbourne Graduate School of Education
University of Melbourne

Dr Claire Atkinson
Director, Quality Assurance Unit
Higher Education Group, DEEWR

Dr Jeanette Baird (Convenor)
Director of SAI Operations and Audit Director
Australian Universities Quality Agency

Mr Alex Barthel
Director, ELSSA Centre, UTS and
Public Officer, Association for Academic Language and Learning
    (AALL)

Ms Sue Blundell
Executive Director
English Australia

Associate Professor Katie Dunworth
Director, International, School of Education
Curtin University of Technology

Ms Anne Holmes
Head of College
Billy Blue College of English
Think: Colleges

Mr Stephen Nagle
Director
Holmes Institute

Associate Professor Sue Starfield
Director, The Learning Centre
University of New South Wales

Ms Catherine Vandermark
Branch Manager
Higher Education Quality Branch, DEEWR

Appendix C Accreditation UK inspection criteria (adjusted to reflect the higher education context)

Notes:

Where providers teach other subjects in addition to ELT, the inspection criteria relate to the management, staff, facilities and resources relevant to the experience of any ELT students.

Some criteria are not applicable to certain types of provider, this is indicated as follows:

- criteria marked s do not apply to sole providers
- criteria marked H do not apply to home tuition providers
- criteria marked N do not apply to first-time new applicants
- criteria marked I do not apply to in-company provision.

Additional criteria apply to the inspection of home tuition (HT) providers, international study centres (ISC) and in-company provision; these are listed after the main criteria.

Evidence will be sought from inspection application forms, interviews with staff and students, on-site and off-site checks, classroom observation, and the documentation listed in the column beside the criteria as appropriate.

The documents are listed next to the first criterion in a section to which they refer but may also apply to other criteria later in the same section.

Please note that where 'any' is used, this means if available/applicable to the provider being inspected.

Management

Standard

The management of the provision will operate to the benefit of its students, in accordance with its publicity and in accordance with the *Declaration of legal and regulatory compliance*.

281

Legal and statutory regulations   M1 Providers will operate at all times in accordance with the declaration made in the *Declaration of legal and regulatory compliance* form.

Please note: Inspectors may spot check elements of the legal and regulatory declaration, as well as awareness of and attention paid to compliance.

Staff management $M2_S$ There will be a clear structure of management and administration for the ELT operation and arrangements to ensure its continuity at all times.

M3 The duties of all staff working with ELT students will be specified.

$M4_S$ There will be effective channels of communication between all involved in the ELT operation (including homestay hosts and group leaders), and between the ELT operation and any wider organisation of which it is a part.

M5 In addition to complying with the statutory requirements, the provider will have and implement appropriate human resources policies for all staff.

M6 Employers will take all reasonable steps to investigate and verify the qualifications and experience of all prospective employees.

M7 The provider will have and implement appropriate induction procedures for all staff.

M8 There will be clear procedures for monitoring and appraising all staff, and for handling unsatisfactory performance.

M9 There will be a formalised policy and procedures to ensure the continuing professional development of all staff in order to meet the needs of the individual, the students and the organisation.

Student administration $M10_S$ Staff will be helpful and courteous to students and there will be sufficient administrative staff and resources to handle the volume of work efficiently.

M11 Students will receive sufficient information and advice on their course choices before arrival and during their stay.

M12 Enrolment procedures will be carried out efficiently and with appropriate sensitivity.

M13 There will be effective systems to maintain up-to-date records of students' local and emergency or next of kin contact details. These will be accessible at all times to the person(s) within the ELT organisation responsible for responding to emergencies.

M14 There will be a clear and effective policy on student attendance and punctuality that will be known and applied to all students; accurate records will be kept and effective arrangements made for following up student absences.

M15 All staff and students will be made aware of conditions and procedures under which a student may be asked to leave the course.

Quality assurance M16$_N$ An appropriate action plan (template available on website), based on the points to be addressed of the previous inspection report, will be submitted in preparation for the next inspection or earlier as required by the ASAC. This plan will include a timeframe and will form part of the next inspection. There will be a satisfactory explanation for points not addressed.

M17 Providers will review systems, processes and practices with a view to continuing improvement. Appropriate action will be taken and recorded.

M18$_H$ The provider will regularly obtain and record feedback from students on all services offered. This will include initial and end-of-course feedback. Feedback will be circulated to relevant staff and appropriate action will be taken and recorded.

M19$_S$ The provider will regularly seek and record feedback from all staff on the services offered. Appropriate action will be taken and recorded.

M20 All students will be made aware of the organisation's complaints policy, which will be written in clear, accessible English. All complaints and the action taken will be recorded in writing.

Publicity – information available before enrolment (Where one medium of publicity is clearly predominant and any other is primarily used to refer prospective students to the main medium, then the secondary medium need not fully meet criteria M23–M27, providing that its contents are accurate and comprehensible.)

M21 All publicity and information (including social media) about the provider and the services it offers will be in clear and accurate English, accessible to non-native speakers, or in translation.

M22 Publicity and information about the provider and the services it offers will be accurate and give rise to realistic expectations about the premises, location, and the extent and availability of the services and resources.

M23 Publicity will give an outline description of each course, including objectives and levels.

M24 Publicity will give accurate information on the courses, including:
- the times of classes, any private study periods and the number of taught hours per week
- course dates and any non-teaching days within the course;
- the minimum enrolment age
- maximum class size.

M25 Publicity will include clear, accurate and easy to find information on:
- the cost of tuition
- the cost of any teaching materials which students are required to buy
- the cost of any accommodation offered
- the approximate cost of any leisure programme not included in the course fees

- the approximate cost of any course related examination fees not included in the course fees
- the requirements for deposits, payment of fees, and the refund policy, including the arrangements and deadlines for cancellations.

M26 Publicity will give an accurate description of any accommodation offered:
- the provider will make it clear if accommodation offered is arranged by an agency
- the types of accommodation offered will be clearly described).

M27 Publicity will give an accurate description of any leisure programme offered.

M28 Any description of staff qualifications and experience will be accurate and apply to the full range of staff at any time. Any classes or courses which are used for teacher training purposes (with unqualified teachers) will be so designated, and will be provided free of charge or at substantially reduced cost.

M29 All eligible provision will be declared for inspection as set out in Section 1.3 **Scope of accreditation**. Any claims to accreditation, or registration of accommodation agencies, will be in line with the guidelines set out in Section 3.1 **Claiming accreditation**, and will not be applied to unaccredited or ineligible provision.

Resources and environment

Standard

The learning resources and environment will support and enhance the studies of students enrolled with the provider, and will offer an appropriate professional environment for staff.

Premises and facilities   R1 Premises, including any external areas, will be adequate in size and number to provide a comfortable environment for students and staff.

R2 Premises, including any external areas, will be in a good state of repair, cleanliness and decoration.

R3 Classrooms and other learning areas will be:
- adequate in size and number
- adequately lit, heated and ventilated
- free from disruptive extraneous noise
- furnished for sufficient flexibility of layout
- arranged so that all students can see, hear and write in comfort.

R4$_1$ Students will be provided with adequate room and suitable facilities for relaxation and the consumption of food. A choice of appropriate food at affordable prices will be available to students on site if not available locally.

R5$_{HI}$ There will be adequate signage to buildings, routes, rooms and exits, and facilities for the display of general information.

R6$_{HI}$ There will be sufficient space for all staff, for meetings, relaxation and the storage of personal possessions, and for teachers to carry out their preparation and marking.

Learning resources   R7 Learning materials will be appropriate to the level, length and type of courses offered and sufficient for the number of students enrolled.

R8 There will be an adequate stock of appropriate, up-to-date materials and resources for teachers, including facilities for the production and reproduction of materials. These resources will be accessible, well maintained and organised.

R9 Any educational technology inside the classroom and elsewhere, will be well maintained with adequate technical support. Staff will be appropriately trained in using the available technology to support learning.

R10$_I$ Any area for quiet study and self-access work will be appropriately equipped and organised.

R11$_I$ Students will receive guidance on the use of libraries and self-access centres where these are available.

R12 There will be a procedure for the continuing review and development of teaching and learning resources and evidence of its implementation.

Teaching and learning

Standard

Teachers will have appropriate qualifications and will be given sufficient support to ensure that their teaching meets the needs of their students. Programmes of learning will be managed for the benefit of students. The teaching observed will meet the requirements of the Scheme.

Academic staff profile   T1 All academic staff will have a general level of education normally represented by a Level 6 qualification on the Ofqual Register of Regulated Qualifications. Exceptionally, the employment of any academic staff without the appropriate general level of education may be acceptable with the provision of a valid rationale.

T2 All teachers will have ELT/TESOL qualifications appropriate to the courses they are teaching.

For information on qualifications, see **4.2 Academic staff qualifications**.
The Scheme expects that:

- teachers of courses for students under 18 will hold at least a TEFLI qualification or have appropriate qualified teacher status

- teachers of courses for adults will hold at least a TEFLI qualification and normally,
- teachers of teacher development courses and EAP courses will hold at least a TEFLQ qualification
- teachers on ESP courses other than EAP will have relevant specialist qualifications or experience at an appropriate level.

T3 There will be a valid rationale for the employment of any teachers without the appropriate ELT/TESOL qualifications.

T4$_S$ The academic manager or academic management team will have an appropriate professional profile to provide academic leadership:

- they will be academically and ELT/TESOL qualified as appropriate to the range of courses on offer; at least one person will have, as a minimum, a TEFLQ qualification
- they will all have at least three years' full-time relevant teaching experience.

T5 There will be a valid rationale for the employment of any academic managers without the appropriate qualifications or experience.

Academic management   T6$_S$ Teachers will be matched appropriately to courses.

T7 There will be effective procedures for the appropriate timetabling of students, teachers, courses and classrooms.

T8 There will be formalised arrangements, satisfactory to students and staff, for covering for absent teachers.

T9 Where enrolment is continuous, attention will be paid to all aspects of academic management affected.

T10$_S$ There will be formalised arrangements, led by an academic manager and covering all teaching sites, to ensure appropriate guidance and support for all teachers in line with the organisation's professional development policy.

T11$_S$ There will be effective arrangements for the observation and monitoring of teachers' performance by a TEFLQ academic manager/TEFLQ member of the academic management team, including appropriate feedback and action planning to improve and develop teaching. Particular care will be taken to monitor and guide inexperienced teachers, those whose classroom performance exhibits weaknesses and those whose student feedback indicates dissatisfaction with their teaching.

Course design and implementation   T12 Course design will be based on stated principles. There will be a coherent and appropriate course structure described in writing for teachers' guidance.

T13 Course design will be regularly reviewed in the light of the different and changing needs of students and feedback from teachers and students.

T14 Written course outlines, appropriate to the course length and type, will be available to students.

T15 Courses will include study and learning strategies that support independent learning and will enable students to benefit from their programmes and continue their learning after the course.

T16 Courses will include strategies which ensure that students can develop their language skills outside the classroom and benefit linguistically from their stay in the United Kingdom.

Learner management   T17$_H$ There will be efficient procedures for the correct placement of students and assessment of starting level so that progress can be evaluated.

T18 There will be procedures for monitoring and for recording students' progress, such as tutorials, and for enabling students to change courses or classes where necessary.

T19 Students will be guided to select the examinations and examination training best suited to their needs and interests.

T20 In the case of examination courses and where there is internal assessment relevant to progression routes, assessment criteria and procedures will be in writing and available to staff and students.

T21 Academic reports will be made available to students on request and, in the case of under 18s, to their parents/guardians.

T22 Students wishing to enter mainstream UK education will have access to relevant information and advice.

Teaching
Knowledge   T23 Teachers will show sound knowledge and awareness of the linguistic systems of English and will be able to provide appropriate models of both spoken and written English.

T24 Teachers will be able to adapt their language to the level of the learners and differentiate between learners with different needs and learning styles.

Planning   T25 The content of the lesson will show that the course objectives and the profile of the specific students in the class have been taken into account.

T26 Lessons will be based on a coherent sequence of activities leading to relevant learning outcomes.

Delivery   T27 Teachers will demonstrate effective management of the classroom environment and resources to promote learning.

T28 Teaching techniques will be appropriate to the focus of the lesson and the needs of the students, and will include feedback and review.

T29 Teachers will demonstrate the ability to manage learning activities and interactions effectively to engage students.

T30 Teachers will be aware of cultural differences and individual characteristics, and will show sensitivity to the group and individuals to ensure a positive learning atmosphere.

Welfare and student services*

(* This section is normally not applicable where the provider only offers in-company provision.)

Standard

The needs of students for security, pastoral care, information and leisure activities will be met; any accommodation provided will be suitable; the management of the accommodation systems will work to the benefit of students.

Care of students   W1 Provision will be made for the safety and security of students on the provider's premises appropriate to their age, background and the location of the provider.

W2 Students will be given pastoral care appropriate to their age, background and circumstances (including any additional support needs). Account will be taken of any special needs arising from religious observance.

W3 A named person or persons will be identified to all staff and students to deal with students' personal problems.

W4 There will be policies and procedures, known to all students and staff, for dealing with abusive behaviour by staff or students (verbal abuse, including harassment, bullying, actual or threatened violence, damage to personal property).

W5 Students will be issued with a 24-hour emergency contact number for the provider in writing, except in the case of organisations enrolling only those students already settled in the local community and with a local support network.

W6 Information on the most appropriate forms of transport between the point of entry to the United Kingdom and the provider or accommodation, and approximate costs, will be available in advance to students. Where transport is offered by the provider, arrangements will be clear, effective and reasonably responsive to unforeseen circumstances.

W7 As appropriate, students will be given advice on:
- local facilities, services and amenities, including, in the state sector, student union membership

- registration with the local police
- banking
- personal safety and the care of valuables
- medical and personal insurance
- local places of worship
- licensing laws
- traffic regulations
- compliance with the law, e.g. in relation to the use of drugs, motoring offences, procedures in case of arrest by the police.

W8 Students will be informed about their rights regarding medical and dental treatment through the NHS. Longer-term students will be encouraged to register with a local GP. Students will have full access to any medical and welfare services available in the organisation.

Accommodation **Please note:** The type of accommodation should be described in the following terms:

- **Homestay accommodation:** the hosts treat the student as a full member of the household, eating together and sharing the common living areas; no more than four students will be accommodated in homestay accommodation at any one time (homes accommodating more than four adult students should not be described as homestay accommodation)
- **Residential accommodation:** in private homes accommodating more than four students, student houses, halls or hostels, catered or self-catering. Residential accommodation where there is no overnight supervision is not suitable for under 18s: please see the additional criteria for *Care of under 18s.*

All accommodation W9 The following will be made available to the student to ensure a comfortable living environment throughout their stay:

- a bedroom and common areas in a proper state of cleanliness and repair
- adequate heating and lighting
- a sufficiently spacious bedroom with natural light, equipped with an adequately sized bed and adequate hanging and drawer space for clothes
- privacy from members of the opposite sex
- a table for private study (where appropriate)
- sufficient washing facilities and access to a bathroom, with baths or showers available daily
- a change of towels and bed linen each week and an adequate supply of duvets or blankets
- a weekly laundry service (especially in the case of under-16s) or clearly explained laundry arrangements.

W10 _H All accommodation allocated to students will be inspected by a responsible representative before students are placed.

W11 All accommodation will be inspected by the provider or their agency at least once every two years.

W12 _H Accommodation registers will be kept up to date with accurate information, including records of visits.

W13 Confirmation of accommodation booked for a student will include accurate and sufficient information about the type of accommodation, location, approximate time and cost of travel between the accommodation and teaching premises, services provided and payment arrangements (including cancellation penalties). Where a student is expected to share a bedroom with another student, this will be clearly indicated in the provider's publicity. Conditions and procedures under which accommodation arrangements can be terminated will be included.

W14 Students will be told who to contact in the case of any problems with their accommodation. At an early stage in their stay, students will be asked by the provider or its accommodation agency if they are satisfied with their accommodation. Problems will be addressed promptly and action taken will be recorded.

W15 Meals in homestay and residential accommodation will be provided as agreed and will offer a well-balanced diet, taking into account any reasonable dietary requirements expressed by students.

Accommodation: homestay only   W16 No more than four students will be accommodated in a homestay at any one time.

W17 _H Hosts will be made aware in writing of the rules, terms and conditions applied by the provider with respect to the provision of accommodation services. Booking and cancellation arrangements will be clear.

W18 No more than two students will be accommodated in the same bedroom unless specifically requested in writing by the students, their agents, parents or legal guardians.

W19 Students with the same first language will not be lodged in the same home at the same time unless written consent of the students or their agents on behalf of their parents or legal guardians is obtained in advance of arrival.

W20 English will normally be the language of communication within the homestay home.

W21 Hosts will ensure that there is an adult available to receive students on first arrival.

Accommodation: residential   W22 Adequate provision will be made for cleaning.

W23 Providers offering residential accommodation will make adequate provision for the care of their students' health.

Accommodation: other   W24 Students will be informed of the implications of their living in bed-sits or flats (tenancy agreements, local taxes, possible loss of contact with speakers of English out of classroom hours, cooking, washing, etc.). Advice will be available in case of difficulties.

W25 Any other accommodation recommended by the provider will be monitored and booking and payment arrangements will be clear.

Leisure opportunities   W26 Students will have appropriate information about and access to social, cultural and sporting events and activities which enhance their experience of studying in the United Kingdom.

W27 Any leisure programmes will be well organised and sufficiently resourced. Where activities form part of a course package, alternatives will be available for activities cancelled for reasons such as poor weather.

W28 There will be effective systems in place to ensure the health and safety of students on all on-site and off-site activities, including written risk assessments and clear guidelines on how to respond to situations where students are at risk.

W29 Any sporting and leisure activities on- or off-site will be under the direction of a nominated, responsible person who has appropriate experience and training.

Care of under 18s*

(* This section is not applicable where the provider never recruits students under the age of 18.)

Standard

There will be appropriate provision for the safeguarding of students under the age of 18 within the organisation and in any leisure activities or accommodation provided.

C1 There will be a safeguarding policy which specifies procedures to ensure the safety and well-being of all students under the age of 18, including safe recruitment (for all roles involving responsibility for or substantial access to under 18s), handling allegations and making referrals, and a named member of staff responsible for its implementation.

C2 The provider will make the policy known to all adults in contact with under 18s through their role with the organisation (including employees, subcontractors, homestay hosts, group leaders and volunteers) and provide guidance or training relevant to its effective implementation.

C3 Publicity (or other information made available to students, their parents or legal guardians before enrolment) will give an accurate description of the level of care and support given to students under 18.

C4 Recruitment materials for roles involving responsibility for or substantial access to under 18s will include reference to the organisation's commitment to safeguarding and inform applicants that:

- references will be followed up
- all gaps in CVs must be explained satisfactorily
- proof of identity and (where applicable) qualifications will be required
- reference requests will ask specifically whether there is any reason that they should not be engaged in situations where they have responsibility for, or substantial access to, persons under 18
- appropriate suitability checks will be required prior to confirmation of appointment.

C5 All current holders of roles involving responsibility for or substantial access to under 18s, and all new appointees to such roles, will have appropriate suitability checks, for example with the Disclosure and Barring Service (in England and Wales) or Protecting Vulnerable Groups Scheme (in Scotland) or Access NI (in Northern Ireland), or Police 'Certificate of good conduct' (outside the United Kingdom), in line with the organisation's safeguarding policy.

C6 Suitable arrangements will be made for the supervision and safety of students outside lessons, normally by:

- the provision of a leisure programme, appropriate to the age, ability and interests of the students (for under-16s, the cost should be included in the course fee).
- ensuring there is sufficient adult supervision for all scheduled activities (excluding classroom teaching) both on-site and off-site, taking into account the nature of the activity, age, gender and needs of the students. (Group leaders and other adults travelling with students under 18 will be responsible only for students in their own group.)
- providing clear rules, appropriate to the ages of the students, for what they may do outside the scheduled lesson or activity times and without supervision, appropriate to the age of the students and the location, and having procedures in place to ensure these rules are adhered to.

C7 Suitable arrangements will be made for the accommodation of students.

- The provider will normally be responsible for providing accommodation and all meals unless alternative arrangements have been made by the parent(s) or legal guardian and confirmed in writing.
- Hosts will be made aware of the rules for what students may do outside the scheduled activity times, and particularly what time they are expected home at night, and will work with the provider to ensure these rules are adhered to.
- A responsible adult (known to and vetted by the provider) will always be present overnight and normally be present when students under 16 are at home.

- Providers will ensure that students under 16 lodged by them or their agency in homestay or residential accommodation will not be lodged with students of 18 years or older.
- In residential accommodation, the ratio of residential adults to students will be at least 1:20 for students aged 12–17, and 1:15 for students under 12. First aid facilities and an appropriately trained member of staff will be available at all times, together with an arrangement with a local doctor in case of emergencies.

C8 Arrangements will be in place to ensure contact between the provider and parents, legal guardians or their nominated representatives concerning the welfare of students.

- The provider will obtain a 24-hour contact number for the parents, or legal guardians of students.
- The provider will give parents, legal guardians or agents of students a telephone number that can be used to contact the provider outside office opening hours.

(Accreditation UK Handbook 2014–15) © British Council 2014. Reprinted with permission.

Index

AALL (Association for Academic Language Learning) 122
Academic English Screening Test (AEST) 209–13
academic literacies 70, 84–7, 129–30
  online resources 167–8
  in tripartite model of language proficiency 88–91, 151–61, 207
academic literacies in the curriculum 89–90, 151–2
  assessment process 157–60, 158*f*
  as a collaborative enterprise 154–61
  embedding approach 89–90, 157–61, 208–9, 222–4
  identification of key literacies 157–9
  innovation 152–4
  see also innovation in English language provision: Australian case study
academic standards 17–19
academic support 63, 64
academic/teaching staff
  and assessment of students' ELP 142–3, 145–6
  and compromise in standards 19
  embedding academic literacies 154–61
  English language competence of 5
  language and discipline 64
  procedural vs declarative knowledge 156–7
  staff profiles 66
  teaching and research 20–3, 51–3
  training and professional development 43–51, 45–7*t*, 156–7
Access Agreements 8
Accreditation UK inspection criteria 66–7, 67*t*, 281
  care of under 18s 291–3
  management 281–4
  resources and environment 284–5
  teaching and learning 285–8
  welfare and student services 288–91
Adams, R. 9

Addison, W. 39, 86, 150
administrative staff 51, 199
AEI (Australian Education International) 56
AEST (Academic English Screening Test) 209–13
Alderman, G. 18–19
Allen, J. P. 73
Anderson, J. R. 156
Arkoudis, S. et al. 90, 98, 108, 109
Aschaffenburg, K. 128
assessment
  of academic literacies in the curriculum 157–60, 158*f*
  of communicative proficiency 76
  discipline-based assessment 107–8, 124, 144
  and ELF 80–1
  and functionalism 75–6
  of general ELP 143
  pair/group assessment 134
  rigour 31, 32
  speaking/listening skills 134
assessment literacy 51, 108–14
Association for Academic Language Learning (AALL) 122
Association of Language and Learning 'Degrees of Proficiency' 59, 62
AUQA *see* Australian Universities Quality Agency
Austin, J. L. 73
Australia
  Bradley Review 9
  IELTS 33, 34, 109, 115
  immigration policy 27, 100
  Knight Review 27
  professional accreditation 33, 34
  regulation 56–62
  student numbers 14, 23, 56
  TOEFL 33
  see also English language standards for Higher Education; Good Practice Principles for ELP; innovation in English language provision: Australian

Lightning Source UK Ltd.
Milton Keynes UK
UKOW01f1854171017
311167UK00012B/253/P